Constantine

ROMAN EMPEROR,
CHRISTIAN VICTOR

Constantine

ROMAN EMPEROR, CHRISTIAN VICTOR

PAUL STEPHENSON

THE OVERLOOK PRESS

NEW YORK

This edition first published in hardcover in the United States in 2010 by

The Overlook Press, Peter Mayer Publishers, Inc.
141 Wooster Street
New York, NY 10012
www.overlookpress.com

Cataloging-in-Publication Data is available from the Library of Congress

Manufactured in the United States of America
FIRST EDITION
2 4 6 8 10 9 7 5 3 1
ISBN 978-1-59020-324-8

In a word, the historical scholar and quite specifically the medievalist, has a twofold duty: one to his own speciality, to his own chosen field of scholarship, where he can justifiably claim expertise, and the other to society which after all maintains him and which makes it possible for him to apply himself with singular zeal to his own research. But this duty to society makes it imperative for him to return to it the fruits of his own research work and learning by putting his specialist work into a broader perspective. In many instances he will do this all the better and with greater success if he tries to apply all his methods, techniques and topics to periods antecedent to and succeeding those which originally fired his research enthusiasm.

Walter Ullmann, *The Future of Medieval History*
Inaugural lecture in the University of Cambridge,
delivered 6 November 1973

Contents

CONTENTS

Maps and Stemmata

Maps

1. The Roman empire in the third century
2. The Tetrarchy in AD 293
3. The empire of the Tetrarchs and Constantine: the twelve dioceses
4. Constantine's Italian campaign, AD 312
5. The first war between Constantine and Licinius
6. Byzantium (Constantinople) and its hinterland in AD 324
7. Constantine's Constantinople, with key later developments
8. The imperial palace complex at Constantinople

Stemmata

1. The relationships and families of the Tetrarchs
2. The family of Constantine

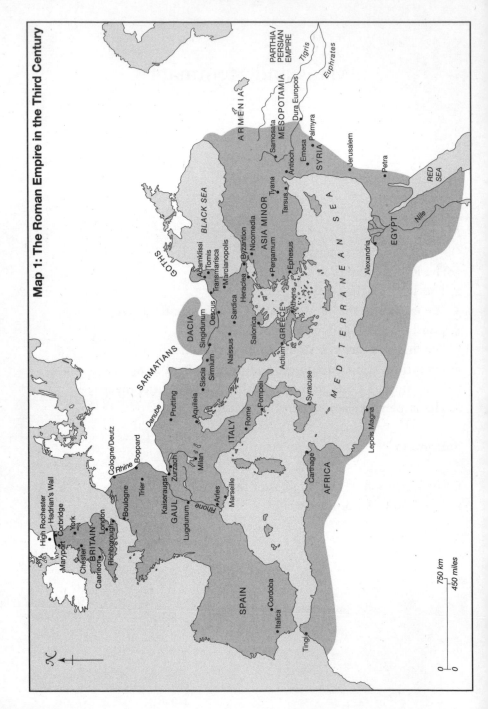

Map 1: The Roman Empire in the Third Century

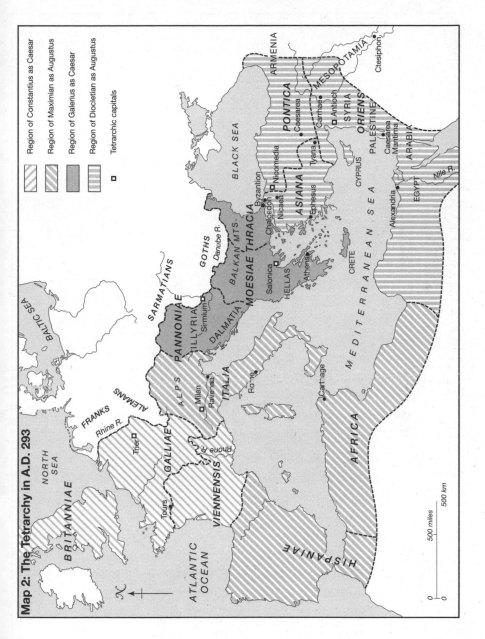

Map 2: The Tetrarchy in A.D. 293

Region of Constantius as Caesar
Region of Maximian as Augustus
Region of Galerius as Caesar
Region of Diocletian as Augustus
Tetrarchic capitals

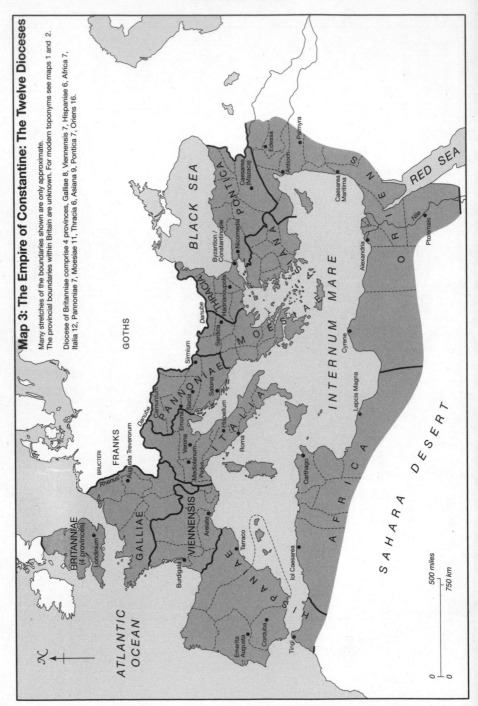

Map 3: The Empire of Constantine: The Twelve Dioceses

Many stretches of the boundaries shown are only approximate.
The provincial boundaries within Britain are unknown. For modern toponyms see maps 1 and 2.

Diocese of Britanniae comprise 4 provinces, Galliae 8, Viennensis 7, Hispaniae 6, Africa 7, Italia 12, Pannoniae 7, Moesiae 11, Thracia 6, Asiana 9, Pontica 7, Oriens 16.

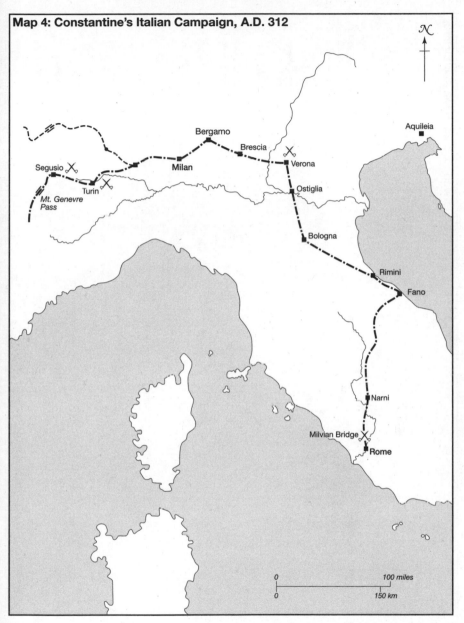

Map 4: Constantine's Italian Campaign, A.D. 312

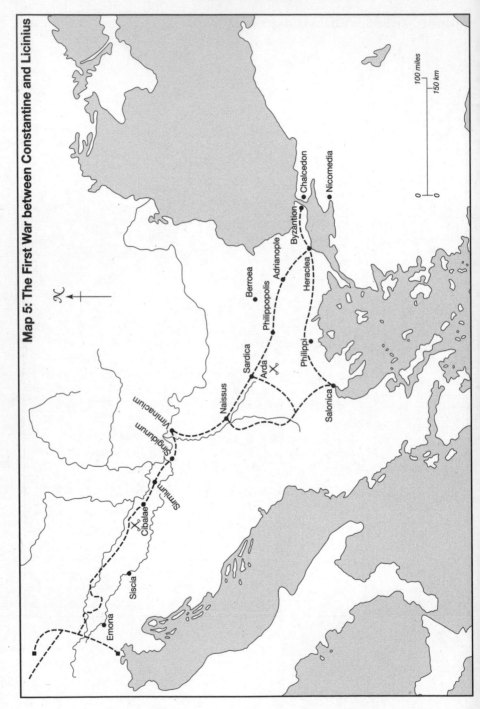

Map 5: The First War between Constantine and Licinius

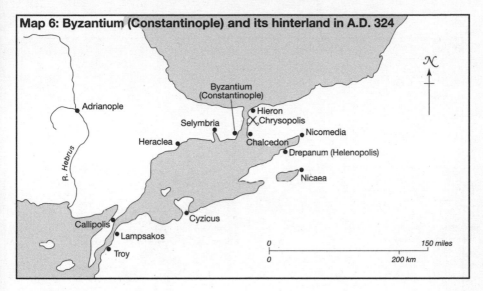

Map 6: Byzantium (Constantinople) and its hinterland in A.D. 324

Adrianople

R. Hebrus

Byzantium
(Constantinople)

Selymbria

Heraclea

Hieron
Chrysopolis
Chalcedon

Nicomedia

Drepanum (Helenopolis)

Nicaea

Callipolis
Lampsakos

Troy

Cyzicus

0   150 miles
0   200 km

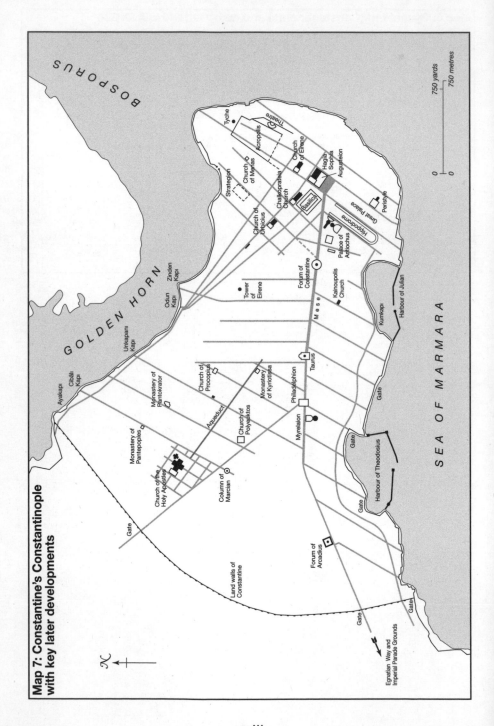

Map 7: Constantine's Constantinople with key later developments

BOSPORUS

GOLDEN HORN

SEA OF MARMARA

Ayakapı
Cibâli Kapı
Unkapanı Kapı
Odun Kapı
Zinden Kapı

Tyche
Theatre
Acropolis
Church of Eirene
Hagia Sophia
Augusteion
Church of Metras
Chalkoprateia Church
Strategion
Church of Urbicius
Basilica
Hippodrome
Great Palace
Peristyle
Palace of Antiochus
Tower of Eirene
Forum of Constantine
Kainoupolis Church
Mese
Kumkapı
Harbour of Julian

Monastery of Panteoples
Monastery of Pantokrator
Church of Procopius
Monastery of Kyriotissa
Church of Polyeuktos
Philadelphion
Taurus
Aqueduct
Church of the Holy Apostles
Column of Marcian
Myrelaion
Gate
Gate
Gate
Gate
Harbour of Theodosius

Land walls of Constantine

Forum of Arcadius
Gate
Gate

Egnatian Way and Imperial Parade Grounds

N

0   750 yards
0   750 metres

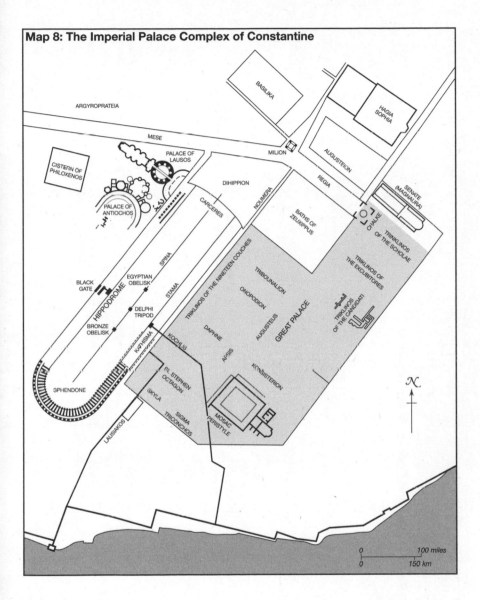

Map 8: The Imperial Palace Complex of Constantine

BASILIKA

HAGIA
SOPHIA

ARGYROPRATEIA

MESE

MILION

AUGUSTEION

PALACE OF
LAUSOS

SENATE
(MAGNAURA)

CISTERN OF
PHILOXENOS

DIHIPPION

REGIA

TRINKLINOS
OF THE SCHOLAE

PALACE OF
ANTIOCHOS

CARCERES

NOUMERA

BATHS OF
ZEUXIPPUS

CHALKE

TRIKLINOS OF
THE EXCUBITORES

SPINA

TRIKLINOS OF THE NINETEEN COUCHES

TRIBOUNALION

BLACK
GATE

EGYPTIAN
OBELISK

STAMA

ONOPODION

TRIKLINOS
OF THE CANDIDATI

HIPPODROME

DELPHI
TRIPOD

AUGUSTEUS

GREAT PALACE

BRONZE
OBELISK

DAPHNE

KATHISMA

KOCHLIS

AEISS

KONSISTERION

SPHENDONE

ST. STEPHEN
OCTAGON

SKYLA

MOSAIC
PERISTYLE

LAUSIAKOS

SIGMA
TRICONCHOS

N

0   100 miles

0   150 km

Stemma 1: The Relationships and Families of the Tetrarchs

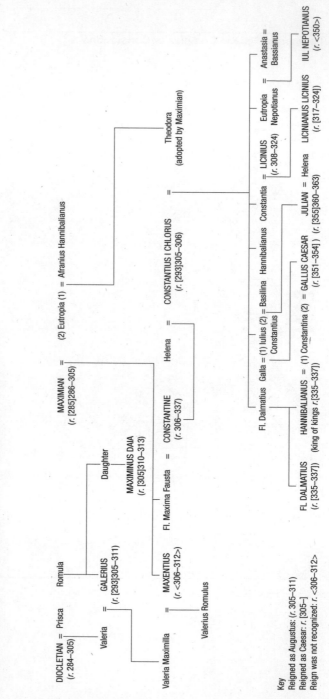

Key

Reigned as Augustus: (r. 305–311)

Reigned as Caesar: r. [305–]

Reign was not recognized: r. <306–312>

Stemma 2: The Family of Constantine

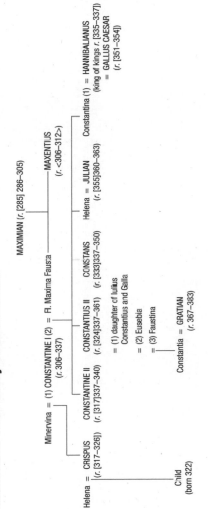

Preface

No life of Constantine is timeless, just as none will have the final word: from the first by Eusebius of Caesarea, so firmly rooted in the concerns of a bishop in the second fifth of the fourth century, to those written in the twentieth century. In 1930 G. P. Baker began his life of Constantine aboard an ocean liner, leaving behind the new skyscrapers of Manhattan to arrive nine days later at the docks of Liverpool. From there he took his reader on a full-day train ride across Lancashire and Yorkshire to old York, where in AD 306 Constantine became the latest Roman general to be acclaimed emperor by his troops. Each life betrays its moment of composition and the preoccupations of its author. Each is written, moreover, in awareness of much, but now never all, that has been said before. This life takes a perspective that complements many accounts and contradicts others that dominate the field in the first decade of the twenty-first century.

The bare bones of Constantine's life are presented fairly consistently in his many biographies. Acclaimed in July 306 at York by a Roman legion following the death of his father, Emperor Constantius Chlorus, Constantine became a Tetrarch, one of four Roman emperors ruling a divided empire. Intent on unifying the empire, he marched on Rome to establish his sole control of its western half, and on the eve of the decisive battle, at Rome's Milvian Bridge in October 312, he had a vision. A cross appeared to him in the sky with an exhortation, generally translated as 'By this sign conquer'. Inscribing the cross on the shields of his soldiers, Constantine drove the followers of his imperial rival Maxentius into the Tiber and claimed the imperial capital for himself. His vision validated, Constantine converted to Christianity and ended persecution of his co-religionists with the defeat in 324 of his last rival, Licinius. Christianity thus emerged from the shadows, its adherents no longer persecuted, its heroes no longer martyred. At Licinius' death, Constantine united the western and eastern halves of the Roman Empire, and presided over the first ecumenical council of the Christian Church, at Nicaea in 325. He proceeded to found a new capital city nearby on the Bosphorus, where Europe meets Asia. This site, the ancient trading colony of Byzantium, became the city of Constantine, Constantinople, a new Christian capital set apart from Rome's pagan past. Thereafter the Christian Roman Empire endured in the east as Byzantium, while Rome itself fell to barbarian hordes in AD 476.

What more is there to say? A good deal, I shall argue in the following pages. I offer here a narrative of Constantine's life in a broader context. I do so by design but also by default, since it is impossible to write a genuine biography of any pre-modern figure. The written sources do not exist or are partial; they have not been preserved or have been preserved by design; they have been altered or miscopied; they cannot simply be mined for data. The same applies to material and visual evidence, which should not be used simply to pad or colour a narrative, although it does so very well. I offer a thicker biography also by design since, as a rather traditional empirical historian, I have always enjoyed narrative. Equally, I have relished the full critical apparatus, which the academic historian employs to demonstrate how she reached her conclusions and how others might find the evidence with which to replicate or refute them. This work, then, a narrative without notes, is as much story as history. I have ventured to use far more imaginative recreation, entertained far more plausible inference, and deployed many fewer probablys and possiblys than I would have thought sensible or feasible if this work were intended solely for a scholarly audience. While I hope my colleagues will read it with forbearance, my greater wish is that the work will appeal to a wider readership. The book makes full use of the remains of the age of Constantine, dwelling on the places where he lived and on the buildings for which he was responsible.

I have not attempted to excise all modern allusions but rather to incorporate them as far as possible, so the reader in the second decade of this century will have a clue where currently to find many of the works of art and architecture here explored. It is my hope that it will prove useful to those who wish to follow in the emperor's footsteps, from York to Trier, from Arles to Rome, from Thessaloniki to Istanbul, and beyond.

A number of colleagues and friends helped as I completed this project. I am especially grateful to Anthony Kaldellis for his lucid and critical commentary on a first draft. Walter Kaegi offered me the opportunity to address some ideas to a learned audience at the University of Chicago. Graham Stewart was instrumental in getting me to consider a popular project, and my agent, Georgina Capel, ensured that it could be done. I am grateful to Richard Milbank, Slav Todorov and Georgina Difford at Quercus, to Ben Dupré for his meticulous editing and Elaine Willis for her indefatigable pursuit of the illustrations.

The book is dedicated to Brooke Shilling.

Introduction

Constantine's rise to sole power began in the empire's most marginal province, Britannia. It is here at a small church at Hinton St Mary in Dorset that the image of Christ appeared for the first time in an extant floor mosaic, which dates from the fourth century and is now in the British Museum (fig. 1). The attribution of the image seems certain, for it has an identifying symbol, the chi-rho: the entwined letters χ (chi) and ρ (rho), the first two Greek letters of Χριστος, Christ. The figure is flanked by pomegranates, which were mythical symbols of death and resurrection. The British Museum's collection of artefacts from Roman Britain also includes a remarkable array of fourth-century objects marked with the chi-rho. It features silver spoons from the Mildenhall silver hoard, silver church plate from Walter Newton, and wall paintings from Lullingstone, Kent. The chi-rho is frequently flanked by the letters alpha (Α) and omega (Ω), the first and the last of the Greek alphabet, alluding to a self-designation by both the godhead and Christ in the Book of Revelation (1.8; 22.13). The earliest securely dated inscription bearing the chi-rho, found under the floor of San Lorenzo in Rome, names the consuls of AD 323 and thus dates from the period of Constantine's sole rule in the west. This was the divine sign Constantine came to believe he had seen in a vision, which a subsequent dream revealed was the guarantee of his victories. It was offered to him, he came to believe, by the god worshipped by Christians, whose number had grown ever larger during his lifetime.

Constantine was born in the city of Naissus, a military settlement sixty-five Roman miles south of the Danube frontier. In the same city

1

and around the same time, Claudius II Gothicus, emperor from AD 268 to 270, died of a 'direful pestilence', probably smallpox, possibly measles. Constantine was no relation to Claudius Gothicus, as he would later claim. He was the son of a barmaid and a young army officer, Helena and Constantius. Helena, Constantine's mother, would have witnessed the epidemic that claimed the emperor's life. Perhaps she joined an exodus from the city, abandoning the sick and injured, while Christians stayed to nurse and nourish them, facing death with fortitude, secure in their belief in salvation. Perhaps she was among those who offered care, or became a Christian as a consequence. She was, as we shall see, the perfect candidate for Christian conversion: a young woman born into a provincial family of modest standing, approaching marriageable and child-bearing age.

The Christian writer Cyprian describes the effect of the plague, which raged most fiercely between 251 and 266, observing that:

the bowels, relaxed into a constant flux, discharge the bodily strength; that a fire originated in the marrow ferments into wounds of the fauces [the arched opening at the back of the mouth]; that the intestines are shaken with a continual vomiting; that the eyes are on fire with the injected blood; that in some cases the feet or some parts of the limbs are taken off by the contagion of diseased putrefaction; that from the weakness arising by the maiming and loss of the body, either the gait is enfeebled, or the hearing is obstructed, or the sight darkened.

And on the fortitude with which Christians faced the disease, he proclaimed:

What a grandeur of spirit it is to struggle with all the powers of an unshaken mind against so many onsets of devastation and death! What sublimity, to stand erect amid the desolation of the human race, and not to lie prostrate with those who have no hope in God; but rather to rejoice, and to embrace the benefit of the occasion; that in thus bravely showing forth our faith, and by suffering endured, going forward to Christ by the narrow way that Christ trod, we may receive the reward of His life and faith according to His own judgment!

Helena, Constantine's mother, was born in around AD 250 in Drepanum, in Bithynia. Today this is the town of Yalova in Turkey, from which ferries sail regularly across the Sea of Marmara to Istanbul, the city founded by Constantine. Helena was likely a Christian before her son was born, and certainly converted before he did (contrary to later claims by Eusebius, whose task was to assign all credit to Constantine). Helena's husband, Constantine's father, was not a Christian, but he was tolerant of Christians, despite instructions from his superiors to act otherwise. Moreover, Constantine, as we shall see, was more than tolerant, acting in the interests of Christians even before his conversion. Their actions are what one would expect of the husband and son of a Christian woman.

There are no portraits of Helena in her youth. The earliest image may feature among those found in fragments at Trier, once decorating the ceiling of the bedroom of Constantine's second wife, the child bride Fausta. By the time Helena appears on coins struck by her son, her image is stylized, a personification of virtue rather than a true portrait. Still, since Helena was not well educated, we might guess that she was beguiling in other ways, sufficient to inspire not just the lust but also the lasting affection of Constantius Chlorus. That is not to suggest that Constantius was born into a noble or wealthy family. He was, like so many men who rose to distinction at this time, a soldier from the Balkans who earned his stripes on the battlefield. Indeed, the efforts made some years later to prove Constantius' descent from the emperor Claudius Gothicus demonstrate that Constantius' origins were far from illustrious. Even when rewritten, the best lineage Constantius could conjure was descent from an emperor of equally humble and obscure background who had risen to power through the ranks of the army.

The life of Claudius Gothicus, preserved only in adapted form compiled a century after his death, the *Historia Augusta*, suggests that: 'Claudius, Quintillus and Crispus were brothers, and Crispus had a daughter Claudia; of her and Eutropius, the noblest man of the Dardanian folk, was born Constantius.' The *Anonymus Valesianus*, also known as the *Origo Constantini* (*The Origins of Constantine*), appears to corroborate this fiction: 'Constantius, grandson of the brother of that best of emperors Claudius, was first one of the emperor's bodyguards, then a tribune, and later governor of Dalmatia.' But a different account is given by Eutropius and Zonaras, to whom we shall return, who identify Constantius

3

as the son of Claudia's daughter, and also by later panegyrical orations, where Constantine is portrayed as Claudius' grandson, suggesting Constantius was Claudius' son. Each version is equally false. We do not know his date or place of birth, nor the names and status of his parents.

Whatever his real lineage, Constantius Chlorus, Constantine's father, became a man of great military distinction. His union, perhaps not legally a marriage, with Helena began shortly before Constantine's birth. The exact nature of their relationship has been disputed, and speculation that Constantine was a bastard was hardly quashed during his reign, when he legislated against the interests of children born to unmarried parents. But there is no doubt that Constantius regarded Constantine as his true son and legal heir, and that his inheritance was growing rather rapidly. Sometime after his son's birth, Constantius became governor of the province of Dalmatia, comprising the lands to the west of Naissus. At that time a provincial governor still supervised both military and civilian hierarchies, overseeing the levying of taxes and the actions of town councils, and maintaining the postal system and all necessary defences. In the generation after, a stricter division between military and civilian functions was introduced, which stripped ambitious soldiers of the means to raise revenue to fund a rebellion. Moreover, the number of provinces was doubled, diluting the power base of any individual governor and subordinating him to a regional 'vicar', who oversaw a group of provinces, a 'diocese'. That the language of provincial government resembles that later employed of church organization is quite deliberate. The vicars were responsible to the emperor's right-hand man, his administrator-in-chief and closest colleague, the Praetorian Prefect. This was the rank attained by Constantius in 289, when he commanded the whole of the western armies, as deputy to the emperor Maximian.

The empire was, at this time, ruled by two emperors, in the west and the east. Helena was no longer a suitable companion for Constantius, and a divorce was engineered so that he could marry Theodora, Maximian's daughter, by whom he had six more children, three boys and three girls. Helena and her son were despatched to the court of the eastern emperor, Diocletian, at Nicomedia, rather near her birthplace. We hear nothing more of her until around 312, but we know more about Constantine, for in that period he became the son of an emperor, and then an emperor himself. However, one cannot begin a study, especially a life, in the middle. If we are to make any sense of Constantine's reign, we must understand the world into which he was born at the end of the third century – a world where his mother, a Christian convert, and his father, a pagan soldier, both of humble birth, could marry and rise to rule the empire. This, then, is our first task. Only then can we turn in earnest to a narrative of Constantine's life and achievements.

Exactly when and how Constantine became a Christian, and the nature of his Christianity, have always been subjects of debate. The Christian historians Lactantius and Eusebius wrote accounts of his conversion while Constantine still lived, and by the fifth century AD it was clear to Socrates Scholasticus and Sozomen that Constantine's reign marked a watershed in the histories of Christianity and the Roman Empire, which henceforth were entwined. Between the two ages the triumph of Christianity and the need to tell its story obscured the truth. Yet certain facts are established as well as any in history. Constantine's reason for embracing Christianity was the guarantee of victory accorded by worshipping the Christian god. Fighting under the symbols of this god, Constantine overcame great odds to seize power and defeat his imperial rivals. To concentrate this divine power on the field of battle, Constantine manufactured a new symbol, the *labarum*, a standard to lead his armies, which was topped with a chi-rho. Christianity, therefore, became the faith of the legions. Such a fact is remarkable when one considers the situation that prevailed before Constantine came to power.

This book demonstrates that Constantine's conversion was not the reason for the rapid growth of Christianity in the fourth century AD. Its rise from minority cult to majority faith was driven by other factors, and Constantine's life happened to coincide with that period when the growth curve went exponential. Drawing on the latest research, the book shows that women were the vectors for the rapid spread of Christianity before Constantine's birth, and also during his lifetime. Constantine's role, therefore, was to handle this explosion and to harness it to his own interests. He promoted a triumphalist brand of Christianity and sponsored

5

an institutional Church that could propagate and sustain the religion. But in doing so, he did not compromise the faith with the novelty of justified violence. His was indeed a militant interpretation of the faith, but this did not represent a fall from a universal pacifist ethic, nor were Christians wholly absent from the army before Constantine. However, Constantine's interest in Church affairs, and his promotion of the interests of bishops, altered the nature of the religion, privileging men and their interests. This made sense to those versed in the organization of Roman state religion and allowed the emperor to address his subjects through their bishops.

The book shows that Constantine's conversion was not a momentary revelation inspired by a vision, but rather was a lifelong process. It also demonstrates that Constantinople, the city of Constantine, was not a new capital to replace Rome, nor was it an especially Christian construction. It was adorned with thousands of pagan statues gathered from across the empire, and its buildings attempted no architectural novelties. Constantine basked in the glory of the Roman past and was not a great innovator. His greatest desire, shared by so many Roman emperors before him, was to be remembered as a victor in battle, no longer merely a man but a demi-god, translated to the heavens or, in his case, heaven. In life Constantine was both unconquered emperor and Christian Victor, the latter the name he took as his own first name, his Christian name. After his death he was considered equal to the apostles, and statues of Jesus' disciples surrounded his tomb. But he considered himself, at various times, a new Alexander, a new Moses, and even a new Christ.

Previous biographical studies of Constantine have focused on his conversion, drawing out its consequences and dwelling on the nature of his faith. Judgements have ranged widely, many shaped by theories first expounded in the eighteenth and nineteenth centuries. Edward Gibbon's condemnation of Constantine's Christianity, which he considered both genuine and destructive, is now read largely for its literary qualities. More provocative to historians has been Jakob Burckhardt's contrary stance, founded on scepticism that the conversion was anything more than a cynical political ploy. The most impressive recent studies have staked out positions between these two stances, presenting compelling accounts of the interaction of faith and power in a new Christian

Roman Empire. This book, addressing these same vital issues, sketches the broader contexts for the developments of Constantine's reign, but places considerably more emphasis on the importance of the army. It considers the crisis of empire in the third century and the political and economic solutions of the Tetrarchy. It sketches the rise of Christianity and the relationship of its adherents and leaders to the Roman state and its ideology. But most importantly and originally, it presents an extended examination of the religious rites and beliefs that defined military life before and under Constantine. It assesses the army's role in making and breaking emperors, and the ideological glue between religion and politics, faith and power: the Roman theology of victory. It demonstrates that Constantine was able to incorporate Christianity, which was not universally hostile to warfare as has often been argued, into this belief system, presenting the Christian god as 'the greatest god', the bringer of victory.

The Romans believed that the gods intervened in human affairs and rewarded the sworn vows of the virtuous and correct observation of religious rites. In war, victory was granted by the gods and appropriate thanks must be given in return. Since the victories of Scipio Africanus the Elder in 200 BC, leading generals had claimed relationships with particular gods or goddesses as bringers of victory. Scipio was granted a *triumphus*, a triumphal procession through the city of Rome, by the senate, which conferred this honour in recognition of his peculiar *virtus et felicitas*, 'manly valour and good fortune'. Both qualities were seen as divinely conferred, and Scipio cultivated the idea by wearing the insignia of the greatest god, Jupiter Optimus Maximus, and depositing the fruits of victory in that god's temple atop the Capitoline Hill. Thereafter, the Roman triumph ended with the dedication of spoils to the god who had granted that particular victory. Most frequently, these were Victoria, Jupiter's handmaiden, and Mars, the god of war in his various forms. Thus when three eagle standards, lost to the Germans in the Teutoburg Forest in AD 9, were recovered, they were placed in the temple dedicated to Mars Ultor, 'the Avenger'.

In the final years of the Republic Pompey and Julius Caesar both claimed a special relationship with Venus, but in different forms: Pompey with Venus Victrix, 'bringer of Victory', and Caesar with Venus Genetrix, 'the mother', as protectress of the Julian dynasty. However, following the establishment of the principate, only the emperor enjoyed divine patronage in war, his 'manly valour and good fortune' serving the interests of his subjects even when he never took the field. The rise of monotheisms in the later empire indicated a still closer relationship of patronage between the emperor and the single 'greatest god', the *summus deus*. Moreover, as the empire entered a period of crisis in the third century, emperors were once again generals, leading armies against 'barbarians' and Romans alike. Divine patronage was especially important in civil wars, where the commander who enjoyed a closer relationship with the greatest god would prevail, for he would become the vehicle for divine will and judgement.

This study demonstrates that Constantine's rise to power and his early actions as emperor were defined by his relationship with his troops, and consequently by his relationship with the greatest god, who would guarantee his, and hence their, victories. Constantine's only means of retaining power in his early years was to lead his men in numerous successful campaigns and to reward them handsomely for their efforts and loyalty. This he did, distributing wealth, including thousands of coins, to his officers and troops with inscriptions declaring their loyalty to him. The emphasis on loyalty, frequently pronounced and inscribed, suggests that in his first decade of power Constantine was never entirely secure. He came close to death by mutiny within four years of his accession, when his father-in-law and rival emperor Maximian persuaded many of his troops to turn against him. Ever more and greater victories were needed, and thus he was set on the path to civil war and sole sovereignty. For this reason he led a seemingly foolhardy invasion of Italy in 312, his sights set on the capture of Rome itself.

Sections of the book employ the terms that Constantine used to describe himself in his official imperial titles, which support this new vision. First Constantine was *invictus*, 'unconquered' and 'unconquerable', an epithet that also described his divine patron, the Sun god – Sol Invictus. Later, as his faith developed but also as political and military circumstances changed, the emperor's devotion to the god of the Christians became more explicit, and he took the title 'Victor'. These were military epithets, and this book presents a new narrative that restores the Roman army to its proper place as the driving force behind Constantine's actions throughout his reign. Christianity to Constantine was the religion of victory. This was first demonstrated at Rome's Milvian Bridge in 312, but only became apparent to Constantine later. The ultimate triumph of the self-consciously Christian ruler was, therefore, at Chrysopolis in 324, when to mark his victory he founded his own 'Victory City', a *nikopolis* that took his own name, Constantinople. Thereafter, Constantine's active promotion and regulation of the faith was a means to ensure stability in his empire and the continued dominance of his family. But Constantine always sustained an iron grip over the army, which remained the chief instrument of his political will. The army embraced Constantine's conversion because it was explained to them within the established Roman theology of victory: Constantine held himself to be, because he truly believed himself to be, the vehicle for that god's will, as demonstrated on the field of battle. His reign is a case study in the interaction of faith and power.

PART I

Faith and Power
in the Third Century

✠

1

Religion in the Later Roman Empire

Roman state religion and imperial cults – The cult of the standards – Private religious devotion and cults – The mysteries of Mithras

The historical magnitude of Constantine's life is explained by one fact: he was the first Roman emperor to convert to Christianity. But Constantine did not make Christianity the official religion of the Roman state, nor was his conversion the reason for the rapid growth of Christianity in the fourth century AD. The remarkable rise of a minority cult to majority faith in the eastern portion of the Roman Empire was driven by other factors, with which Constantine's life happened to coincide. His task was to handle the religious tumult and to harness its energy to his own interests. In doing so, he made the Christian faith acceptable and accessible to those whom it would have had greatest difficulty reaching, far from the urbanized provinces of the east. Constantine identified aspects of Christianity that correlated best with his own expectations of a religion. In particular, he saw the god of the Christians as the bringer of victory, the 'greatest god' (in Latin, the *summus deus**) who had hitherto been misidentified as Zeus or Jupiter, or as the Sun. Constantine's militant interpretation of Christianity was founded on the Roman understanding of the interactions between faith and power. In order to understand the profound changes this brought about for the later Roman world, and for Christianity, we must first understand a little more about both.

We may best start by looking at the official cult practices of the Roman state. These were not what we now unthinkingly call pagan, which is a pejorative term invented by Christians, most likely contrasting their urban religion with the rustic beliefs of the countryside. The

---

* A glossary can be found below, at p. 309, which explains some Latin and Greek terms.

'pagan' was a *pagus*, not merely of the countryside, but a 'bumpkin' or 'redneck'. Alternatively, he was a 'civilian' (another meaning of *pagus*), not a *miles Christi*, 'a soldier of Christ'. This latter distinction would have struck a soldier of the second century as quite ironic, for it was within the ranks of the army that Christianity spread most slowly, while the diverse cults embraced and tolerated by the Roman state flourished. It is also when dealing with the army that records are clearest.

The army was the most powerful instrument of state during Constantine's lifetime, and it was at its head that he forged his new empire. The Roman army was held to be the Roman people at war, although of course it embraced only one part of the people: men. We shall turn more fully to women in the next chapter, for they were the driving force behind the rise of Christianity. The religious life in the Roman army may best be understood in three categories, all of which together comprise *religio*, a Latin term that cannot, alas, simply be translated as 'religion'. The first category is the official religious life of the army as a whole, which was distinct from the religious beliefs of individual soldiers. It was prescribed by the state and intended to sustain the link between the Roman people at peace, civilians, and the Roman people at war, the army. Over time it evolved into a means to guarantee the link between the army and the emperors through cultivation of imperial cults, as is reflected in the official calendar distributed by every new emperor to every unit in every part of the empire. The second category comprises religious practices prescribed within each unit, with the state's sanction, which were intended to build morale and ensure unity. Rituals were concentrated on the military standards and took place within army camps. The third category, by far the largest, embraces the private religious devotion of the soldiers, which generally took place beyond the limits of the camp. Soldiers recognized a multitude of gods and worshipped in a multitude of fashions, from private prayers to individual divinities to participation in the rites of hierarchical cults which mirrored the structure of the army itself. The latter, for example the cult of Mithras, reinforced elements of unit solidarity and thus were actively encouraged by the state. At certain times, moreover, the veneration of particular gods was prescribed to serve the ends of the state as a whole, for example the worship of the Syrian Sun god by the emperor Elagabalus (AD 218–22). However, thousands of surviving inscriptions suggest that individual worship was devoted primarily to private prayer and to the consequent fulfil- ment of particular vows. That is to say, beyond participation in ritual at the behest of the state and the unit, a soldier would seek divine patronage for specific endeavours and give an offering of thanks if the prayer was answered. All three elements were linked, and each in turn requires further elaboration.

Roman state *religio* and imperial cults

As Cicero had observed in the century before the birth of Christ, the Romans 'excel all other peoples in religiosity and in that unique wisdom that has brought us to the realization that everything is subordinate to the rule and direction of the gods'. Religion and politics were inextri- cably entwined, and performing the rituals prescribed by the state was essential as it ensured the public weal and protected all families, all communities, from harm. Consequently, refusal to honour the gods was to be punished severely. As Rome's power expanded, so it absorbed local cults, integrating rituals or allowing them to continue as supplements, not alternatives, to state rituals.

The calendar of state ritual was, at core, a product of the Augustan age, which coincided with the lifetime of Christ. It was intended to regularize public religious practices in both civilian and military spheres. However, it was revised and updated regularly to reflect imperial succes- sion and apotheosis, and dynastic and ideological imperatives. It was circulated to every magistrate in every city and to every commander of every army camp. The camp is an instructive place to observe the state aspect of *religio*, as a third-century army calendar has survived. Discovered in 1931–2 within the Temple of Artemis Azzanathkona at Dura Europos, Syria (see map 1), the so-called *Feriale Duranum* can be dated by its entries to the reign of Severus Alexander (AD 222–35). It was one of several Latin papyri, all dated AD 200–50, which must have belonged to the Twentieth Cohort of Palmyrenes. The extant papyrus shows clear signs of hard usage, including repairs, for example backing pieces with other fragments of papyri, used and blank. While buried, the *Feriale* was partially eaten by worms, creating many lacunae. However, a fairly full calendar has survived for 19 March to 5 August, with modest fragments for early January, early March and later September. Many familiar Roman celebrations are, therefore, missing, including Saturnalia and Lupercalia, which took place in December and February. But others are present, including the Quinquatria, a festival to Minerva (19 March) and the birthday of the City of Rome (21 April).

Two celebrations in January had particular significance for the army. The honourable discharge (*honesta missio*) was celebrated on 7 January, if one trusts the heavily reconstructed text. And on 3 January the annual oath, the *sacramentum*, was sworn to the emperor, and a new altar to Jupiter Optimus Maximus, 'the best and greatest' god, was dedicated by each unit. Consequently, the old altar, which had been used the previous year for all prescribed ritual, would be buried. To demonstrate that this did indeed take place, we may travel from Dura in Syria to the opposite end of the empire, to Maryport (Alaunum) in Cumberland, in northern Britain (see map 1). There, twenty-one altars dedicated to Jupiter Optimus Maximus have been found buried in a series of pits 350 yards north-east of the fort, surely on the edge of the parade ground. Although some date from as late as the Severan period, sixteen altars date from the arrival at the site of the First Cohort of Spaniards (*cohors I Hispanorum*) in *c*.AD 122–5, to their departure in *c*.139–40. Dedications were evidently annual over a period of around fifteen years.

The core ritual was public sacrifice of cattle. Indeed, cattle alone are sacrificed in the *Feriale Duranum*, and the pouring of libations, offerings of wine to the deity in question, was plentiful, ensuring a regular distribution of beef and booze to the troops. However, this is not to suggest that prescribed ritual was mere artifice, any more than observing a weekly Sabbath indicates a preference for rest over worship. Furthermore, the spacing of holidays is hardly regular, demonstrating that tradition outweighed convenience. No soldier was permitted to absent himself from the ritual, nor from participating in communal elements, for example vows offered to the emperors. And the third-century *Feriale* demonstrates a predominant concern for the imperial cult, particularly celebration of the birthdays of deified emperors (*divi*). Twenty-three of forty-one extant entries concern *divi* (seventeen) and deified empresses (*divae*, six). One might detect a preference for military emperors, including Trajan, Antoninus Pius, Marcus Aurelius, Septimius Severus, and Caracalla, plus the deified Julius Caesar and the mortal Germanicus, who were never emperors.

The ubiquity of rituals commemorating Rome's most successful generals in the *Feriale* is not because we are dealing with the army, but because the *vir militaris*, the leader who was successful in war, was remembered most fondly by all Romans. But the imperial cult is better regarded as a series of related imperial cults, for it took distinct forms throughout the empire. Cults appear to have emerged spontaneously in the eastern provinces, where ruler cults were long established, and more frequently to have been transplanted to the western provinces from Rome. In the words of G. W. Bowersock, the imperial cult 'provided an unparalleled guarantee of loyalty throughout a vast and varied empire, and it served to engage the more affluent and better educated provincials in the ceremonies of devotion to the ruling power'.

In addition to veneration of the *divi*, due honour was accorded to images of the reigning emperor and his family members, which were to be found in every camp and municipality throughout the empire. Formally, it was not the man who was worshipped but his divine quality (*numen*). However, there was a fine line between the veneration of the emperor's *numen* and the valorization of the man. Inscriptions to the divine qualities (*numina*) of the emperors abound in military contexts in Britain. For example, a small slate dedication tablet 'to the *numen* of the Augustus' found near the watergate of the legionary fortress at Chester was most likely set up by a common soldier who could not afford more elaborate monuments. One who could erected a sandstone altar. Temples proliferated to facilitate the veneration of the *numen* of the living emperor. Among the first monuments to the Roman conquest was the erection in Colchester of a temple to the living emperor Claudius. It was here that the earliest colonists were burnt alive by Boudicca, queen of the Iceni.

The veneration of the divine qualities of the living emperor is evident as early as the reign of Augustus, when Tiberius dedicated an altar to his *numen*. Such veneration had proliferated to include emperors living and dead by the reign of Caligula, when, according to Suetonius, Artabanus, king of the Parthians, made peace with Rome and 'venerated the Roman eagles and standards and images of the Caesars'. The Praetorian Guard, the imperial bodyguard based in Rome, regularly incorporated imperial portraits onto their standards. However, the cult took off in the provinces in the mid-second century and flourished into the third, promoted by the Antonine and Severan dynasties. In Britannia and Asia Minor some intriguing miniature busts of emperors have been discovered at cult sites, which might have baffled historians were it not for the fact that they can be read together. The bronze heads found at Willingham Fen in Cambridgeshire have small pegs at their bases. A rod discovered at Ephesus has two small holes in its top, for the insertion of the head of a relevant emperor, perhaps on the appropriate imperial birthday. It thus becomes a sacred sceptre. An inscription from Ephesus attests to 'icons' of Trajan, Plotina and Augustus being carried in processions for the Artemis cult.

Observing the rapid escalation in veneration of the emperors, the eminent classicist Arthur Darby Nock was inspired to ask himself, 'do the emperors, at least in the third century, overshadow the gods?' Although he believed not, he drew attention to the portrayal of gods as divine 'companions' (*comites*), affording protective companionship to emperors. The title *comes*, commonly employed on coins, implied equality, not subordination. Moreover, gods were at this time, as art historian Ernst Kantorowicz demonstrated in a classic study, increasingly portrayed like emperors, wearing military uniforms and carrying arms. The imitation by gods of emperors inverted the established practice of emperors being portrayed in the guise of gods.

By the age of Constantine, cults of the living emperor had stood at the heart of the state's religious ceremonial for two centuries, albeit in diverse forms throughout the empire. Full participation in prescribed imperial cults by soldiers and civilians was essential, because divine support for the head of state was guaranteed only by correct and universal observance of ritual. Soldiers could more easily be obliged to participate, and any recalcitrance more readily punished. It is in this area that we shall dwell in the next chapter, when we meet Christians serving in the Roman army, who evince for the first time, and under pressure from certain writers, an unwillingness to swear oaths to two masters, the emperor and their god. They wish to separate politics from religion and to obey Christ's command to 'Render therefore unto Caesar the things which be Caesar's, and unto God the things which be God's' (Luke 20:25). But the loyalty of each soldier had to be beyond question, to the emperor, to the state and to his unit. To that end, the army calendar incorporated two dates of especial importance, replicating festivals enjoyed in both urban and rustic settings, but placing at the centre of the celebration the objects most revered by the army – the military standards.

The cult of the standards

On 10 May, and again on 31 May, were held the *rosaliae signorum*, rose festivals where the military standards, which will have played a role in all other camp rituals, themselves became the objects of veneration. It is important to note that the *rosaliae* did not originate in the camps, but rather were universal festivals marking the transition from spring to summer. Since the occasion called for the decking of something with roses, what could be more appropriate in a military context than the standards? This act appears to be depicted on a decorative carving found in three fragments of a pilaster discovered at Corbridge (Corstopitum), a fort at Hadrian's Wall.

The *genius*, or guardian spirit, of each unit or division resided in its standard. *Genii* have been identified for most divisions of the army, from the entire army (*exercitus*) down through the legion or auxiliary unit, vexillation or specialist cohort, to the smallest constituent unit, the infantry *centuria* or cavalry *turma*. Troops appear to have venerated most fervently the *genius* of their century; for example, at the legionary fortress of Chester (Deva) in Britannia, numerous altars inscribed in dedication to the *genii* of centuries have been found. According to Roman military historian Michael Speidel, 'by far the largest number of chapels, altars and statues are dedicated to the *Genius centuriae* . . . because the soldiers attached to their *centuriae* the strongest feeling of identity and belonging'. This is an observation of the utmost importance, supported as it is by an abundance of epigraphic evidence, for it goes to the heart of a very modern concern in war studies. It has frequently been observed that the modern soldier feels the greatest loyalty to his or her immediate peers and comrades in an infantry company or squadron (60–250 personnel, 2–6 platoons), a platoon or troop (25–40 personnel), and more particularly a squad (8–10). This insight, based on sociological studies of 'primary group' dynamics, was offered in a seminal study of German Wehrmacht morale published shortly after the Second World War by Edward A. Shils and Morris Janowitz. It was developed by Janowitz in his sociological studies of the professional soldier through the period of the Vietnam War. Where small unit or 'primary group' relationships were characterized by daily intimate association and co-operation, the group cohered and remained effective, even as loyalty to a higher cause was increasingly absent.*

The Roman century would have had a nominal strength of eighty men and thus was the equivalent of a small company, at least twice as large as a modern infantry platoon. So one might posit that the Roman methods of fighting, employing larger units than are standard in modern warfare, led to variations in notions of group solidarity. Still, it is hard to dismiss the notion that men also felt close, perhaps the closest, bonds with members of their *contubernium*, i.e. men with whom they shared a tent or billet. While such proximity might have led to tensions that would have hindered rather than helped on the battlefield, one can imagine just as easily that competition between *contubernia* within the century and competition between *centuriae* in the cohort might lead to demonstrations of battlefield valour. The *genii* represented the spirit of the century and thus personified a very real common feeling.

Genii, either carved on altars or portrayed in statues, were usually

---

* Far more recently, small unit efficacy has become the focus of much theorizing and planning by those responsible for training US troops for the 'Global War on Terror' (GWOT). In the bewildering acronymic jargon of the modern military one reads of the need for greater recognition of the fact that 'victory rests with small units' in the 'contemporary operating environment' (COE) and that this must be reflected in 'mission rehearsal environments' (MRE), i.e. exercises. Recognition of the supremacy of the small unit has become a predicate of those calling for the transformation of the US military, to meet the challenges of modern warfare, where 'stability operations and support operations' (SOSO) are at the core of most missions. As the COE has changed, increasingly the smallest units, squads and platoons, operate independently, heightening the tendency for soldiers to fight not for a cause but to protect and impress their closest friends and comrades.

shown as young, nude, beardless men holding a *cornucopia* and a bowl for the wine libation. These might be venerated individually, but when the unit wished to call upon its *genius*, it turned to its standards. The standards were housed in the *aedes*, a building at the centre of the camp that served both as a chapel and as a treasury. The standard-bearers (*signiferi*) were also charged with overseeing the unit's coffers. Numerous inscriptions have survived recording corporate vows and offerings to the standards. Two fine examples have survived from the fortress of High Rochester (Bremenium) in Northumbria, Britain, north of Hadrian's Wall, where an auxiliary cohort from northern Spain was stationed in the first half of the third century.

To the genius of our Lord and of the standards of the First Cohort of Vardulli and of the unit of scouts of Bremenium styled Gordianus, Egnatius Lucilianus, emperor's Propraetorian Prefect [set up this altar] under the charge of Cassius Sabinianus, tribune. (*RIB** 1262)

This first inscribed altar was discovered where one would have hoped, within the treasury of the fortress. It is dated quite precisely by the mention of Egnatius Lucilianus, who governed Britannia Inferior from AD 238 to 241. A second altar was found in a bath house, where it appears to have been transferred after a fire, for it is heavily burnt and split in two.

To the genius and standards of the First Loyal Cohort of the Vardulli, Roman citizens, part mounted, one thousand strong, Titus Licinius Valerianus set this up. (*RIB* 1263)

This cannot be dated so precisely, but one might posit that the altar of *c*.238 took this one's place when it was replaced according to the prescriptions of the *Feriale* that the altar be broken, buried and replaced each year as an act of renewal and rededication.

At the legionary fortress of Caerleon (Isca Silurum), Britannia, the following inscription was unearthed in 1800:

To the *numina* of the *Augusti* and the *genius* of the Second Legion Augusta in

---

* *RIB* is the standard abbreviation for *The Inscriptions of Roman Britain*. Full details of this, and every text to which we shall refer, may be found in the bibliographical essays that complete this book. A list of frequently used abbreviations can also be found at the end of the book.

honour of the [eagle standard?] . . . the senior centurion gave this gift; dedicated 23 September in the consulship of Peregrinus and Aemilianus [AD 244], under the charge of Ursus, *actarius* [military clerk] of the same legion. (*RIB* 327)

The date of the dedication, 23 September 244, corresponds with that given in the *Feriale* as the birthday of the deified Augustus, when an ox would be sacrificed. This would have had especial significance for an Augustan legion, since it would also be the legion's birthday, and hence that of its eagle.

These were official dedications as prescribed in the *Feriale*. A more personal offering can be identified by a statue base found in 1925 at Chester, in what would have been a barrack block, which is dedicated to the 'Genius of the standard-bearers of the Twentieth Legion Valeria Victrix, Titus Flavius Valerianus gave this gift to his colleagues'. The dedicant was evidently a *signifer*, and the *genius* he venerated that of the standards he and his colleagues protected. A legionary fortress such as Chester would have housed one of the most sacred and enduring standards, the eagle standard of the legions. These were awarded at first in silver and later in gold, at the inception of the legion. Divisions and units also had standards, most commonly incorporating a flag called a *vexillum*. In addition, regimental emblems and images of the emperors would be carried into battle, and in the third century one might see also cruciform trophies and dragon standards.

Standards were taken into battle, as depicted on the monuments raised by the emperor Trajan in Rome and at Adamklissi (near Tomis, now in modern Romania). They transmitted the soterial power of the *genii* to those fighting under them. So diverse and numerous were the standards that additional, mundane functions might be served. Standards demonstrated to troops where each unit was stationed before battle, and in battle they showed that the line was being held. Narratives, for example those of Caesar, relate where soldiers fought before or behind the standards. They identified the position of unit commanders and hence facilitated the relay of battle orders. They served as points of muster for units when an order to reform was given. At all costs the standard was to be defended, for its loss generally meant the end of the unit, if one remained to be disbanded. Soldiers knew this, and thus could be motivated to follow the standards into the most treacherous conditions. Caesar records that the eagle-bearer of the tenth legion leapt into the sea off the coast of Britain, obliging his comrades to follow. Still more precariously, both Plutarch (*Aemilius Paulus*, 20) and Livy (34.46) record that the standards might be thrown among the enemy to spur legionaries to advance further into the mêlée. Few standards were lost, despite this practice, but most famously the general Varus lost three eagles in AD 9 when three legions were annihilated. These were recovered over the following decades and deposited in Rome's temple of Mars Ultor, 'the Avenger'.

Military eagles (*aquilae*) appear never to have been replaced, and many were heavily restored. The latest known representation of an eagle is found on the gravestone of Titus Flavius Surillio, eagle-standard-bearer (*aquilifer*) of the Second Legion Adiutrix (fig. 2). The carved stone, which was set up in Byzantium, the future Constantinople, in *c.*AD 213, shows the *aquilifer* holding the standard in his right hand as it rests in a cup supported by a strap suspended from his shoulder. Surillio's eagle sits on a base atop a shaft, peering to its right with lowered wings. It is quite distinct from the regular style of raised wings and head turned forward, and this suggests that it may be the same eagle depicted on Trajan's Column in Rome. Immediately below the eagle's base, on the shaft of the standard, one can see the head of an indeterminate animal. Far clearer is a ram's head at the base of the shaft, which consequently has been added to the list of legionary emblems of the Second Legion Adiutrix.

Surillio's eagle was surely that presented to the legion upon its foundation in AD 69, and the gravestone suggests that it had acquired few accretions. In contrast, the standards of smaller divisions acquired numerous wreaths or crowns, which commemorated particular victories, as well as disks, moon sickles, images of men or animals, and even ships' prows. We have several depictions of flag standards, *vexilla*, for example on the columns of Trajan (fig. 3) and Marcus Aurelius, and on the monument at Adamklissi. Third-century flag standards associated with known units can be seen in carved reliefs from Benwell (Condercum) and Corbridge in Britain, and on a bronze roundel depicting men from two British legions. The Corbridge relief which depicts the rose ceremony also shows the *vexillum* between two more pilasters. The standard is fairly simple, being a shaft planted in the ground. Upon the shaft, one quarter of the height to the flag, one sees a horizontal S-shaped device. The flag has a broad border on the top and sides, perhaps of embroidered brocade or embossed metal, and a narrower fringe of tassels below. Above the flag is the bottom of a disk or crescent, mostly lost, which perhaps was surmounted by a lance point. On the body of the banner one reads in two lines 'the flag standard of the Second Augustan Legion'. The only surviving *vexillum*, in the Pushkin Museum in Moscow, bears no such inscription. Nor does the flag standard depicted in a fresco in the Temple of Bel at Dura Europos, where a tribune named Terentius is shown performing a camp ritual (fig. 4).

The cult of the standards, therefore, was an additional element in the elaborate body of camp ritual which ensured that the Roman soldier expressed openly, regularly and ceremoniously his loyalty to the emperor, to the gods who protected the Roman state and people, and to his unit. It was held that through these common actions the Roman army, as the Roman people at war, would secure victories in war and the benefits of peace. None of the rites, however, addressed in their entirety the spiritual needs of the individual. These were met by prayers to any number of gods and by membership in various cults.

Private religious devotion and cults

The Roman was generally free to worship any and all deities according to his or her own conscience. And the first thing one must observe is that the place of Jupiter Optimus Maximus, 'the best and greatest', at the head of the pantheon of gods worshipped in state *religio* did not diminish his appeal to individuals. By far the greatest number of inscriptions, the clearest surviving evidence for patterns of private devotion, attest to the veneration of Jupiter in western parts of the empire and North Africa. A chart of fifteen cults produced by the classicist Ramsay MacMullen from analysis of the indices of catalogues of Latin inscriptions shows how all other deities paled in comparison, with Jupiter's closest peers being his traditional companions, notably Mercury, and his sons Dionysus (Bacchus) and Heracles (Hercules). Of female gods

Diana (Artemis) and Venus (Aphrodite) have fewer attested adherents than Fortuna, the goddess of fortune, but that can easily be explained by the nature of individual prayer, since good luck in any sphere could be attributed to fortune. Apollo, Mars and Silvanus were as popular overall as Asclepius and Mithras, and more so than other cults of personal salvation, including those of the Great Mother (Cybele), Isis and Serapis, and Jupiter Dolichenus (a distinct variant of 'the best and greatest' god, to whom we shall turn shortly).

Inscriptions provide indications of relative rather than absolute popularity. Exclusivity of worship was rare, as almost everything was held to be protected by a specific deity or *genius*. Shrines devoted to the veneration of ancestral spirits, Lares, who preserved families and their memories, were maintained in private households. And tens of thousands of surviving inscriptions suggest that individual worship was devoted primarily to private prayer and to the consequent fulfilment of particular vows to all manifestations of supernatural power. Men, women and children prayed for health and safety for themselves and for their families. They sought divine patronage for specific endeavours and gave an offering of thanks if the prayer was answered.

Military inscriptions have survived abundantly, revealing that men prayed to particular gods or *genii* with specific entreaties and requests, vowing in return to erect an altar, statue or plaque. Such prayers were frequently answered, and when the lucky recipient fulfilled his vow, he left behind a record that often reveals the nature of his prayer. Vows to gods were made to ensure that a soldier would not embarrass himself before his comrades, or allow his comrades to die or be injured, or sustain injury or die himself. Colleagues who were left behind might erect dedications to their colleagues, in fulfilment of vows for their safe return. For example, 'the soldiers on garrison duty' at Corbridge erected an altar 'To Jupiter Optimus Maximus, for the welfare of the detachments of the Twentieth Legion Valeria Victrix, and of the Sixth Legion Victrix'. They also swore vows to abstract concepts, which the Romans deified and of which the most popular was fortune, the goddess Fortuna. In military contexts, concord and discipline were also venerated, since both would serve units well in battle. We find three such dedication slabs at Corbridge, including one to concord between the same legions, the Sixth Victrix and the Twentieth Valeria Victrix. More commonly, vows were to a warrior god or goddess, and of the many thousands we cite only two from Benwell, on Hadrian's Wall, to Mars, who bears the epithets 'preserver' (*conservator*) and victor; and two inscriptions from the Rhine frontier fortress of Castellum Matiacorum (modern Mainz-Kastel in Germany), which attest to the erection of an altar in AD 224 and to the reconstruction of a temple in 236, both dedicated to the warrior goddess Bellona.

Vows were fulfilled upon returning to camp having undertaken duties and obligations; upon returning to find friends and family in safety and good health; and, ultimately, upon returning home. Those stationed far from home, and who campaigned in various lands, took few chances in spreading their prayers around, as the following inscription found at York makes plain: 'To the African, Italian and Gallic Mother Goddesses, Marcus Minicius Audens, soldier of the Sixth Legion Victrix and a river pilot (*gubernator*) of the Sixth Legion, willingly, gladly and deservedly fulfilled his vow.' This is the only dedication to the African 'Mother Goddesses' in Britain and was likely erected by a recruit from Africa who fought in both Gaul and Italy. Another African officer stationed far from home, at Maryport, erected an altar of red sandstone, dedicated 'To the genius of the place, to Fortune the Home-bringer, to Eternal Rome, and to Good Fate, Gaius Cornelius Peregrinus, tribune of the cohort, decurion of his hometown of Saldae in the province Mauretania Caesariensis, gladly, willingly and deservedly fulfilled his vow.' Devotion 'to Fortune the Home-bringer' suggests a desire not merely to return safely to camp, but ultimately to a native land, to settle in a veterans' canton. In the event that one did not return home, one's prayer to die swiftly and painlessly may have been answered, and colleagues might erect a gravestone, like that to Titus Flavius Surillio, the 'eagle-bearer' (*aquilifer*), and undertake the necessary rites to ensure passage to an afterlife.

Private prayers and the fulfilment of vows were far more significant considerations for individuals than those prescribed by the state. It is here that we approach most clearly rituals that today are considered religious, rather than rites which appear political and were intended to promote loyalty to the state and its symbols, jingoism, community spirit and unit solidarity. Again, one must avoid the temptation to separate the political from the religious, but more than singing a national anthem or pledging allegiance to a flag, these inscriptions attest that the traditional gods could attend to the spiritual needs of individuals. However, as Rome expanded, they were joined by new deities with great appeal from beyond the traditional pantheon. Most notably, cults promising personal salvation became remarkably popular in the second and third centuries AD. MacMullen attributes this, somewhat oddly, to the expense of maintaining the traditional religion. When and where the task of supplying the most splendid temples to house the gods or of staging the most splendid festivals in their honour was too great, many would turn to other deities, whose demands were less aristocratic. But this, to an extent, ignores the fact that membership of certain cults, including Christianity, offered members things that state religion did not: a sense of belonging to an elect group; the promise of health and victuals; and the certainty of eternal life.

A series of seven sarcophagi from the tomb of the Calpurnii, now housed at the Walters Art Museum in Baltimore, provide a host of symbols associated with the worship of Dionysus, also known as Bacchus and Liber Pater. Most famous is the triumphal procession of Bacchus in a chariot pulled by two panthers (but elsewhere by leopards, tigers, centaurs or elephants), carved in c.AD 180. A slightly later sarcophagus of equal artistry depicts Victories holding a shield of valour, the *clipeus virtutis*, on which is a bust of Bacchus (fig. 5). In their other hands they hold slim cruciform trophies, which have been misidentified as *vexilla*, flag standards without flags. They are, however, clearly precursors to the Christian crucifix, symbols of victory over death, which guarantee the eternal life of the faithful, in this case devotees of Dionysus. An extremely early example of this can be seen in the so-called House of Dionysus at Paphos, Cyprus, where in a Hellenistic pebble mosaic dating from the fourth century BC a sea monster, Scylla, is depicted holding a long, thin cross. Within the same complex, far later mosaics depict the luxuries enjoyed by a prosperous merchant who was a devotee of Bacchus. One (fig. 6), dated c.AD 150–75, shows Dionysus atop his triumphal chariot, pulled by two leopards (or perhaps panthers) led by Silenus, the god of the dance of the wine-press. A satyr bearing a large jug, a *krater*, and wine-skins is stepping onto the chariot. Dionysus is holding a long, thin staff rather similar to Scylla's but without the cross-bar: it is his pinecone-topped *thyrsos*. In the nearby House of Aion, a mosaic dating from Constantine's reign, *c*.325–50, shows Dionysus' chariot pulled by centaurs. This is the type we shall meet again later, in examining Constantine's Great Cameo (see p. 217), which is entirely contemporary with it. Its message is quite different to that of its second-century neighbour. No longer the god of wine and excess, Dionysus is virtuous, the world's saviour, offering his initiates secret knowledge of immortality and rebirth. Where his chariot rolls grow flowers, and he is attended not by a wine-bearing satyr but by a girl carrying a *liknon*, a basket bearing the secret of rebirth, a phallus (fig. 7).

Many cults offered a vision of paradise after death, but those that offered specific earthly benefits, like Dionysus', grew most rapidly. Of some popularity was the cult of Asclepius, to whom healing shrines and temples were dedicated throughout the Mediterranean world. Once a man and now a god, Asclepius was worshipped as both healer and saviour, a channel between divinity and humanity, as a prayer reveals:

Asclepius, child of Apollo, these words come from your devoted servant. Blessed one, god for whom I yearn, how shall I enter your golden house unless your heart incline towards me and you will heal me and restore me to your shrine again, so that I may look on my god, who is brighter than the earth in springtime? Divine blessed one, you alone have power. With your loving kindness you are a great gift from the supreme gods to mankind, a refuge from trouble.

The sacred stories of Aelius Aristides, written in the AD 140s, praise Asclepius for healing his toothache, earache, asthma and fever, all suffered by the author before he visited the god's sanctuary at Pergamon (modern Bergama in Turkey). The cult of Asclepius remained popular even after Constantine's reign, when the healing miracles of scripture saw Christ enter into direct competition with Asclepius. Indeed, in early Christian art Christ is portrayed most commonly in miracle scenes, and where Asclepius carried his staff wrapped with a snake, Christ is commonly shown holding a magician's wand.

Of similar vintage in Rome to the worship of Asclepius, although older in origin, was the cult of the Great Mother (Magna Mater), also known as Cybele. This was brought to Rome from Phrygia, Anatolia, in 204 BC. According to Livy, this was because Rome's Sibylline Books of prophecy suggested she would bring victory in the war against Carthage. This was indeed the case, and within two years the Second Punic War was brought to a successful conclusion by the Roman general Scipio Africanus, who forced Hannibal to accept peace after the Battle of Zama. As a consequence, Scipio was granted a *triumphus*, a triumphal procession through the city of Rome where he wore the insignia of Jupiter Optimus Maximus and deposited booty in the temple atop the Capitoline Hill. Thereafter, the Roman triumph ended with the dedication of spoils to the god or goddess who had granted that particular victory. Most frequently, these were Victoria, Jupiter's handmaiden, and Mars, the god of war in his various forms. But the role of Cybele was universally acknowledged, and she was granted a temple atop the Palatine. In Ovid's later account, the meteorite that became the head of her cult statue was first placed in the Temple of Victory, while her adjacent temple was completed.

Cybele was venerated in the state calendar each year, on 4 April, when patricians held banquets to mark the day of her arrival in Rome. This became the start of a week-long festival aimed at the plebeians, the Megalesia, during which plays (including four of those extant by Terence) were performed, and later chariot races were held. From before her arrival in Rome, the goddess had been tended by priests, called Galli, who were self-castrates, given to drenching themselves in perfumes and sporting extravagant wigs and colourful robes. The Galli and their ecstatic rites, involving a procession with flutes and drums, made Cybele somewhat peripheral to regular Roman state *religio*. Only Phrygians were allowed to become priests and take part in the Megalesian procession. Nevertheless, additional rituals later adhered to the cult, including the day of blood on 24 May, when worshippers were washed in blood. The following day, 25 May, marked the rebirth of Attis, Cybele's castrated consort, three days after his demise. This was also the day that Christians had taken as the date of Christ's death. Death, blood sacrifice and resurrection emerged at the core of the worship of the Great Mother in the first centuries AD, which made it particularly distasteful to Christians.

St Jerome changed her title from Mother of the Gods (*mater deorum*) to Mother of Demons (*mater daemoniorum*). She was also equated with the whore of Babylon (Revelation 17:3–6), 'the woman drunk with the blood of the saints, and with the blood of the witnesses of Jesus'.

Cybele was quite markedly a civilian goddess, and both relative to other cults and absolutely on the basis of her own adherents, she appealed to women. Inscriptions attesting vows to her come from the interior lands of the empire, not from the frontiers. Where she was worshipped in army camps, it was as Bellona. Cybele featured on the coins of the emperor Antoninus Pius (AD 138–61), and it is late in his reign that we first hear of the *taurobolium*, a ritual which was carried out by others for the benefit of the emperor, apparently another accretion to the imperial cults. In this rite, a bull was slaughtered on a platform, below which initiates would lie, to be baptized by its blood. That at least is according to the lurid description, probably reflecting a Christian disgust for and pastiche of the practice, provided by Prudentius in his *Crowns of the Martyrs*. It is possible that the first performance of the rite was merely the regular sacrifice of oxen prescribed in the religious calendar (*feriale*).

The popularity of Cybele cleared the path to Rome for a still more powerful goddess, Isis, who arrived from Egypt claiming to be the supreme divinity, head of the whole pantheon. Designated the consort of Serapis by Manetho and Timotheus, two men charged in *c*.300 BC by Ptolemy I with establishing a hierarchy for the multitude of Egyptian gods, she swiftly reigned supreme. Supreme was not, of course, unique, for the Ptolemies practised not monotheism but henotheism, the belief in a greatest god, who surpassed in power all other deities. Isis' arrival in Rome was not uneventful, for she did not, like Cybele, bring in her wake a longed-for victory. The senate banned her worship in 58 BC, and both Augustus and Tiberius considered the cult incompatible with traditional beliefs, seeing to the destruction of altars and temples and to the crucifixion of some priests. But a festival to Isis was granted by Caligula (d. AD 41), who took part in her mysteries, and thereafter she remained a fixture in Rome.

Isis gave birth to her son Horus without prior intercourse, and thus she was an archetype for the virgin mother. Her greater appeal, like that of Cybele and Dionysus, was to promise triumph over death to her followers. Just as she had resurrected her twin brother Osiris to dwell eternally with her, so she might offer that reward to her devotees. In the later second century, a famous hymn to Isis was offered in the only Roman novel to survive in its entirety, Apuleius' *The Golden Ass*. The novel's hero, Lucius, has a rare bond with the goddess, who visits him in his dreams (as Christ will later visit Constantine, more than once). Entering the priesthood of Isis, Lucius undergoes an initiation, during which time he suffers a ritual death, a vision and its illumination. He emerges to set himself on a platform before the people, at one with the goddess. This rare literary record of a Roman's conversion has a great deal in common with the story of Constantine's epiphany, as we shall see in later chapters.

Isis proved to be rather popular in Italy, and MacMullen advances the notion that here adherents of Isis were predominantly slaves and freedmen from the east. This cannot be proven and seems rather similar to outdated explanations for the rise of Christianity, which held that it was most popular among the poor and downtrodden, to whom its message would most appeal and who had most to gain in the next world. Lucius' particular bond with the goddess notwithstanding, Isis, like Cybele, appealed especially to women. Since women did not so frequently inscribe their names and vows on stone, the extent to which Isis was venerated may be under-represented in the historical record. Moreover, soldiers, who inscribed more than most, do not feature much in Isiac lists. Only two temples to Isis have been found in military contexts in the west. This does not hold for the east, but the presence of soldiers in or near towns and cities with temples to Isis is a likely explanation for this. Nevertheless, according to the relative survivals of inscriptions, worship of Isis reached a peak under the soldier emperors Septimius Severus and his son Caracalla, in the first third of the third century AD. This peak may, in fact, merely represent the height of the habit of inscribing, as it was exactly contemporary with the epigraphic apogee of the cult of Jupiter Dolichenus (Jupiter of Doliche).

The earliest inscription attesting to the presence of the cult of Jupiter Dolichenus is from Lambaestis in Africa, dating from AD 125–6. The cult of Jupiter Dolichenus first appears in the west in the later 120s, attaining a peak of popularity around 200 and fading after the death of Septimius Severus. In that one hundred years there are enough inscriptions to earn the cult a place in MacMullen's league table of fifteen, which covers a far longer period. Almost all are associated with the army. The cult was relatively unpopular to the east of its point of origin, Doliche (modern Dülük in Turkey). Recently, however, a fine relief of the god standing atop a bull, his familiar pose, within a temple dedicated to Jupiter Dolichenus has been uncovered at Balaklava, near Sebastopol (modern Ukraine). A magnificent bronze from Mauer-an-der-Url, in the province of Noricum, similarly depicts Jupiter standing on the back of a bull. The god holds in his lowered right hand a thunderbolt and in his raised left hand a double-headed axe (although the axe-head is lost). He sports a Phrygian cap, but also an imperial cuirass and a sword with an eagle-headed hilt, suggesting an instance of *imitatio imperatorum* that was so popular in the third century.

Since no literature pertaining to the rites of Jupiter Dolichenus has survived, interpretation must dwell on such imagery, as well as on some important reliefs discovered at Rome and Corbridge, the fort on Hadrian's Wall. Both of these show an image of the sun, a god with a solar crown. He is paired on one relief with the moon, a goddess, suggesting their centrality to the cult's doctrines. The Roman inscription was set up by a priest of Jupiter Dolichenus, one Marcus Ulpius Chresimus, 'to the Unconquered Sun for the salvation of the emperors and to the genius of their [unit of bodyguards]'. It seems likely that Ulpius was a member of that unit, as well as a priest in the cult.

An association of Sol Invictus with Jupiter Dolichenus appears to be confirmed by the discovery at Corbridge of the first known dedication by a provincial army unit to the Unconquered Sun, set up in AD 162–8.

To the Invincible Sun, a detachment of the Sixth Legion Victrix Pia Fidelis set this up under the charge of Sextus Calpurnius Agricola, the emperor's pro-praetorian prefect. (*RIB* 1137)

At Corbridge one finds also an altar dedicated 'To eternal Jupiter Dolichenus and to Caelestis Brigantia and to Salus, Gaius Julius Apolinaris, centurion of the Sixth Legion, at the command of god [set this up]'.

Thus, the oriental god was set beside a very local goddess, of the Brigantes, who dominated what is now Yorkshire.

That the cult was well established among soldiers in Britannia by the mid-second century is demonstrated not only at Corbridge but at many other sites, including Caerleon, where a sandstone altar (now lost) was found in 1653. It was dedicated: 'To Jupiter Best and Greatest, of Doliche ... Fronto Aemilianus ... Calpurnius ... Rufilianus, legate of the emperors [set this up] at the bidding [of ?].' Continued interest in the cult is attested by part of a dedication slab found in 1811 in the river Ribble at Ribchester, which can be dated quite certainly to AD 225–35. Here a temple had been dedicated by legionary centurion Titus Floridius Natalis 'according to the reply (*ex responsu*) of the god' Jupiter Dolichenus. However, shortly afterwards, one finds systematic destruction of temples along the Rhine and Danube frontiers, apparently instigated by the emperor Maximinus Thrax (AD 235–8). The cult may have been fairly wealthy – finds of bronze and silver support this – and perhaps the emperor was hoping to fill his coffers. This may not have been a wise policy, as Maximinus died at the hands of his own troops shortly afterwards.

A particular feature of the cult, surely associated with its popularity with the army, was an attachment to cultic standards. Impressions of some of these suggest close parallels with military standards, although others end in a crescent, perhaps alluding to the moon goddess. Standards are portrayed on four of the six bronze votive tablets dedicated to Jupiter Dolichenus that have been discovered at sites bordering the Danube. These tablets are all triangular, resembling a spear tip, and two indeed have sockets welded to the bottom which would have been attached to rods, perhaps to be carried during rites alongside the standards they depict.

The mysteries of Mithras

Only slightly more is known about the rites of the greatest military cult, that of Mithras, alternatively Mithra, which reached the peak of its popularity in the later second to early third century. The cult offered personal salvation to its initiates, who proceeded to that goal through seven grades, each a new level of understanding. These levels represented the seven planetary spheres, through which one passed to reach the door to the eighth sphere, where Mithras dwelt in his solar invincibility. Born on 25 December, according to some accounts from a virgin (but in others sprung from a rock, a tree or an egg), Mithras was the intermediary between the god of light and the god of darkness. He slaughtered the first-born, a bull, from whose blood living creatures were created and wherein lay their salvation. Having defended mankind against evil, Mithras ascended to heaven in a solar chariot, not unlike Elijah's chariot of fire (2 Kings 2:11). He became one with the Sun, as *deus Sol invictus Mithras*, 'the God, the Unconquered Sun, Mithras', or perhaps better, 'the Unconquered Sun God Mithras'. The notion of a god descending to save mankind and ascending to rejoin the godhead is common with Christianity, of course, but the tension between descent and ascent are omnipresent in Mithraic art. Mithras' solar chariot ascends, pulled by four horses, while its pair, the moon's chariot, descends yoked to two. These are evidently akin to motifs employed by those who worshipped Jupiter Dolichenus.

The principal iconography of Mithraism is a scene of sacrifice and redemption, the iconological equivalent of the crucifixion in later Christian churches. It is widely known from archaeological excavations, and one might cite as examples the relief discovered during excavations of the temple of Mithras, a Mithraeum, at Walbrook in the City of London, now displayed in the Museum of London, or the sculpture now in the Vatican Pio Clementine Museum (fig. 8). Here, in a scene called the tauroctony ('bull-slaying'), Mithras is shown cutting the bull's throat so that the blood may flow onto the earth. Mithras looks away from the bull, his eyes gazing towards the heavens. Many other elements are omnipresent, others only frequently or occasionally visible. The sun and moon usually appear, and one must imagine that the Vatican Pio Clementine Museum sculpture was displayed before a relief or fresco showing them. Other symbols represent stellar constellations. The snake represents Hydra, the dog Canis Minor, the crab Cancer. One might also expect to see a lion representing the constellation Leo, and the twins Gemini, and a raven for Corvus. The tauroctony displayed in every Mithraeum was, therefore, a view of the heavens, extending from Taurus, the bull, in the west, usually to Scorpio in the east. It is unlikely that the sacrifice of a bull actually took place within the Mithraeum. It was simply too small and was underground. One cannot easily imagine initiates coaxing a bull into a tunnel at night, still less holding it still for sacrifice. More certain to have taken place is the common meal, the second iconographical scene universally displayed in Mithraea: a banquet of initiates feasting and servants (or the lower-ranked?) wearing animal masks waiting on them. Equivalent to the Christian Eucharist, this was where initiates drank sacrificial wine, symbolizing blood, and ate together of the flesh. Benches on which initiates reclined have been excavated.

The cult of Mithras was open only to men, and it had many civilian adherents. About one third of those who inscribed vows to Mithras did so in Italy, with almost half of them in Rome itself and many at Rome's port of Ostia, where fifteen separate small Mithraea have been excavated. But as the cult spread, it appealed particularly to soldiers. The cultic hierarchy reflected that of the army, and one proceeded through the ranks by undergoing real and symbolic feats of endurance, some involving heat and cold, perhaps including branding (or the threat of it) with white-hot steel, another the rejection of a crown at sword-point (to which we shall return in the following chapter, with Tertullian's account). One can imagine a rite where the initiate expects to be run through with a sword and submits to this, finding himself blindfold and apparently transfixed. Thus we might explain a trick sword discovered in a German Mithraeum, which comprised a hilt and blade tip, joined by a large metal loop designed to fit around the upper body.

Mithraea were found throughout the empire in the vicinity of military camps, for example at Prutting, south-east of Munich near the river Inn, at the German border with Austria, which continued in use until the end of the fourth century. We find another at Dura Europos in Syria, base of the Twentieth Palmyrene Cohort. Britain, as a heavily militarized part of the empire, provides copious evidence for Mithraism. In the bath building outside the legionary fortress of Caerleon was found an inscription: 'To the invincible Mithras, the well-deserving [. . .]s Iustus [. . .] of the Second Legion Augusta, set this up.' We know that the same cavalry unit of Vardulli that honoured the *genius* of their standards erected a temple to Mithras at High Rochester, for which we have the dedication slab:

Sacred to the invincible god, the sun and companion, for the welfare and safety of the emperor Caesar Marcus Aurelius Antoninus Pius Felix Augustus: Lucius Caecilius Optatus, tribune of the first cohort of Vardulli, with his fellow devotees [erected this building], vowed to the god, built from the ground. (*RIB* 1272)

The same tribune was responsible for a dedication in AD 213 to the Celtic bear god Matunus, for the welfare of the emperor Caracalla, found seven miles from High Rochester. Evidently, devotion to Mithras need not be exclusive, and indeed one suspects that many initiates were also adherents of Jupiter Dolichenus.

The absence of a Mithraeum does not demonstrate absence of worshippers of Mithras. It is known that adherents were satisfied worshipping their god in the temples of others, for example those of Hermes, Dionysus and Isis. Until recently, there was an absence of evidence for the worship of Mithras in the vast province of Egypt. But now we have a lacunose text on papyrus which appears to be a catechism for new initiates to Mithraism. The editor of the papyrus, Brashear, identifies the text largely on the basis of the term 'little lion', known elsewhere only from a Latin inscription which employs the term to designate a junior grade in the Mithraic hierarchy. Other words and phrases thus fall into place, such as 'father', and 'night . . . you are called . . . becoming fiery . . . in a trench . . . being girdled . . . death . . . very sharp . . . hot and cold'. Mithraic rites are known to have been nocturnal and subterranean, and these terms all suggest an initiation ritual.

The papyrus, which dates from the fourth century AD, preserves fragments of a conversation in question-and-answer form, although not a single complete pair of question and answer survives. It is a theoretical dialogue to take place according to prescription, between a highly ranked initiate and an initiand. The papyrus was found at Hermupolis (Damanhur), just outside Alexandria, most likely during excavations in 1906, and is now in the Egyptian Museum in Berlin. Sources for a Roman army presence at Hermupolis begin to turn up only in the mid-fourth century, just as Mithraism was on the decline elsewhere. Moreover, since the text is written in Greek not Latin, it is clearly not a product of the military establishment. Perhaps, therefore, it was an ad hoc local production translated from a Latin version, which may have been introduced slightly earlier by the army. Little more can be said, except that Constantine, brought up in army camps, was perhaps an initiate of the mysteries of Mithras.

2

The Rise of Christianity

Women and the spread of Christianity – Christianity as an urban phenomenon – Christian exceptionalism and martyrdom – Early Christian attitudes to warfare – Christians in the Roman army – Military martyrs and warrior saints

Christianity falls into the category of private religious worship, which would normally be allowed to operate as a spiritual supplement to official Roman state cults. At the time of Constantine's birth, Christianity was a faith growing rapidly. Its popularity can be attributed in large part to its message, some of which it shared with contemporary cults that promised personal salvation. It has been estimated that the number of Christians grew at a rate of forty percent per decade, through reproduction and conversion. From a tiny pool of believers, the number of Christians grew slowly at first, but eventually exponentially. The period of exponential growth began in the later third century, when from around one million in AD 250, there were more than six million Christians in AD 300, and almost thirty-four million in AD 350. The total population of the empire remained relatively constant at this time, with few reported epidemics or famines after a devastating pandemic of measles or, more likely, smallpox in the 260s. Thus, in the century that embraced Constantine's reign, the empire went from having a tiny minority to a majority of Christians.

Our task is to determine the impact of the emperor's conversion: whether it allowed Christianity to continue to grow at the pace it had established by making advances into new areas. That is, to see whether the fact that Constantine adopted the faith allowed it to spread from the cities of the eastern Mediterranean, where it had made great headway before his birth, into the empire's northern and western provinces, into inland cities and towns, and also into army camps. First, then, we must assess how Christianity grew before Constantine.

38

Women and the spread of Christianity

Why did Christianity grow, and at the expense of which religions? The answer is vast and complicated, but for the sake of clarity it may be reduced to sex, health and arithmetic. These are to the fore in compelling studies by the sociologist Rodney Stark, which have changed the way we see the religious landscape of the later Roman Empire.* Most converts to Christianity in the earliest centuries were Hellenized Jews. Christianity was a cult, whose adherents bruited a new set of beliefs but still lugged around a great deal of cultural baggage. That baggage, notably the books that the Christians called their Old Testament, was familiar to Hellenized Jews, as was the language in which it was written: Greek. Only the Jews of Palestine spoke and read Hebrew and Aramaic, whereas the vast majority in the diaspora spoke Greek and read their holy books in an authoritative Greek translation, the Septuagint, so called for the seventy (or seventy-two) Jewish scholars who produced it. After AD 70, as the Jewish Wars set the population of Palestine against the Romans, there was a still better reason for the diaspora Jews to distance themselves from their co-religionists, and many, it would appear, embraced Christianity. Jewish converts made up the bulk of new Christians for at least two centuries. But as the number of Christians began to rise rapidly in the third century, most converts were former adherents of the traditional Roman gods, whom we know as pagans, employing a pejorative term coined by the Christians. Pagans converted for a number of very good reasons, many of them spiritual and intellectual. But the most profound reason is surely the indisputable fact that Christianity offered a better life to women and their children.

Women endured a lowly status in the Graeco-Roman world because they were proportionately few and thus, as a precious commodity, carefully controlled by men. If the population of the Roman Empire was sixty million at the time of Constantine's birth, only around twenty-four million of these were women. Given that boys are more problematic in

---

* It is important to note that this interpretation remains controversial and has provoked many dissenting opinions. Some are presented in the bibliographical essays appended to this book.

the womb, more sickly as infants and more inclined to die at a young age in military activity or by violence, this figure is quite remarkable and can be explained only by the fact that baby girls were frequently murdered. It was rare for all but the wealthiest families to raise more than one daughter, however many were born, and infanticide was the surest way to dispose of unwanted girls. It was legal, philosophically justified and widely practised. An infamous letter sent by a man to his pregnant wife in 1 BC instructs her: 'if it's a boy keep it, if it's a girl throw it away.' One can no longer point to a drain in Ashkelon, in southern Israel, where a hundred skeletons of discarded infants have been found, as corroboration. DNA analysis on nineteen femurs from the pit has revealed fourteen to be of boys. Still, the weight of evidence suggests that far fewer girls than boys were allowed to grow to maturity, that is to child-bearing age, and consequently the general rate of reproduction in the late Roman world was kept artificially low. One must add to this the high rate of infant mortality and the death of mothers in childbirth or from complications and infections arising from it. Moreover, abortion was widely practised, although the gruesome descriptions one may read in Roman medical treatises make one wonder why women did not run the lesser risk of full-term delivery. The answer, of course, was men. Roman husbands and fathers had complete control over their wives' and daughters' fates, and could order that abortions be carried out as surely as they could order the exposure of a healthy baby girl.

Christianity offered a new vision, where both abortion and infanticide were forbidden, and virginity before marriage was prescribed. Christians discouraged marriage below a certain age and banned consummation of a marriage between a man and a child bride, such that the average age of marriage for Christian women became twenty, whereas for pagan women it was twelve. One must add that the rate of reproduction among pagans was very low: men favoured birth control (including anal and, less commonly, oral sex), indulged in homosexual sex, took concubines and patronized both male and female prostitutes, who in turn favoured various methods of birth control and abortion when necessary. All of these practices were forbidden to Christians, as most were to Jews. Roman men who converted to Christianity were obliged to have vaginal intercourse with their wives, and if pregnancy resulted, were obliged to have a child and raise it, regardless of its sex. Moreover, a Christian woman would have a community to support any resistance she offered to the directives of a pagan husband to do otherwise. As a consequence of this moral code the Christian population reproduced far more effectively than other Romans, and there were rapidly far more Christian women than pagan women, as a proportion of their communities.

According to modern sociological observation, setting aside the advantages outlined thus far of conversion to Christianity in its earliest centuries, women are far more likely than men to convert to any new religious faith, particularly one with a strong spiritual dimension. Thus, the conversion of women to Christianity in greater numbers need not be accounted for wholly by the higher status accorded to women and the greater care taken of children of both sexes. But given that women did convert, for a variety of reasons, they would often then persuade their husbands to accept or join their new faith. And once men converted, if they were of sufficient status, it was expected that the whole household, including slaves and perhaps even clients and freedmen, would also convert, thus augmenting a local Christian community considerably. That there were relatively high rates of intermarriage between Christian women and pagan men was inevitable given the disparity between numbers of pagan women and men. Moreover, such intermarriage was not banned by the Church. St Paul expected it, although that was a function of his having written when there were perhaps fewer than one thousand Christians in total. But the fact that Tertullian, writing Christian tracts from the later second century, condemns interfaith marriage so vociferously demonstrates how prevalent the practice still was. Thus, the male pool of potential secondary converts was large, and even if the husband remained a pagan, the Church prescribed that children of such marriages be raised as Christians. So it was that entire families of Christians emerged, even if the father refused to convert.

There are interesting contrasts to be drawn here with other henotheistic and monotheistic cults that appealed principally, or were open exclusively, to men. These could not be inherited religions, for only mature men could enter some cults, for example that of Mithras. Without women, there was no possibility that a cult would grow into a church.

Moreover, military men worshipped for specific reasons, notably their safety in battle, and swore vows to that end. They were drawn to military cults for the camaraderie and hierarchy that mirrored camp life. Once they left the camps, however, and were allowed to live with their wives, these constraints no longer applied. Certainly, those who lived in colonies – settlements of discharged army veterans – would be able to continue with former practices if they chose, but in different groups, as their comrades in arms might remain elsewhere on active duty and the need to pray to military gods was no longer so apparent. Others, however, with their prior connections sundered, might enter new networks and manifest new spiritual needs. A maxim central to Rodney Stark's analysis applies here: 'To the extent that we value our relationships with others, we will conform in order to retain their esteem.' One might easily find former adherents of military mystery cults now drawn to Christianity, even with its explicit 'love command' as articulated in its New Testament. We shall turn to this shortly. Where the 'love command' was subverted, and where one might wish to retain the esteem of a trusted commander (or indeed of an emperor who now openly identified himself as a Christian and surrounded himself with other Christians), one might expect to find many new converts to Christianity.

Christianity as an urban phenomenon

Religions, like diseases, spread most effectively in urban contexts. Christianity was not unique in this, but over time it began to define itself by its urban context. Christians chose to group all traditional religious practices under the heading 'paganism', for the pagan (in Latin *paganus*) was by definition 'of the countryside (*pagus*)' – what we might call in various argots a 'bumpkin', 'hick' or 'redneck'. Although at any one time perhaps seven or eight of every ten Romans would live in the countryside, they were not out of reach. These country folk regularly made their way into the cities of the empire, driven by the search for opportunity, advancement, an education, a career, or by crop failure and blight, famine and war. The mortality rate in the empire's cities was high, so there was always room for newcomers. And immigrants were prime targets for conversion, as they had left behind their firmest bonds, to family and friends. They would be most open to the approaches and kindness of strangers.

Life in late Roman cities was nasty, brutish and short. It was not, however, solitary, as the population density of Roman cities was far greater than in most modern cities. The population density of Rome itself was far greater than modern Manhattan (even with its vertical emphasis), dwarfed London, and once one accounts for the vast areas given over to public works and spaces, surpassed Mumbai and Kolkata. The Tiber was a morass of filth, and the streets were, for the most part, open sewers, as indeed were most of the sewers. Faeces rained down from tall buildings, ancient tenement blocks that frequently burnt or fell down. In a rare reversal of fortunes the poorest, who occupied the highest floors, might survive more easily in a collapse, as there was less to fall on their heads. In such crowded and unsanitary quarters, accidents and diseases were daily concerns, and Christian women were particularly prone to the latter, since childbirth led to both immediate and chronic infections, compromising immune systems already sorely tested by the ubiquity of excrement and bad water.

Rodney Stark highlights two epidemics that swept across the Roman Empire: one in AD 165–80, which was most likely smallpox and was described by Galen; and another which began in AD 260, which was measles or smallpox and was described by Cyprian (see p. 2 above). Both had high, if disputed, levels of mortality. Stark opts for a fairly high thirty percent mortality rate. Even if his figures are flawed and his message daubed with the broadest brush, still it is persuasive: Christians nursed their sick and therefore saved far more lives than pagans, who more frequently abandoned theirs. That is to say, there was no imperative for non-Christians to nurse those to whom they had no close relationship. Consequently, non-Christians did not develop immunity, as did certain Christians who survived early exposure and were able to move among the diseased freely. Instead, by fleeing the site of an outbreak, pagans acted as vectors for the spread of the disease. Of those who fell ill but were nursed, most, perhaps two-thirds, survived. Of those who were abandoned, less than a third survived. Moreover, Christians did not nurse only their own but offered succour to sick pagans. Between those whom they saved and those who witnessed their greater rates of survival and selflessness, the Christians found many fresh converts. Furthermore, where pagan social networks were fractured or destroyed by death and displacement, new Christian networks emerged. And within these circles, Christians offered explanations for the epidemics: it was not random, but rather God's means of separating those who worshipped correctly and those who did not. Or: Christians who died would be rewarded, for they would join their Lord and later be reunited with loved ones who had survived. Paganism offered no justifications, no promises and no systematic nursing.

By its community nursing programmes, Christianity became more efficient than other cults in maintaining its own social networks and recruiting individuals from others that fractured. This it did in cities where it had established a substantial presence, and Stark's analyses of thirty-one Roman cities with populations over 30,000 demonstrate statistically what common sense has suggested to others. Stark's statistical research demonstrates that:

– Cities closest to Jerusalem, the point of origin of Christianity, had communities of Christians earlier than others; and once Rome had established a large Christian community, this acted in similar fashion.
– Cities furthest from Jerusalem, and later from Rome, took far longer to Christianize.
– Cities with a Hellenic culture absorbed Christianity more ably than others, for reasons explored above, namely that the new faith 'maximized' the value of pre-existing knowledge (especially for Hellenized Jews).
– Larger cities absorbed Christians more easily, if with a slightly lower correlation than that between Christianity and Hellenism, because the larger a population, the more easily a deviant group can reach critical mass to sustain its enterprises.
– Port cities of the eastern Mediterranean, just as they were more susceptible to trade-borne disease, were more receptive to new religious ideas; they had greater turnover in population and were ethnically more diverse.
– Consequently, port cities had established Christian churches sooner than any others.

– Many of these considerations apply also to the cults of Cybele emanating from Phrygia and of Isis emanating from Egypt, both of which flourished in the Hellenic port cities of the eastern Mediterranean in the years before Christianity took hold.

These are but a few of the observations in Stark's *Cities of God*, a compelling study, albeit one that repeats a great deal from his earlier *Rise of Christianity*. Together, these works allow us to observe that the task left to Christianity in Constantine's age was to establish itself more effectively in the vast rural landscape, more especially in the north-western provinces, which were never urbanized and whither ideas had further to travel. To this we might add that Christianity needed to make ground in those places where one might expect most resistance, for example in the army camps where state *religio* and masculine cults were best established. A map plotting the locations of Mithraea in the third century shows that their distribution is almost a mirror image of that of Christian churches, being concentrated primarily in inland areas, disproportionately in the sparsely populated but heavily militarized frontier provinces of the north and west. Again, we shall return to these matters, for they are crucial to understanding the impact of Constantine's reign.

Christian exceptionalism and martyrdom

How, then, did Christianity rise with so little state interference? The answer is that it did and also that it did not. The Roman state was generally tolerant of religious faiths so long as they did not interfere with state *religio* and so long as they were not considered barbaric, decadent or corrupting. Thus, certain oriental cults met with disfavour in conservative Roman circles, but only two religions were regularly proscribed and their communities actively persecuted, for limited periods of time and in certain areas. In the province of Britannia, the northernmost of the Roman world, druidism was outlawed for its practice of human sacrifice, and on occasion its priests were hunted down and executed. Far more common and widespread, although still infrequent, was persecution of Christians, who proved to be useful, frequently enthusiastic, scapegoats for misfortunes that befell the state.

Few cults posed any threat to the state, and those that proved popular were absorbed into the system as supplements, rather than alternatives, to ancestral beliefs. Christianity was different, for its adherents were nominally forbidden to participate in the state religion and it had particular misgivings about the veneration of the emperors. How energetically and regularly this prohibition was applied one cannot know, but at the insistence of certain fundamentalist writers and community leaders, Christians periodically resisted directives to participate in public rites. As the Christian population grew, such recalcitrance was considered a significant betrayal of the interests of the state. This was surely the cause of the crises that struck the empire in the third century, pagans believed, and it had to be punished severely. And so in the mid-third century one encounters for the first time systematic persecution of Christians across the empire. We shall turn to this below. But while they were a tiny minority in a sea of pagans, this caused little concern, and they were made scapegoats at little political cost, as for example in the AD 60s, when Nero blamed Christians for the fire he had set in Rome. Those killed at that time, later legend holds, included St Peter. A half-century later, Pliny the Younger was content to carry out Trajan's orders to persecute Christians in his province of Bithynia, but sought guidance from the emperor on correct procedure. The exchange is worth citing at length. Pliny asks:

It is my practice, my lord, to refer to you all matters concerning which I am in doubt. For who can better give guidance to my hesitation or inform my ignorance? I have never participated in trials of Christians. I therefore do not know what offences it is the practice to punish or investigate, and to what extent. And I have been not a little hesitant as to whether there should be any distinction on account of age or no difference between the very young and the more mature; whether pardon is to be granted for repentance, or, if a man has once been a Christian, it does him no good to have ceased to be one; whether the name itself, even without offences, or only the offences associated with the name are to be punished. Meanwhile, in the case of those who were denounced to me as Christians, I have observed the following procedure: I interrogated these as to whether they were Christians; those who confessed I interrogated a second and a third time, threatening them with punishment; those who persisted I ordered executed. For I had no doubt that, whatever the nature of their creed, stubbornness and inflexible obstinacy surely deserve to be punished. There were others possessed of the same folly; but because they were Roman citizens, I signed an order for them to be transferred to Rome.

Trajan replies:

You observed proper procedure, my dear Pliny, in sifting the cases of those who had been denounced to you as Christians. For it is not possible to lay down any general rule to serve as a kind of fixed standard. They are not to be sought out; if they are denounced and proved guilty, they are to be punished, with this reservation, that whoever denies that he is a Christian and really proves it – that is, by worshipping our gods – even though he was under suspicion in the past, shall obtain pardon through repentance. But anonymously posted accusations ought to have no place in any prosecution. For this is both a dangerous kind of precedent and out of keeping with the spirit of our age.

As the letters reveal, when read in full, Christianity was considered a problem by Trajan because it categorically forbade adherents to participate in the state *religio*. Even those who were not citizens were held accountable and put to death, whereas citizens were shipped off to Rome, one might suggest to die in the arena for the edification of the plebs. But all were given a number of opportunities to recant, and only the most ardent would have preferred death to such a lapse. The number that refused to recant, according to the compelling hypothesis of G. W. Bowersock, was greatest exactly when and where Pliny governed: Asia Minor in the second century.

Christian martyrs rejected engagement with the world of paganism, and with it Roman authority. If the number of Christians who died in this manner for their faith was extremely small, their sacrifice was enacted publicly and theatrically. Ignatius, bishop of Antioch, condemned to die in the arena in the reign of Trajan, was allowed a triumphal journey to Rome punctuated by preaching and letter-writing. His greatest concern was that rich friends in the city would intervene and save him, and this he wrote to prevent, for he revelled in his celebrity, knowing his name would live forever in this world, even as his entry into the next was guaranteed. Those who could witness neither Ignatius' journey nor his ultimate sacrifice were regaled with his story by Polycarp and later by Eusebius of Caesarea, who collated the tales of all the male martyrs of Palestine.

As pagans witnessed the martyrs' willingness to die and the brutality with which the state punished their conviction, most could not fail to be impressed. What sort of god must these zealots worship that he offered them no protection and delivered them not from the hands of their accusers? Few would initially have appreciated the perspective of the Christians – that their god did not work for their protection in this world but rather delivered them from its pain to the place he had prepared for them, presided over by Christ. Their sacrifice mirrored that of their Lord, and the most fortunate of them would be executed in the same manner, on the cross. In choosing death, the martyrs firmly rejected the Roman predicate that divinities intervened in human affairs to offer protection or victory, and thus they refused to acknowledge the premise on which they were persecuted: that their refusal to sacrifice had brought down divine retribution upon the Romans. This point is striking, as we shall see how enthusiastically some Christians embraced the apparent intervention of their god in human affairs, as he ordered the death of the persecutors at the hand of his champion, Constantine. This was the resurrection of the Old Testament god, who had strengthened the right arms of the Hebrews and directed the slaughter of their enemies. But this must wait a short while longer.

If the theatricality of the martyrs impressed the masses, witnessing their sacrifices in the empire's public spaces, Christianity was explained to the educated by others. Philosophically inclined pagans who observed the sacrifice of the Christians may have been impressed by their adherence to a Socratic principle, albeit practically reversed. Christians died for that in which they believed, whereas Socrates had died for refusing to assert that in which he believed, or did not. The educated were engaged in debate by Christian apologists, whose task was to interact with those of other faiths and to build bridges. Apologists explored the role of classical education and culture, *paideia*, in the emergence and development of Christian thought and practice, and explained their beliefs in terms others could comprehend. Such intellectual engagement kept Christianity within the public realm, preventing it from becoming an entirely closed sect. The apologists' task became easier as others turned towards forms of henotheism – belief in a greatest god who reigned over other, lesser deities. These are generally conflated with pagan monotheisms – forms of belief in a single god. Two of the foremost apologists, Tertullian and Origen, held influential views on warfare, to which we shall now turn, for they present the essential background to understanding Constantine's interpretation of the faith.

Early Christian attitudes to warfare

One cannot overstate the essential messiness of early Christianity, which was not a monolithic set of beliefs but countless local sets of ideas and practices. Moreover, we know primarily the views of an elite group of scholars whose writings have been preserved, most frequently because they suited later tastes for reasons of style and theology. Therefore, to attempt to discern one coherent Christian attitude to warfare in the centuries before Constantine is wrongheaded. However, before this was made plain by the revolution in studies of late antiquity, estimable scholars, often moved to write by personal and denominational convictions or formed by experiences of modern war, had compiled long lists of pertinent quotations from scripture and the Church fathers. The pacifist line was expounded most fully in English shortly after the First World War by C. John Cadoux, who intended 'to show how strong and deep was the early Christian revulsion from and disapproval of war, both on account of the dissension it represented and of the infliction of bloodshed and suffering which it involved'. The quotations he presented were intended to 'show further how closely warfare and murder were connected in Christian thought by their possession of a common element – homicide'.

The crux of the pacifist interpretation of early Christianity is the New Testament's 'love command', the familiar instructions to 'turn the other cheek' and to 'love thy neighbour', presented in Christ's Sermon on the Mount, as preserved in the Gospel of Matthew (5:38–45). This is evidently still the modern popular understanding of the early Christian position on war, and it runs as follows in the King James Version:

Ye have heard that it hath been said, An eye for an eye, and a tooth for a tooth: But I say unto you, That ye resist not evil: but whosoever shall smite thee on thy right cheek, turn to him the other also. And if any man will sue thee at the law, and take away thy coat, let him have [thy] cloke also. And whosoever shall compel thee to go a mile, go with him twain. Give to him that asketh thee, and from him that would borrow of thee turn not thou away. Ye have heard that it hath been said, Thou shalt love thy neighbour, and hate thine enemy. But I say unto you, Love your enemies, bless them that curse you, do good to them that hate you, and pray for them which despitefully use you, and persecute you; That ye may be the children of your Father which is in heaven: for he maketh his sun to rise on the evil and on the good, and sendeth rain on the just and on the unjust. For if ye love them which love you, what reward have ye? do not even the publicans the same? And if ye salute your brethren only, what do ye more do not even the publicans so? Be ye therefore perfect, even as your Father which is in heaven is perfect.

Widely reported by the evangelists is Christ's aversion to the sword, of which his assertion that 'all who take the sword shall perish by the sword' is emblematic, foreshadowed by the prophecy in Isaiah (2:2–4) that at the end of days: 'He shall judge among the nations, and shall rebuke many people: and they shall beat their swords into plowshares, and their spears into pruning-hooks: nation shall not lift up sword against nation, neither shall they learn war any more.' But a coherent pacifist ethic cannot be identified in the New Testament, because Jesus never addressed the matters of military service or killing in war.

Militant language is frequently employed in the New Testament, although not to encourage violent actions. Christians are increasingly urged to 'fight the good fight' (1 Timothy 1:18). St Paul was particularly fond of military metaphors and referred to missionaries like himself as *milites Christi*, 'soldiers of Christ'. Paul compared his service to that of an army officer. He urged the Thessalonians to gird themselves with the breastplate of faith and love and the helmet of salvation; the Corinthians to don the armour of righteousness; and the Ephesians (6:17), having girt their loins with truth, to add to these the shield of faith and 'the sword of the Spirit, which is the Word of God'. Consequently, it was rather common for patristic authors to employ military language. This cannot be taken as an endorsement of warfare, but it does reflect the ubiquity of strife, and of soldiers, in the world they occupied. As Cadoux astutely observed, 'they were fond of speaking of the Christian life itself as a warfare and of themselves as soldiers of Christ. Scripture taught them to think with reverence and esteem of the warriors of old as men acting with the approval and under the guidance of God. Many of them looked forward to a great military triumph of Christ over his enemies at the end of the age.' Here he is thinking of the New Testament's clearest contradiction to the 'love command', the message of its last book, the Book of Revelation, where Christ turns not the other cheek but comes in majesty to avenge wrongdoing, seated on a white horse, 'just in judgement and just in war', a sword projecting from his mouth to smite the nations. 'For he it is who shall rule them with an iron rod and tread the winepress of the wrath and retribution of God,' we are told. He is identified by the inscription on his robes: 'King of kings and Lord of lords.' But Revelation was a problematic text for the compilers of the New Testament and was generally rejected before the fourth century. It was most likely the changed circumstances of Constantine's reign, and the influence of Eusebius of Caesarea, that saw Revelation become part of the canon.

Patristic authors frequently use militaristic imagery, often to draw a contrast with their message. For example, Clement of Rome, who was pope until AD 98, in his First Epistle to the Corinthians, urges his addressees to turn to peace and to follow peaceable rulers, but he employs the language of war:

Christ is our leader, and we His soldiers. Let us then, men and brethren, with all energy act the part of soldiers, in accordance with His holy commandments. Let us consider those who serve under our generals, with what order, obedience, and submissiveness they perform the things which are commanded them. All are not prefects, nor commanders of a thousand, nor of a hundred, nor of fifty, nor the like, but each one in his own rank performs the things commanded by the king and the generals. The great cannot subsist without the small, nor the small without the great.

A century later, Clement of Alexandria employs military language to contrast soldiers with Christians, stating that their trumpets were the Gospels. The most abundant use of military analogies is to be found in the writings of Cyprian, bishop of Carthage (d. AD 258), who considered the world to be the battlefield of the army commanded by Christ, whose soldiers fought battles known as persecutions against forces arrayed behind the devil.

Marcion, who led a movement within the Church of the second century to differentiate Jehovah, the god of Israel, from the god of the New Testament, the Stranger, did not consider the devil to be the principal problem. Christ was the messenger of the Stranger, who dwelt in a heaven above that of the Creator and wished to liberate the souls of man trapped in the 'hyle' of Creation by the angry god worshipped by the Jews. Marcion's arguments placed opponents in the awkward position of having to defend the atrocities of the vengeful Old Testament god or to explain away the war history as allegory. Most adopted the latter course. Indeed, although Marcionism was perhaps the most widely practised form of Christianity in second-century Syria, we know of Marcion's ideas only through the lengthy refutation penned decades later by Tertullian (c.155–230).

Origen (185–c.254), Tertullian's younger contemporary, took on another dead second-century thinker, the philosopher Celsus, whose views represented an archetype of the challenges posed by the Roman state to Christian communities. Origen denies that Christians are seditious and assigns to them the task of praying for the victories of those who fight righteous wars for Rome. Among Celsus' charges is that if all converted to Christianity and thus neglected state *religio*, the empire would inevitably fall to the barbarians:

Celsus: 'You surely do not say that if the Romans were, in compliance with your wish, to neglect their customary duties to gods and men, and were to worship the Most High, or whatever you please to call him, then he will come down and fight for them, so that they shall need no other help than his. For this same God, as you yourselves say, promised of old this and much more to those who served him, and see in what way he has helped them and you! They, in place of being masters of the whole world, are left with not so much as a patch of ground or a home; and as for you, if any of you transgresses even in secret, he is sought out and punished with death.'

Celsus attempts to queer Origen's pitch by observing the sorry fate of the martyrs. But Origen will have none of it:

The question stated is, 'What would happen if the Romans were persuaded to adopt the principles of the Christians, to despise the duties paid to the recognized gods and to men, and to worship the Most High?' This is my answer . . . God rejoices in the agreement of rational beings, and turns away from discord. And what are we to expect, if not only a very few agree, as at present, but the whole of the empire of Rome? For they will pray to the Word, who of old said to the Hebrews, when they were pursued by the Egyptians, 'The Lord shall fight for you, and ye shall hold your peace'; and if they all unite in prayer with one accord, they will be able to put to flight far more enemies than those who were discomfited by the prayer of Moses when he cried to the Lord, and of those who prayed with him. Now, if what God promised to those who keep His law has not come to pass, the reason of its non-fulfilment is not to be ascribed to the unfaithfulness of God. But He had made the fulfilment of His promises to depend on certain conditions, namely that they should observe and live according to His law; and if the Jews have not a plot of ground nor a habitation left to them, although they had received these conditional promises, the entire blame is to be laid upon their crimes, and especially upon their guilt in the treatment of Jesus.

Evidently he is not seeking out Jewish converts, but Origen has now identified scapegoats for the failure of the Christian god to deliver on a promise. On the other hand:

If all the Romans, according to the supposition of Celsus, embrace the Christian faith, they will, when they pray, overcome their enemies; or rather, they will not war at all, being guarded by that divine power which promised to save five entire cities for the sake of fifty just persons.

Evidently, Origen did not expect Celsus' supposition to come to pass, for although the pace of conversion of Romans to Christianity was healthy during his lifetime, he could not have anticipated the exponential increase that took hold at the end of the third century. But Origen appears to have had a fairly low opinion of the quality of most Christians. They were, to his mind, too weak generally to disengage themselves from society and act as 'soldiers of Christ'. He thought that task should fall to ascetics, the monks who had begun to replicate Christ's isolation in the deserts of North Africa and Syria, fighting demons on his behalf and for the good of weaker fellow Christians engaged in civilian life.

Origen was later described by Eusebius as 'possessed with such a passion for martyrdom' that he urged it upon his own father. Origen was a passionate youth, who began his career as a literal interpreter of scripture, apparently giving up wearing shoes and even, possibly, castrating himself, after reading Christ's admonition in Matthew (19:12). However, after his early days, as an instructor to catechumens, he turned to more mature reflection, and to allegory. He saw the Bible as an extension of the incarnation and recognized that it was essential for its words to penetrate minds so that listeners might partake of the body of Christ. Scripture was, he wrote, 'the one perfect and harmonized instrument of God, which from different sounds gives forth one saving voice to those willing to learn.' Each word of scripture had, potentially, three senses: literal, moral and spiritual, although not all had all three. This corresponded to humans, with body, soul and spirit. All scripture had spiritual elements, but not all could be interpreted literally. Thus, he was among the first to interpret the more martial books of the Old Testament allegorically. His gloss on the Book of Joshua, among the most violent in the Old Testament, is a tour de force. Origen suggests that the narratives were preserved to teach us spiritual lessons. Joshua, who in Greek bears the name 'Jesus son of Nun', prefigures Christ. Origen interprets the conquest of Canaan by the Israelites as an allegory for each Christian's lifelong spiritual struggle. Therefore, he states, the heretics are wrong to regard the god of the Old Testament as cruel, just as they provide no justification for religious violence. But Origen would not have been surprised to find Christians serving in the army, as they certainly did in his lifetime.

Christians in the Roman army

The first suggestion that Christian soldiers were actively campaigning is to be found in accounts of the Danube campaign of Marcus Aurelius in AD 173. According to Apollinarius of Hierapolis, whose work is not extant but is cited by Eusebius in his *Ecclesiastical History* (*HE** 5.5) and later by Tertullian (*Apology* 5), Christian soldiers of the Twelfth Legion Fulminata prayed for rain to alleviate thirst, and it came in the form of

---

* Since I shall refer to Eusebius of Caesarea's *Ecclesiastical History* very frequently, the abbreviation *HE* will often be used. Those who wish to consult the text, available in a Penguin translation and online, will find the chapter and section numbers useful.

a lightning storm, appropriate to their name, the 'thunderstruck legion'. It is not true that the legion received the name 'thundering' from the emperor at this time. The episode is depicted on the Aurelian column in Rome (fig 9), where Marcus Aurelius is himself shown praying and on contemporary coins; it is also mentioned by the pagan historians Dio Cassius and Capitolinus, both of whom attribute it to prayers to a pagan god, either Jupiter Pluvius or Hermes Trismegistus. None makes mention of Christians.

This record, then, is equivocal, but Tertullian provides unequivocal evidence that Christians served in the Roman army in the late second century and early third century. Tertullian was well informed about army life, although there is no corroboration for St Jerome's later claim that he was the son of a North African centurion. Tertullian gives numerous examples in his *Apology* (chapters 4, 37, 42), perhaps aimed at grumbling pagans, of Christians serving faithfully. There is no indication of widespread disfavour for such service, and Christian soldiers of his time who felt obliged to justify their position did so by reference to Old Testament precedents, some of which Tertullian enumerates in chapter 19 of his tract 'On Idolatry':

But now inquiry is made about this point, whether a believer may turn himself unto military service, and whether the military may be admitted unto the faith, even the rank and file, or each inferior grade, to whom there is no necessity for taking part in sacrifices or capital punishments. There is no agreement between the divine and the human sacrament, the standard of Christ and the standard of the devil, the camp of light and the camp of darkness. One soul cannot be due to two masters – God and Caesar. And yet Moses carried a rod, and Aaron wore a buckle, and John the Baptist is girt with leather and Joshua the son of Nun leads a line of march; and the People warred: if it pleases you to sport with the subject. But how will a Christian man war, nay, how will he serve even in peace, without a sword, which the Lord has taken away? For albeit soldiers had come unto John, and had received the formula of their rule; albeit, likewise, a centurion had believed; still the Lord afterward, in disarming Peter, disarmed every soldier.

This tract was written later in Tertullian's career, when he had become a Montanist. A heretic in the eyes of the later Church, Montanus declared that the Holy Spirit had offered him new revelations. Montanus' 'new prophecy' has been eradicated from the written record, but Tertullian implies that it was concerned with church discipline rather than doctrine and held that Christians who fell from grace could not be redeemed. This would explain his new rigour in condemning military service, for he identified the impossibility that an active soldier could extricate himself effectively from the religious world of the camps, where devotion to the emperors and to the *genius* of the legion and its standards was required.

Indeed, Tertullian's disapproval of Christian participation in military matters is not principally provoked by the potential for violence occasioned by army life. Rather, his particular distaste is for the requirement for all soldiers in the Roman army to participate fully and regularly, without fail or resistance, in state *religio*, according to the dictates of the religious calendar, the *feriale*. In his *De corona*, 'On the Crown', Tertullian condemns Christian soldiers who do not display the courage of their convictions, but instead wear the symbols of idolaters, in this case the laurel wreaths of victors. The author recounts a tale for edification and emulation of a soldier who refused to wear the wreath and was consequently martyred.

Very lately it happened thus: while the bounty of our most excellent emperors was dispensed in the camp, the soldiers, laurel-crowned, were approaching. One of them, more a soldier of God, more steadfast than the rest of his brethren, who had imagined that they could serve two masters, his head alone uncovered, the useless crown in his hand – already even by that peculiarity known to every one as a Christian – was nobly conspicuous. Accordingly, all began to mark him out, jeering him at a distance, gnashing on him near at hand. The murmur is wafted to the tribune, when the person had just left the ranks. The tribune at once puts the question to him, 'Why are you so different in your attire?' He declared that he had no liberty to wear the crown with the rest. Being urgently asked for his reasons, he answered, 'I am a Christian'. O soldier! Boasting thyself in God. Then the case was considered and voted on; the matter was remitted to a higher tribunal; the offender was conducted to the prefects. At once he put away the heavy cloak, his disburdening commenced; he loosed from his foot the military shoe, beginning to stand upon holy ground; he gave up the sword, which was not necessary either for the protection of our

Lord; from his hand likewise dropped the laurel crown; and now, purple-clad with the hope of his own blood, shod with the preparation of the gospel, girt with the sharper word of God, completely equipped in the apostles' armour, and crowned more worthily with the white crown of martyrdom, he awaits in prison the largesse of Christ.

The account, which continues through fifteen chapters, demonstrates several things. First, it clearly shows that it was not unusual for Christians to be on active military duty in c.AD 200. Only one man here is said to deserve the name Christian, but there are several, perhaps many others in this single, albeit fictive, unit who accept the wreath of victory and thus occasion Tertullian's scorn. Second, it shows that the issue of idolatry, insofar as wearing the crown was such an act, was not considered a major problem by most Christians, even though the wreath appears to have been a sacred symbol to those who worshipped Mithras, as Tertullian later reveals. Third, it shows that some Christians questioned the wisdom of the soldier's stand, believing him naive and foolish to make such a show and thus to question the faith of others, who are willing to accept the garland. In gaol he becomes truly a soldier of Christ, fighting the good fight against persecutors and earning the martyr's crown, blessed in Tertullian's eyes but clearly a fool in the eyes of less rigorous believers.

De corona is the only work in early Christian literature devoted uniquely to the military. It is also the only work to preserve a coherent description of an aspect of Mithraism: its last chapter recounts the initiation of a worshipper to the third rank, that of 'soldier' (*miles*). Still condemning those Christian soldiers who do not support their Christian comrade in casting off the crown, Tertullian writes:

Blush, ye fellow-soldiers of his, henceforth not to be condemned even by him, but by some soldier of Mithras, who, at his initiation in the gloomy cavern, in the camp, it may well be said, of darkness, when at the sword's point a crown is presented to him, as though in mimicry of martyrdom, and thereupon put upon his head, is admonished to resist and cast it off, and, if you like, transfer it to his shoulder, saying that Mithras is his crown. And thenceforth he is never crowned; and he has that for a mark to show who he is, if anywhere he be subjected to trial in respect of his religion; and he is at once believed to be a soldier of Mithras if he throws the crown away – if he say that in his god he has his crown. Let us take note of the devices of the devil, who is wont to ape some of God's things with no other design than, by the faithfulness of his servants, to put us to shame, and to condemn us.

In his later writings, which include *De corona*, Tertullian urged Christians to sacrifice themselves, rather than sacrificing beasts to false idols, both those of the state religion and those of the cult so favoured by soldiers, Mithraism. His firm line is that 'if one is pressed to the offering of sacrifice and the sheer denial of Christ by the prospect of torture or of punishment', one is less of a Christian than one who 'dreads denying [Christ] and [is willing] to undergo martyrdom'. More than wearing the crown, Tertullian condemns any soldier's willingness to swear the *sacramentum*, the regular oath of loyalty to the Roman emperor, since baptism was the only sacrament that they should observe. He uses the same term for both, as he does when comparing a soldier's regular duty as nightwatchman to his Christian duty to keep vigil, fasting. But nowhere does he condemn soldiers for being soldiers. Rather, he echoes the admonition of John the Baptist to Roman soldiers, as recorded by the evangelist Luke (3:14): 'And the soldiers likewise demanded of him, saying, And what shall we do? And he said unto them, Do violence to no man, neither accuse [any] falsely; and be content with your wages.' These were not, of course, Christian soldiers, but John does not advise them to leave the service. Rather, his wish is to ensure that they do not exploit their monopoly of violence for personal gain, at the expense of others. He is concerned with extortion, not killing. Jesus did not condemn a centurion for his service, but rather healed his servant (Matthew 8:5–13; Luke 7:1–10).

Beyond the limited scope of Tertullian's refined prose, there must have been many and varied prescriptions for regulating the behaviour of Christian soldiers, so that they would not violate the tenets of their faith. Some are preserved in extant church orders. These documents, including the third-century *Apostolic Tradition*, were manuals for church leaders, so that they might correctly instruct and discipline Christian communities and order the liturgy. They were regularly revised and updated, and circulated, each version drawing on the last and perhaps several others. So they reflect the changing views, over time and space, of Christian thinkers on a variety of subjects, including warfare and military service. They bear witness most clearly to the diversity of early Christianity, revealing that attitudes were mutable and can only be understood in their appropriate geographical and temporal contexts. As importantly, they are not the works of refined intellectuals writing for educated readerships, but practical guides used by those who recruited and educated converts in communities across the empire.

The *Apostolic Tradition* survives in Latin, Coptic, Ethiopic and Arabic translations, although a Greek original has been lost. All versions concern themselves with military service, in a section advising Christian leaders on screening potential converts. All prescriptions are different. The Coptic and Arabic versions allow for soldiers to be baptized as Christians and accepted into a community, so long as they swear not to kill and so long as they are not men of rank. The Ethiopic version is stricter, banning all soldiers from becoming catechumens; it determined that such a vocation rendered them senseless to the Christian message. (The Latin version of this chapter is missing.) Soldiers in command positions were excluded in all versions, and the reason for this must be that they were incapable of absenting themselves from the quotidian idolatrous rituals of army life. The familiar issue of the soldier's oath, the *sacramentum*, is raised, and it is held in all versions to be incompatible with the Christian sacrament of baptism. All versions forbid confirmed Christians and catechumens from enrolling voluntarily in the army (which would require them to swear the oath). This implies two things: first, that this was not an unfamiliar event; and second, that those who were conscripted were not to be penalized, but their behaviour was to be moderated.

Military martyrs and warrior saints

The most popular early martyr stories involved not powerful men, like Ignatius or Polycarp, but women. This is hardly surprising, given that women drove the spread of Christianity. St Thecla's story circulated as early as the second century, although the notion that she met her end by diving into a pool of man-eating seals was perhaps later. Still more favoured was the *Passion of Saint Perpetua*, a woman of noble birth executed in the theatre at Carthage. Her story was made all the more compelling by the fact that she wrote much of it herself, while in gaol. The interest in female martyrs was to wane, however, as one encounters the first systematic persecution of Christians projected across the entire empire in the reign of Decius (AD 249–51). It was at this time that Origen achieved his greatest desire, appearing among those listed by Eusebius as being tortured and martyred. Evidently, it was now rather dangerous to be either a bishop or a Christian soldier, for the reluctance of soldiers to participate fully in state ritual was rather obvious. And so it was that a universal decree issued by Decius, that all participate in an empire-wide sacrifice, eat the sacrificial meat, and swear that they had always sacrificed, led to recalcitrance in the camps and the first notable martyrdoms of Christian soldiers. Able neither to flee, like some notable bishops (but unlike the pope Fabian, who died a martyr in January 250), nor to hide in urban crowds or the Pontic hills (like Gregory Thaumaturgus), soldiers volunteered themselves for martyrdom. Thus we meet four Alexandrian troops with splendidly contrived names – Ammon, Zeus, Ptolemy, Ingenuus – who die alongside an old man, Theophilus, whom they are supposed to have taken to trial. They apparently followed the example of the equally apocryphal Basilides, whose story is told earlier by Eusebius. A soldier charged with guarding a condemned woman, Potamiaena, he is suitably impressed by her endurance and by the fact that she appears to him in a vision three days after her death and offers him a crown. This he accepts and is converted and promptly beheaded.

It is during Decius' reign that we meet the first of the great warrior saints of Byzantine tradition, St Mercurius. A far later and entirely fictional *Passion* sees Mercurius visited by an angel, converting, and refusing to abjure Christ before the emperor himself, who invites him to sacrifice to Artemis. Later still, the story migrates to the fourth century, when Mercurius is believed to have hurled the javelin that killed Julian the Apostate, thus securing an imperial future for the faith of Constantine. The stories of the military martyrs became notable only later, because only later was a Christian empire in need of warrior saints. Initially, the deaths of Christian soldiers were treated no differently to those of bishops or others, because no Christian writer in the religion's first three centuries formulated a fully developed ethical theory of pacifism, according to which the actions of soldiers might be measured differently. But it is clear that most who were later considered orthodox found the notion of killing repugnant, and to heretics like Marcion it was abhorrent. Tertullian took a firmer line against military service when he became a Montanist, but he was not alone in appearing more concerned with the idolatry of army life than with the prospect that a Christian soldier might kill. This point serves to illuminate how diverse were those in the first three centuries who called themselves Christians and considered their views orthodox. What was orthodox could only be enforced when the state's monopoly of violence was seen to back decisions taken by bishops at well-attended meetings, synods, sponsored by the administration and directed to serve the best interests of the state by the promotion of a single, universal viewpoint. At that time, what was orthodox and what was heretical took on new meaning. But this came later, and as we shall see, Constantine was instrumental in the change, and willing, indeed anxious, to enforce unity. For now, the Christian Church was a loose agglomeration of disparate communities, and many views could be expressed.

3

The Unconquered Emperor and his Divine Patron

The crisis of empire – The emperor and the army –
The Roman theology of victory – The unconquered emperor
and the Sun – Aurelian – Christ the true Sun

The rise of Christianity coincided with a sustained period of crisis for the empire. It was held by many to be the cause of the crisis, and for that reason one finds, for the first time in the mid-third century, a systematic persecution of Christians throughout the empire. At the same time, in response to the crisis but in fact contributing far more effectively to its perpetuation, one witnesses a dramatic increase in the political power of the army. Through the third century, the army was the only instrument of state that could raise up and strike down emperors. To retain power, therefore, third-century emperors struggled with only limited success to maintain control over their errant soldiers. In the half-century between the end of the Severan dynasty (193–235) and the foundation of the Tetrarchy (in 284), the subject of our next chapter, more than fifty men claimed the title emperor. Twenty-two of these were universally recognized, of which the vast majority were both acclaimed and later murdered by troops under their command. All but two of the recognized emperors who reigned from AD 251 until 284 died in this manner, the exceptions being Valerian (253–60), who was captured in battle with the Persians, and Claudius II Gothicus (268–70), who died of 'a most grievous pestilence', probably measles or smallpox.

The instability associated with ephemeral and brutal reigns compounded problems that Rome might otherwise have dealt with quite comfortably. It is beyond the scope of this study to sketch the empire's troubles at length, but it is important to outline the developments that paved Constantine's path to power. Constantine was, in York in AD 306, merely the next man to be raised up by his army, and his greatest fear, quite logically and legitimately, was that he would be the next to die at their hands. The likelihood of his demise declined with time and success, the latter defined exclusively in terms of victories in war. This was the legacy of Rome's third-century crisis.

The crisis of empire

It has become fashionable recently to diminish the problems faced by the Roman empire in the middle years of the third century – to attribute more to literary construction than to barbarian invasion and to deny the situation its traditional appellation, 'the crisis of empire'. The threats to the Roman frontiers in the third century may have been no greater than in some earlier or later periods, and the nature of surviving histories may indeed skew the picture. Eyewitness accounts by Cassius Dio and Herodian cover only the first four decades. For the remainder of the century we are largely reliant on the *Historia Augusta*, compiled by an ingenious and disingenuous scholar at the end of the fourth century. However, one cannot ignore the fact that foreign threats were pressing and regular, and that they were largely the unhappy consequence of Roman victories. Whereas the Parthian empire to Rome's east had presented a large and soft target, a perfect source of booty and prestige, the vacuum created by Severan success against the Parthians unleashed Ardashir, satrap of Fars, from his tutelage. His ambition rested on military accomplishments, and thus he directed his aggression against Rome. From the mid-220s, a new power, the Sassanian Persian empire, replaced the Parthians as Rome's eastern foe, with conflict intensifying during the reign of Ardashir's son, Shapur I (241–72).

At the same time, the Germanic and Gothic peoples of the north pressed regularly across the Rhine and Danube frontiers. Scholars no longer regard the Goths and Alemans as coherent peoples, two of many shunting each other across the steppes of inner Asia into Europe. Instead, it is now recognized that their appellations, created in the Latin annals of their literate enemies, mask as much as they reveal about barbarian identities. The Goths and Alemans were armies, not peoples, who shared goals (accrual of wealth, social advancement), not signifiers of ethnicity (brooches, hair-styles). However, a key means by which Goths and

Alemans cohered as groups was by following kings who attacked Roman outposts in search of plunder and prestige. While not as disruptive as invasions by whole peoples, increasingly frequent raids by efficient armies could not simply be ignored. Foreign invasions both provoked and exacerbated failures in the imperial system, and for two decades splinter states existed in Gaul and Syria, both claiming to be Roman, but denying grain and taxation revenues to the empire.

The leaders of the Gallic and Palmyrene empires failed to secure support within the empire's core provinces, but many other pretenders and usurpers enjoyed, for better or (mostly) for worse, the title 'Emperor of the Romans'. When there was no stability at the heart of government, the fiscal demands of running the army were crippling to the state economy, which was but a small part of the broader economy. Only a small fraction of the Roman economy was ever monetized, being that part of it which was of direct interest to the state. Certainly, Roman citizens needed bronze coinage to buy bread, where this was not distributed to them in major cities and where they did not produce their own. But the coinage was provided so that those who sold bread and grain might acquire coinage to pay their taxes. This was still more the case with gold and silver coins, which were issued exclusively to support the state economy: to meet the demands of government, to pay the army, and to facilitate the levying of taxes. The fact that some precious metals entered general circulation, serving the secondary function of facilitating trade in very large volumes or luxury goods, was of only slight interest to most emperors, so long as enough was recouped each year. In times of war disruptions to the system of taxation were inevitable, as revenue-generating lands were under threat or lost for periods of time. Southern Gaul and Egypt, both lost for protracted periods, were two of the leading tax-exporting regions, whereas Italy and the city of Rome, which were never lost, enjoyed tax-exempt status under the *ius Italicum*. The loss of productive lands was exacerbated by the destruction of crops by foreign or Roman forces wishing to deny provisions to enemies in foreign or civil wars and by the requisitioning of crops to feed troops. Landholders, having no crops to sell, were denied the means to pay taxes on their lands. Romans had endured this in the past, of course, but the problems of the mid-third century saw fighting increasingly within the frontiers, and between dozens of emperors, each unable, and in many cases unconcerned, to raise sufficient revenue to meet more than the ever-increasing demands of the army.

Each ephemeral emperor would immediately concern himself solely with the army: defending the frontiers with garrisons and fortresses; keeping troops constantly in the field and ensuring that they were properly supplied and provisioned; distributing cash bonuses to the army, known as donatives, upon accession and to reward victories; ransoming captives. Nothing beyond the camp would seem immediately pressing, and except for crisis management little revenue would be diverted to finance the regular workings of government. Beyond the army, the state was starved of the taxes it needed to function and of the opportunities and means to raise them. The situation was greatly exacerbated by the epidemic which persisted through the 250s and 260s and killed up to thirty percent of the population of the Roman empire. Dead citizens tilled no fields and paid no taxes. This was a tipping point. Where sufficient gold and silver could not be recouped to meet the demands of the state economy, the only immediate solutions open to an emperor were to debase the currency and increase rates of taxation. Thus, the fineness of the precious currency decreased, and consequently inflation rose rapidly. Sellers, recognizing the diminished value of currency, raised prices accordingly. And even as taxation rates rose, the government recouped ever less precious metal to re-strike coins. According to Gresham's Law, which states that bad money drives out good, Romans who could afford to do so hoarded older coins with higher gold or silver content, paying taxes in the debased currency. Moreover, the wealthy were always far more able to extract tax concessions from the state, or indeed to resist the demands of armed tax-gatherers. So the burden fell ever more on the poor, who were ever less able to pay.

The story of this fiscal crisis is told not by hyperbolic literature but in the numismatic record: in the ever-diminishing fineness of gold coins; in the explosion in numbers of low-value coins in circulation after AD 200; and in the breakdown of monetary unity across the empire, with patterns of circulation for different provinces diverging wildly. Coins, struck to meet immediate needs in particular locations, were no longer circulating through a centralized system. The fate of the 'double denarius', later called the *antoninianus* after its originator, is instructive. The emperor better known as Caracalla (211–17) introduced the coin in AD 215. Although its face value was, perhaps, twice that of the regular silver *denarius*, the double was only fifty percent heavier and contained the same amount of silver. Production was stopped for twenty years, from 219 to 238, and when it recommenced, the coin was one-sixth lighter. By the reign of Gallienus, the regular *denarius* had been stopped altogether, and after 260 the silver content of the *antoninianus*, once fifty percent, was reduced to a silvering on the surface. At this time production of the 'silvered' coins escalated rapidly, with finds in hoards suggesting that the number of new coins struck was three times higher than usual. This was surely a response to the loss of tax-exporting regions, most notably Gaul and Egypt, and therefore to the loss of currency in those provinces. Even with the 'restoration' of the 270s, Aurelian's *antoniniani*, although back to full weight, were one part silver to twenty parts copper.

The emperor and the army

Making war was always the most important duty of a Roman emperor. Augustus, in his *Res Gestae*, made this plain, listing his campaigns and victories before all else. Later emperors composed war narratives, sending despatches from the field to the senate. One usurper, Maximinus, to whom we shall return below, also sent pictures of his personal exploits, although this may have been because he was unwilling to present himself in Rome and nobody might otherwise know what he looked like. Emperors wrote autobiographies, for example Trajan's account of his Dacian wars, of which but one line survives. That shows at least that he wrote in the first person, unlike Julius Caesar, who wrote in the third. But if victory in war was always a crucial factor in sustaining an emperor, the ability to lead and reward the army became the only imperial quality that mattered in the third century.

The rise of the army began with the Severan dynasty, which ruled with various interruptions from the accession of Septimius Severus in April 193 to the murder of Severus Alexander and his mother, Julia Mamaea, near Mainz in March 235. Septimius Severus attempted to legitimize his usurpation by declaring himself the son of Marcus Aurelius. But his right to reign was established on the battlefield, where he won significant victories in Mesopotamia, at various times taking the triumphal epithets Arabicus, Adiabenicus and Parthicus Maximus to mark his victories over the Arabs, the Adiabeni and the Parthians. The last victory he celebrated in 204 with a triumphal entry at the head of his army into the city of Rome, where a monumental archway was raised through which it would march. Septimius endeared himself further to the army by increasing pay by one half and by allowing enrolled soldiers to marry. He died after an eighteen-year reign in York, Britannia, on 4 February 211. No reign would last as long until Diocletian's.

Government under the Severans was in the hands of a select group that cohered around the emperor. This was most notable in the case of the youth Severus Alexander, who was in thrall to his mother and murdered by his troops, who came to despise him as a 'mummy's boy'. Notable features of the period were an increased reliance on the army to maintain authority. Large stipends were paid to officers and generous distributions made to the rank and file. The army's gain was largely at the expense of the senate, which was marginalized by the autocratic, military regime.

The Severan emperors projected themselves aggressively as 'fellow soldiers'. Septimius Severus rode at the head of his line of march bareheaded in rain and snow, so that he could be seen clearly bearing the same hardships as his men. He ate and slept as they did in the open and served as a figure for them to emulate as well as to serve. Severus' son, whom he named Lucius Septimius Bassianus, followed his example, and the name by which he is better known, Caracalla, is that of the hooded tunic he had worn in the army camps from boyhood. Caracalla saw himself as a new Alexander the Great and is described as having modelled not only his portraits on Alexander's, but his very gaze and posture, the tilt of his head and his flowing locks. When he marched against the Persians, Caracalla chose deliberately to follow in Alexander's footsteps, and on that journey drank from cups and bore weapons he alleged had belonged to his hero. He even enrolled a phalanx of Macedonians. It was a shock to many when he was killed by his men. His replacement, Macrinus, had been Caracalla's Praetorian Prefect and spent the whole of his fourteen-month reign with the army in the east. He was clearly in thrall to his men and dispensed with the infamous punishment of decimation, whereby every tenth soldier in a disgraced unit, selected by lot, was put to death by his comrades. Macrinus made the punishment one-tenth as severe, instituting the *centesimatio*. Senior soldiers, who were most likely to rise against him, were given a pay rise, whereas new recruits were not.

Maximinus Thrax (235–8), who engineered the death of the last Severan, Severus Alexander, went further still, taking part personally in battles. This was exceptional, for the emperor was not expected to risk his life in the battle line. Although this might have been the ultimate demonstration of bravery to his 'fellow soldiers', it was generally regarded as unnecessary and foolhardy. The emperor should stay back and direct tactics. Maximinus had been responsible under Severus Alexander for enrolling and training recruits, who remained loyal to him throughout. But Maximinus fared poorly despite this. He was the first of a seemingly endless stream of men who claimed the title of emperor, only to be killed by the very troops who raised them. This was often a practical measure, to prevent a battle. That is to say, in order to avoid becoming further enmeshed in civil wars, the army looked to its own interests, raising champions for as long as they were useful, then cutting them down. This was the case with Maximinus, whose demise is worth pondering for what it reveals of the mood of the army. An account is provided by Herodian, written shortly after the events described. We meet Maximinus at Aquileia in northern Italy, where he has set a siege, hoping to proceed thence southwards in an aura of victory. However, the citizens resist his assault ably, inspired by one Crispinus:

It is reported that Crispinus persevered in prosecuting the war because there were many people inside the city [of Aquileia] who were experts in the art of reading omens and entrails, and who announced that the signs were auspicious. The Italians place particular faith in this kind of divination. Some oracles were also spread around to the effect that the local god was promising the Aquileians victory. The god, whose worship is extremely popular, was called Beles and is identified with Apollo. Some of Maximinus' soldiers said that his image appeared frequently in the sky fighting for the city. I am not sure [Herodian avers] whether the god really appeared to some of the men or whether it was imagination. They were anxious to avoid the disgrace of being unable to overpower a crowd of townsfolk that was numerically inferior, so wanted it to appear that they had been defeated by gods and not men.

Clearly, Maximinus' patron god could not overpower Beles. His soldiers were maimed, blinded and disfigured by the burning pitch that the Aquileians poured down upon them. Moreover, the troops, to prevent supplies being taken into the city, had burnt the local vines and fruit trees. As their siege dragged on, they began to starve. Action was necessary, and the Second Parthian Legion acted decisively.

Suddenly the soldiers ... decided to murder Maximinus, so that they could abandon the long interminable siege, and stop laying waste to Italy for the benefit of a tyrant who was condemned and hated. With great daring they went towards Maximinus' tent at noon and tore down his image from the standards [of the Praetorian Guard] with the assistance of the guards. When Maximinus and his son emerged from their tent to try to negotiate, the soldiers killed them without a hearing.

Maximinus was killed to end a civil war, and a similar desire to end or avoid battle with fellow Romans saw to the demise of many other emperors and pretenders. Indeed, only one legitimate emperor, Philip the Arab (244–9), died after engaging in battle with a fellow Roman, Decius (249–51). On the other hand, in an era when plunder was an excellent source of income for a soldier, an emperor had constantly to be willing to fight if the army so demanded. Probus (276–82), who was responsible for establishing the first fortifications that later became known as the Saxon Shore in Britain, was murdered by his own troops because he had no great expedition planned. This dynamic has been observed in later centuries, notably during Charlemagne's campaigns against the Saxons and Avars, which were intended to secure booty to reward his troops and shore up his prestige. Emperors, it would appear, could be disposed of by the army if they demanded battle against the men's wishes, and equally if they showed a lack of desire to fight. Never was a telling phrase, coined by Tiberius, truer than in this period, when handling the army was 'like holding a wolf by the ears'.

The prevailing motivation was often simply the army's desire to install yet another general, who would thus owe his men substantial rewards and, potentially, booty, as he strove to prove his mettle and bolster his prestige in foreign wars. Frequent usurpation created a constant demand for coins, as every emperor was expected and required to distribute donatives upon his accession. Failure to do so would lead very swiftly to his demise. Victories helped, as booty could be secured and either distributed in pieces or melted down and struck as coinage. Following a successful campaign, the emperor would distribute mostly bronze coins, but also gold and silver for officers. Nevertheless, expensive campaigns did not always pay for themselves. The coins distributed to soldiers in great numbers bore legends that may not have been legible to them, for many could not read. Still, images must have been clear enough: bound captives beneath standards, emperors in helmets or laurel crowns, or the goddess Victoria carrying a wreath or the trophy, to which we shall turn shortly.

Each emperor would address the army formally when distributing donatives after a victory or upon accession. One might suppose that an informal address often preceded acclamation, as the pretender needed to gauge the likelihood of gaining the support of his troops. The imperial speech (*adlocutio*) was delivered from a platform that was a permanent feature of all camps. A travelling version might be carried on campaign and erected when necessary. The emperor would be accompanied on the platform by key advisers, including the unit commander. He might also here introduce his sons, and their claims to succeed, to the troops. For example, Septimius Severus, when he knew he was soon to die, appeared on the rostrum with Caracalla. The emperor's message was always straightforward, as his men were generally poorly educated but understood and appreciated a direct address from their commander.

Once raised up by the army, third-century emperors were generally keen to secure recognition from the senate in Rome. This was always granted. Additionally, the Arval brethren, a priestly college in Rome composed of senators, would sacrifice for the good of the emperors and look after their interests while they were away from Rome. This barely affected the army's propensity to act just as it pleased in dispensing with emperors of whom the senate had approved. Indeed, the only lasting effect of recognition by the senate has been to recommend many

1. Bust of Christ, with the chi-rho and pomegranates. Detail of a mosaic discovered at Hinton St Mary, Dorset, now preserved in the British Museum. (The Granger Collection/TopFoto)

2. Gravestone of Titus Flavius Surillio (d. *c*.AD 213), *aquilifer* of the Second Legion Adiutrix, now in the Istanbul Archaeological Museum. (akg-images/Erich Lessing)

3. Roman flag standards (*vexilla*) and other *signa* depicted on Trajan's Column, Rome, represented here on the facsimile in London's Victoria and Albert Museum. (Author)

4. (Above) A flag standard (*vexillum*) depicted in a fresco in the Temple of Bel at Dura Europos, where a tribune named Terentius is shown performing a camp ritual. (Yale University Art Gallery, Dura-Europos Archive)

5. A sarcophagus from the tomb of the Calpurnii, now at Baltimore's Walters Art Museum; it depicts Victories bearing cruciform standards and a 'shield of virtue' showing Dionysus' head. (Author)

6. The triumph of Dionysus, his chariot pulled by leopards or panthers. A late second-century mosaic in the so-called House of Dionysus, Paphos, Cyprus. (Author)

7. The triumph of Dionysus again, his chariot pulled by centaurs. A fourth-century mosaic in the so-called House of Aion, Paphos, Cyprus. (Author)

8. Tauroctony, the ritual bull-slaying sacred to initiates of the mysteries of Mithras, now displayed in the Pio-Clementine Museum, Vatican. (Scala/Museo Pio-Clementino)

9. The 'thunderstruck' legion and the rain miracle depicted on the column of Marcus Aurelius in Rome. (The Granger Collection/TopFoto)

10. The Gemma Augustea, produced in c.AD 10 to mark a victory of Tiberius over the Dalmatians. A trophy is raised on the battlefield in its bottom-left corner. It is now in the Kunsthistorisches Museum, Vienna. (Luisa Ricciarini/TopFoto)

11. The Ludovisi Sarcophagus, depicting Gallienus (or another mid-third-century emperor) as an unconquerable emperor (Invictus Augustus), without a helmet in the midst of battle. Rome, Museo Nazionale, Romano. (Author)

12. Oversized bronze statue of Trebonianus Gallus, displayed in New York's Metropolitan Museum of Art. (Scala/The Metropolitan Museum of Art/Art Resource)

13. A small statue of Sol Invictus striking a pose rather similar to Trebonianus Gallus (c. AD 190). (Museum of Fine Arts, Boston, Massachusetts/Bridgeman Art Library)

14. A mosaic depicting Christ-Helios, in Mausoleum M, the tomb of the Julii beneath the Vatican. (Topham Picturepoint)

15. Porphyry statues of the Tetrarchs, located in the south-east corner of the southern facade of the Basilica of San Marco in Venice. (Scala/St Mark's Basilica)

16. Porphyry statue of the Tetrarchs, now in the Vatican Museums. (Photo: Scala/Vatican City)

17. The Arras medallion, showing London submitting to Constantius, 'Restorer of the Eternal Light'. The original has been stolen. There is an electrotype in the Museum of London. (The Granger Collection/TopFoto)

18. Pier of the Arch of Galerius in Salonica, modern Thessaloniki, Greece, to be found very close to the Rotunda of Galerius. (Author)

19. Detail from the Arch of Galerius, showing the emperor in single combat with Narses, ruler of the Persians. (Author)

20. Detail from the Arch of Galerius, showing the Tetrarchs together in victory. The *Augusti* are enthroned in the centre, the Caesars standing to either side. (Author)

usurpers to posterity as legitimate, while others who ruled for longer and more successfully are denied the title Roman emperor. Since emperors travelled to Rome to secure recognition, the city retained some of its prestige. But this must be measured against the fact that most emperors now spent the greater part of their short reigns in the field, or at a series of important centres elsewhere, including Trier, Sirmium and Sardica, within striking distance of the Rhine and Danube frontiers; Salonica and Nicomedia, on major roads between east and west; and Antioch, whence one might strike at Persia. We shall turn to several of these in later chapters, to explore the effects of being designated an imperial city. This was truly a significant feature of the period, reflecting centrifugal tendencies that were expressed also in the emergence of ephemeral mini-empires, in Gaul and North Africa. There was no desire, it seems, for these regions to separate entirely from Rome, but where the regional rulers could not secure recognition and could not march on Rome, there emerged for the same short period, AD 260–73, two autonomous empires: the Gallic empire, and the Palmyrene empire. Both were called Roman by those who ruled them, intending eventually to rule from the centre. Both also were symptoms of the inability of one man to control the whole empire.

The Roman theology of victory

In the words of J. B. Campbell, in his authoritative study *The Emperor and the Roman Army*, 'Ultimately the Roman emperor did not rely for his survival on political parties, or the support of groups of senators or *equites*, or on mass popular support based on elections or assemblies, but on military strength and the personal loyalty of his army.' We have sketched some attempts by emperors to secure the personal loyalty of the army, by portraying themselves as 'fellow soldiers', addressing the troops regularly in person, providing opportunities to secure plunder, and, above all, through the distribution of donatives, in coins and bullion. Such practical measures alone clearly did not work, and thus there were also attempts to consolidate the bond between leader and followers on emotional and spiritual levels. The bond was, as we have seen at some length, at the core of the army's religious life.

Emperors attempted to bind the army to them more firmly through powerful oaths. The most potent, the *sacramentum*, was sworn to the emperor by each soldier upon recruitment, when the recruit was also obliged to wear around his neck a lead seal, a dog tag, bearing the image of the emperor. He was thus 'branded' the emperor's man. The oath was sworn by every soldier each year thereafter, on 3 January, and upon the accession of a new emperor. Additional oaths were sworn during regular ceremonial, and we have observed the development at this time of imperial cults that appear to promote the veneration of the emperor's person, as well as his 'divine quality' (*numen*). There is evidence that the troops took their oath of loyalty seriously and considered it a personal oath to the emperor rather than to the state. Individual emperors seem to have tinkered with it to improve their own standing or chances of survival. Alas, we have only one full version of the *sacramentum*, preserved in a later Christian context and probably reworked to suit the tastes of Theodosius I (d. AD 395).

Correct ritual observance was required of all Romans to secure divine support for the state and its leader, the emperor. The requirement that the people, most notably the army, participate fully in state *religio* remained in force, of course, and it is for this reason that persecution of Christians was mandated first of all in the army camps. But increasingly the onus was on the emperor to prove that he enjoyed the patronage of a powerful god, who, if propitiated by correct ritual, would deliver victory. This, in essence, is what Jean Gagé seventy-five years ago called the 'Imperial Theology of Victory'. The term 'theology' is used in a precise manner, to designate the interpretation and understanding of the nature of god, or the gods, and by extension their roles in delivering victory in battle. (It does not refer to the study of religions or of Christianity in particular.) A Roman commander would need to demonstrate a host of qualities to secure the favour of a divine patron, but the reward of victory rested squarely on two characteristics with which he must be endowed: *felicitas* and *virtus*.

Felicitas is most commonly translated into English as 'good fortune', but that does not accurately represent the concept. Being essential to victory, *felicitas* was a divine gift, not in the keeping of any mortal. Cicero is quite clear on this: *felicitas*, unlike fortune (*fortuna*), which might be both good and bad, was a reward for the deserving. More particularly, *felicitas* was the reward for *virtus*. This latter term is usually translated rather generally as 'virtue', but in this context a more accurate rendering would embrace 'manly aggressiveness', 'bravery' and 'valour'. Sallust, Cicero's contemporary, identified this human quality, rather than divine favour, as the principal cause of victory, but as republic gave way to empire, the valour of the emperor became a superhuman quality. Indeed, it was most commonly translated into later Greek as *dynamis*, which in Homer means bodily strength but which by the fourth century AD is used regularly to designate the Christian god.

During the third century there was no longer a balance between human *virtus* and divine *felicitas*, but rather one observes an 'absolutist theology [of Victory] involving the notion of an invincible (*invictus*) emperor, possessed of a supernatural *virtus* procuring an eternal and universal Roman victory'. That last clause is a quotation from Rudolph Storch, who observed astutely that this escalation mirrored both a decline in Roman military fortunes and the rise of monotheistic beliefs. *Invictus* means both 'unconquered' and 'unconquerable'. Neither quality was enjoyed by any emperor of the third century, but this did not prevent all from claiming it. The notion that invincibility was an imperial quality, intimately associated with *virtus* and *felicitas*, was as old as the empire.* However, this was not reflected in official imperial titulature until the third century, mirroring the rise of an absolutist theology of victory.

It has been suggested that the title *invictus* was applied to emperors rarely. However, it appears quite frequently in military contexts throughout the empire. For example, a third-century altar found in 1693 at Chester (Deva), in Britain, was dedicated:

For the welfare of our Lords the most invincible emperors, to the guardian spirit of the place Flavius Longus, military tribune of the Twentieth Legion

---

* The sense persists. Recent observers of the 'Third Rome', a title claimed for Moscow as early as the fifteenth century, when Byzantium fell to the Ottoman Turks, may be interested in anachronistic comparisons which will age rapidly in print. Still, biographies of Constantine are always of their age, so one might note without inordinate fear of censure that on 2 October 2007 it was reported in the *New York Times* that Paralympic ski champion Mikhail B. Terentyev took to a Moscow stage in his wheelchair to proclaim to the then president of Russia: 'Vladimir Vladimirovich, you are lucky ... And while you are president, the luck accompanies Russia.' *Felicitas* is the reward for *virtus*, the manly aggressiveness with which judo champion Putin defended Russia's national interests.

Valeria Victrix, and Longinus, his son, from Samosata, fulfilled their vow. (*RIB* 450)

At the other end of the empire, far nearer the birthplace of Flavius Longus, one of the papyrus morning reports of the Twentieth Palmyrene Cohort, stationed at Dura Europos in Syria, begins with an oath to 'stand watch at the standards of the Emperor Marcus Antonius Gordianus Pius Felix Invictus Augustus'. This oath to Gordian has been dated to 27–8 May AD 239.

As emperors fell ever more rapidly to the swords of their own men, symbols of divinely inspired victory, always ubiquitous in imperial art, acquired new meanings. The goddess Victoria, who would later mutate into the angel of Byzantine art, appears everywhere bearing a laurel wreath, the shield of valour (*clipeus virtutis*), or most notably the trophy. The trophy (*tropaeum*) was, in origin, a pole or tree trunk with a cross-beam upon which were hung the arms and armour, notably the breast-plate, helmet and shields, of a vanquished foe. Initially it appears to have been raised on the battlefield. The first reference to a battlefield trophy is in Florus' description of a victory over the Allobroges by the third Domitius Ahenobarbus (consul in 122 BC) and Fabius Maximus. A trophy being raised on a battlefield can be seen on the *Gemma Augustea*, produced in *c.*AD 10 to mark a victory of Tiberius over the Dalmatians (fig. 10). On a grander scale, one can see trophies depicted half-way up Trajan's Column in Rome. The monumental *Tropaeum Traiani*, 'Trajan's Trophy', erected in *c.*AD 107–9 at Adamklissi to celebrate Trajan's successful Dacian campaigns, takes the form of a trophy and also portrays trophies carried by victorious Roman troops.

Representations of trophies were a commonplace on Roman coinage from the last century of the Republic until the early third century AD. They were most often shown placed between bound captives or borne by the goddess Victoria. In each case the trophy shown commemorated a specific victory. However, quite suddenly the trophy disappeared from imperial coins during the reign of Macrinus (217–18) and did not re-appear until that of Gallienus (253–68). Now it was shown carried by the emperor, no longer representing a specific victory but rather appearing as a visual equivalent of the title *invictus*, and there is even evidence that it was used as an imperial standard. On the Ludovisi Sarcophagus, "on view in the Museo Nazionale Romano, in Rome" an emperor is shown mounted in the middle of a battle scene (fig. 11). Roman legionaries in crested helmets, mounted and foot soldiers, are engaging 'barbarians', who wear no helmets nor any clear ethnic markers, being distinguished from the Romans by their curly hair. Diana Kleiner, an eminent commentator on Roman sculpture, notes that of the Romans only 'the Ludovisi general is bare-headed and holds no weapon. The implication is that he is insuperable and will be victorious without protection or weaponry.' He is *invictus*, and thus one might clearly understand the presence on the edge of the battle of a trophy, borne on the shoulder of a Roman legionary.

The Ludovisi Sarcophagus is exceptional in being the only extant battle sarcophagus produced after their Antonine hey-day of AD 160–200. And the general has now been identified as the very man who reintroduced the trophy to Roman coins: Gallienus. The trophy depicted on the sarcophagus serves a symbolic function, corroborating the bareheaded emperor's invincibility. But it is also possible that Gallienus carried the trophy into battle as an imperial standard, to ensure his victory. As we shall see, a similar idea was seized upon by Constantine, who devised his own cruciform battle standard, the *labarum*. It was forged in the form he claimed to have seen in a vision that foretold his victory. The vision is later described as a 'cross-shaped trophy formed of light', using the now familiar term in Greek (*tropaion*).

The unconquered emperor and the Sun

As the empire's crisis deepened in the middle years of the third century, Roman emperors resorted more fully to rhetoric, becoming unconquerable generals whose actions in war demonstrated the support and manifested the will of a single greatest god (*summus deus*). Emperors had long shared the characteristics of the gods, and their divine qualities (*numina*) were worshipped in the camps. Emperors appeared divinely nude in sculpture, for example – and there are many examples up until the end of the second century – the bronze of Septimius Severus on display at the Cyprus Museum in Nicosia. In contrast, the more-than-life-sized nude of Trebonianus Gallus at New York's Metropolitan Museum of Art is the only large-scale bronze to survive from the third century (fig. 12). Gallus, if Gallus it is, is shown in a pose freely emulating that of Alexander the Great, glancing heavenwards and holding aloft a lance, based on a lost prototype by Lysippus, which depicted the hero in full battle armour and helmet. The nude emperor, therefore, presents a striking contrast to his model. Emulation of Alexander (*imitatio Alexandri*) was, as we have noted, much in vogue in the third century, but the preferred Alexander type was no longer the man, but Alexander in the guise of a god, Alexander-Helios, Alexander the Sun. The emperor as Alexander the Sun wore a solar crown, from which the sun's rays projected, and raised his right hand in a gesture of imperial or divine majesty and benediction. He wore a uniform, standing erect, in the pose of a living trophy.

In the third century, emperors were portrayed as generals, uniformed and armed, and gods as emperors, no longer nude, nor simply bearing their traditional accoutrements, but rather wearing cuirasses and helmets and bearing weapons. This was not, of course, an absolute contrast, but a further blurring of the distinction between patron gods and client emperors, who now shared divine characteristics and were filled with supernatural *virtus* that ensured their victories: until it did not, and they were replaced. One meets for the first time in the third century the gods Jupiter Invictus, Mars Invictus and Hercules Invictus, each 'unconquerable', each portrayed on coins in military dress. A god almost invariably portrayed in military garb is Jupiter Dolichenus, wielding his double-headed axe. More striking is the fact that Mithras is not portrayed thus in iconography discovered within Mithraea, but it is perhaps through devotion to this god of the camps that the military emperors, many of whom must have been initiates of the mysteries, evinced a devotion to Sol Invictus 'the Unconquered Sun'. This fact deserves more consideration than it has so far received from experts, for where initiates could not reveal any details of the mysteries, and therefore of their devotion to the Unconquered Sun God Mithras, they might openly venerate Sol Indiges, a solar deity long within the Roman pantheon, who was venerated on the Quirinal and in the circus and was reborn as Sol Invictus.

Sol came to the fore in the reign of Septimius Severus, whose wife Julia Domna was daughter of the chief priest of the Sun god at Emesa (modern Homs), Syria. Upon relocating to Rome, she appears to have brought a suitable priest, as eight inscriptions have been discovered in Trastevere naming one Julius Balbillus, six of which identify him as a *sacerdos* (priest) of Sol. On two occasions, Sol is identified as Elagabalus, the Syrian god worshipped at Emesa in the form of a black stone, probably a meteorite (and thus common to the worship of Cybele, Sol Elagabalus and later the god of the Muslims). But Septimius was wary of presenting such a deity to the Roman people, who preferred anthropomorphic gods with Roman equivalents. Thus, from AD 197, he struck coins annually to Sol, and on the reverse declared himself AUG INVICTUS, 'unconquered emperor'. Hitherto, Sol was most commonly portrayed on his four-horsed chariot, a *quadriga*, streaking towards the sky – a pose which remained popular. Now the god was depicted for the first time standing unattended, in the pose of Alexander-Helios, wearing a solar crown and with his right hand raised as if in benediction or acknowledgement (fig. 13, and compare with fig. 12), a gesture described by art historian Richard Brilliant as a 'conventional and ecumenical sign of radiant power'. But more particularly, it was the way an emperor would hold his hand when he was about to address his troops, in *adlocutio*, or when receiving the acclamations of a cheering crowd during a triumphal entry, the *adventus*.

Sol was by no means Septimius Severus' only patron, and he appears to have considered Jupiter his principal patron during a long and successful military career. His son, Caracalla, displayed a preference for the moon over the sun, venerating the goddess Luna. Caracalla struck coins to Sol regularly, but as son to a companion of Jupiter, he also favoured Jupiter's sons, Hercules and Dionysus. It was not a general, therefore, but a man quite without military standing who introduced the Sun as his sole imperial patron. A priest of the Sun god at Emesa, in Syria, before he acceded to the throne as Marcus Aurelius Antoninus (AD 218–22), he is better known by the name of his god, Elagabalus. Elagabalus the emperor was unpopular in Rome for wishing to institute the worship of Elagabalus the god alongside regular state rituals. He wore his priest's costume on state occasions and placed his cult title, 'the most mighty priest of the invincible Sun god', before that of *pontifex maximus*, chief priest of the various cults, within the imperial titulature. He struck coins to no other god and declared Sol Elagabalus to be protector of the emperor (*conservator augusti*). But the *conservator* could not protect the young priest from his own guards, who murdered him and his mother. The black rock which he had imported to Rome from Emesa was sent back, and Sol Elagabalus was not worshipped in Rome thereafter. Sol Invictus, however, remained, now striking additional poses and communicating additional messages.

In AD 238, when Gordian III, aged thirteen, was raised to the throne by the senate, coins were struck demonstrating his solar credentials. Sol is depicted handing the young emperor a globe, symbol of world domination, suggesting an established connection between the worship of the Sun and imperial legitimacy. It seems clear that those claiming to succeed the Severans observed the established iconography they had propagated and recognized the value of Sol's patronage. There are no known coins depicting Sol struck by the usurpers Gallus, Decius or Aemilianus, but the Sun was favoured by Valerian (253–60) and consequently by his son, Gallienus (253–68), as a guarantor of Rome's *aeternitas*, the eternal endurance of the empire in the face of ever-mounting troubles. Sol featured yearly on Gallienus' coins, and a new type emerged, featuring a winged horse, akin to Pegasus, but in fact a symbol of the Unconquered Sun identified as Sol, as the inscription reveals: SOLI CONS AUG, 'To Sol, Protector of the Augustus'. Sol appears thus to have been recruited as a patron for Gallienus' new cavalry corps, with the four horses of the Sun's familiar *quadriga* and the flying chariot itself suitably condensed. More significantly, Gallienus was the first emperor to strike coins which featured on their obverse the inscription 'unconquered emperor' (*invictus augustus*), with a reverse portrait of the unconquered Sun god, named in full as Sol Invictus. Previously, the god had enjoyed that epithet only in private inscriptions, mostly by adherents of Jupiter Dolichenus and those initiated into the mysteries of Mithras. One suspects that Gallienus, who spent his entire adult life in the army, must be numbered among these. We have already seen what efforts Gallienus made to portray himself as 'unconquerable', and this extended to the promotion of the

Unconquered Sun. According to the later (and largely unreliable) *Historia Augusta*, Gallienus . . .

gave orders to make a statue of himself arrayed as the Sun and greater than the Colossus [a pre-existing statue of the Sun god, erected by Nero with that emperor's face], but it was destroyed while still unfinished. It was, in fact, begun on so large a scale that it seemed to be double the size of the Colossus. His wish was that it should be placed on the summit of the Esquiline Hill, holding a spear, up the shaft of which a child could climb to the top. The plan, however, seemed foolish to Claudius and after him to Aurelian.

If the plan did indeed seem foolish to these men, it was not the reason that they, with other senior army officers, conspired to bring about Gallienus' death in 268. Claudius II (268–70) promptly proclaimed himself Sol Augustus, the Sun emperor. What he meant by this remains unclear, but it does not suggest an aversion to the Sun god. A glance at his coins might suggest that Claudius did not especially venerate Sol, striking coins dedicated to Jupiter the Victor and to the rarely seen Neptune, and even altering Gallienus' Sol Invictus type so that it displayed Hercules instead of the Sun god opposite the inscription 'unconquered emperor'. But Sol featured on a rather large proportion of the coins struck in his short reign, and also on those of the still shorter reign of Quintillus, his brother. Aurelian (270–5) went far further, and his reign deserves careful consideration, for it presents a case study of the imperial theology of victory in action and serves as a model for Constantine's actions in the early years of his reign.

Aurelian

Aurelian was a successful cavalry commander in his mid-fifties when Claudius II acceded to the throne. He had flourished in a milieu where rapid deployment of smaller, mobile units had come to dominate military strategy, and achieved high command during the apogee of the crisis under Gallienus. Most recently he had taken part in the campaigns that secured Claudius II his triumphal epithet, Gothicus Maximus, by the defeat of the Goths at a set-piece battle near Naissus (modern Niš in Serbia) in AD 269. Claudius' reign was cut short in 270 when, about to turn east to confront the rebel Palmyrene empire of the self-styled empress Zenobia, he fell victim to 'the plague'. Quintillus, Claudius' younger brother, was acclaimed by the army, but when Aurelian, commander of the cavalry, threatened civil war, Quintillus' troops turned against him and he committed suicide. Aurelian succeeded.

The brutal imposition of authority was more admired than feared by the Romans, but Aurelian was remembered as a particularly stern disciplinarian. While still a cavalry officer, according to the gloriously fictitious account in the *Historia Augusta*, Aurelian indulged in some *imitatio Alexandri*. But in this instance, it was not to magnify his achievements but to inspire respect in his troops:

He was alone among commanders in inflicting the following punishment on a soldier who had committed adultery with the wife of a man at whose house he was lodged: bending down the tops of two trees, he fastened them to the soldier's feet and let them fly up so suddenly that the man hung there torn in two – a penalty that inspired great fear in all.

Alexander is recorded as having employed this punishment, and the readers of this life would have been expected to make the association.

Aurelian travelled to Rome late in 270, not only to secure approval of his succession from the senate but also to begin a programme to rebuild the city's crumbling walls. This he did less to defend the populace and more to project his vision of eternal Rome, even as the empire endured for the first time in its history the presence of two secessionist states in its core provinces. Aurelian's achievement was to restore the integrity of the empire, in 272–3 defeating Empress Zenobia of Palmyra to recover Egypt and Syria, and in 274 crushing C. Pius Esuvius Tetricus to recover Gaul. Consequently, he took the title *restitutor orbis*, 'restorer of the world', and attributed his victories to Sol Invictus. He erected a new temple to this god in Emesa, and following a triumphal entry into Rome in 274, where Zenobia and Tetricus were paraded in defeat, he dedicated another still greater temple to the Unconquered Sun on the Campus Agrippae. To tend to this cult, he established a new priesthood of Sol, the *pontifices deo Soli*, whose members were drawn from the senatorial aristocracy and were distinct from all earlier *sacerdotes* of Sol

Elagabalus. There were also games devoted to the Sun, the *agones Soli*, which were celebrated annually on 25 December.

Why, one must ask, was Sol Invictus credited with delivering victory and allowing Aurelian to restore the empire? We are reliant almost solely on the *Historia Augusta* for our answer, and the tale is highly suspect. However, it makes comprehensible those of Aurelian's actions that are attested archaeologically – in the temple he erected at Rome, in the coins he struck, and in inscriptions by the priesthood of the Sun that endured after the emperor's death. The account involves an imperial vision of a philosopher-redeemer, the battlefield manifestation of a god to the commander and his men, and the glorious observance of the theology of victory in action.

Setting out for war, Aurelian commanded that the senate consult the Sibylline Books, Rome's famous books of oracles, kept meticulously updated shortly after the events they predicted had unfolded. They revealed that victory would be secured by correct propitiation of the gods. 'I wonder, revered fathers,' Aurelian informed the senators, 'that you have hesitated so long to open the Sibylline Books, as if you were consulting in a gathering of Christians and not in the temple of all the gods.' This would appear to be clear evidence that the author of this part of the *Historia Augusta* is addressing an audience of Roman senators in the later fourth, not third, century. But we cannot assume, consequently, that everything else here recorded is merely a response to Christianity's rise. Rather, the tale as it unfolds suggests that a story circulated during Aurelian's reign, the key elements of which were later recorded and embellished by our author. Most significantly, we may surmise that the story was known to Eusebius, and he used it when rewriting the tale of Constantine's vision, as we shall see in chapter 7.

The reason given for the delay in consulting the books is rooted in a now familiar discussion about the nature of imperial *virtus*, manly valour, and its divine or human origins. Thus, one senator, Ulpius Silanus, reminded his peers:

I often said in this body, when the invasion of the Marcomanni [a Germanic people] was first announced, that we should consult the commands of the Sibyl, make use of the benefits of Apollo [a cognate of Sol], and submit ourselves to the bidding of the immortal gods; but some objected, and objected too with cruel guile, saying in flattery that such was the valour (*virtus*) of the emperor Aurelian that there was no need to consult the deities, just as though the great man does not himself revere the gods and found his hopes on the dwellers of heaven. Why say more? We have heard this man's message asking for the help of the gods, which never causes shame to any. Now let this most courageous man be helped.

Aurelian, however, failed to defeat the Marcomanni, and 'there would have been no victory for Rome . . . if the power of the gods, after the Books had been consulted and the sacrifices performed, had not confounded the barbarians by means of certain prodigies and heaven-sent visions'. There is no indication that these visions are the same as that which Aurelian alone experienced en route to his decisive battle with Zenobia. As he was encamped before the city of Tyana, contemplating the fate of the rebels within . . .

Apollonius of Tyana, a sage of the greatest renown and authority, a philosopher of former days, the true friend of the gods, and himself even to be regarded as a supernatural being, suddenly appeared to Aurelian as he was withdrawing to his tent . . . [saying] 'Aurelian, if you wish to conquer, there is no reason why you should plan the death of my fellow citizens. Aurelian, if you wish to rule, abstain from shedding the blood of the innocent. Aurelian, act with mercy if you wish to live long.' Aurelian . . . at once stricken with terror, promised him a portrait and statues and a temple . . . For who among men has ever been more venerated, more revered, more renowned or more holy than that man [Apollonius]? He brought back the dead to life, he said and did many things beyond the power of man.

Apollonius is clearly here presented as a counterpart to Christ. According to a third-century life composed by Philostratus, Apollonius was an exact contemporary of Christ, who prayed thrice daily to the Sun. He is credited with the prayer: 'O, thou Sun, send me as far around the world as is my pleasure and thine; and may I make the acquaintance of good men but never hear anything of bad ones, nor they of me.' Unlike Christ, who would in a vision urge Constantine on to the slaughter of his foes, Apollonius provokes Aurelian's clemency. Consequently . . .

The whole issue of the war was decided near Emesa in a mighty battle fought against Zenobia and Zaba, her ally. When Aurelian's cavalry, now exhausted, was on the verge of breaking ranks and turning about, suddenly by the power of a supernatural agency, as was afterwards made known, a divine form spread encouragement throughout the infantry and rallied even the cavalry. Zenobia and Zaba were put to flight, and a victory was won in full. And so, having reduced the East to its former state, Aurelian entered Emesa as a conqueror, and at once made his way to the temple of Elagabalus, to pay his vows as if by a duty common to all. But there he saw the same divine form which he had seen supporting his cause in the battle. Wherefore, he not only established temples there, dedicating gifts of great value, but also built a temple to the Sun at Rome.

The form that appeared to Aurelian and his troops is not revealed, but it should be recalled that the god of Emesa was worshipped in the shape of a black rock. There are here remarkable similarities to Constantine's vision, but only in the form recorded by Eusebius, according to which Constantine, as we shall see, had both a dream of Christ and a vision. Eusebius also produced a treatise refuting a now lost work by Sossianus Hierocles, which advanced an extended comparison between Apollonius and Christ that favoured the miraculist from Tyana. However, there are notable differences also: Apollonius appears to Aurelian while he is awake some time before the battlefield vision, whereas Christ appears to Constantine while asleep on the eve of battle, in order to explain an earlier vision. The vision that Aurelian shared with his troops occurred in the midst of battle, inspiring his men to snatch victory from defeat. Constantine's men had no vision during the battle, nor indeed immediately before, but relied on their commander to remind them of an earlier sign they had observed, and by his command to daub it on their shields. These distinctions will become clearer once we turn to the accounts of Constantine's vision. For now it is important to record that Aurelian's actions demonstrate clearly that he attributed his victories to Sol and that this must be interpreted within the established framework of the imperial theology of victory.

Aurelian's vision is known to us only from the *Historia Augusta*, a source compiled after Eusebius' account of Constantine's vision and in that form evidently responding in some fashion to it. Nevertheless, it was not entirely a later fiction, but rather drew on an earlier story that was known by and served as a template for Constantine's actions. It would be easy to suggest cynically that he did not believe in divine patronage, but used the idea and its symbols to inspire his men to action. But this would be to introduce modern sensibilities. Certainly, the Romans were masters of propaganda and persuasion, but they also lived in a world filled with gods who provided very real benefits and rewards. For Aurelian's men at Emesa, therefore, like those who fought for Maximinus Thrax at Aquileia, it was quite natural to see the actions of a particular local god behind their successes or failures. Aurelian's achievement was to establish that god, Sol, at the pinnacle of the Roman pantheon, where Elagabalus had earlier failed, as the true greatest god (*summus deus*). There he would be equated with Apollo, or with Jupiter, or indeed with Christ.

Christ the true Sun

From the time of Aurelian dates the most striking image to have emerged from the excavations conducted beneath the Vatican. In the tomb of the Julii (mausoleum M) is a mosaic of the Sun god, seven rays projecting from a nimbus around his head (fig. 14). He is riding a solar chariot pulled by white horses, two of which are visible. A cape flies out behind his left shoulder. The god's right hand, now mostly lost, appears to be raised in benediction, familiar from other third-century representations of Sol. The left hand, also damaged, holds a globe. The halo and solar rays are standard, but are also evocative of earlier images of Apollo, in the guise of Helios, for example a wonderful medallion from a floor mosaic discovered at El Djem in Tunisia, which dates from the later second century. Thus the figure has been identified as Apollo-Helios. But more frequently, Sol of the Julii has been identified with Christ, largely because of his location and juxtaposition with scenes from the life of Jonah.

Jonah is similarly juxtaposed with the Sun in a less impressive fresco at Rome's Domitilla catacombs. The story of Jonah was a favourite among early Christians, for whom the scenes were elements of a language of symbols. But his significance is best illustrated by the Jonah Marbles at the Cleveland Museum of Art (AD 270–80), among which sculptures of Jonah swallowed by the whale, and then disgorged, represent the death and resurrection of Christ. There is no reason to suppose that members of the same family could not be devotees of both Sol and Christ, nor indeed that they could not appreciate their equivalences. As our consideration of the conversion of Constantine will demonstrate, Sol and Christ might easily be regarded as cognates, and the veneration of the former treated as a stepping-stone to the fuller appreciation of the latter. And so, just as Jonah's encounter with the whale was a metaphor for Christ's descent and resurrection, so was the setting and rising of the Sun, as foretold by Isaiah (60:1): 'Arise, shine; for thy light is come, and the glory of the Lord is risen upon thee.'

Two further elements of the mosaic decoration of mausoleum M, a fisherman and a man holding a staff, are ubiquitous early Christian motifs. Both are presented alongside a sun-crowned god on a striking sarcophagus, dating from the mid-third century and discovered at La Gayole in Provence. One sees here also a teaching scene and a person standing with hands outstretched in prayer (*orans*). The scene suggests the progression of the person buried within through education, revelation and the power of prayer, from worship of the Sun to that of Christ. This was exactly the path recommended by Clement of Alexandria, who saw worship not merely as a polytheistic fallacy but rather as a monotheism a step below that of Christian worship. For Clement, moreover, Christ is the Sun:

And the Lord, with ceaseless assiduity, exhorts, terrifies, urges, rouses, admonishes; He awakes from the sleep of darkness, and raises up those who have wandered in error. 'Awake,' He says, 'thou that sleepest, and arise from the dead, and Christ shall give thee light' – Christ, the Sun of the Resurrection, He 'who was born before the morning star', and with His beams bestows life.

Likewise for Origen, Christ is the Sun of Justice, that part of the godhead that manifested itself to mankind, to illuminate the earth and dispense justice. In his polemic against Celsus, Origen observed the difference between worshipping the Sun and that which the Sun represented:

Those, indeed, who worship sun, moon, and stars because their light is visible and celestial, would not bow down to a spark of fire or a lamp upon earth, because they see the incomparable superiority of those objects which are deemed worthy of homage to the light of sparks and lamps. So those who understand that God is light, and who have apprehended that the Son of God is 'the true light which lighteth every man that cometh into the world', and who comprehend also how He says, 'I am the light of the world', would not rationally offer worship to that which is, as it were, a spark in sun, moon, and stars, in comparison with God, who is light of the true light.

While pagans would have observed the Sun god in his familiar chariot, Christians looking at the image of Sol in the Mausoleum of the Julii would have seen none other than the Light of the World. And the same must surely apply to those who, a century later, looked up into a cupola in the small church of San Aquilino in Milan to see Christ in a chariot streaking across the sky. Perhaps the prayer of Ambrose, *Splendor paternae gloriae*, composed in Milan, was intoned beneath this very image. It is now known to English-speakers as the hymn 'Splendour of God's Glory Bright':

> O splendour of God's glory bright,
> O Thou that bringest light from light,
> O Light of light, light's living spring,
> O day, all days illumining.
> O Thou true Sun (*verusque Sol*), on us Thy glance,
> Let fall in royal radiance,
> The spirit's sanctifying beam,
> Upon our earthly senses stream.

4

The Tetrarchy

The first Tetrarchy – Jovians and Herculians – The Caesars at war – The army of the Tetrarchs – The Great Persecution – Lactantius: On the Deaths of the Persecutors

With a better understanding of the Roman empire in the third century, one can approach Constantine, who fused the vigour of the Christian faith with the power of the army. Constantine exploited the traditional interaction between faith and military power, the imperial theology of victory, to construct for himself the image of 'unconquered emperor'; he took as his patron the 'greatest god', whose identity was revealed to him in a vision; and later, having established his hold on power, he transformed himself from 'unconquered emperor', a style enjoyed by so many of his predecessors, to Christian Victor, a title unique to Constantine. His response, however, was not to the situation at the death of Aurelian, when Constantine was but an infant, but to that which prevailed in the first decade of the fourth century. At that time, the Roman empire was ruled by four emperors, two junior with the title Caesar, and two senior with the title Augustus. Together they were known as the Tetrarchs. One of these was Constantine's father, Constantius Chlorus, a junior emperor who was subordinate to Maximian in the west. To the east, the junior emperor was Galerius, subordinate to Diocletian.

The first Tetrarchy

Diocletian, commander of the imperial bodyguard, was acclaimed emperor by his troops near Nicomedia in Bithynia (Izmit in modern Turkey), in November AD 284. He attained power in the same manner as so many of his predecessors, but he retained it in a manner no other had achieved. Through the period of crisis one of the commonest acts of a recent usurper was to seek recognition of his son as Caesar, which designated a junior emperor and heir or occasionally, as Augustus, co-emperor. Diocletian emulated this but removed the dynastic element, and hence harnessed the dynamism of new men to the new system, obviating the tendency to place teenaged puppets on the throne, such as Severus Alexander and Gordian III. He could then campaign without the fear, which every one of his predecessors had felt and to which most had succumbed, that appointing a successful general was tantamount to signing his own death warrant. If the emperor himself could not win all battles – and no man could fight on northern and eastern frontiers simultaneously – then he had better hope that his appointed general failed to win any spectacular victories.

According to a papyrus record from Egypt dated March 285, Diocletian was called Diocles upon his accession, but he took for himself the more imperial style Gaius Aurelius Valerius Diocletianus. His first act was to dispose of Aper, the Praetorian Prefect with whom he had conspired to kill Numerianus, elder son of Carus (282–3). Before May 285 Carus' second son, Carinus, was murdered by his own troops in Moesia to avoid battle with Diocletian. Shortly after that, perhaps on 21 July 285, Diocletian took a trusted subordinate, Marcus Aurelius Maximianus, or Maximian, as his Caesar. This was not a radical departure from recent precedent. Valerian had appointed Gallienus immediately to the rank of Augustus, and more recently Carus had involved his sons in his rule, first as Caesars and later as Augusti. Countless others had tried and failed to ensure the succession of their son or sons. But Diocletian had no son, only a daughter, whom he later married to Galerius. He needed a general whom he could trust to operate in the west while he campaigned to the east, one who would not view success as an opportunity for rebellion. Early victories against the Bagaudae in Gaul saw Maximian elevated to Augustus before the end of May 286. With no higher position to which he might aspire, the second emperor remained loyal.

Soon after his appointment, Maximian entrusted a subordinate, Carausius, with the construction of a fleet to clear the seas between Gaul and Britain of pirates. Carausius was an expert sailor and was immediately successful. However, he kept much of the recovered booty for himself and was called to account by Maximian. Rather than face retribution, he rebelled and swiftly established control over north-western Gaul and southern Britain. Maximian made extensive preparations to quash the rebellion, spending a year building ships. And while thus occupied, he relied increasingly on his Praetorian Prefect to carry out the duties Diocletian had entrusted to him. The prefect, Flavius Constantius, whom we know better as Constantius Chlorus, was a popular and effective commander. He led his army as far as the Danube, capturing a barbarian king and devastating the lands of the Alemans. His success was a threat, and Maximian moved to secure his loyalty by engineering Constantius' marriage to his daughter Theodora. Constantius embraced this arrangement at the expense of his existing union with Helena, mother of Constantine. That he proceeded to father six more children over the next decade, in between battles, suggests no lack of enthusiasm for his new, younger bride. But it also implied no derogation of Constantine, his first-born son.

Diocletian's establishment of a Dyarchy, the rule of two emperors, was clearly an ad hoc measure to ensure that he did not suffer the fate of so many predecessors. But within a few years of his elevation Maximian had become a liability, no longer able to lead his army effectively, having failed perhaps twice to defeat Carausius. Since he could not entrust the task to Maximian, Diocletian himself struck against the northern barbarians in 288 and 289. In 290, his attention was required on the eastern frontier, and he marched the length of the empire to Syria. But shortly afterwards, he transferred his base from Nicomedia in Asia Minor to Sirmium on the Danube. This was not the situation he had anticipated in appointing Maximian, who could not now have been saved if his army desired his removal. A natural successor, Constantius, was poised to take over. But Maximian and Constantius were linked by marriage, and Diocletian had reason to worry. The emphasis placed by orators at this time on *concordia*, 'harmony', between the imperial colleagues suggests that all was not harmonious. Diocletian anticipated either that Constantius and Maximian would conspire against him, obliging him to take the field against them both; or that Constantius might raise the banner of revolt against Maximian. Recent experience reduced the likelihood that Maximian would triumph in such a clash, and his demise would oblige

Diocletian to march against Constantius. A resolution was required, one which would prevent a return to the familiar cycle of military acclamation and civil war, and which would allow a concerted effort to be directed against Carausius, the latest pretender.

The senior emperor convened a summit in Milan in winter 290–1. Senators arrived from Rome to add further gravitas to the event, or at least to offer an additional veneer of legitimacy to the radical constitutional reform that was resolved. A deal was struck that Constantius was to be appointed Caesar, junior emperor, and would remain subordinate to Maximian. But Diocletian would also appoint a Caesar, and his choice was his own Praetorian Prefect, Galerius Maximianus. The elevations did not take place until 293, and the reason for the delay of two years is unknown. The years 291 and 292 are peculiarly obscure, but we can be fairly sure that the Augusti did not meet again between January 291 and spring 293. On 1 March 293, the Roman empire had for the first time four recognized emperors who had undertaken to rule as one, as a Tetrarchy.

Jovians and Herculians

By 287 the imperial colleagues had begun to use the adjectival epithets Jovius and Herculius, 'of Jupiter' and 'of Hercules'. Jupiter was, of course, the father of the gods, and more specifically father of the semi-divine Hercules. Diocletian, as the Jovian, might achieve all he desired alone, but frequently relied on his Herculian subordinate Maximian to execute his wishes. This was a clever improvisation which appealed greatly to the orators charged with praising the emperors. One, named Mamertinus, offered in 289 a speech in honour of Maximian to mark Rome's birthday, a piece which is replete with references to Hercules. It is explained that Maximian's task is to assist Diocletian:

For just as all useful things . . . come to pass for us through different divinities but nevertheless flow from the supreme creators, Jupiter, ruler of the heavens, and Hercules, pacifier of the earth, so in all the most splendid exploits, even those carried out under the leadership of others, Diocletian makes the decisions, and you carry them out. It is through your good fortune, your *felicitas*,

Emperor, that your soldiers have already reached the ocean in victory, and that already the receding waves have swallowed up the blood of enemies slain upon the shore.

The language here is familiar, within the imperial theology of victory. The junior emperor, Maximian Herculius, owed his victories to his *felicitas*, his divinely bestowed good fortune, and to the instructions of Diocletian Jovius, which he carried out to good effect. In fact, this last passage misrepresents the scale of Maximian's victory, rather than merely exaggerating. The 'ocean' in question is today's English Channel, and the blood is that of the soldiers of the rebel Carausius, whom Maximian could not defeat and whose successes provoked the elevation of the Caesars. By that innovation, the symmetry of the 'divine' relationship between Diocletian-Jupiter and Maximian-Hercules was destroyed. This, of course, presented no problems to orators, who saw the manifest opportunities to praise the new arrangement for its arithmetic. One, speaking in 297, observed:

in addition to the concerns and interests of the state, that kindred majesty of Jupiter and Hercules also required a similarity between the entire world and heavenly affairs in the shape of Jovian and Herculian rulers. For indeed all the most important things depend upon and rejoice in the number of your divinity, for there are four elements and as many seasons of the year, the world divided fourfold by a double ocean, the orbits of heavenly bodies (*lustra*) which return after four revolutions of the sky, the Sun's team of four horses, and Vesper and Lucifer added to the two lamps of the sky.

Constantius, although the senior of the two Caesars, was formally adopted into the junior Herculian line. Galerius was adopted into the senior Jovian line and married to Diocletian's daughter, but he was the junior Caesar and hence the most junior of all four emperors. The situation was complicated further when the Caesars took patron gods of their own, with Constantius favouring Mars, popular in the west, and Galerius venerating the eastern favourite Sol Invictus. More troubling than this tinkering with the pantheon was the fact that Maximian, unlike Diocletian, had a son who was effectively sidelined by the convention. Maxentius was then still a youth, a little younger than Constantine. But there were evidently still hopes that he might one day succeed, and some time later Maxentius was married to the daughter of Galerius. Constantine similarly became a pawn in the great game, despatched to the east with Diocletian and Galerius, a potent incentive to Constantius to remain loyal and a reminder that the rhetorical unity of the Tetrarchs required serious underpinnings.

The harmony between the four emperors is illustrated by a porphyry statue, carved from the purple marble quarried only in Egypt, which has survived as plunder taken from Constantinople by the Fourth Crusade. It is now located in the south-east corner of the southern facade of the Basilica of San Marco in Venice (fig. 15). Four emperors are depicted, each clasping the eagle-headed hilt of his sword with his left hand and the shoulder of a fellow emperor with his right. This requires that one of each pair lean across his partner, affecting a manly embrace. The embracer in each pair sports a beard of light stubble, and he is slightly taller than the embraced. Only these marks of maturity and stature distinguish the Augusti from their Caesars, for in all other ways the men are identical. Their facial features are the same, as are their military costumes. One of the Caesars has lost his left foot, presumably when he was ripped from his base in Constantinople in 1204. All Tetrarchs have both feet, and indeed short beards, in a second set of porphyry pairs, now held in the Vatican (fig. 16, illustrating two). Instead of hilts, they hold in their left hands orbs, imperial insignia symbolizing earthly dominion. Once again the embracer in each pairing must be considered the Augustus, for his eyes are slightly higher than those of his Caesar. All look upwards, like so many heavenwards-gazing Alexanders (see below, p. 207), but with the close-cropped hair and angular, masculine chins of soldiers. Their squat legs and powerful, oversized arms convey strength abstractly.

The porphyry statues reflect an ideal of concord and co-operation that certainly did not exist between the Tetrarchs. The emperors were rarely together, perhaps only once and briefly in two decades. They all travelled constantly, spending summers in military compounds and winters in various provincial capitals. Edicts, imperial pronouncements, issued by each emperor were held to have effect throughout the empire, but rarely were they enforced universally. Each emperor was largely autonomous in his own territory, and although there was no absolute

schematic division of imperial territories in 293, each of the four emperors went back to where he was most needed and where his personal
authority was established. These regions were, roughly and in modern
terms: Maximian in Italy, Spain and North Africa (Tunisia and Algeria);
Constantius in northern France and the Benelux countries, southern
France and Britain; Diocletian in eastern Turkey, Palestine and Syria,
and Egypt; and Galerius in western Turkey, the Balkans, and Austria-
Hungary (see map 2).

The porphyry statues also, in their abstract and blockish manner,
convey an ideal of haughty power to which the emperors aspired, jointly
and individually. Increasingly through the third century, as we have
seen, emperors had drawn parallels between themselves and the gods,
and as emperors were shown with divine attributes, so gods were
portrayed in imperial dress or military costume. But Diocletian took
this a stage further, seeking to elevate himself above those who, like
him, might aspire to ultimate power. For a man of such humble birth,
interposing distance between himself and those who would challenge
his authority was not simple, as the author Aurelius Victor observed,
but it could be achieved with silks and gems and titles:

He [Diocletian] was a great man, yet he had the following characteristics: he
was, in fact, the first who really desired a supply of silk, purple and gems for
his sandals, together with a gold-brocaded robe. Although these things went
beyond good taste and betrayed a vain and haughty disposition, they were
nevertheless trivial compared to the rest. For he was the first of all after Caligula
and Domitian to permit himself to be called 'Lord' in public and to be worshipped
and addressed as a god.

Aurelius Victor ascribed the new style to Diocletian's low birth, but
in that he was hardly unique. Indeed, after the Severans, all third-century
emperors were equestrians, not senators, and many shared the author's
given name, Aurelius, which was given to all new citizens without an
established family upon the extension of citizenship by the Antonine
Constitution of 212. This was formalized upon recruitment into the army,
when a full name was required for the rolls. One might recall that
Constantine's chosen forebear was Marcus Aurelius Claudius (Claudius
Gothicus), who was replaced by Marcus Aurelius Aurelianus (Aurelian),

who a decade before Diocletian permitted himself to be called 'Lord and god', *dominus et deus*. Still, the point is well taken that Diocletian greatly elaborated imperial ceremonial, establishing a distance between emperor and subject that could only be crossed, figuratively and literally, with the assistance of his court eunuchs, employed for the first time in numbers by the imperial household in emulation of the Persians. He greeted visitors in immense reception halls, where his elevated throne would tower above all else. Yet still the minion would be required to offer the emperor his obeisance in a low bow, and only the most eminent would be permitted to kiss the bejewelled sandal. Constantine would later emulate this scheme in all its parts at his court at Constantinople.

A new imperial architecture emerged as the backdrop to this elaboration of ceremonial. Huge basilicas were constructed in each imperial city to serve as reception halls of the god-emperors, one of which still stands, rebuilt at Trier. The eyes of a visitor now are cast up towards the ceiling of the tall chamber, but then none were permitted to meet the gaze of the emperor, which in any case would itself be upwards, in commune with a divine patron. And divine patronage was needed, as ever, most urgently on the field of battle.

The Caesars at war

Immediately upon his elevation as Caesar, Constantius set to his assigned task of crushing Carausius. In 293, he drove the rebel out of north-western Gaul, to Britain. This was no mean feat, as Carausius had widespread support and wealth at his disposal. He was the only man claiming the title emperor who at that time was able to mint coins in silver. These expressed his claim to rule alongside Diocletian and Maximian, whose heads were shown behind his own. The defeat led to Carausius' murder by his deputy, Allectus, who strengthened the walls of the British shore castles in anticipation of an assault. Constantius turned to the Rhine frontier, before settling affairs with Allectus in 296. The campaign to recover Britain is well covered in a panegyrical oration delivered in 297, and from this we learn that Constantius was himself still at sea, adrift in the mists of the English Channel, when the initial victory was won by his Praetorian Prefect, Asclepiodotus. The orator does his best to obscure this fact, which would have been well known to all his listeners, mentioning neither Asclepiodotus' name nor his title, and he does so within the traditional framework of the imperial theology of victory. Hence, the success is attributed directly to Constantius' *felicitas* and to his demonstration of *virtus* in setting off first from Boulogne (although he failed to reach the shore opposite). Constantius' subsequent triumphal arrival at London is praised most highly. The event is also commemorated on a celebrated medallion, found at Arras in 1922 (fig. 17), which shows on its reverse a woman, representing the city of London, kneeling before the emperor, her back to her fortified gates, her hands raised in supplication and thanks to the mounted warrior. He appears to float, larger than life, above the river Thames, on which a warship rests at anchor, having delivered the city and the province back to Rome. In this way, as an inscription hails, Constantius had become the 'Restorer of the Eternal Light' of Rome. But the victory was not his alone. The Caesar shared his success with his three colleagues, and all took the cognomen Britannicus Maximus. Later they would also take Persicus Maximus, to mark the victory over the Persians, in which campaigns Constantine cut his military teeth.

Constantine was not with his father in Britain but had been despatched to the east and put to work in the army, learning the skills that would earn him the respect and loyalty of his troops in later years. When Constantius became Caesar, Constantine achieved the rank of military tribune, and a later tale has the young officer offered the insignia of his new status by Fausta, daughter of the emperor Maximian, who would later become Constantine's wife. Constantine spent the period after 293 between the eastern frontier in battle with the Persians and the Danube frontier fighting the Sarmatians. There are no contemporary representations of Constantine's youthful exploits – we may dismiss a suggestion that he is depicted alongside Galerius' rearing horse in the battle scene on the Arch of Galerius, to be discussed shortly – but we know that he played a role in Galerius' campaigns and that this was later held to be heroic. According to the *Origo Constantini*:

When Constantine, then a young man, was serving in the cavalry against the Sarmatians, he seized by the hair and carried off a fierce savage, and threw him at the feet of the emperor Galerius. Then sent through a swamp by Galerius, he entered it on his horse and made a way for the rest to the Sarmatians, of whom he slew many and won the victory for Galerius.

This took place in 299 and thus was the fourth such victory over the Sarmatians during Diocletian's reign. The four Tetrarchs each took the title Sarmaticus Maximus IV alongside Persicus Maximus II, which Galerius had secured for them all by a major victory in 299. Constantine certainly fought in Galerius' campaigns against the Persians, which initially went poorly. The Romans lost the Battle of Carrhae (modern Harran, in eastern Turkey) in 296, but Galerius returned in full force in 298, marching as far as the walls of the Persian capital Ctesiphon. Constantine would later recall this campaign in his *Oration to the Saints*, when he had seen the ruins of Memphis and Babylon.

The Romans entered Ctesiphon, one hundred years after Septimius Severus had done the same. The campaign was celebrated in stone on an arch erected in Galerius' honour in Salonica (or Thessaloniki, in Greece), his base between *c.*AD 298 and 303 (fig. 18). The friezes include, on the north-east side, a representation of the victorious battle, where Galerius is depicted in a pose rather similar to that of the emperor on the Ludovisi Sarcophagus (figs. 11, 19). Although his head has been defaced, it is clear that he, unlike his men or his foes, wears no helmet. His horse is rearing up, trampling a Persian, who is trying to unsheathe his sword, even as the emperor engages the mounted Sassanian ruler, Narses, son of Shapur I. This is an entirely fictive image of single combat, intended to personalize the victory of the unconquerable emperor. On the frieze immediately beneath this, the four emperors are depicted together, the two Augusti enthroned, their Caesars standing beside them (fig. 20). Their faces are missing, but Diocletian is sitting to the right of Maximian (to the left as we look at it), with Galerius standing beside him. Constantius stands at Maximian's left hand. Victoria offers the Augusti laurel wreaths, and Fortunes hold trophies, as the emperors elevate personifications of the liberated provinces of Syria and Britain. Beneath the feet of the Augusti and beside their subordinates, we see images of deities of the earth and ocean, demonstrating the power of four as it had been described by the panegyrist of 297. Beneath this is a badly abraded line of seven Victorias, each bearing an illegible symbol and together offering an intriguing suggestion that Galerius' devotion to Mithraism and its seven spheres is here illustrated. One recalls that his patron deity was Sol Invictus and wonders whether overt references to personal beliefs were to be suppressed in favour of the common gods of the Tetrarchs. Thus, on the south-east side of the arch, Diocletian and Galerius are depicted together, offering a victory sacrifice at Antioch to the patron gods of the Tetrarchy, Jupiter and Hercules, who are depicted frontally enthroned on the altar, although Galerius was not a Herculian but rather the junior Jovian emperor (fig. 21). The victory over Persia, the greatest a Roman had enjoyed for a century, rendered the juniority of Galerius moot.

The army of the Tetrarchs

The Tetrarchs were all soldiers, emperors by dint of their ability to lead men and of their success in war. Diocletian, Maximian and Constantius had all served as Protectors (*protectores*), to which position only the most capable of soldiers were promoted from all other units. Protectors served many functions, for example rounding up the sons of veterans for enrolment in the legions, but in times of war they were to be found with the emperor. Gallienus had established a cavalry corps of Protectors which accompanied him always, reacting swiftly to military needs across the empire. During Diocletian's reign, and perhaps before, one notes a further development in the structure and stature of the Protectors. A corps had been established, which was known simply as his 'retinue' (*comitatus*), but which later took the title Domestics (*domestici*), meaning defenders of the imperial household. The role of guarding the emperor had traditionally fallen to the Praetorian Guard, which had failed to protect a good number of third-century emperors, including Maximinus Thrax in 238. Commanders of the Praetorian Guard, Praetorian Prefects, had benefited from proximity to the emperor by elevation to the throne, for example Macrinus in 217 and Philip the Arab in 244. The retinue of Protectors, therefore, was formed in no small part to protect the emperor from the Praetorians, although Diocletian had himself failed in that task when he had commanded the

Protectors attending the emperor Carus and his sons Carinus and Numerianus. He played a role in all of their deaths, and immediately afterwards slew his principal competitor for elevation, the Praetorian Prefect Aper. The Praetorian Guard henceforth enjoyed a far less privileged position, many of its cohorts rarely leaving Rome and thus rarely seeing emperors. Diocletian and Galerius both considered disbanding the Guard, resenting having to pay the elevated stipends and donatives demanded by the Praetorians (half as much again as for regular troops), and anticipating that it would be an unstable force of uncertain loyalty in the city. This proved to be the case, as we shall see.

The Tetrarchs, as soldiers, devoted particular attention to reforming the military. Lactantius, a Christian author to whom we shall turn in detail shortly, claims that they quadrupled the size of the army, each emperor competing to lead the largest force. He wilfully misrepresents the situation, but his claim has some foundation in fact: there were many more units, but not as many more troops as this might suggest. John Lydus, writing in the sixth century, states with disconcerting precision that Diocletian maintained an army of 389,704 and a navy of 45,562. If he is broadly accurate, then around AD 300 it would have required 20,000 new recruits each year to maintain the fighting strength of the army, to replace those lost to discharge, disability and death. Diocletian introduced conscription, formalizing the custom that sons of veterans were obliged to serve. But this could not rapidly produce battle-ready troops, and consequently some established legions were broken into two, with the new units distinguished as senior and junior. The junior legion comprised largely new recruits, bolstered and commanded by a cadre of distinguished troops from the original legion, which formed its first cohort. The senior legion was depleted, but all legions now comprised fewer than the regulation 5500 men.

In addition, new elite infantry legions were formed bearing the telltale names Joviani and Herculiani. Once again, the best men were drawn from established legions, which would have remained understrength. If these new legions were attached at first to Diocletian and Maximian in turn – and certainly Diocletian travelled with the first Jovian legion in his retinue – soon they were serving where needed. Legionaries bearing the mark of a Herculian legion – Hercules bearing his club – can clearly be seen on the Arch of Galerius, participating in the Jovian Caesar's Persian campaign (fig. 22). When additional manpower was needed for expeditions, ad hoc groupings known as vexillations were formed by drawing men from several units. It was logistically simpler to move some from several places, rather than all from a few camps, which might then prove to be vulnerable to attack. The newer recruits, or those who had proved less able, would be left behind as garrisons. Vexillations were commanded by tribunes, the rank held by Constantine.

Although many young Romans were conscripted into the legions, the bulk of new troops recruited by the Tetrarchs were 'barbarians', who formed new auxiliary units. Many were recruited from peoples settled along Roman frontiers, or from peoples against whom the Tetrarchs won victories. The auxiliary unit known as the Regii was formed by Constantius in 298 from a group of Alemans who had been trapped on an island in the frozen river Rhine. They joined his army as a group and served under their own king, Crocus (hence their name, meaning 'of the king'). Crocus and the Regii would serve a crucial role in the elevation of Constantine. The unit of Regii was paired with that of the Batavi, probably raised at the same time from among the Franks settled next to the Rhine. The purpose of pairing was to maintain unit morale and promote excellence through competition, and this was achieved very well by trading on established rivalries. One month the Batavi might have been fighting off Aleman raiders, the next fighting beside them against their kinsmen. The Cornuti and Bracchiati were similarly recruited from among the Franks at this time, fighting together but distinguished by their eponymous horned helmets and armbands.

There were clear precedents for the formation of imperial units from recently conquered barbarians. Aurelian had used two thousand Vandals vanquished in 271 and bound to him by a treaty as a guard unit. But the Regii and Batavi and the Cornuti and Bracchiati were permanent palatine units (*auxilia palatina*), bolstering the imperial bodyguard. They provided additional security for the emperors, for as barbarians their leaders would never have been accepted as alternative rulers by the rest of the army. Moreover, the kings owed their loyalty to the emperor himself, and not to a series of intermediate officers under whom they may have served or by whom they may have been promoted. Just as Byzantine emperors in later centuries would surround themselves with fierce Anglo-Saxons and Rus, the Varangian Guard, so Constantius Chlorus, and following him Constantine, were accompanied by the barbarian *auxilia palatina*.

Providing for a vast and growing army was a complex task, which has been elucidated by a cache of papyri discovered at Panopolis, near Ptolemais, in Egypt. The task was made considerably harder by galloping inflation in the last decades of the third century. Diocletian attempted, piecemeal, to re-establish some sense of order, starting with currency reform as early as 293–4. Gold coins were struck, and a new silver coin of high value, the *argenteus*, was issued thereafter from new mints that were placed in provincial cities under the direct control of the Augusti and Caesars. However, despite these attempts to restore confidence in the currency and to ensure its widespread circulation, the state economy continued to falter. High-grade coins were withdrawn from circulation and hoarded by those fortunate enough to receive them, and silver did not make its way back to the centre, where it was needed to finance the essential functions of government.

Diocletian's administrative reforms allowed closer regulation of taxation, and consequently imposed a heavier tax burden across the empire. For this he was condemned by several authors. But the reforms stuck. More and smaller provinces were created from older, unwieldy units, and civilian and military matters were entrusted to different bureaux. Provincial governors, no longer soldiers, answered to 'vicars' who oversaw the administration of groups of provinces, or 'dioceses' (see map 3). Each vicar answered to his regional Praetorian Prefect, no longer the commander of the Praetorian Guard but rather the deputy of each Tetrarch and head of his civil service. Indeed, the creation of Praetorian Prefectures seems to have been intended in large part to allow the emperors to concentrate on their main task: commanding the armies. These developments were modified over the following decades, and we shall return to them in chapter 10, in addressing Constantine's administration.

Several attempts were made to institute a regular fifteen-year tax cycle, known as the indiction, which would prevail through the Byzantine period. But sufficient funds were still not reaching the imperial coffers, and rather than once again raise the overall tax burden on his subjects, Diocletian determined to recalibrate the relative value of the coinage and to fix prices for essential goods and services. In September 301 an edict was issued that doubled the value of the high-grade silver coin, the *argenteus*, from 50 to 100 copper coins, *denarii*. Thus the purchasing power of the state, which collected taxes in silver, was instantly doubled. Two months later, in November 301, an attempt was made to impose maximum prices, in an edict posted throughout the eastern provinces, where it has survived in more than forty inscriptions. Indeed, Diocletian's edict of maximum prices is the best-attested epigraphical document of antiquity.

The prices of more than thirty items, including wheat, barley, lentils and beans, were fixed according to the measure employed by military quartermasters: the army *modius*. That amount of grain or pulses would feed an eight-man *contubernium*, the army's smallest unit, for one day, providing about a dry litre per person. The daily grain allowance, the *frumentum*, was supplemented by the *cibaria*, including meat and drink. But not all items monitored were on a soldier's or quartermaster's daily shopping list. Thus, in the edict slabs of pork and beef were distinguished from best fig-fed pig's liver (16 *denarii* per pound) and smoked Lucanian beef sausage (10 *denarii* per pound), or still more expensive items like dormice (40 *denarii* for ten) and peahens (200 *denarii* each). Salaries were also capped for those who might provide services to the military. Thus, a camel-driver or ass-driver was to be paid no more than 25 *denarii* a day, whereas a shipwright for seagoing vessels might command 60 *denarii* (and consequently take home 10 thrushes for his wife or concubine to roast). Other craftsmen were unlikely regularly to have been required in a camp, where many could as easily wield a brush as a sword. However, the price edict specified that a wall painter could expect only half as much as a figure painter, whose 150 *denarii* would buy him one whole hare.

The state was to be the only real beneficiary of the new strictures. Small-holders and hunters, who transported their wares to market, treated currency largely as a unit of account, needing coin only to pay taxes, and even that burden might frequently be commuted. Thus, most in the wider economy were unaffected by the dearth of coin in circulation and by the inflated price of an army *modius* of wheat or brace of hares. They could barter one for the other. The soldier did not enjoy this luxury, for he was paid in coin. This was apparent to the emperor, who condemned inflation as the result of profiteering. The preamble to the edict of maximum prices explains that Diocletian was most troubled that a soldier 'is deprived of his donative and salary in the transaction of a single exchange, and that the whole world's entire tax contributions for the maintenance of armies are spent on the profits of thieves'. Price-fixing was, of course, no solution, since those who would police the system, the municipal councils and local potentates, were the very men who would benefit from higher prices and laxer controls. Arriving at a place where the edict was enforced, a seller might simply take his wares to another where it was not.

Pay and conditions had traditionally made life in the army attractive, but this was no longer the case at a time when recruitment targets had risen. An Egyptian papyrus of 299–300 reveals that legionaries and cavalry troopers received an annual stipend of 600 *denarii*, paid in three instalments. Auxiliary troops had always received less than legionaries, but this shortfall was offset by an additional allowance of 200 *denarii* for rations. At these rates, even if the price edict had been enforced, a soldier would have been paid in a year what a wall mosaicist made in ten days, or a carpenter in twelve. But this was but a fraction of a soldier's annual pay, as a far greater proportion was now paid in donatives, lump-sum payments associated with celebrations in the ritual calendar marking the birthday and accession day of each emperor. As there were now four emperors, donatives were paid four times as frequently. A distinction was drawn between Augusti and Caesars, but which emperor one served directly did not affect the size of one's donative. Hence, a legionary could expect to receive 1250 *denarii* for each celebration of an Augustus, and 625 for that of a Caesar, although since the junior emperors were elevated together, on 31 March 293, the donative would be 1250 *denarii* on that day also. An auxiliary soldier was far less privileged, receiving only 250 *denarii* for celebrations of the Augusti and 125 for those of the Caesars. In times of financial crisis, the fact that barbarians were willing to accept far less to serve in the army explains a great deal of their attraction to the Tetrarchs.

The Great Persecution

In the years after the Persian victory, Diocletian found himself with no military campaign to lead, nor one to plan. In 299 he had swapped stations with his victorious junior, shuttling between Antioch in Syria and Nicomedia in Bithynia. Galerius moved to Salonica, to live in the shadow of his arch. The Caesar had attained such prestige by his victory over Narses that he eclipsed the Augustus; clearly Jupiter was working through Diocletian's subordinate, to the credit of both, but to the greater glory of the younger man. While Galerius ensured order at the Danube frontier, Diocletian toured the eastern provinces of the empire he had ruled for two decades, now at peace. He was no longer young, and his attention had been fixed for some time on the type of empire he would leave behind. Unable to tame the economy, Diocletian turned his controlling urges to the state's moral and spiritual health, promoting a fictive return to traditional Roman values. Thus, in 295, an edict issued in Damascus specified that Roman laws of marriage were valid everywhere, and any unions contracted under other conventions were not only void but 'like the lustful promiscuity of cattle or wild animals'. Conformity with Diocletian's notion of *romanitas*, 'Roman-ness', was to be ensured in the face of regional and local variation even at the cost of social cohesion.

The Augustus had only a poor, perhaps no, knowledge of Greek, the language spoken by citizens of his capital at Nicomedia and the *lingua franca* throughout the eastern provinces that he regularly toured. His Illyrian peasant upbringing and decades in the army camps made Latin his preferred tongue, and seeking to make a virtue of his shortcoming he made the revival of Latin a core element in his programme of cultural renewal. It had never been un-Roman to speak Greek, which was the core of a rounded education. But now all official business was to be conducted and recorded in Latin, even where all parties spoke Greek. The new emphasis on Latin was not to appear anti-intellectual: professors of Latin were appointed in the imperial capitals, and it is due largely to this revival that such a variety of Latin panegyrical material has survived, to elucidate the otherwise opaque decades of the Tetrarchy.

Mamertinus and Eumenius composed and delivered eloquent Latin orations in the major cities of Gaul: Trier, Arles and Autun. And in Nicomedia, Lactantius, a North African professor of Latin rhetoric, rubbed shoulders with the administrator-cum-polemicist Sossianus Hierocles and the philosopher Porphyry. These last two men are often held up as the intellectual architects of a revived attack on Christians, which was so vicious and protracted that it became known as the Great Persecution.

Living in the east and moving constantly through the provinces, Diocletian became increasingly intolerant of religious differences. He was no longer willing to countenance claims by Christians, like Origen, that they prayed in their own way for his well-being. Their forms of worship, their ways of being Roman, clashed with his own limited conception of *romanitas*. Riding beside Diocletian on a protracted trip through Egypt and Syria in 301–2 was the military tribune Constantine, who observed the aging emperor's consternation at the antics of adherents of various religious sects. In March 302, a letter was despatched from Alexandria, where Diocletian had recently arrived, to Julianus, the proconsul of Africa, instructing him that: 'Excessive leisure sometimes provokes ill-suited people to cross natural limits and encourages them to introduce false and outrageous forms of superstitious doctrine . . . No new belief should criticize the religion of old.' The targets for this rescript, whose new religion challenged the old, were Manichaeans, followers of Mani, whose practices and popularity Diocletian had observed with disgust. He found their religion to be too 'Persian', which is somewhat ironic, for just a few years earlier the followers of Mani had been persecuted in Persia for not being Persian enough. The Persians similarly persecuted Buddhists, Jews and Christians. In Diocletian's Roman empire there were few, if any, Buddhists, and the Jews had long enjoyed the right to pray to their own god for the good of the emperor and the state. The Christians, however, had never enjoyed that right, and their observances, accepted since the reign of Gallienus, once more came under scrutiny.

The Manichaean precedent should have given Christian leaders pause: those who would not relinquish their scriptures were to be burnt with them; and those whose status allowed them greater leniency were to spend the rest of their lives in the slave mines. But still they provoked the Augustus. In Antioch in the autumn of 302 a Christian deacon from Caesarea Maritima named Romanus disrupted the religious observances that preceded court proceedings. Diocletian ordered him gaoled and his tongue removed. He was killed a year later. This was perhaps still fresh in his memory when, late in 302, Diocletian travelled from Antioch, Constantine still at his side, to spend the winter in Nicomedia. There both Sossianus Hierocles and Porphyry delivered lectures to the court on a subject that chimed well with Diocletian's sentiments. Sossianus, like Pliny two centuries earlier, was a governor of Bithynia faced with a familiar problem: the unwillingness of Christians to sacrifice. He observed that followers of Christ had been duped into believing he was a god by the miracles he had performed. But had not Apollonius of Tyana performed yet greater miracles at the same time? Had he not forbidden gossip that he was divine? Did Apollonius not urge his followers to see him, in his piety and asceticism, merely as a channel for divine grace? And did he not urge them all to continue to sacrifice? Sossianus' message was simple and clear, and he would later apply it practically, torturing a dissident Christian bishop whose name, Donatus, would come to bear greater meaning during the so-called Donatist schism.

More complex commentary was offered by Porphyry, the philosopher, who averred that respect for Jesus was compatible with traditional religion. Oracular pronouncements of Apollo and Hecate had affirmed the wisdom of Jesus, but equally had shown that he was a spiritual guide, not a god. Christians, Porphyry held, deserved pity and instruction, so that their error would become clear. But those who persisted in worshipping Jesus as a god merited punishment. Porphyry did not set out an unequivocal case for persecution, and the notion that his agenda mirrored Diocletian's deserves critical scrutiny. His observation that Christians were wrong to believe that a soul united to a body (i.e. Christ) could be worshipped could equally be aimed at those who venerated the emperor. The line between the Augustus and his *numen* was ever blurry, and never more so than during the reign of the heavenward-gazing Tetrarchs. Furthermore, the philosopher had recently written a treatise condemning sacrifice, *On Abstinence from Killing Animals*. Although he did not seek to bind those in public or active life, including soldiers and sailors, to vegetarianism, he recommended it to intellectuals. He quoted a story of Apollonius of Tyana, who claimed to have been told a story by a swallow, and of a friend 'who used to tell how he was fortunate to have a slave boy who understood the speech of birds. Everything they said was a prophecy announcing what would soon come to pass. But he lost his ability to comprehend when his mother, fearing that he would be sent to the emperor as a gift, pissed in his ear.' The emperor would likely have welcomed such a gifted boy, for he revelled in oracles, but he held sacrifice above all else, and here his views were far from consonant with Porphyry's intellectual agenda. Sacrifice was the core of state *religio*, and correct observation was a foundation of Diocletian's reactionary project.

Years before Porphyry spoke at court, Diocletian had set his stall against those on his palace staff who would not sacrifice. According to Lactantius:

Diocletian's anxious disposition made him an investigator of future events; and while he was busy in the east, he was once sacrificing cattle and looking in their entrails for what was going to happen, when certain of his attendants who knew the Lord [i.e. Christians, like Lactantius] and were present at the sacrifice placed the immortal sign on their foreheads; at this the demons were put to flight and the rites thrown into confusion. The diviners began to get agitated at not seeing the usual marks on the entrails, and as if they had not made the offering, they repeated the sacrifice several times. But the slaughter of victim after victim still revealed nothing; and finally their *Tagis*, the chief of the diviners, said that the reason why the sacrifices were not yielding an answer was the presence of profane persons at the rites. Diocletian then flew into a rage; he ordered that not only those who were attending the rites but all who were in the palace should sacrifice, and any who declined should be punished by scourging. He also sent letters to commanders ordering that soldiers too should be compelled to perform the abominable sacrifices, and that any who disobeyed should be discharged. But this was as far as his anger went: he did nothing further against the law and religion of God.

It is noteworthy that Diocletian began not by persecuting but by purging Christians from his immediate staff and from the army, both directly under his control. The decision taken at Nicomedia in spring 303 was far more stringent. When the Augustus and his eastern Caesar, Galerius, met, they considered ways to oblige all to participate once again in state *religio* and to reduce the influence of certain Semitic cults. Constantine was still with the Augustus at this time, and one must conjecture, therefore, that he participated in the deliberations. Later apologists would assign the greater part of the blame, however, to Galerius, who is the villain of Lactantius' account. From him we learn the details of the first edict of persecution, issued on 24 February 303. One day earlier, on the festival of the Terminalia, the termination of Christian worship commenced. The pun is Lactantius', who records the destruction of the Christian church at Nicomedia, which could be seen from the imperial palace, by gangs armed with tools and weapons.

The first edict of persecution has survived only in Lactantius' account, but it is fairly certain that it ordered the destruction of churches and of scripture, the loss of rights and status by Christians, and the use of sacrifice as a test. Among the more revealing asides is that Diocletian obliged his daughter Valeria and his wife Prisca 'to be polluted by sacrifice', strongly suggesting that they were Christians. Universal sacrifice was not, however, mandated, nor was death prescribed for Christians in particular. It was unnecessary, since the regular penalties for resisting an imperial edict included torture and death, and that was the fate of some who refused to hand over Christian books. Therefore, for the first time in half a century, we hear of Christian martyrs, for example Felix, bishop of Tibiuca in Africa. A second edict of persecution was issued, later in 303, ordering the imprisonment of all Christian clergy. The tightening of the screw may be related to the fires set in the imperial palace at Nicomedia, blamed on Christians but which Lactantius claims were Galerius' handiwork. A third edict gave gaoled clergy the opportunity to apostatize and earn release, thus losing authority over their communities and breaking down hierarchies of resistance. Indeed, the rapid issue of a general pardon, providing for the release of all held in imperial prisons to celebrate Diocletian's twentieth year in power, must have sown confusion in many communities, obliging them to ask: was our priest released in the general pardon, or was he an apostate? The third edict, therefore, may be considered a device intended merely to facilitate rumour-mongering. However, a fourth edict marked a return to the full persecution of the reigns of Decius and Valerian, moving from efforts to decapitate communities to attacks on individual Christians of every social status. All citizens were ordered to sacrifice before official witnesses. Those who refused were first tortured and then burnt.

Lactantius: *On the Deaths of the Persecutors*

Exactly why Diocletian determined to reinstitute the persecution of Christians has generated much debate, starting with the observations of the contemporary Christian writer Lactantius, who fled the persecution in Nicomedia to settle in the lands ruled by Constantius. Lactantius wrote *On the Deaths of the Persecutors* in 314–15, shortly after the Great Persecution had come to an end. His hero, therefore, is the man who brought an end to persecution: Constantine. Lactantius was in no doubt that the chief instigator was Galerius, the bull-necked son of a priestess. But the meeting at which Diocletian is alleged to have been persuaded by his junior took place behind closed doors, and the most Lactantius could have heard was rumour. Still, he wished to attribute the greatest crimes to the man who suffered most and whom Constantine grew to hate. Galerius died painfully shortly after rescinding the order of persecution, possibly of cancer, if we are to trust Lactantius' description which draws heavily on the biblical demise of Antiochus. Galerius, like Decius and Valerian, suffered divine retribution, whereas Diocletian, with whom Constantine had spent some important, perhaps happy, years, ended his life cultivating cabbages at his palace in Split. Despite the fact that Constantius died only shortly after the edict was promulgated, Lactantius plays down any role for Constantine's father, revealing only that the edicts were despatched to him to enforce, and that he, 'to avoid appearing to disagree with the instructions of his seniors, allowed the churches . . . to be destroyed. But the true temple of God, which is inside men, he left unharmed.' The fourth emperor, Maximian, as we shall see, died at Constantine's command.

The failure of the Great Persecution was inevitable, as there were in AD 303 simply too many Christians for it to work. There was sure to be resistance in every community, and the actions of the martyrs gave it focus. Those who witnessed their willingness to die, and the brutality with which the state punished their conviction, could not fail to be impressed. Nor were pagans convinced that the slaughter of fellow citizens for their beliefs could be in the best interests of the state. After all, as we have noted, the Roman way had always been to promote tolerance. And so it was not so much the spectacular protests of the Christian minority as the growing disgust of the pagan majority that put an end to the persecution.

Lactantius' *On the Deaths of the Persecutors* is the best and fullest account of the period 303–13 and thus is indispensable. But it is also an angry screed, with no known model in Greek or Latin literature, nor in Christian apologetic. Not only did Lactantius delight in the misfortune and demise of the persecuting emperors, he also attributed them to the intervention of the god of the Christians, defending the interests of the faithful. Such an approach rejected the very premise on which martyrs had accepted death at the hands of their persecutors: that their god did not meddle in earthly affairs to bring misfortune upon Roman emperors. This was the first step in articulating a new Christian triumphalist rhetoric, which we shall explore more fully in later chapters. In doing so, Lactantius drew on an Old Testament model, the Second Book of Maccabees, which still forms an accepted part of the Orthodox canon. Thus, the opening refrain of each text thanks God for punishing the wicked, and the agonizing death of Galerius mirrors that of Antiochus Epiphanes (2 Maccabees 9). And just as Judas Maccabeus is promised divine aid in a dream before his victory over Nicanor, so Constantine dreams that he will conquer his rival Maxentius. It is to this that we may now turn.

PART II

Constantine Invictus

✠

5

Constantine Invictus

*The second Tetrarchy – Constantine's accession – Trier –
A vision – The road to Rome – The Battle of the Milvian Bridge
– Constantine Invictus and the theology of victory*

Constantine, aged around thirty, was an experienced campaigner who had traversed the empire on several occasions. Through the 290s he had fought at both the empire's frontiers, against the Sarmatians at the Danube and the Persians at the Euphrates. In 301–2, he had ridden in peace through North Africa at the side of the senior ruler of the Roman world, Diocletian, and returned with him to the imperial capital of Nicomedia. He was a member of Diocletian's inner circle and may have been more than an observer at the instigation of the Great Persecution. Around the same time, Constantine shared his bed with a young woman named Minervina who bore him a son, Crispus. We know neither the date of Crispus' birth nor whether Minervina died in childbirth or shortly afterwards. However, it would appear that the infant was entrusted to Constantine's mother, Helena. In 303, Constantine travelled to Rome with the aging Diocletian, to participate in a splendid affair to mark Diocletian's *vicennalia*, the beginning of the twentieth year since his accession. It was also the tenth anniversary of the elevation of the Caesars and thus the *decennalia* of Constantine's father Constantius, whom he had not seen for many years. Constantine, like Diocletian, had never visited Rome. In the western empire it was the largest city and had the largest concentration of Christians. Diocletian would leave in a foul mood, never to return. Constantine, in contrast, would return in triumph a decade later, to become sole ruler of the western Roman empire.

The second Tetrarchy

Various monuments were prepared to mark the Roman festivities of 303. Five pillars were set up in Rome's forum, before the rostra, each standing on a base carved with the image of an emperor sacrificing and surmounted by a statue of a Tetrarch. The fifth column was Jupiter's. Only fragments of these have survived, the best showing Constantius, although the columns can be seen clearly in a relief on Constantine's arch (fig. 23). A new triumphal arch was also built across the Via Lata, called, with a splendid lack of invention, the New Arch. Through this passed a triumphal procession, moving belatedly through the imperial city to mark the great victory over the Persians. The procession surely ended at the temple of Jupiter on Rome's Capitoline Hill, although no source mentions this explicitly.*

All four emperors were to attend this grand composite celebration of Tetrarchy, and they convened shortly before in northern Italy. It was here determined by Diocletian, in a manner quite unprecedented, that he would abdicate the throne, at the same time obliging his fellow Augustus Maximian to retire. Maximian was upset by this plan and later forced to swear an oath to fulfil his obligation in Rome's Capitoline temple of Jupiter. The fact that the abdications would not take place immediately suggests that, as a concession, Maximian was to be allowed similarly to celebrate his *vicennalia*, which would fall in 305–6. Leaders have always, it seems, been impressed by round numbers, and this was particularly the case with Romans for whom such lavish parties were thrown. The two Caesars would, consequently, become Augusti, and two new Caesars would be promoted in 306. The choice of junior emperors was clear, for both Maximian and Constantius had grown sons groomed for empire and tested in war: Maxentius and Constantine.

Proceeding to Rome, Diocletian did not receive the welcome he desired or expected, for a number of reasons. The citizens felt no special affinity for an emperor they had never seen and whose policies had stripped their city of many of its privileges. Moreover, a great

---

* This point is significant, as far too much has been made of the fact that the terminus of Constantine's triumphal procession through Rome in 312 is also unmentioned.

number were suffering once more under the edicts of persecution issued in the east, which Maximian was willing to enforce in his territories. The catalyst for unrest was an unforeseen tragedy: during the celebrations part of the circus structure collapsed, killing 13,000 spectators. No number of exotic animals or Persian prisoners could quiet the crowd, which jeered the triumphant Diocletian. He left the city enraged and in haste for Ravenna, never to return to Rome. Departing thence to return to Nicomedia, he contracted an illness which worsened through the winter. Indeed, towards the end of 304 it was rumoured that the emperor was dead, and he did not appear in public again until March 305. His health may have returned somewhat, but his authority would not, and into the breach stepped Galerius, the eastern Caesar.

Galerius arrived in Nicomedia intent on bringing pressure to bear on the eastern Augustus, and told him, by Lactantius' account, that 'If Diocletian refused to give way . . . he would look to his own interests, so as no longer to remain junior emperor at the bottom of the list.' His threat was backed with an increasingly large army, and the tired Augustus gave way. The date of the abdications was brought forward by a year, and instead of elevating the sons of Maximian and Constantius, the new Caesars were both to be close associates of Galerius. The conversation, which Lactantius cannot have heard, still deserves to be set out as the Christian author reported it a decade later:

DIOCLETIAN: 'What shall we do then?'

GALERIUS: 'Maxentius is not worthy of it . . . If he has shown such contempt for me as a private citizen, what will he do as an emperor?'

DIOCLETIAN: 'But Constantine is popular and will rule in such a way that he will be judged better and more merciful than his father.'

GALERIUS: 'But in that case I shall not be able to do what I want. We must appoint men who will be in my power, who will fear me, and do nothing but what I command.'

These men were Severus and Maximinus Daia, the first a trusted subordinate of Galerius and perhaps a relative, the second certainly Galerius' relative by blood and probably also by marriage. Since we are reliant on Lactantius, we know little more about the background of these men, but later pagan sources confirm that Maximinus Daia was Galerius' nephew and the keenest of persecutors.

The announcement was made on 1 May 305, before the assembled officers of the eastern legions. All eyes, Lactantius claims, were on Constantine, still at Diocletian's side, so it was with shock that the soldiers witnessed Diocletian remove his own purple cloak and throw it across the shoulders not of Constantine but of Maximinus. On the same day in the west, Maximian invested Severus with the purple.

Galerius had his way, and Constantine lost both his powerful patron and the promise of empire. But his father, Constantius, now held the title of senior Augustus, and in that capacity he demanded that his son be returned to his side. To comply, Galerius realized, would be to acknowledge Constantine's right to succeed his father, for it was to hand him an army that would both acclaim and support him. But this he did, sending Constantine on his way later in 305. It seems certain that an agreement was reached before Constantine's departure for Gaul that he would become Caesar upon his father's death and that he would acknowledge Galerius as senior Augustus in the east and Severus as Augustus in the west. The agreement was later suppressed by Constantine, who concocted a far more romantic tale of midnight flight. Taking advantage of a bout of drunkenness during which Galerius gave him leave to depart, Constantine did not wait for morning and sobriety, but took to the road, hamstringing post horses as he went lest he be pursued. Lactantius was happy to report this fanciful story, as was the pagan author Zosimus in an account openly hostile to Constantine. Both recount that Constantine arrived at his father's side just shortly before Constantius' death. In fact, Constantine arrived far earlier, meeting his father in Gaul and travelling to Britain with him before the end of 305 to suppress the Picts. It was on this trip, at York, that Constantius died. Led by Crocus, king of the Alemans who comprised the Augustus' bodyguard, and by now accustomed to serving the senior emperor, the legions had no desire to see their man kowtow to any eastern despot. Nor, it seems, did they wish to recognize the claims of Constantius' younger sons, by his wife Theodora, who were all present at his death. As the mother and her children, the eldest no more than ten years old, stood by, the troops acclaimed Constantine alone as Augustus on 25 July 306.

Constantine's accession

Acclamation as Augustus was more than Constantine expected, and certainly more than Galerius had agreed in 305. Many military acclamations were carried out with the threat of violence to the *imperator*, should he refuse to accept the great honour his men had chosen to bestow upon him, and this may explain why Constantine accepted the senior title. But he did so for only as long as it took him to confirm his place in the second Tetrarchy, by writing to Galerius and accepting from him the lesser rank of Caesar. Constantine was not the next Carausius: he was no pretender, to be crushed regardless of his apparent qualifications to rule. Nor did he threaten the established principle that only those nominated by the senior Augustus might be regarded as legitimate, for his accession came with Galerius' imprimatur. Constantine was set to become the new Caesar by tacit agreement in 305, and his elevation to that rank was recognized with little fuss by Galerius in 306. The Tetrarchy was thus reconstituted as follows, in order of precedence: Galerius, Augustus of the east; Severus, Augustus of the west; Maximinus Daia, Caesar of the east; Constantine, Caesar of the west.

Henceforth, Constantine struck coins identifying himself as 'Caesar', but also as the 'Prince of Youth' (*princeps iuventutis*). This was a title of Republican origin, once used to identify the leading boy in the Game of Troy. It later passed to the chief of the equestrian order, but under the principate came to be used to designate the scion of the imperial house who was designated to succeed. It carried no implication of youth: although Constantine was still a young man, he was no longer a youth in Roman terms. Upon their promotion to the rank of Caesar in 293, Constantine's father and Galerius, both in their mid-forties, had minted bronze coins with the reverse legend 'To the Prince of Youth' (PRINCIPI IUVENT). The title had clearly been sanctioned by the Augusti and reflected the juniority of the Caesars, but at the same time indicated the certainty of their succession. Early in 307, therefore, Constantine's coins echoed those of his father, reproducing the image of the emperor standing holding a spear in his right hand and a globe in his left. They also reflect the fact that he had accepted the junior rank willingly.

At the same time, a fifth emperor began striking coins also claiming the title *princeps*, but his accession was not sanctioned by Galerius. In the words of the Anonymus Valesianus, 'After Constantius died in Britannia and his son Constantine succeeded him, Maxentius, the son of Herculius, was suddenly hailed as emperor by the Praetorian Guards in the city of Rome.' Maxentius, son of Maximian, twice passed over for imperial office, was acclaimed emperor in Rome on 28 October 306, and chose the title 'prince' as a sop to the citizenry. No longer would they be ruled by a distant and lofty 'master', or *dominus*, he announced. Instead, the days of the first Augustus would return, and Maxentius would govern as 'first among equals'. Of course, there was some distance between this rhetoric and the reality of Maxentius' regime. Maxentius' rise to power in Rome was, like Constantine's, initially a military affair. With no emperor resident in Rome, the celebrated Praetorian Guard, once the imperial bodyguard, now had no body to guard, and its strength had been reduced by Diocletian to ten cohorts. Those who remained had retained their extra salary, but for how long they must have wondered. Galerius had made matters still worse, planning to disband the remaining cohorts of under-employed Praetorians and transfer the men to frontier garrisons on lower wages. Moreover, after the tax regime across Italy had been overhauled, there appeared no reason for Rome to remain exempt. The city had never paid taxes, but from autumn 306 it would, according to Galerius. The two policy initiatives were related, as the Praetorians were the only force capable of resisting the new taxation policies, by supporting the interests of senators who wished to pay less than their due. Still, the manner and scale of resistance was unforeseen. Furthermore, Maxentius' first act upon his usurpation was to rescind the order of persecution, which appears to have been enforced in Rome by both his father and by Severus. He thus secured the support not only of the army and the senate, but also of the powerful community of Christians. Safe behind the Aurelian walls, the citizens of Rome awaited the consequences of their actions under their new leader.

Galerius, occupied with a campaign against the Sarmatians later in 306, despatched Severus to crush Maxentius. Leading his army to Rome, Severus did not anticipate that he would face not just Maxentius, but Maximian too. The former Augustus had been tempted from retirement by his son, who summoned him to Rome and invested him once again with imperial office. Nor did Severus anticipate that his troops, many of whom had served the retired Augustus for long years, would swiftly change sides. He was forced to withdraw to Ravenna, where he was trapped and voluntarily handed over his insignia of office. Severus was taken prisoner and held at a villa outside Rome for as long as he was useful. When Galerius himself marched against Rome in autumn 307, Severus was murdered, lest he become a greater problem. The western empire, consequently, lacked an Augustus, and Constantine might legitimately have expected to be promoted. He had remained distant from events unfolding in Italy, overseeing projects in Britain in spring and summer of 307. However, upon receiving news of Severus' capture, Constantine saw the tide turning against Galerius and agreed to meet Maximian at Trier. On that occasion he implicated himself fully in the rebellion of the Herculians: he married Fausta, Maximian's daughter and Maxentius' sister, and at the same time received from Maximian the insignia of an Augustus, in place of Severus.

In September 307, Constantine's elevation and nuptials were celebrated by a panegyrist at Trier, the first of five Latin orations delivered to Constantine which have survived.

For what more precious thing could you give, or could you receive, since with this marriage of yours, Maximian, your youth has been renewed through your son-in-law, while you, Constantine, have been enhanced by the name emperor (*nomen imperatoris*) through your father-in-law. And so we give you the most heartfelt thanks in the public name, eternal princes, because in rearing children and wishing for grandchildren, you are providing for all future ages by extending the succession of your posterity, so that the Roman state, once shaken by the disparate characters and fates of its rulers, may at last be made strong through the everlasting roots of your house . . . for you are propagating the state not with plebeian offshoots but with imperial stock . . . that the reins of our common safety be not handed down, subject to change through new families, but may last through all ages, emperors forever Herculian.

Emphasis is placed appropriately on the joys of marriage and the anticipated product, imperial children. But the orator states far more, and in a manner that attacks the very premise of the Tetrarchy – the notion that the title emperor should be conferred upon those best able to serve the interests of the state (viz. the army), regardless of birth and lineage. The two families here linked were, in fact, both plebeian, but now had been elevated and were semi-divine, Herculian. Equally noteworthy is the fact that the orator alludes not at all to Maximian's own son, Maxentius, who had for a year claimed the title emperor. Nor is Constantine's son Crispus, born of Minervina, mentioned despite the fact that Constantine is later praised for having resisted the pleasures of youth by marrying young. The Herculian line is to flourish through Constantine's union with Fausta, and Constantine will assume the mantle Maximian had borne under Diocletian two decades before. As the older man surveys from a 'pinnacle of command the world . . . and with a celestial nod decide[s] the fate of human affairs', the younger will 'traverse the frontiers tirelessly where the Roman empire presses upon the barbarian peoples, to send frequent laurels of victory to the father-in-law'.

The panegyric is essential to the reconstruction of Constantine's early years. It is the earliest surviving source devoted to the young emperor, and it alone suggests that Minervina was Constantine's legitimate wife, not his concubine, as many have claimed. The fact that no mention is made of a divorce may not, however, be taken as evidence that Minervina had died. Rather, it is proof only of the orator's obsequious prurience. Still, we hear a little of Constantine's first campaigns and 'important tribunates', by which he had demonstrated his great 'valour' (*virtus*) and earned the right to be called emperor. His elevation by Maximian's hand was foretold in a 'picture in the palace at Aquileia, placed in full view of dinner guests', which shows 'a young girl adorable for her divine beauty' offering to Constantine, 'still a lad, a helmet gleaming with gold and jewels, and conspicuous with its plumes of a beautiful bird'. The girl, it is implied, is Fausta, although the image dates from between 293 and 296, when Constantine was raised to the rank of tribune and sent east. Fausta was born only around that time, and was still a girl of fourteen or fifteen years old on her wedding day. The orator ends by addressing Constantius Chlorus, 'whom the Sun himself took up to heaven on a chariot almost visible'. The son who was first to make him a father was now 'similar in appearance, similar in character, and equal in imperial power'.

Maximian left Trier as senior Augustus and returned to Rome. If he expected Constantine to do his bidding, as the panegyrist had suggested, he was soon disappointed. Constantine would not honour Maximian's command that he harry Galerius' troops as they withdrew across the Alps. He turned his attention instead to the Bructeri, a barbarian tribe. Nor was Maximian's son more receptive to his claims of seniority. Maxentius was fortified by having withstood Galerius' siege and resented his father's posturing: had he not recalled Maximian and raised him up, and not vice versa? The relationship between father and son soured, and Maximian decided to eliminate Maxentius. Expecting the troops he had won from Severus and Galerius to support him, Maximian took to the tribunal in the forum, standing before the five pillars of the Tetrarchs, ostensibly to address the people on the state of affairs. Instead he grabbed the purple cloak from Maxentius' shoulders and declaimed against him. But the son did not yield. Acclaimed by the Praetorian Guard, Maxentius had retained their loyalty through two sieges and did so still in the face of his father's machinations. The Praetorians forced Maximian to stand down and flee the city. In April 308, thwarted, he headed north to join his son-in-law Constantine in Gaul, and was received warmly.

Constantine was playing a waiting game, secure in his control of the western provinces and aloof from the turmoil in Italy. At the start of 308, unlike in 307, he had acknowledged Galerius' choice of consuls for the year, surely hoping to secure acknowledgement in return from the eastern Augustus. The office of ordinary consul had once held great power in Rome but now was a mark of prestige, awarded only to men of wealth and influence. Consuls gave their names to the years, for Romans did not yet, of course, count by *Anni Domini*. The appointment of consuls was an imperial prerogative, and to acknowledge the selection was to accept the authority of the senior emperor. The arrival of Maximian, which might have upset Constantine's attempts at rapprochement with Galerius, had by virtue of the rupture with Maxentius become an opportunity. When, in November 308, Galerius convened a summit at Carnuntum, a military camp on the Danube in Pannonia, Maximian attended. One must imagine Constantine expected his interests to be represented by his father-in-law. However, upon arriving Maximian was confronted by Diocletian, summoned from his retirement palace to force his partner back into seclusion and to preside over a new settlement of Galerius' devising. On 8 November 308, the Tetrarchy was, once again, reformed with a new Augustus. But neither of the Caesars was promoted. Instead, Galerius' most trusted general, Licinius, was made emperor *ex nihilo* and elevated directly to the highest honour, senior to both Constantine and Maximinus Daia, who were reconfirmed as Caesars. This was unacceptable to both men, whose dates of elevation made them both senior to Licinius. Constantine continued to use the title Augustus, and some time later Maximinus also began to use it. However, for now the settlement was sealed by the dedication of a temple to Mithras at Carnuntum.

Returning to Gaul, Maximian renounced once again his claim to the purple, but he continued to harbour both resentment and ambition. While Constantine toured his provinces, building and distributing largesse, his father-in-law hatched yet another plot. In autumn of 309, as Constantine marched north to campaign on the Rhine, pausing to begin construction of a bridge at Cologne, Maximian headed south to Arles. There he announced that Constantine was dead, seized the treasury and mint, and distributed large donatives to the troops. For the third time he was acclaimed emperor, and unlike in Rome, troops flocked to him willingly. When news of the usurpation reached Constantine, he turned south with his small field army, facing a seven-hundred-kilometre journey by land and river. Maximian took the opportunity to move from Arles to Marseille, which could be defended more easily, and awaited his arrival.

An orator, who later spoke in praise of Constantine, performs contortions to make it appear that Constantine's forces were loyal only to him; that Maximian secured favour only through lavish expenditure, whereas Constantine's men broke camp even as he was 'distributing travel allowances', scorning the money. Such special pleading reveals quite how shaky was Constantine's hold over his army, and obscures how reliant he was on a few core units which had accompanied him north. Nor does the panegyrist manage to conceal the failure of Constantine's attack on Marseille:

O Emperor, upon your first arrival and at the first attack of your army, neither the height of the walls of this same Marseille nor its host of towers, nor the nature of the terrain would have delayed you from taking the harbour and city immediately, had you wished it . . . But what remarkable pity you displayed, Constantine, which ever preserves its sense of duty even amidst arms. You gave the signal for retreat and put off your victory, so that you might have the opportunity to pardon all.

Maximian, ruler of the west for two decades, resisted the ineffectual siege and retained the support of much of the western army. However, he was willing to negotiate terms with Constantine, which likely allowed both to retain their imperial titles. We know nothing with certainty, for what followed is obscured by Constantine's later propaganda. By the time Lactantius wrote his *On the Deaths of the Persecutors*, in 314–15, the inconclusive clash at Marseille had been recast not only as a 'delayed' victory for Constantine but as a rout. Maximian is held to have been delivered to his son-in-law by the citizens and to have been pardoned by him. Some months later Maximian was dead, allegedly by his own hand. This required that a story be fabricated, which Lactantius gladly disseminated. It bears great similarities to numerous tales of betrayal.

Maximian, encouraged by having once escaped [from his attempt at usurpation] with impunity, devised yet another plot. Calling his daughter Fausta to him, he urged her with a mixture of entreaty and cajolery to betray her husband, promising her another who would be worthier of her. He asked her to allow their bedroom to be left open and only carelessly guarded. She promised she would do this, but then promptly reported the matter to her husband. A scenario was then devised to ensure that he would be caught in the act of committing the crime. A worthless eunuch was planted in the emperor's room to die in his stead. Maximian rose in the dead of night . . . killed the eunuch and then rushed out proclaiming what he had done. Suddenly, Constantine revealed himself on the other side of the room with a band of armed men . . . and [Maximian] was rebuked for the impiety of his crime, and finally given free choice as to the manner of his death, 'he bound the noose for an unseemly death from a lofty beam'.

Thus it is implied with a poetic flourish, borrowing from Virgil's account of the death of Queen Amata in the *Aeneid*, that Maximian hanged himself. It seems rather likely that he was given some help.

Trier

Constantine alone now ruled the western provinces north of the Alps. He did so from his base at Trier, which boasts of being the oldest city in Germany. Trier rose to prominence during the third-century crisis, when as the chief city of the province of Gallia Belgica it became the second city of the breakaway Gallic empire. While the rebel emperor Postumus was acclaimed in Cologne, Postumus' ephemeral successor, Victorinus, was based in Trier, and there he restored a large house and installed a mosaic which announced his new position as tribune in Postumus' Gallic Praetorian Guard. Postumus' rebellion demonstrated how crucial it was to maintain an imperial presence in Gaul, at the heart of the north-western provinces, projecting Roman authority to Britain, Spain and the Germanies. Diocletian had recognized this when he established Maximian in Trier. However, when Maximian proved unable to control his provinces and failed to quell the rebellion of Carausius, the situation in Trier deteriorated significantly until Constantius Chlorus was raised to the rank of Caesar. This we have explored.

The presence first of Maximian and then of Constantius in Trier made the city truly an imperial centre, which required the monumental setting for imperial government. A mint was established by Constantius in 293, which became the principal mint of the western provinces, striking coins in all metals. The setting for the interaction of public and emperor was radically overhauled. Trier's amphitheatre, which like the colossal structures in Rome and Arles dated from the Flavian period (shortly before AD 100), was renovated, and a new stadium was constructed to stage chariot races. The famous Porta Nigra, added in a hurry in the later second century, shows signs of repair at this time. Large new imperial baths were constructed, although the presence of equally large public baths, the so-called Barbarathermen, suggests that the motive for their construction was ostentatious munificence rather than public health. These are the largest surviving baths outside Rome, and their design and construction echo Rome's Baths of Diocletian and Baths of Maxentius. They were probably begun under Constantius but completed by Constantine, for a coin dating from 314 has been found within a construction trench.

Most impressive within Trier's modern cityscape is the large basilica erected as an imperial audience chamber and hall of justice. It still stands to its full height of one hundred Roman feet (although the current building was reduced by air raids in 1944 and reconstructed according to careful plans), and is two hundred feet long and a hundred feet wide (fig. 24). The walls of the basilica were constructed in red tile, with each course levelled by mortar in a style that would become a signature of Byzantine architecture. Originally, however, this would have been covered with grey plaster. High windows fill the hall with light, now illuminating bare brick, but once highlighting marble revetment, frescoes and mosaic floors. The panegyrist of 310 refers to this hall in its incomplete state, and thus we can be fairly sure that it was the work of Constantine. This has been confirmed numismatically, as the latest coin found within the walls of the structure was struck in 305. Upon discovery, it showed few signs of wear, and thus had not circulated widely before it was lost in the building materials.

The development of Trier is celebrated on a gold coin struck by Constantine, showing the city's walls, jetties and wharves. An imperial palace that no longer survives has presented an even more intriguing picture of life in Constantine's Trier. In fact, it has left us fifteen pictures, each reconstructed from a myriad tiny pieces, fragments of painted panels from the ceiling of a chamber, which scholars believe once belonged to Constantine's young wife Fausta. The fifteen panels, in three rows of five, include seven scenes in which *putti*, little winged Cupids, convey objects associated with imperial status or ceremonial: a flaming altar, a purple cloak, a cornucopia. In an eighth scene, to the right of the central panel, a young girl is herself conveyed by a *putto*. Her hairstyle is the same as the young woman of the central panel. This is Fausta herself, before and after her marriage. The remaining five scenes are both personifications and, perhaps, portraits: an older woman, nimbate (haloed) with a jewellery box from which she pulls a string of pearls, who has often been identified as Helena (fig. 25); a nimbate woman playing a lyre; two older men, guarding each of the doors; and a philosopher, whom some claim to be Lactantius. These pictures are now the prized possessions of Trier's Diocesan Museum.

The decoration of this part of the palace was completed shortly before Constantine left Trier, if one can trust a freshly struck coin from 315, which was found among fragments of mosaic, intermingled with chunks of the ceiling frescoes. When Constantine left Trier, to base himself in Sardica (modern Sofia, now the capital of Bulgaria) and Sirmium (modern Sremska Mitrovica in Serbia), he left the thirteen-year-old Crispus in the city. As we shall see in the following chapter, on 1 March 317 Crispus was raised to the rank of Caesar, at the same time as Constantine's second son, also called Constantine, born to Fausta in Arles in August 316. Fausta returned to Trier, where coins were henceforth struck in the names of both Caesars, Crispus and Constantine. Both were too young to rule, so the administration of Gaul and the western provinces was entrusted to a Praetorian Prefect. But when Crispus reached eighteen, he was given greater responsibilities. He also then married Helena – not to be confused with the older Helena, Constantine's mother – who swiftly produced a son. A close family they were, and this is the message conveyed by the magnificent sardonyx cameo preserved in Trier's Stadtbibliothek, which has since 1499 been incorporated into the ornate cover of a gospel book (fig. 26).

The Eagle Cameo, also known as the Ada Cameo after the gospel book it now adorns, is cut from a three-layered sardonyx. The artist has carved through each of the top two layers to depict a scene. The uppermost layer, the colour of dried blood, shows two eagles, their wings raised as if preparing to fly. Their chests point outwards, but their heads are turned inwards so that they look up at the imperial family depicted behind them, and more particularly at the central figure, a young boy. The second layer, in milky white suffused as if with imperial purple from the third ruddy layer beneath, contains images of five people, from left to right: a veiled woman, a laurel-wreathed man, a small boy, a woman, and a second larger boy. These are Constantine's mother Helena, Constantine, his son Constantine, his wife Fausta, and his elder son Crispus. It has often been stated that the two boys were Constantine's sons by Fausta, Constantine and Constantius. However, there is no reason at this stage to conjecture that Constantine conceived of his family as a unit without Crispus. Therefore, it seems more likely that the cameo was carved in Trier before the birth of Constantius on 7 August 317. Moreover, the location of the smallest figure, the younger son, in the very centre, between Constantine and Helena, suggests that he is the object of celebration. Thus, the most likely reason for the cameo's production was the birth of Constantine II in the summer of 316. The imperial family can be seen only from their necks up, sitting in a circus box, perhaps in the new hippodrome at Trier, perhaps at Arles, attending games staged to celebrate the birth.

A vision

By summer 310, with Maximian dead, there were five men claiming the title Augustus. Four decided to recognize each other. The odd man out remained Maxentius. The Tetrarchy, therefore, took on a new form, but it was ephemeral. Galerius was sick and, like Diocletian before him, was planning to abdicate and retire to his birthplace, Romuliana (modern Gamzigrad in Serbia), where he had begun to build a palatial complex. Archaeologists have uncovered a number of monuments that echo features of Galerius' earlier capital, Salonica, including a four-columned arch (*tetrapylon*) and two mausolea atop a nearby hill. Carved reliefs from the site show six emperors in pairs: two retired Augusti, Diocletian and Maximian; two reigning Augusti, Galerius and Licinius; and two Caesars, Maximinus and Constantine. The obvious date for Galerius' planned retirement would have been his *vicennalia*, the date at which he would have reigned for twenty years, on 1 March 312, but he did not make it to that celebration. Lactantius took great pleasure relating his death as divine punishment for his persecutions, describing his repulsive symptoms and the failure of pagan doctors and prayers to heal him:

A malignant ulcer appeared on the lower part of his genitals and spread more widely. Doctors cut and then treated it. But once a scar had formed, the wound split open and a vein burst such that the flow of blood threatened his death . . . the cancer attacked the whole adjacent area, and the more that was cut away the more it grew . . . Doctors of renown were brought in from all sides, but human hands could achieve nothing. They then turned to idols, praying to Apollo and Asclepius, begging for a remedy. Apollo prescribed his cure, and the malady worsened considerably. Death now was close, and had taken hold of his lower parts. His entrails putrefied from the outside, and his whole bottom dissolved in decay . . . As the marrow was assailed, the infection was forced inwards and took hold of his internal organs. Worms were born inside him. The stink pervaded not just the palace but the whole city. And this was not surprising, for the channels for his urine and excrement were now conflated. He was consumed with worms and his body dissolved and rotted amid insufferable pain . . . Cooked meats still warm were placed near his dissolving buttocks so that the heat would draw out the worms . . . This had gone on continually for a year when at last, subdued by his ills, he was compelled to confess God. Already dying he issued the following edict [ending persecution].

Lactantius cites the edict in full. The story has much in common with the account of the death of Antiochus, persecutor of the Jews in the Second Book of Maccabees. Lactantius must have been struck by the remarkable coincidences, and borrowed Antiochus' worms and stench. But insofar as his account is trustworthy, it suggests that Galerius contracted cancer of the scrotum or testes, which was not detected until the tumour had grown too large to treat and had spread to his bowel; or more likely, that he had contracted bowel cancer, which metastasized, presenting visibly in the area of his perineum.

Licinius was present at Galerius' death, most likely at Sardica, and was entrusted with the care of his wife and daughter. But Galerius' natural heir in the east was Maximinus Daia, who pursued the persecution of Christians with more vigour even than his mentor, before and after Galerius' deathbed retraction. While Licinius delayed at Sardica, Maximinus made for the palace at Nicomedia to press his claims to seniority. Henceforth, Licinius and Maximinus would be at loggerheads, struggling to demonstrate mastery in the east. A temporary peace agreed near Chalcedon would not hold. Licinius remained, in name alone, senior ruler in the west. However, looking east from his base at Sardica, he had no influence on Constantine in Gaul and Britain, nor on Maxentius in Italy and Africa. And those two men, in the aftermath of Maximian's death, turned on each other, staging a propaganda war that presaged a more bloody confrontation. Maxentius and Constantine were sons of peasant soldiers from Illyricum, but both manufactured and disseminated claims to ancient lineage, and hence pitted two ancient Roman families against each other. Constantine became the champion of the *gens Flavia*, the new Flavian dynasty, whose right to rule was challenged by the fictive scion of the *gens Valeriana*, Maxentius the new Valerian. Maxentius claimed the patronage of Mars, father of the founders of Rome, Romulus and Remus, and the avenging god of war. In return, Constantine demonstrated his privileged relationship with Apollo, and propagated a story that he had experienced a divine vision that proclaimed his fitness to rule.

According to a panegyrical oration, a speech in praise of Constantine delivered in Gaul in 310, the emperor had recently experienced a vision of Apollo, who had appeared accompanied by the goddess of victory, Victoria, to offer Constantine laurel crowns. These were marked with the numerals XXX, which foretold that he would rule for thirty years. The panegyrist's interpretation of the scene reflected an established form. The appearance of numerals within a wreath was widely known from the VOTA coins, bronze coins struck in huge numbers to be distributed as donatives, largely to the army. The coins were given in return for public prayers, *vota*, offered on five- and ten-year anniversaries for the continuation of imperial rule. By the fourth century such prayers were offered specifically for the renewal of the *virtus Augusti*, the emperor's manly courage, so that he might continue to rule victoriously with divine favour. They were offered at the beginning and end of the anniversary year, upon the date of accession. Romans counted inclusively, so in both July 310 and July 311 Constantine enjoyed public prayers from his army in Gaul, and issued VOTA coins to mark his *quinquennalia*, the fifth year of his reign.

Looking more closely at the panegyrist's account of Constantine's vision, one notes how it corresponds with contemporary efforts to set the emperor apart from his imperial colleagues and rivals. The bestowal of a laurel wreath by Victoria is a ubiquitous motif in art, both Roman and later, and its presence in the dream is unremarkable. The key figure is Apollo, near whose temple Constantine had his vision, and it was to this temple that he now hurried to give thanks for his recent achievements: the construction of the bridge over the Rhine at Cologne; the quelling of barbarian unrest across the river; and, most significantly, the rebellion and defeat of Maximian. Apollo was Constantine's new patron deity, and he took various forms. Most notably, however, Constantine was no longer a Herculian and no longer tied to the gods assigned to his father and to him by Maximian. The transition is worth spelling out, for it is clear on his coins and elsewhere, and on monumental art as we shall see shortly.

On succeeding to his father's position in 306, Constantine had become a Herculian and client of Mars. His earliest coins reflect his relationship with Mars, who appears on the reverse as his father and preserver (MARTI PATRI CONSERVATORI). However, in 310, if not before, Constantine rejected his adoptive patrons and advanced the novel claim that both his father and he were directly descended from the emperor Claudius II Gothicus, whose patron god was identified as Sol Invictus, 'the Unconquered Sun'. Sol was an eastern cognate of Apollo, of whom Constantine had a divine vision. In this way Constantine emulated Septimius Severus, the last usurper successfully to establish a dynasty. Septimius had claimed to be the son of Marcus Aurelius, and first placed Sol Invictus on his coins. Claudius II was among the last emperors to rule alone, and Constantine, according to the new logic, had a greater claim to rule than his rival Tetrarchs. No longer content to be a junior Herculian, Constantine's new style echoed that of Aurelian, who had struck coins commemorating the deified Claudius Gothicus and portrayed himself wearing the crown of Sol Invictus.

In claiming the patronage of Apollo-Sol, Constantine distanced himself from the claims circulated just a few years earlier that he was Maximian's true son and heir, who would produce Herculian children and grandchildren for the ages. But he was also resisting Maxentius' more recent propaganda, which emphasized his illegitimate birth – a son of Constantius certainly, but by Helena, whom Maxentius claimed was a concubine, not a wife. Constantine was not of imperial stock like Constantius' sons by Theodora, who were sons and grandsons of reigning emperors. Maxentius claimed no other parentage than Maximian, but Constantine spread rumours in turn that he was the son of a Syrian, with whom his mother had fornicated behind Maximian's back. Legitimacy and imperial lineage were once again live issues, and the meritocratic basis of the

Tetrarchy was abandoned. Thus, in the east even Licinius began to claim descent from Philip the Arab, who had reigned from 244 to 249.

We can understand, therefore, the presence of Apollo in the vision described by the orator in 310, and may doubt that Constantine truly experienced a vision in Gaul in that year. There is a compelling set of reasons for Constantine to have embraced the Sun god as his patron that does not require it. The orator who supplies our information was certainly disseminating useful propaganda, that Constantine was descended from emperors and visited by gods. Furthermore, Apollo was worshipped at an important temple in the orator's district, which gave him a further reason for elaborating upon the truth.

The road to Rome

A second panegyrical oration, delivered to Constantine in Trier in 313, alludes to divine revelation and places emphasis on his fortitude in marching on Italy in the face of adverse omens. Besides supplying the only extant account of Constantine's vision of Apollo, the anonymous orator describes in greatest detail his actions in the years after the death of Maximian. The occasion for delivering his oration was the staging of triumphal games in Trier, where Constantine despatched thousands of captive Franks to their deaths in the arena. This is recalled fondly: 'What is lovelier than this triumphal celebration in which he employs the slaughter of enemies for the pleasure of us all, and enlarges the procession of the games out of the massacre of the barbarians?' These hapless barbarians were captured upon Constantine's return from a far greater victory: the victory over the forces of his imperial rival Maxentius throughout northern Italy and, ultimately, before the gates of Rome.

The orator explores Constantine's march on Italy, providing valuable insights into his victories before his arrival at Rome's Milvian Bridge. We hear, as Constantine himself would have heard, that his departure from Gaul was widely considered foolhardy, as he took just a fraction of his troops. Most were left behind to guard the Rhine frontier, although surely Constantine travelled most comfortably with those he trusted in battle. His journey would be swift and hard, but the men he took had accompanied him before in that manner, to Marseille from Cologne.

So one should not be surprised that he preferred to leave behind a larger, more cumbersome force of untried soldiers to defend the Rhine frontier against incursions. More worrisome was the fact that sacrifices undertaken before the campaign did not bode well for its outcome. Constantine paid no attention, however, as he had access to a higher power, the greatest god, who communicated to him personally:

Could you have had such foresight, Emperor, that you were the first to embark upon a war . . . when all your associates in imperial power were inactive and hesitating? What god, what majesty so encouraged you to perceive on your own, when almost all comrades and commanders were not only quietly muttering but even openly fearful, that the time had come to liberate the city [of Rome]? You must share some secret with that divine mind, Constantine, which has delegated care of us to lesser gods and deigns to reveal itself to you alone.

This passage refers only to a singular god and has frequently been used to explain that Constantine had, before the oration was delivered, openly declared his devotion to this unnamed deity, identified later as the god of the Christians. But this is far from clear, indeed it is left deliberately obscure. The lesser gods, whose rites presaged ill for the emperor, are subordinate but separate, left as much in the dark as Constantine's subjects. Their counsel was sought too by Constantine's imperial colleagues, and perhaps they, through soothsayers and diviners, had persuaded Licinius not to march against Maxentius, as was his duty as senior emperor in the west. Or perhaps it was the example set by both Severus and Galerius, who failed to take the city. Constantine put all to the test, observing, as others did not, that Maxentius' circumstances had changed. Constantine was urged on by his belief in the theology of victory and the faith he now placed in his Gallic troops, numbering fewer than 40,000 against 120,000 fielded by Maxentius (see map 4).

The bulk of Maxentius' army was already stationed in northern Italy, under the command of his Praetorian Prefect Ruricius Pompeianus. Pompeianus had made his base at Verona, which suggests that he, and Maximian, had expected an attack not from the north-west but from the north-east. That is, they had anticipated that Licinius would launch an invasion from Pannonia. Instead, Constantine's forces fell upon them at Susa (modern Segusio), which at forty miles west of Turin defended access to the Po Valley. Unwilling to set a siege, which would halt his rapid advance and allow Pompeianus to send reinforcements, Constantine had his troops launch a frontal assault on the city, throwing torches at the gates and placing ladders up against the walls. The fire took hold and spread rapidly through the city, and in the panic Constantine was able to take control. He was merciful, commanding that the fire be doused, and thus set an example to other cities, that to surrender would earn his mercy. The defenders of Turin, however, learnt another lesson: not to be trapped inside their own walls. When Constantine arrived, he found a large force arrayed in battle order.

The enemy was not widely spread out . . . but their battle line was arrayed in the form of a wedge, with the flanks extending downhill to the rear. If you [Constantine] had joined battle with them at the outset, they would have turned and surrounded your men as they were engaged in fighting. But since you foresaw this, you sent men ahead on both sides to obstruct them and at the same time, if there were any lurking in ambush, to drive them out. You yourself, when the stubborn point of the enemy's formation had been driven back and their whole line turned to flight, advanced and completed a slaughter equal in size to the numbers that reinforced their battle line. They were routed and cut down right to the walls of Turin, and when they reached the gates already fastened by those within they closed them off by the mass of their own corpses.

The lesson was learnt in Mediolanum (modern Milan), which was delivered to Constantine without resistance. He entered the city, formerly Maximian's capital, in a victorious procession, greeted by the leading citizens as the rest cheered. Now only Verona, where Pompeianus commanded the bulk of Maxentius' forces, lay between Constantine and his goal.

The panegyrist provides another battle narrative, less full than for Turin but equally revealing. Pompeianus took refuge within the city, expecting the river Adige both to supply and water the city and to defend it from Constantine's approach along the valley. However, an advance force took a path through the mountains and was able to cross the river where it was narrower and out of range of enemy archers. Constantine's men, therefore, converged upon the city from both east and west, forcing Pompeianus to sally forth to engage the smaller advance force. He broke through their line and rode off to summon aid, while Constantine pressed his siege. Returning with reinforcements, Pompeianus met Constantine's army drawn up in a double battle line, barring access to the city. This was evidently a brutal encounter in which Constantine's forces were heavily outnumbered. The emperor took to the field himself, fighting alongside his 'fellow soldiers' and earning the orator's qualified praise. It was, after all, reckless for a commander to relinquish his post and enter the thick of battle. Unlike Xerxes, or Augustus at Actium, Constantine led by example, but so did Pompeianus who died on the field. Constantine's battle-hardened troops won the day, and some were alleged to have asked: 'What were you doing, Emperor? To what fate had you abandoned us if your divine valour (*divina virtus*) had not protected you?' This encounter, more than those before and that which would follow, cemented Constantine's belief that his interests were protected by a patron without rival. The identity of this singular god would shortly afterwards be revealed, as Constantine descended without further resistance upon Rome.

The Battle of the Milvian Bridge

It was both customary and necessary in fighting a civil war to absorb defeated forces into one's own army. Had Constantine conscripted the men who had followed Pompeianus at Verona, his army might have approached Maxentius' in size. But what it lacked in size Constantine's force made up for in experience and, now more than ever, confidence. Their commander would take no chances in diluting his fighting force and would not trust the captives from Verona to remain loyal if arrayed against their comrades. Instead, he commanded that their swords be hammered into manacles, not ploughshares, and did this by 'divine instigation' (*divino . . . instinctu*). The significance of this phrase will become apparent later. And so his forces arrived before Rome somewhat depleted from the campaign and with the prospect of setting a lengthy siege. Instead, within days they fought and won the decisive Battle of the Milvian Bridge. Accounts of this encounter have been coloured by later rewriting and legend, not least the idea that Constantine experienced a vision of a cross in the sky which foretold his victory. This was, in fact, a clever retelling of the vision of Apollo, which we shall, therefore, treat in its proper place, in an account of Constantine's developing Christianity and his consequent revision of key moments in his rise to power (see below, p. 183). It is quite distinct from Lactantius' account of a dream, contained in his *On the Deaths of the Persecutors*, completed before 315.

Lactantius states that having arrived with his forces at the Milvian Bridge, which spanned Rome's river Tiber, 'Constantine was advised in a dream to mark the heavenly sign of God (*caeleste signum dei*) on the shields of his soldiers and then engage in battle'. Divinely inspired dreams were common among emperors and pretenders, and those foretelling victory in battle had many Roman precursors, including the visions of Scipio Africanus, Sulla, Julius Caesar, Germanicus, and, as we have seen, Aurelian. A still more important model for Lactantius is Judaeo-Christian, being the Old Testament dream of Judas Maccabeus, upon which the author drew here as he did in describing the death of Galerius. One must wonder, therefore, whether Lactantius was once again highlighting a noteworthy coincidence, or altering information to fit his model. He continues: '[Constantine] did as he was commanded [in the dream], and by means of a slanted letter X with the top of its head bent around he marked Christ on their shields. Armed with this sign, the army took up its weapons.' Lactantius is referring to the Latin letter X, not the Greek chi, the vertical bar of which when slanted curved to form a P. It would appear, therefore, that he is describing a staurogram, a variant on the chi-rho Christogram. The presence of this mark on the shields of Constantine's troops is supported later by Eusebius, but nowhere else at this time.

It is certain that Roman shields bore designs, to express allegiance and to identify members of a unit to each other in the thick of battle. Several of these can be discerned on the Arch of Constantine, to which we shall turn in the next chapter. A Gallic unit in Constantine's army, the Cornuti, is clearly depicted on the arch wearing their horned helmets and carrying shields depicting their emblem, two confronted goats' heads. On the Arch of Galerius in Salonica, one can discern three distinct designs on separate shields: Hercules holding his club (fig. 22), and elsewhere a fleur-de-lys and an eagle. However, no shield of the fourth century has survived to prove Lactantius' claim, and there are few contemporary representations of the chi-rho design on shields. A green glass beaker kept in Cologne's Römisch-Germanisches Museum has a crude design cut into it portraying a soldier standing between two *vexilla*, flag standards, marked with six-pointed stars (fig. 27). The soldier, who has generally been identified as one of Constantine's German bodyguards, has two spears strapped to his back and holds a large oval shield in front of himself, masking his whole body between his shoulders and calves. The shield bears a design, but it is not the chi-rho. Rather, it is a cross formed of two intersecting lines, each formed of four lozenges. The symbols most likely are not Christian, since on another shield displayed on the same beaker there is only cross-hatching. Similarly, one type of copper coin struck for Crispus, Constantine's eldest son, in Trier in 322–3 features the chi-rho on the shield that he holds. However, on coins of the same issue the shield bears at least five alternative designs, including the head of Medusa and two variants of Victory crowning the emperor. A bronze steelyard weight of Constantine, produced in the sixth century but perhaps modelled on a fourth-century statue, holds a shield on which the chi-rho is visible. Finally, Constantine's second son, Constantius, is depicted on a silver dish found in the Crimea next to a soldier whose shield bears the chi-rho. We shall look more closely at this in the last chapter (fig. 60). Alas, one cannot be certain that any or all of these are not artists' fabrications, and so Lactantius' claim cannot be corroborated.

The account written closest to the events here recounted, the now familiar panegyrical oration of 313, makes no mention of a vision or of a dream on the eve of battle. Rather, it suggests that Constantine's army arrived at a forced march to find Maxentius' battle line positioned with the river Tiber behind it, between the soldiers and the city. Maxentius had cut the eponymous Milvian Bridge, apparently to prevent his enemy from advancing on the city, rather than to steel his own men by denying them a route of escape. There remained a means of retreat for Maxentius and his retinue, across a pontoon bridge constructed of boats. This, however, proved the cause of their demise. As the battle was engaged,

Maxentius' guard was unable to resist the first assault of Constantine's cavalry. They retreated across the pontoon, which gave way under their weight. Horses and riders were thrown into the river, and although Maxentius almost made it across, 'After the Tiber had swallowed up the impious, the same Tiber also snatched up their leader himself in its whirlpool and devoured him, when he attempted in vain to escape with his horse and distinctive armour by ascending the opposite bank.'

Why did Maxentius come out to meet Constantine on 28 October 312? On two earlier occasions, he had allowed Severus and Galerius to camp beyond the city's stout Aurelian walls, while he remained within. But matters had changed by October 312, and the citizens of the city, who had once stood gladly behind their ruler, the first to base himself in Rome for a century, had turned against Maxentius. Much of the blame was the emperor's own, because he had failed to expand his rule beyond the Italian peninsula. For the first time citizens of Italy bore the full burden of financing their government, and whereas threats by Diocletian and Galerius to effect such a reform had earned Maxentius support in 306, by 312 he had raised taxes on Roman citizens for five years. The promise to restore Rome to the heart of a revived empire had turned into the burden of supporting a separatist state, no longer sustained by tax revenues generated in the provinces. Only Africa remained with Italy under Maxentius' control, and not without considerable problems. In 308–9 the pretender Domitius Alexander rose in rebellion, and the regular grain shipments from Africa to Rome were ended for at least one sailing season. Maxentius may have lost Africa as a consequence of his breach with Maximian, for the latter had formerly commanded the legions stationed there. Africa had been recovered capably by troops sent from Italy under Maxentius' Praetorian Prefect, Ruricius Pompeianus. But for a year the citizens of Rome suffered depleted grain supplies that were not easily replenished in the city. Furthermore, the actions of Maxentius' troops, slaughtering many in the African cities they had 'liberated', led to his vilification, and he had vented his anger in Rome itself, attacking certain senators and ordering the Praetorians to kill protesters.

As Maxentius sat within Rome, tensions grew each time news arrived of Constantine's victories over the forces ranged against him in northern

Italy. When Verona fell, the beleaguered citizens in Rome had only their walls on which to rely, and Maxentius had no ally who would arrive to lift the siege. He feared for his life if a siege was set and had no option but to march out of the city and trust to battle. But before he did so, he had, like Constantine, to ensure that it was widely known that his efforts enjoyed divine support. So he consulted the city's Sibylline Books, which had, forty years earlier, predicted Aurelian's victory at Palmyra; and lo, it was seen that the time was perfect and that Rome would be liberated from a tyrant. Unfortunately, the outcome of battle demonstrated that he was the tyrant. At least this was what the credulous would later believe, accepting the claims of Constantine's propaganda that Maxentius was addicted to hollow superstition and that the hand of God had drawn him forth in his arrogance from the city that previously he had not left. They would also believe that Maxentius was so loathed in the city that his death was the liberation predicted by the oracle. His demise was, indeed, dramatic and deserving of such tales, but it was a pale victory compared to that at Verona.

Constantine Invictus and the theology of victory

Shortly after his victory at the Milvian Bridge, Constantine took *invictus*, meaning both 'unconquered' and 'unconquerable', as part of his official titulature. Besides an inscription at Rome, we have two letters from the poet Porfyrius addressed to 'Master Constantine, the most pious and unconquerable Augustus' (*Domino Constantino maximo pio invicto . . . Augusto*), and 'Unconquered Constantine the Greatest Augustus' (*Invictus Constantinus Maximus Augustus*). Constantine was only the latest emperor to adopt this epithet, but he did so for quite specific dynastic reasons. His patron was Sol Invictus, who linked him to his chosen forebear, Claudius Gothicus, leaping neatly over the period of the Tetrarchy to establish the renewed domination of the Flavians. Constantine now feared nobody. He had earned the full support of his army, who knew that his divine patron would deliver victory even in the direst circumstances.

One cannot overemphasize how much Constantine relied on his troops and how close he came in 308 to losing their loyalty, as had so many usurpers through the third century. After Maximian's death he needed a series of successful campaigns to demonstrate his fitness to rule and to secure booty to reward them. One can see how frequently he distributed the fruits of victory, not only in medallions but also in gold clasps, brooches and rings proclaiming the faith of the army. One might detect in this some special pleading. How embarrassing would it be to launch a coup wearing a cloak pinned with a badge of one's loyalty? Who would willingly wear a buckle or pin proclaiming faith to an emperor he had recently murdered? The sense of unease is nowhere more clearly expressed than on the coins Constantine struck, praising the army and its loyalty.

Unlike monumental art or written sources, which are snapshots subject to alteration and revision, Constantine's coinage provides a running commentary on his reign, and in particular on how the emperor conceived of his power and actions. This can be seen most clearly in the interplay between obverse and reverse images and inscriptions on his gold, silver and bronze issues. In the words of Patrick Bruun, a leading numismatist and scholar of the Constantinian age, 'The obverses in script and picture convey the official conception of the *sacri vultus* [sacred countenance] adorned with appropriate emblems of power . . . [whereas] the reverses draw the factual background, whether it is a warlike incident, a ceremonial act or the prevailing sentiment pictorially expressed by an allegory, a symbol or a personification.' On his earliest coins Constantine projects himself as a general. He exalts his army on medallions and regular bronze issues widely distributed as donatives, dedicating them to 'the Valour of the Army' (VIRTUS EXERCIT), and to 'the Faith of the Army' (FIDES EXERCITUS). Gold coins struck at Trier between 309 and 313, thus from the very moment when he had defeated Maximian, celebrated the 'Glory of the Gallic Army' (GLORIA EXERCITUS GALL).

Constantine's victories in war were the key to his ability to control his army, and the need to remain victorious explains why he chanced all on a risky assault on Rome, where so many had failed before. He feared for his own position and needed to prove that he had divine support. Taking Rome also, of course, offered him the chance to secure senatorial support and legitimation, in a manner emulating so many third-century usurpers. But Constantine was also devoted to his men and pleased to reward them. Many emperors between Trajan (d. AD 117) and Constantine are recorded as referring to their troops as 'fellow soldiers' in extant works of history. But Trajan was the last man for two centuries to issue an extant public document that makes specific reference to his 'fellow soldiers' (*commilitones*). He also uses the term in letters to Pliny the Younger. The next public document to refer to the emperor as a fellow soldier was issued by Constantine, in a law that was incorporated later into the Theodosian Code. In fact, Constantine refers to his 'fellow veterans' (*coveterani*), and one might guess that he is referring particularly to those who had fought in his protracted wars, perhaps even his personal retinue, in his earliest campaigns.

6

Constantine and Rome

Maxentius in Rome – Adventus Constantini – The Arch of Constantine – Meanwhile: Licinius and Maximinus Daia – Constantine confronts Licinius

At the end of 2006, archaeologists announced a most remarkable discovery on Rome's Palatine Hill: the insignia of a Roman emperor, hitherto known only from descriptions and depictions on coins, had been unearthed. A sceptre, in the form of a flower clasping a blue-green ball, and three additional glass and chalcedony spheres were found wrapped in silk within wooden boxes. Alongside them were four javelins, three lances and a base for planting standards (figs. 28 and 29). These had been buried, it was conjectured, to prevent them falling into the hands of the owner's vanquisher. In this way, one small part of Maxentius' imperial legacy survived his defeat by Constantine. All else was rapidly swept up in a process of revision and rebranding: *damnatio memoriae*, which erased the memory of the emperor now called only 'tyrant'.

Maxentius in Rome

When Constantine entered Rome, he saw a city that had been altered substantially in Maxentius' short reign. The city's defensive walls had been supplied within living memory by Aurelian, but they were repaired and heightened and the gates strengthened to withstand sieges set by Severus and Galerius. Structures within the walls were built anew in areas devastated by fire in 283, and outside the walls a new imperial complex was completed adjacent to the Appian Way, between its second and third milestones in the region called *ad catacumbas*, after its Christian catacombs. Diocletian and Maximian had not neglected Rome, which remained a centre of symbolic importance for the empire and a unifying feature in Tetrarchic ideology. Nor did the Tetrarchs neglect the damaged fabric of the city, as one later source, the anonymous Latin Calendar of 354, records:

Many public works were erected by these emperors: the senate house, the Forum of Caesar, the Basilica Julia, the Theatre of Pompey, porticoes II, nymphaea III, temples II [to] Isis and Serapis, the New Arch and the Baths of Diocletian.

However, as the names make clear, all but the last of these were reconstructions. The erection of the Baths of Diocletian was the only major new project, aimed at securing the favour of the urban unwashed. They were begun by Maximian on his first recorded visit to the city, in 298–9, when he was returning from campaigns in Africa, but they were not completed until 305–6, as is revealed by an inscription recording their dedication to the two retired Augusti, two reigning Augusti and two Caesars. In the meantime, in 303, Diocletian had also made his first recorded visit to Rome, to celebrate the twentieth anniversary of his accession. This was the reason for the construction of the second new structure, the New Arch, a triumphal arch spanning the city's Via Lata. But when the old Augustus left the city prematurely and intent on reforms, Maxentius was thrust to the fore by the Praetorian Guard, jealous of their privileges. Maxentius needed a broader support base and achieved it through grand public building campaigns.

Maxentius' building projects represented a conscious revival of Rome's status as an imperial capital and reminded citizens of their place at the heart of the empire: an empire divided and supplied in recent years with a number of competing imperial cities. We have explored Constantine's Trier, an imperial centre of recent development to rival Diocletian's Nicomedia and Galerius' Salonica. To this list one must add Maximian's preferred residence at Milan, and two other cities favoured by Diocletian: Sirmium on the Danube, while he was actively campaigning, and Split on the Dalmatian coast in retirement. Each city served as a centre of administration, with an imperial court at its heart. Maxentius emulated these developments, creating a new imperial complex on the Appian Way. An imperial villa, of fairly modest proportions, served as the residence and reception halls. From the villa a covered path ran to the new circus, giving Maxentius direct access to a box overlooking the 10,000 seats. This complex, more than anything within the city's walls, demonstrated his commitment to Rome. An inscription of 311–12 discovered there announces that Maxentius was an 'unconquered emperor', *invictus augustus*. But he was also then the father to a recently departed son, whom he had divinized and buried in the family mausoleum, a rotunda facing the villa. Two inscriptions discovered in 1825 at the circus commemorate the son, who had been named for this family and, perhaps not entirely fortuitously, after the founder of Rome. His name was Valerius Romulus.

The need to site this mausoleum outside the *pomerium*, the formal boundary of the city, has been suggested as the reason for locating the entire complex outside the city's defensive walls, where so recently imperial rivals had encamped. The mausoleum was depicted on coins that Maxentius minted after Romulus' death, which projected a new image for himself and the Valerian dynasty (*gens Valeriana*). For the first time these coins bore the names and images of the Tetrarchs, but only those who had recently died, and only those who had been related to Maxentius by blood or marriage. Constantine (Maxentius' brother-in-law by his marriage to Fausta, and very much alive), Licinius and Maximinus were ignored. The relationship between the dead and the living was spelt out on the coins: 'to the divine Romulus son of Maxentius Augustus' and 'to the divine Maximian father of Maxentius Augustus'. More contentiously, following Galerius' death in May 311, Maxentius struck coins to him addressed by his formal name, Maximian Junior: 'to the divine Maximian father-in-law (*socer*) of Maxentius Augustus'. Most provocative were the coins 'to the divine Constantius, kinsman (*cognatus*) of Maxentius Augustus', which claimed Constantine's own father for the Valerii. The obverse of these coins featured a bust of Maxentius below the phrase AETERNAE MEMORIAE, 'to the eternal memory'. Constantine was suitably provoked.

Within the city Maxentius erected buildings that projected the deep roots planted by his chosen family, the *gens Valeriana*, in Rome's soil. His location of choice was the Velia, a low ridge that projects from the northern side of the Palatine. One of the seven hills on which Rome was founded, it was associated in legend with the most famous of the

Valerians, P. Valerius Publicola, one of the first consuls. Rather conveniently, the Temple of the City that adorned the Velia was destroyed in a fire in 306, allowing Maxentius to erect a huge basilica, eighty metres long, twenty-five wide and thirty-five tall. Its shell may still be seen, although on signs one must seek the Basilica of Constantine for reasons that will be explored shortly. Even more impressive was the Temple of Roma and Venus erected beside the Velia, between Maxentius' basilica and the Flavian amphitheatre (the Colosseum). Dedicated by Hadrian in AD 135, the temple had been damaged in the fire of 283, and again in 306. Maxentius' reconstruction was the largest temple in Rome and the largest devoted to the goddess Roma ever to be constructed. On the side of the basilica away from this temple, at the foot of the Velia, was erected a far smaller sanctuary, but one with greater personal meaning, for it may have been constructed atop the ancestral tomb of the Valerii. Maxentius dedicated this temple to his dead son Romulus and his namesake.

Together these buildings comprised the Forum of Maxentius, which with his imperial complex on the Appian Way illuminated Maxentius' dedication to the city and its history. This message was disseminated also by his officials. An inscription on a marble plinth was raised by Furius Octavianus, keeper of the sacred buildings of Rome, on 21 April, probably late in Maxentius' reign. The date is Rome's birthday, the *natalis urbis*, and the plinth was discovered near the Lapis Niger, traditionally regarded as the tomb of the original Romulus. It reads:

To Unconquered Mars, Father, and to the founders of his eternal city. Our Lord Imperator Maxentius Pius Felix, Unconquered Augustus [dedicated this statue].

On top was once found a statue, possibly of Mars but perhaps of his sons, the founders of the eternal city, Romulus and Remus. It has even been suggested that the *Lupa Capitolina*, the majestic bronze in the Capitoline Museums of the she-wolf suckling those infants, once sat atop this plinth, although there are also claims that Maxentius relocated that sculpture to the Lateran, where it was attested through the Middle

Ages (fig. 30).* A base has been found there with four depressions exactly aligned with the feet of the wolf. The parallels between Maxentius and Mars are clear: both are fathers of the city and, more literally, of sons named Romulus; both are unconquered. Constantine's arrival ended the reign of Mars and Maxentius.

Adventus Constantini

Constantine's victory required the eradication of Maxentius' legacy. This was achieved by traditional Roman means: *damnatio memoriae*, damning Maxentius' memory and appropriation of his legacy. The most common label attached to Maxentius was 'tyrant', the worst type of leader. In the city of Rome the term was redolent of the rhetoric of the killers of Julius Caesar, and still earlier of the champions of the Republic who had despatched the *reges superbi*, those kings bloated with pride who had oppressed Rome. In this latter context, one must note the remarkable coincidence between the phrase 'by divine instigation' (*instinctu divinitatis*) found in the inscription on the Arch of Constantine and the suggestion that the proud king Tarquin was driven out 'by instigation of the gods' (*instinctu deorum*, where gods are certainly plural). Nazarius, who in 321 delivered a panegyric in praise of Constantine, spoke of the 'loathsome head of the tyrant' paraded through Rome and then despatched to Africa, so that the crowds in Carthage might also witness Constantine's victory. Charged with such an edifying task, even the winter winds co-operated, speeding the ship south across the Mediterranean with its grisly cargo. 'Tyrant' alone would suffice in future to identify Maxentius, as we shall see on the dedicatory inscription attached to Constantine's arch. The Calendar of 354 states simply of the year 312: 'The tyrant was cast out.'

Before Nazarius, the anonymous orator of 313, whom we met at length in the previous chapter, provides details of Constantine's *adventus*, his entry into Rome after the defeat of Maxentius. Constantine's first act

---

* Since this chapter was written, it has been revealed by researchers at the University of Salerno, employing radiocarbon and thermoluminescence dating techniques, that the bronze in the Capitoline Museums was sculpted in the thirteenth century AD. The twins were added in the fifteenth century. We must suppose, therefore, that we possess only a copy of an original piece, now lost.

was to recover Maxentius' body from the Tiber, for the citizens had to know that their emperor was truly dead:

The swirling river rolled along the bodies and arms of other enemies and carried them away, but that one it held in the same place where it had killed him, lest the Roman people should long be in doubt whether it was to be believed that the man, the confirmation of whose death was sought, had actually escaped . . . Then after the body had been found and hacked up, the whole populace of Rome broke out in vengeful rejoicing, and throughout the whole city where it was carried affixed to a spear that sinful head did not cease to suffer disfiguration.

It has often been noted by those wishing to add a Christian twist to Constantine's actions that no mention is made by the orator of a visit to the temple of Jupiter Optimus Maximus on the Capitoline, the established terminus of a triumphal procession. The author of the panegyric knew and borrowed from an earlier oration in praise of Maximian, delivered in 307, which makes specific mention of Capitoline Jupiter, but he failed to incorporate these details. However, no weight can be placed on this argument from silence, for no account of a ceremonial act can be read as a plain record of what happened and why. Rather, the retelling of ritual serves a purpose in itself, as Philippe Buc has advised historians of medieval Europe: to establish the superiority of one account and the interests of its author. Similar insights inform Mary Beard's recent study of the Roman triumph, which offers commentary on the procession under scrutiny.

Constantine's procession appears to have been a formal *triumphus*, a rare and carefully staged celebration of specific military victories that was voted for the emperor by the senate. Although instances had increased during the later third century, between 31 BC and AD 235 only thirteen formal triumphs were staged in Rome for nine generals, with four holding more than one. Augustus staged three on three successive days, folding his civil wars into foreign victories. His actions reflected distaste for the formal celebration of victories in civil wars, and that this remained the case is demonstrated by Septimius Severus' refusal of a triumph in 195 lest it appear to be for victory in a civil war. Severus subsequently failed properly to celebrate his great victories over foreign foes, perhaps because of gout, which meant he could not stand during the processions associated with the dedication of his triumphal arch in Rome.

Constantine may have had similar scruples about staging a formal *triumphus* to celebrate victory in a civil war, although his return to Rome in 315 suggests that he, like Augustus, would gladly fold domestic successes into those over foreign 'barbarians'. In 312 there was simply no time to stage such an event – gathering prisoners and booty to display, decking the city in banners and flowers, arranging groups along the route to shout acclamations, and much more besides – between the battle on 28 October and the imperial entry into Rome on the very next day. One cannot assume from the fact that crowds cheered Constantine that Maxentius had been universally unpopular. A victorious general riding at the head of a long line of battle-hardened, largely Gallic and German troops might convince many to hoot encouragingly. Nor need we trust the orator of 313 in his portrayal of Maxentius, 'that monster' who had dispensed Rome's treasures 'to gangs of men hired to rob citizens . . . and while he enjoyed the majesty of that city which he had taken, he filled all of Italy with thugs hired for every sort of villainy'. One wonders whether the orator is referring here to Maxentius' loyal soldiers, who fought Constantine across the north of Italy, or his tax-collectors. The damning of Maxentius' memory was well advanced by 313, so every clichéd atrocity is attributed to him. A sustained comparison between Constantine and Maxentius illustrates the point:

He was Maximian's illegitimate changeling (*suppositus*), you the true son of Constantius Pius; he was of a contemptibly small stature, twisted and slack in limb, his very name mutilated by a misapplied appellation, you (it suffices to say) are in size and form what you are [the audience could see the emperor] . . . you were attended by respect for your father, but he, not to begrudge him his false paternity, by disrespect; you were attended by clemency, he by cruelty; you by virtue devoted to a single spouse, he by lust befouled with every kind of shameful act; you by divine direction, he by superstitious mischief; he, finally, by guilt for the despoiled temples, the slaughtered senate, the Roman plebs destroyed by famine, you by thanks for the abolition of calumnies, the prohibition of delation (*delatio*), the avoidance of shedding even murderers' blood.

The most striking accusation here is that Maxentius was not Maximian's true son, but rather was a *suppositus*, someone introduced into the family falsely, not truly of the *gens Valeriana*. A rumour had been started that Eutropia, Maxentius' mother, had conceived him by a Syrian, perhaps even a dwarf. Small wonder that he shared none of Constantine's chaste Roman qualities and dabbled in magic rather than trusting in true divinity. This is rather comical, given that so recently Constantine had invented for himself an imperial lineage, projecting an entirely false descent from Claudius II. Indeed, it would appear likely that the reason such emphasis was placed on Maxentius' illegitimacy is that similar stress had recently been placed on Constantine's birth by Helena, who upon Constantine's accession was not Constantius' widow, if she ever had been his wife.

The final list of Constantine's merciful concessions suggests that he was actively courting the plebs by dismissing court cases and freeing criminals. He is portrayed as cancelling Maxentius' aberrant methods of policing, and it is stated that false accusations would no longer be heard, but nor would those that might be true, for *delatio* means 'the giving of information against someone in order to have that person's crimes come to the notice of the proper authorities'. There arose from this the tradition that Maxentius had persecuted the senate and that Constantine had freed one hundred senators from fetters, all of whom joined his joyous parade. Thus, in 321, the rhetor Nazarius claimed of the *adventus*: 'Leaders in chains were not driven before the [emperor's] chariot, but the nobility marched along, freed at last. Captive foreigners did not adorn that entrance, but Rome was now free.' And just as those whom Maxentius was alleged to have oppressed were liberated, so were his enforcers dismissed. The Praetorian Guard, by whose intrigues he had come to power, whose support had allowed him to vanquish his father, and who had fought beside him at the Milvian Bridge, was disbanded. Constantine was able to achieve what Diocletian and Galerius could not, and dispensed with that overpaid and dangerous corps. He similarly abolished the *equites singulares*, the emperor's horse-guard, razing their camp on the Caelian Hill and in its place erecting a new building, a grand basilica that adjoined the Sessorian Palace, where Constantine based himself while in Rome and which he gave to his mother Helena in 326, upon determining to settle permanently elsewhere. The new building was a basilica, rather similar to the one he had constructed in Trier, which later became a church. And this new basilica also became a rather famous church, St John in Lateran, seat of the bishops of Rome before the construction of St Peter's. This gift was accompanied by a host of rich furnishings including, according to the (far later) *Book of Pontiffs*, 'a silver paten weighing twenty pounds . . . a golden chalice weighing two pounds. Five service chalices each weighing two pounds . . . twelve bronze candlestick chandeliers each weighing thirty pounds'. The weight of the items was a measure of their value, and hence of the esteem in which Constantine held their recipient, the bishop of Rome.

The *equites singulares* had remained loyal to Maxentius throughout his reign, and his end was their end. Consequently, Constantine damned their memory as he did that of his rival. It is remarkable that all of Constantine's Christian buildings in Rome were connected in some way with their destruction or that of the Praetorian Guard. Not only did St John in Lateran replace the camp of the horse-guard, but a church dedicated to St Marcellinus and to St Peter, two Christians martyred in Rome, was constructed at the site of their unit's graveyard, at the Via Labicana, and this was associated with a mausoleum in which Constantine planned for his own mortal remains to be interred. It would come instead to house his mother's. The Praetorians fared little better: their cemetery on the Via Nomentana was replaced with a church dedicated to St Agnes and St Constantius, also local martyrs. It is hard indeed not to reach the conclusion that Constantine wished to assert that his victory over the Praetorians and the horse-guard was achieved through the power of the god of the Christians, but we cannot say whether he wished this immediately, in 312, or somewhat later, as we do not know the exact dates at which the churches were founded. We do not know these dates, but we do know that Constantine's were not the first imperial churches in Rome. Maxentius had already sponsored a building dedicated to St Crisogonus in Trastevere. This information was later suppressed, so that all would equate Constantine's victory with that of Christianity.

Damning the memory of Maxentius has made the task of identifying his building projects most difficult, as they were the easiest to appropriate. They were raised in such a short period as to have no distinctive style, and certainly not one distinct from that attributed to Constantine. In the words of Aurelius Victor, 'All the works that [Maxentius] had built with such magnificence, the Temple of the City and the basilica, were dedicated by the senate to the merits of Flavius [i.e. Constantine]'. Constantine discontinued use of Maxentius' circus on the Appian Way and enticed the crowds back to the Circus Maximus by adding new rows of seats. The tragic collapse of a decade before, during Diocletian's *vicennalia* festivities, would in any event have commended repairs. A bust identified as either Constantius Chlorus or Claudius Gothicus has been found within Maxentius' villa, and the fact that one cannot distinguish between the two possible honorands seems only to support the point that Constantine was seeking to make: the Valerians had given way to the Flavians. The Valerians were no longer. Nowhere is this clearer than on coins Constantine had struck in Rome modelled closely on those struck by Maxentius to honour his divinized relatives, including Constantine's father. Just as fortunes were reversed, so is the commemorative inscription, now MEMORIAE AETERNAE. The image of the Valerian mausoleum was removed and replaced by an eagle of consecration or the Herculean lion or club, and the images are of Claudius Gothicus, Constantius and Maximian.

The buildings on the Velia were similarly rededicated to the scion of the Flavian house. An inscription at the Temple of Romulus reads: '[Dedicated] to Flavius Constantinus Maximus triumphant Augustus, by the senate and people of Rome.' The Basilica of Maxentius became the Basilica of Constantine, and the conqueror still more literally took on the parts of Maxentius, for within the tall basilican apse stood a colossal statue of its founder. This was taken and the head reworked to resemble Constantine. Several colossal body parts, including the famous head, were found in 1486 within the basilica and can now be seen a short distance from there in the courtyard of the Capitoline Museums (fig. 31). The oversized eyes have always attracted attention, and fourth-century viewers, unlike today's, believed that they projected beams, thus both surveying and possessing the buildings he had appropriated. This statue is referred to by Eusebius in his *Ecclesiastical History* (*HE*), who added further that 'perceiving that his aid was from God, he immediately commanded that a trophy of the Saviour's be put in the hand of his own statue'. Eusebius continues (*HE* IX.9.11):

And when he had placed it, with the saving sign of the cross in its right hand, in the most public place in Rome, he commanded that the following inscription should be engraved upon it in the Roman tongue: 'By this saving sign, the true proof of valour, I have liberated your city freed from the yoke of the tyrant and moreover, having set at liberty both the senate and the people of Rome, I have restored them to their ancient distinction and splendour.'

Eusebius revised his account and expanded it greatly in a later work, the *Life of Constantine*.* But both accounts of the statue and the 'saving sign' post-date 325, when Constantine felt quite differently about his victory. A second colossal statue reveals more clearly Constantine's initial feelings upon entering the city of Rome in 312 and again in 315. The Colossus was made for Nero, and its head was his on the body of the Sun god. It had been altered several times over the centuries, most recently to resemble Maxentius' dead son Romulus. This much is revealed by an inscription which adorned its base and which was incorporated into a further structure, one most likely raised for Maxentius but now rededicated to Constantine: the famous Arch of Constantine.

The Arch of Constantine

In July 315 the senate celebrated Constantine's victory and *decennalia* together, in stone, by dedicating a triumphal arch in Rome and offering *vota* – prayers of thanks for his continued rule (fig. 32). Recent excavations suggest that the arch, like the basilica and temples that had been recently rededicated to Constantine, had been erected for Maxentius. The arch is placed at the endpoint of his building project, and as one approached it, its archway framed the colossal statue of Nero/Romulus/ Sol. The most recent head, of Romulus, was replaced with that of

---

* Since I shall refer often to Eusebius of Caesarea's *Life of Constantine*, the abbreviation *VC* (*Vita Constantini*) will be used. Those who wish to consult the text will find the chapter and section numbers useful. In most cases I have used and quoted from the English translation by Cameron and Hall. The reader will recall that Eusebius' *Ecclesiastical History* is referred to by the abbreviation *HE*.

Constantine. It has been suggested that this very head is the bronze in the Capitoline Museums, and indeed it has suitable attachments. However, the hair and eyes seem more in keeping with Constantine's later image, forged after 324 (fig. 47).

One might ask why, in 312, Maxentius was constructing a triumphal arch, for surely he had neither the time during Constantine's rapid march south, nor indeed the hubris to anticipate a victory so brazenly. It seems more likely that the monument was an element of the general triumphal ideology within which Maxentius presented himself as the 'Unconquered Prince', whose divine companion was Mars Invictus. Had he not driven off two imperial rivals, Severus and Galerius, who had marched on Rome? And had his expeditionary force not delivered Africa from the pretender Domitius Alexander? Still, one might wonder at the timing of the arch's construction, as it stood virtually complete in 312. Perhaps the best explanation is that the *ludi saeculares*, the secular games, were scheduled to be celebrated in 314. The secular games were held in Rome to mark the start of each new *saeculum*, a period of 110 years. Although Philip the Arab (b. AD 204) had staged millennial games in the city in 248, to celebrate the thousandth anniversary of the city's foundation, there had been no secular games since those under Septimius Severus in 204. The centrepiece of Severus' celebrations had been the triumphal arch completed in 203 to mark his victories over the Parthians, amongst others. Maxentius' ostentatious *romanitas* made the celebration of the games inevitable, and the precedent of the Arch of Severus, the architectural model for the new Arch of Maxentius, would appear to confirm the association between recent victories, planned festivities and construction.

Maxentius had his arch decorated with sculptures taken from earlier monuments. This saved the time and expense of carving new panels, and there may well have been much available to plunder, following the fires of 293 and 306, particularly from the Hadrianic monuments on the Velia. All Maxentius' projects at this site reused second-century materials. Furthermore, Maxentius had the recent example of Diocletian's New Arch, erected just a decade before, which employed reliefs from a Claudian or Antonine structure (now to be seen at the Boboli Gardens in Florence). In the form that it can be seen today, the monument can be considered nothing other than the Arch of Constantine. However, if one posits Maxentius' own inspiration for many of the choices, the arch's overall scheme becomes comprehensible, for many reliefs do not display triumphal imagery, but rather showcase generic imperial qualities. They were chosen to remind Rome's citizens of the city's constant renewal and the centrality of the figure of the emperor to that renewal, for once again an emperor was resident among them. Moreover, the sculptures placed Maxentius in the line of succession from great emperors of the past, notably Trajan, Hadrian and Marcus Aurelius.

The upper register of the arch consists of eight relief panels taken from an existing monument, possibly a triumphal arch, erected in honour of Marcus Aurelius by his son Commodus. In four panels above the lateral archways, either side of the central inscription, on the south face, we see: the appointment of a foreign king, *rex datus*, reflecting the emperor's universal dominion; his *adlocutio*, or speech to the troops, emphasizing concord, *concordia*; the *lustratio* ritual before the military standards, illustrating piety, *pietas*; and the presentation of barbarian prisoners, again beneath the standards, where the emperor might exhibit clemency, *clementia*. On the north face we see: the emperor's *adventus*, the arrival in Rome, representing *felicitas*, and the consequent triumph overseen by Victoria, who flies above with a laurel crown; his *profectio*, the departure on campaign which symbolizes his *virtus*, manly valour; the emperor's distributions and largesse, reinforcing the quality of *liberalitas*, generosity (fig. 33); and finally a second scene depicting the submission of the vanquished, beneath four standards (fig. 33). As the panels are *spolia* – material carved earlier for another purpose and then collected for reuse by Maxentius – one might understand the emphasis on traditional Roman imperial virtues and actions. Maxentius did not wish to become Marcus Aurelius, but rather to highlight the qualities of the great second-century emperor that he shared. That Constantine retained these demonstrates that the scenes also suited his needs, but his appropriation of the arch as a monument to his victories required that the heads be re-cut with his own features. The heads on the figures one sees today were replaced in 1732 during restoration work ordered by Pope Clement XII.

Eight tondi, round sculpted panels, from a Hadrianic monument occupy the arch's middle register, flanking the central archway and surmounting the side archways on the north and south sides of the monument. On the southern face of the arch, the emperor and his comrades gather before an archway, probably a gateway, suggesting that they are just outside the city. To ensure success, in the next panel they sacrifice to Silvanus, god of the woods. They proceed to a bear hunt in panel three, where the mounted emperor is shown with spear raised, ready to strike (fig. 34). On the fourth roundel, the last on the south face, a sacrifice of thanks is offered to Diana, goddess of the hunt (fig. 34). On the arch's north face, the first of four tondi depicts the emperor mounted once again, in the act of running down a boar. Next, a sacrifice to Apollo is the best-preserved image of an imperial figure and his two companions, the second to the right holding the reins of a horse. In the third panel a lion has been killed, and the hunters stand over their trophy. Finally, an emperor appears veiled, sacrificing to Hercules. For Maxentius, the scenes may simply have displayed the prowess and piety of his predecessor, Hadrian, while engaged in the most imperial of pursuits, the wild beast hunt. However, all of these scenes might be interpreted metaphorically, as victories over diverse barbarian peoples represented by the various beasts. This was surely Constantine's preferred interpretation. His re-cut features have survived in at least some of these scenes, as have those of a second imperial figure who appears in five scenes and was once believed to be Licinius. Scholars of this persuasion posited a secondary message: Constantine and Licinius are at peace, and Dyarchy, the rule of two emperors, has supplanted Tetrarchy, the rule of four. This was possible, for the two men were bound to each other from 311. However, the second figure has now been identified as Constantine's father, Constantius Chlorus, and thus the scenes serve to demonstrate the piety of the imperial *gens Flavia*. It is Constantius, not Constantine, who is shown sacrificing. Moreover, only in these sculptures are all the imperial figures shown nimbate, with haloes. This invites the possibility that these heads were re-cut, once again, before Constantine's visit to Rome in 326, for by then he had foresworn participation in sacrifice and was regularly depicted nimbate. We shall return to these themes later.

Four panels from a monument of Trajan, known commonly as the

Great Trajanic Frieze, feature on the inner walls of the central archway and on the eastern and western sides of the uppermost register. In each of the frieze panels Trajan's head has been replaced by Constantine's. On one side of the central passage Trajan as Constantine sits astride his horse in the mêlée of battle, his cloak flying above his left shoulder. As he tramples on one barbarian, his right hand is raised to strike down another. The eagle-bearer is a pace behind him, indicating that he is at the front of the battle line. Only one legionary precedes him. Battle scenes on the eastern and western sides of the arch fill out the action. On the second panel in the central archway, Trajan as Constantine is crowned by Victory and greeted by Virtus, a divine figure representing his 'manly valour' whose features are remarkably similar to those of the goddess Roma.

The separation and largely out-of-sight placement of these four panels, the most elegant and most clearly martial of the reused elements, suggests that they may have been chosen by Constantine and fitted where space allowed between Maxentian elements. One might also suggest that Constantine chose the eight free-standing barbarians, Trajan's Dacian captives, which stand atop each of the arch's columns (fig. 33). The fourth-century elements of the arch that can be ascribed with certainty to Constantine's initiative are: the frieze which depicts his campaign of 312; the inscriptions, still clearly visible on either side of the archway, offering thanks for his ten years as emperor (*votis X*) and prayers that he will reign for twenty (*votis XX*); the arch-spandrels and pedestals; and the dedicatory inscriptions (fig. 35) on both north and south faces that read:

TO EMPEROR FLAVIUS CONSTANTINUS MAXIMUS

FATHER OF THE FATHERLAND, THE SENATE AND ROMAN PEOPLE,

BECAUSE WITH DIVINE INSTIGATION AND THE MIGHT OF HIS INTELLIGENCE,

TOGETHER WITH HIS ARMY HE TOOK REVENGE BY JUST ARMS ON THE TYRANT

AND HIS FOLLOWING AT ONE AND THE SAME TIME,

HAVE DEDICATED THIS ARCH MADE PROUD BY TRIUMPHS

The god is identified in Latin by a singular form: this was the *summus deus*, the greatest god and divine patron working through Constantine's intelligence and the might of his army. It was the theology of victory in action. The identity of this singular god is implied by a sculpted tondo, which depicts Sol on his *quadriga* (four-horsed chariot) rising out of the ocean, and by its pair, which shows the moon descending on a two-horsed chariot, a *biga*. The Luna (Moon) tondo is immediately above the start of the narrative sequence, Constantine's departure from Milan, on the arch's western side, while the Sol tondo surmounts its denouement on the eastern side, Constantine's ceremonial entrance (*adventus*) into Rome (fig. 36). Between these, on the southern face of the arch, are portrayals of the siege of Verona and the Battle of the Milvian Bridge (fig. 34). On the northern face are shown the triumphal celebrations in Rome, with Constantine delivering a speech and distributing largesse. The goddess Victoria is Constantine's constant companion. At the siege of Verona she hovers behind to crown him. At the Milvian Bridge, Constantine's image (now destroyed) was depicted flanked by the goddesses Roma and Victory. As he enters the city of Rome, the reins of the horses pulling Constantine's *quadriga* are held by Victory. Similarly, on the fourth-century arch-spandrels and pedestals, symbols of victory are omnipresent. On the pedestals placed either side of the main archway Victories, trophies and soldiers stand over defeated enemies. In spandrels framing the main archway to both north and south, Victories are depicted carrying trophies. These would all have appeared entirely appropriate to Constantine, representing the Roman theology of victory as he understood it.

A gilded bronze statue of Constantine atop his own *quadriga*, no longer in place, surmounted the arch above the central inscription. It was a further indication of the identity of the singular divinity and his correspondence with Constantine. Even more striking, but until recently overlooked, was the alignment of the arch, placed slightly off the triumphal way (*via triumphalis*), with the colossal statue of Nero now sculpted anew to bear the face of Constantine and the radiate crown of Sol Invictus. The alignment one can attribute to Maxentius, who must have pictured his divinized son appearing framed by this new triumphal arch. With both appropriated by Constantine, the statue would have appeared to the emperor and his processing troops at various points on his triumphal journey to the Forum behind the arch. Initially, its head would have framed his own gilded statue atop the arch. As the emperor moved closer, to around thirty-five metres from the arch, Sol would have been framed by the archway. Drawing still closer, the statue would have become indistinct until Constantine emerged through the archway, when Sol would have appeared to him suddenly, echoing the story of his vision as disseminated in 310.

It has been argued that the predominantly pagan senate was responsible for this monument, and the deities portrayed announced its understanding of Constantine's vision and his divine patron. The dedication is theirs, in the dative, as are the inscriptions above the Trajanic panels in the central passageway, 'to the liberator of the city' and 'to the establisher of peace'. But to insist on a senatorial reading contrary to Constantine's own understanding is to ignore the correspondences between the arch and the range of coinage Constantine produced, which disseminated a clear message: Sol Invictus was the guarantor of Constantine's victory. For five years before the arch was dedicated, Sol had appeared on Constantine's gold, silver and bronze coins and was the central element of Constantinian propaganda directed at all levels of Roman society. Most frequently, Constantine issued coins modelled on those of his claimed forebears Claudius Gothicus and Aurelian, which featured on their reverses an image of Sol Invictus as his 'companion' (*comes*). These coins were dedicated SOLI INVICTO COMITI, 'to the Invincible Sun, preserver of the Augustus'. On coins where Sol is not thus invoked on the reverse, Constantine himself is frequently featured on the obverse wearing a radiate crown – a crown from which project spikes or triangles representing solar rays (fig. 37). In 313 a gold coin struck for Constantine by his mint at Ticinum shows on its obverse the emperor and Sol Invictus together. The bust of Constantine wearing a laurel wreath is superimposed over the bust of Sol, identical but for his radiate crown. Sol's profile is visible behind the emperor's, at his right shoulder as they both face left. The resemblance between the emperor and the god recalls the panegyric of 310, where Constantine is reminded 'You did see the god, and recognized yourself in the likeness of him'. To complete the picture, Constantine holds a shield on which Sol's *quadriga* is shown rising from the ocean. The reverse depicts Constantine's triumphal entry into Rome. The inscription on the obverse hails Constantine as *invictus*. A remarkably similar image was used later on gold medallions minted at Ticinum in 315–16, although on these Constantine held an orb in his left hand, not a shield (fig. 38). Evidently, Constantine resembled his patron god in every way.

Meanwhile: Licinius and Maximinus Daia

In February 313, Constantine and Licinius met in Milan. Two years earlier, confronted with an alliance between Maxentius and Maximinus Daia, Licinius had agreed to marry Constantine's younger half-sister, Constantia. At Milan the wedding was celebrated, and the emperors cemented their agreement by issuing a famous joint letter commanding universal religious toleration, known commonly as the Edict of Milan. Versions of its text have been preserved in both Eusebius' *Ecclesiastical History* and Lactantius' *On the Deaths of the Persecutors*; the latter, the more complete and accurate, begins:

When I, Constantine Augustus, and I, Licinius Augustus, happily met at Milan and had under consideration all matters which concerned the public good and security, we thought that among all the other things that would profit men generally that which merited our first and chief attention was reverence for the divinity. Our purpose is to grant both to the Christians and to all others the freedom to follow whichever religion they might wish; whereby whatsoever divinity dwells in heaven may be appeased and made propitious towards all who have been set under our power.

At the time of the pronouncement Constantine had already eliminated his western rivals, but Licinius had still to deal with his eastern foe, Maximinus Daia. The principal account, completed by Lactantius before 315, is fascinating in portraying Licinius as Constantine's fellow champion. Eusebius, in contrast, would amend his first account of Licinius, preserved in his *Ecclesiastical History*, adding a chapter to its final book (*HE* X.8) to vilify the emperor for his reversal. He would later portray Licinius as the foil to the hero of his *Life of Constantine* and omit mention of his role at Milan (*VC* I.41.3). But for both Eusebius and Lactantius, the greater villain is Maximinus Daia. Already established as worse even than his sponsor Galerius, Maximinus was swept back into the spotlight by resisting Galerius' dying wish that the persecution of Christians be ended. It was against him, then, that the Edict of Milan was directed, and Lactantius reminds us that Licinius' task was to ensure that Maximinus complied.

Having received Galerius' instruction to repeal the persecution in 311, Maximinus Daia had acted cautiously. While Galerius still lived, he moderated his actions. Whereas Constantine and Licinius had set about releasing Christians condemned to the empire's gaols and mines, and restoring property that had been seized from them, Maximinus instructed his subordinates no longer actively to pursue Christians, but to take care not to publicize the edict of toleration. Following Galerius' death, Maximinus was no longer checked, and responded enthusiastically to appeals for a renewed persecution in the vast lands under his control, which stretched from the Asian shore of the Bosphorus to Antioch and beyond. Indeed, it was claimed that he solicited such petitions, including one preserved as an inscription at Arycanda in Lycia, in what is today southern Turkey. This was addressed to him and to Constantine and Licinius:

The gods, your kinsmen, most illustrious emperors, having always shown manifest acts of kindness to all who have their religion earnestly to heart and pray to them for your perpetual health, our invincible lords, we have thought it well to have recourse to your immortal sovereignty and to request that the Christians, who have long been disloyal and still persist in the same mischievous intent, should at last be put down and not be suffered by any absurd novelty to offend against the honour due to the gods.

In the further reaches of his realm, the bishops of Emesa (modern Homs in Syria) and Alexandria were both beheaded, and the Christian scholar Lucian of Antioch was brought to Nicomedia, where Maximinus condemned him to death. Such cruelty came naturally to the morally depraved ruler, Lactantius noted, supplying a long rhetorical diatribe that dwelt on Maximinus' sexual depravities, which prefigure a myth of the high Middle Ages, the *droit de seigneur* (or *droit de cuissage*), the right to deflower local virgins.

As Constantine prepared to meet Maxentius before the walls of Rome, according to Eusebius (*HE* IX.8), Maximinus was making war on the

Armenians, who were 'from a very early date friends and allies of Rome, a Christian people and zealous adherents of the Deity'. In fact, Maximinus was in Syria and nowhere near the Armenians, who converted some years later, under their king Tiridates. By the time Constantine and Licinius convened at Milan, Maximinus was back in Nicomedia, having marched his army west in the depths of winter, leaving the corpses of pack animals along the route. On short rest his troops pressed on to Byzantium, a city on the European shore of the Bosphorus (see map 5). Licinius had left a garrison in Byzantium, which Maximinus attempted first to win over with bribes and then to displace by force. The garrison resisted for eleven days – long enough to send word to Licinius, who hurried east. Maximinus, meanwhile, sailed across the Bosphorus into Europe, meeting resistance from another of Licinius' garrisons at Heraclia in Thrace (ancient Perinthos, modern Marmara Ereğli). As Maximinus' force, numbering 70,000 men, proceeded north-west, Licinius and his army of 30,000 had reached a staging post eighteen miles beyond Adrianople. According to Lactantius, 'As the armies approached each other, it seemed that a battle would shortly take place. Maximinus then made a vow to Jupiter that, if he won the victory, he would obliterate and utterly destroy the Christian name.' Licinius, in turn, on the eve of battle with Maximinus, had a divine vision to rival Constantine's. This he translated into a means to galvanize his troops to battle. In a dream an angel appeared before Licinius and 'told him to rise quickly and pray to the supreme god with all his army; the victory would be his if he did this'. Thoughtfully, the angel provided the words of the prayer:

Supreme God, we beseech you; holy God, we beseech you. We commend all justice to you, we commend our safety to you, we commend our empire to you. Through you we live, through you we emerge victorious and fortunate. Supreme, holy God, hear our prayers, we stretch our arms to you; listen, holy, supreme God.

Lactantius notes further that: 'This [prayer] was written out and distributed to the officers and tribunes, so that they could all teach them to their own troops. Confidence grew among them all with the belief that victory had been announced to them from heaven.' Suitably neutral with regard to which supreme god was being worshipped, the prayer appeared acceptable to all, and the troops intoned it three times on their knees on the field of battle, before engaging and defeating Maximinus' forces.

Such a sympathetic account of Licinius' progress was excised from later accounts. Eusebius, in the revised version of his *Ecclesiastical History* (*HE* IX.10), quite naturally attributed Licinius' victory to the Christian god's favour, but he made no mention of the vision or prayer. It seems most likely that Constantine and Licinius had composed the prayer together, in Milan, and perhaps also contrived the notion that a divine or angelic visitation would be the natural medium for such words to be revealed to an emperor. Thus, the troops of the Dyarchy were obliged to acknowledge a singular highest god, the same god as had brought Constantine to supreme power in the west and would allow Licinius to attain similar authority in the east. But we must beware of following Lactantius and Eusebius uncritically in identifying Licinius' patron god as the Christian divinity, for a contemporary work of art suggests Sol Invictus was still at large.

A cameo in the Cabinet des Médailles in Paris, which is generally believed to portray Licinius celebrating his victory of 313, shows an emperor on a four-horsed chariot or *quadriga* advancing over the bodies of the vanquished, holding a globe in his left hand and a spear in his right (fig. 39). Personifications of the sun and moon present globes, and two Victories flank his chariot, one bearing a *vexillum* (flag standard), the other a *tropaeum* (trophy). Recently the cameo had been re-dated to the later fifth century, but Martin Henig has related it to a second cameo of the early fourth century and highlights similarities between the two. The latter, an agate cameo, depicts a youthful clean-shaven ruler in a style typical of the Tetrarchy, wearing an imperial diadem. He holds in his left hand a sceptre which rests on his shoulder, and in his outstretched right hand a globe. He faces forwards standing in a moving *quadriga*, his cloak (*paludamentum*) billowing behind him and his four horses rearing on their hind legs. The scene closely resembles contemporary portrayals of Sol's chariot, and that association is made certain by the scene depicted on a golden plaque in the Hermitage in St Petersburg, which was manufactured in AD 60–70 to adorn a priest's crown (fig. 40). This shows Nero as Sol astride a *quadriga* drawn by rearing, galloping horses. His cloak billows behind him, to his left, and in his outstretched right hand he holds a staff or wand, perhaps a whip. He wears a radiate crown and stares forwards, above his head a sickle moon and star-shaped sun. Henig has suggested that the agate cameo was produced to mark Licinius's victory over Maximinus. Here, then, we find Licinius portrayed as Constantine's counterpart, his victory over Maximinus equated with the defeat of Maxentius, both attributed publicly to Sol Invictus.

Constantine confronts Licinius

Following his victory at the battle on 30 April 313, Licinius made for Nicomedia. There he repealed Maximinus' persecution and on 13 June had erected for all to see an inscribed version of the letter he and Constantine had formulated in Milan. He instructed that copies of the letter be despatched to all cities and towns in the eastern realm and that they be displayed prominently attached to rulings by local magistrates, so that the will of the emperors would no longer be suppressed. Maximinus, who had fled the battlefield, was pursued to Tarsus, where he committed suicide. Lactantius invented a suitable denouement: the poison Maximinus ingested failed because he was so engorged with food and wine, leaving the man deranged for four days; in that time, he pounded his head so hard against a rock that his eyes popped out, allowing him finally to see the true god. While attesting to his conversion, Lactantius fails to corroborate Eusebius' claim that Maximinus also issued an edict recanting his anti-Christian ordinances. Both stories seem rather unlikely.

Having rejoiced in the painful deaths of the persecutors, both Lactantius and Eusebius recount rather dispassionately that Licinius cleaned house. Statues of Maximinus, like Maxentius branded 'tyrant', were cast down throughout the empire. His wife, his eight-year-old son and his seven-year-old daughter were all put to death at Antioch. So were other potential rivals: Valeria, daughter of Diocletian and Galerius' widow, was murdered; her mother Prisca and her adopted son, Candidianus, met the same fate. Candidianus had been betrothed to Maximinus' young daughter. Severianus, son of the ephemeral Augustus Severus, was executed. Now, only two imperial families remained, that of Licinius and that of Constantine, united through Constantia who, in 315, produced a son, Valerius Licinianus Licinius. Licinius' hopes and claims for his son immediately became an issue between the emperors.

Since his marriage to Fausta in 307, when she was still a child, Constantine had not produced a second son. Initially, one imagines, he did not attempt to consummate the marriage, but by 316 Fausta was perhaps eighteen years old, and it may have appeared that she was barren. Constantine moved, therefore, to ensure the succession of Crispus, his only son (by Minverina), who was by now twelve or thirteen. Still too young properly to play a role in administering the empire, Crispus was to become a Caesar alongside a second man, Bassianus, a Roman senator who was certainly old enough to govern. While Licinius was married to Constantia, one of Constantine's three half-sisters, Bassianus was married to another, Anastasia. This wedding had most likely taken place during Constantine's sojourn in Rome from July to the end of September 315. Bassianus was, therefore, brother-in-law to both Augusti and was to be entrusted with Italy, including Rome.

The status of Italy, and more particularly of Rome, had been a bone of contention between the Augusti. Constantine's acquisition of Rome in 312, and with it the whole of Italy, had violated Licinius' interests. Licinius, the older Augustus, had been named senior ruler of the west at the council of Carnuntum in November 308 and charged with the duty of removing the usurper Maxentius. This formal reconstitution of the second Tetrarchy had recognized Constantine's right only to the title Caesar, but from 310 to 312 he had proceeded to usurp both the title and the role assigned to Licinius, as well as the patron god of the late Galerius, Sol Invictus. Neither of the Augusti resided in Rome: Constantine shuttled between Arles and Trier in Gaul, while Licinius established his court at Sirmium in Pannonia. But both coveted Rome, and the arch erected there by the senate for Constantine was a monumental poke in Licinius' eye. Rome continued to laud Constantine.

On coins minted in Rome in 315 to mark the start of his *decennalia*, Constantine was exalted with the invocation 'To the Happy Victory of the Eternal Prince' (VICTORIAE LAETAE PRINC PERP). One must imagine that this reflects an actual acclamation offered by his troops during the victory celebrations. No coins celebrating Constantine's *decennalia* were minted in lands under Licinius' control, nor are there any surviving inscriptions that mark the occasion. This indicates strongly that relations between the two men had soured considerably since 313. Perhaps Bassianus' promotion was to remove Italy from the purview of either Augustus and so bring them closer together. More likely it was a ploy to disinherit Licinianus, promoting an alternative imperial line which Licinius was sure to reject and providing Constantine with a *casus belli* and the support of Bassianus. But there was an unexpected twist, for in the winter of 315–16 it became apparent that Constantine would have a second child after all. On 7 August 316, in Arles, a son was born whom he named Constantine. One tradition holds that Fausta was not the mother, and this led to rather confused coverage in later sources, notably Zosimus in the sixth century, some two hundred years later. However, Julian the Apostate, Constantine's nephew, who was hostile to his uncle and his sons, would claim that Fausta was mother to three emperors.

What happened early in 316, and indeed immediately after the birth of the young Constantine, is obscured by Constantine the father's later propaganda, but it is clear that Bassianus had ceased to be an asset, becoming instead a threat to the succession of Constantine's offspring. Licinius discerned this, and according to the *Origo Constantini* persuaded Bassianus to do his bidding:

Through the influence of Senicio, Bassianus' brother who was loyal to Licinius, Bassianus took up arms against Constantine. He was seized while still preparing himself, and at Constantine's order was convicted and executed. When Senicio, as the person responsible for the plot, was demanded for punishment, Licinius refused to hand him over, and the peace between them was broken.

Constantine got his *casus belli*, at Bassianus' expense. While we cannot be certain that Licinius did persuade Bassianus to rebel, or indeed that Bassianus even took up arms (for Constantine had invented a similar story to justify his murder of Maximian), there is no indication that Licinius was unhappy with the outcome. He ordered statues of Constantine to be thrown to the ground at Emona (modern Ljubljana in Slovenia), which sat on the frontier between their two realms, and thus declared war.

In October 316 and again in January 317 the armies of the two Augusti met in battle (see map 5). Constantine's forces appear to have won the first encounter at Cibalae (modern Vinkovci), between the rivers Drava and Sava, but the second clash on the Arda plain, south-east of Sardica, was less clear-cut and equally indecisive. The account offered by the *Origo Constantini* seems almost balanced:

Both their armies were taken to the plain of Cibalae. Licinius had 35,000 men, infantry and cavalry; Constantine commanded 20,000 foot and horse. After an indecisive battle, in which 20,000 of Licinius' infantry and part of his armoured cavalry were killed, Licinius escaped under cover of darkness to Sirmium with the greater part of his horse. From there, having collected his wife and son and his treasury, he went to Dacia. He made Valens, commander of the frontier, a Caesar. Then, when a huge force had been gathered by Valens at Adrianople, he sent ambassadors to Constantine, who had established himself at Philippopolis,* to discuss peace. The ambassadors returned frustrated, and having resumed war they fought again on the plain of Arda. After a long and indecisive battle, Licinius' men gave way and fled in the darkness. Licinius and Valens turned away towards Berroea, believing (which was true) that Constantine would pursue them by heading further towards Byzantium. So when Constantine was forging ahead eagerly, he learnt that Licinius was at his rear. Just then, when his soldiers were weary with battle and the forced march, Mestrianus was sent to him as an ambassador to sue for peace, at the request of Licinius who promised henceforth to do as he was told. Valens was commanded to return to his former rank, and when this was done peace was confirmed between the two emperors, and Licinius held the provinces of Oriens, Asia, Thrace, Lesser Moesia and Scythia.

This meant that Constantine had acquired the rest of the Balkan lands west of Thrace, a significant addition to his holdings encompassing the region of his birth, Moesia and Pannonia, and all of Greece. This was a substantial concession and suggests that Licinius' forces were as depleted as the *Origo*'s (exaggerated) figures propose. Zosimus (II.18–19) claims that the fighting was particularly brutal and supplies similarly high figures. A further later source, Peter the Patrician, suggests that Licinius' ruse, turning aside to Berroea rather than heading straight to Byzantium,

---

* Philippi is also offered as a location, for which see map 5. Philippopolis (modern Plovdiv, Bulgaria) appears to make more sense, given where the battle took place.

had allowed him to capture much of Constantine's retinue and baggage train, and this may have forced Constantine's hand, preventing him from pressing a third battle. The demotion of Valens was less of a concession from Licinius, who later saw that he was murdered. Caesars were clearly now expendable, mere pawns in the end game of the Augusti. Unless, that is, they were the sons of the Augusti.

At Sardica on 1 March 317, the peace was sealed by the promotion of the sons of the Augusti, all three at once, to the rank of Caesar. Constantine was recognized unequivocally as senior Augustus and established his new capital at Sardica. He resided there for much of the next seven years, while his sons were sent back to Gaul, Crispus presiding at court in Trier. Licinius withdrew further east, establishing his court at Nicomedia, formerly home to Diocletian, Galerius and, most recently, Maximinus Daia. The emperors continued to mint coins in each other's names, and one finds Licinius portrayed on coins with Constantine's patron Sol on the reverses, and Constantine with Licinius' patron Jupiter. However, neither emperor was satisfied with joint rule, and the battle for supremacy would soon be rejoined. That war, unlike in 316–17, would be pitched as a clash between their patron deities, for by then Constantine was openly a Christian.

21. Detail from the Arch of Galerius, showing the
Tetrarchs sacrificing at an altar on which are depicted
Jupiter and Hercules. (Author)

22. Detail from the Arch of Galerius, showing the
shield-badge of a soldier in a Herculian legion.
(Author)

23. The columns of the Tetrarchs, erected in the Forum in Rome, here shown in relief on the Arch of Constantine in Rome, eastern end of the northern facade. (Author)

24. Constantine's Basilica (Basilika) at Trier, exterior view. The reception hall was shortly afterwards converted into a church. The current structure has been rebuilt. (Author)

25. Woman with pearls, often identified as Helena. Detail from one panel of the ceiling paintings from a site identified as a bed-chamber in the imperial residence at Trier. (R. Schneider/Bischöfliches Dom- und Diözesanmuseum Trier)

26. The Eagle Cameo, also called the Ada Cameo, preserved in Trier's Stadtbibliothek. (Stadtbibliothek Trier MS 22 Ada-Evangeliar)

27. A green glass beaker depicting shield designs, kept in Cologne's Römisch-Germanisches Museum. (Römisch-Germanisches Museum zu Köln)

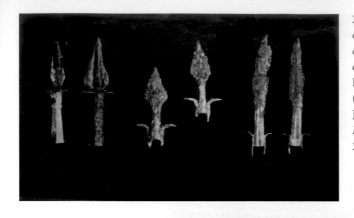

28. The imperial insignia of Maxentius: the tops of ceremonial lances unearthed during excavations on Rome's Palatine Hill. (Reproduced from Jean-Jacques Aillagon, ed., *Roma e i barbari*, Milan 2008)

29. The imperial insignia of Maxentius: glass spheres unearthed during excavations on Rome's Palatine Hill. (Reproduced from Jean-Jacques Aillagon, ed., *Roma e i barbari*, Milan 2008)

30. The Lupa Capitolina, the bronze in Rome's Capitoline Museums of the she-wolf suckling Romulus and Remus, recently identified as a medieval copy. (Author)

31. Parts of a colossal statue of Constantine, now to be found in Rome's Capitoline Museums. (Author)

32. Arch of Constantine, southern facade, Rome. (Author)

33. Upper-register panels from the Arch of Constantine, northern facade, depicting the emperor's distributions and largesse, and the submission of the vanquished beneath four standards. The panels are from the reign of Marcus Aurelius, while the free-standing barbarians to either side are Trajanic. (Author)

34. Two Hadrianic tondi on the Arch of Constantine, southern facade, depicting a bear-hunt, where the mounted emperor is shown with spear raised, and a sacrifice of thanks to Diana, goddess of the hunt. Below is a Constantinian frieze depicting the Battle of the Milvian Bridge. Above is the inscription Sic XX, a prayer for the emperor to reign for twenty years. (Author)

35. Dedicatory inscription on the Arch of Constantine. (Author)

36. The eastern side of the Arch of Constantine. In the centre there is a tondo depicting Sol ascending in a *quadriga* above a relief of Constantine's *adventus* into the city of Rome. (Author)

37. Gold coin showing Constantine wearing a radiate, or solar, crown. (Scala/BPK, Bildagentur für Kunst, Kultur und Geschichte, Berlin)

38. Gold medallion, struck at Ticinum in 315–16, depicting Sol and Constantine jugate. Their features are identical, and almost uniquely they are both facing left. A very similar image was first used on a nine-*solidus* medallion struck at Ticinum in 313.
(The Trustees of the British Museum)

39. Cameo of Licinius, now to be found in the Bibliothèque nationale de France in Paris.
(Bibliothèque nationale, Paris, France/Giraudon/ The Bridgeman Art Library)

40. A golden plaque depicting Nero as Sol, standing upon a *quadriga*, in the Hermitage Museum, St Petersburg.
(The State Hermitage Museum, St Petersburg)

7

Constantine's Conversion

*A Christian education – The setting Sun? – Legislating toleration
– The battle for toleration – Eusebius and the* labarum *–
A common vision?*

The son of monotheists, brought up to venerate a single 'greatest god', Constantine was an ideal candidate to embrace the empire's fastest-growing faith, Christianity. As the sociologist John Lofland observed, upon close scrutiny of the Moonies in the early 1960s, conversion proceeds most easily within groups where potential recruits already have close associations, friends or relatives. Moreover, the process of conversion changes how one conceives of a new faith and its oddness. For example, Lofland witnessed new Moonies changing their opinions and denying that they had ever felt ambivalent about the cult. Having embraced Christianity and lived for a decade among Christian intellectuals, Constantine no longer saw that his choice was strange, still less that it had been a long process. In place of the story of his struggle to identify his god, and to smooth over the contradictions between his past and current views, he told a tale that those who would promote conversion more widely embraced and disseminated. Chief among these was Eusebius, whose view of Constantine's conversion has been accepted ever since. His is the story of the emperor's moment of revelation before the Battle of the Milvian Bridge that has persisted through the centuries.

Observers of the Fourth Rome, the USA, in the first decade of the twenty-first century are familiar with tales of conversion and redemption While politicians in western Europe,* Greece to America's Rome,

---

* Excepting Tony Blair, who confessed that God had guided him to war, but only once he had left public office. The archetypal 'candidate' is George W. Bush, whose redemption is held to have taken place at a moment in 1986, but also from the time of his marriage in 1977; and yet it is clear that his problems had not been entirely resolved by 1991, when he attended a state dinner for Queen Elizabeth

have done their best to conceal any religious convictions they might nurture, aspirants to executive office in the United States have embraced theirs and expounded them publicly, clamorously, juxtaposing middle-aged sobriety with admissions of youthful indiscretions. For the powerful, conversion is Pauline: a moment of revelation rather than decades of gradual refinement. Revelation is decisive, for the powerful must make decisions quickly and with conviction. It reveals an intimate relationship between the candidate and a higher power, the *summus deus*, whose hand might then be seen to guide him or her to powerful office, and who will remain a source of strength and inspiration, directly and regularly.

But conversion is never a momentary phenomenon; it is only held to have been upon reflection and with hindsight. Revelatory conversion has been recast by sociologists as the 'peripety paradigm'. A term employed by dramatists and those who study modes of composition, peripety is a moment of sudden change, which one expects in literature and in the retelling of a life. For Constantine's conversion, in the account related by Eusebius, was the emperor's own tale presented in terms that Eusebius, as a churchman of the early fourth century, understood. He was sure to equate the road to the Milvian Bridge with the road to Damascus. If Eusebius realized that conversion was a life-long process which brought one closer to divinity, he may have equated it with monasticism, the phenomenon intended to facilitate and perfect that process, which emerged in the deserts of North Africa during Eusebius' lifetime. The life of the first monastic hero, Antony (d. AD 356), was composed after Eusebius' death. As a fourth-century work of spiritual biography, it may be compared to Eusebius' *Life of Constantine*. But Constantine was no

---

11 hosted by his father, President George H. W. Bush. A stump speech delivered in June 2007 by Barack Obama, then a Democratic party candidate in the 2008 presidential election, is also paradigmatic: 'One Sunday, I put on one of the few clean jackets I had, and went over to the Trinity United Church of Christ on 95th Street on the South Side of Chicago. And I heard Reverend Jeremiah A. Wright deliver a sermon entitled 'The Audacity of Hope' [which is also the title of Obama's second book]. And during the course of that sermon, he introduced me to someone called Jesus Christ. I learned that my sins could be redeemed. I learned that those things I was too weak to accomplish myself, he would accomplish with me if I placed my trust in him. And *in time* [my italics], I came to see faith as more than a comfort to the weary or a hedge against death, but rather as an active, palpable agent in the world and in my own life.' Obama's story is the more convincing for containing no dates.

ascetic hero. He was mired in the business of mundane power, and his conversion saw the victory of the Christian Church over its persecutors. That victory was fragile and incomplete at his death, despite the efforts he made through the last two decades of his life.

A Christian education

As early as 312, Constantine may have recognized the god of the Christians as a manifestation of the greatest god, the *summus deus*. Christians saw in this recognition an end to their recent persecution. But was Constantine at that point a Christian? Had he been converted by the events of 312? These questions cannot be answered, for they are framed incorrectly. Constantine's actions after 312 reveal a man with sympathy and concern for the Christians in his empire. Like his father, he forbade persecution of Christians throughout his lands, even when Tetrarchic colleagues pursued adherents of the faith most fiercely. Nor was Constantine's concern simply to end violence between different religious communities. Letters written soon after the Battle of the Milvian Bridge demonstrate the emperor's desire to end factionalism *within* the Christian community, lest this bring down divine wrath upon the emperor. The sentiment is as authentic as the letters, for it reflects Constantine's conception of the *summus deus* as a grantor of victory, which might be rescinded as surely as it was given. Constantine's concern for Christians was founded in a practical desire to ensure divine favour for his own enterprises, and this facilitated the emperor's conversion from veneration of a *summus deus* that he portrayed in the traditional iconography of Sun worshippers, to his public recognition of the god of the Christians as the true 'greatest god'. This process took the course that it did because Christians had been freed from persecution by his victories, and consequently some of the most eloquent and persuasive were drawn to Constantine's court.

The most notable scholar to join Constantine at Trier, and according to a compelling recent study by Elizabeth DePalma Digeser, perhaps the architect of the emperor's developing religious policy, was Lactantius. According to Digeser, Lactantius, whose writings we have already consulted frequently, was at Constantine's court at Trier as early as 310. At that time he was appointed tutor to Constantine's son Crispus, responsible for instructing the young prince, then aged six or seven, in Latin literature. (Digeser quite rightly observes that those who suggest Lactantius arrived at Trier only in 317 must explain why Crispus, almost a grown man in charge of Gaul, would then still require a basic education.) It was at Constantine's court, therefore, and not in Nicomedia under Galerius and Licinius, that Lactantius wrote his tract *On the Deaths of the Persecutors*, the earliest apologetic for violence committed in the Christian cause. Lactantius saw Constantine as his god's tool for punishing those who had so recently persecuted his co-religionists, and will have read aloud each chapter to the emperor as he completed it. The emperor will also have been among the first to hear Lactantius' greater work, the *Divine Institutes*, which was composed in its first form between 305 and 310.

The *Divine Institutes* were begun in Nicomedia, as a response to the musings of those philosophers who had justified the Great Persecution, notably Porphyry and Hierocles (see *DI* 5.2.1). Monotheism was, Lactantius held, Rome's original religion, and the idea of many gods was introduced in error. He attacks the folly of the philosophers who have failed to see the truth: that religion and wisdom are inseparable, and that only through Christianity is true wisdom attainable. Only those who reject the many gods for the one may be wise and just. Whereas Porphyry had advocated repression of those who would not participate in established rituals, Lactantius exposes such false rites as the veneration of dead men and demons. And in a digression in the fifth book of seven in the *Divine Institutes*, Lactantius presents, according to its recent translators (Bowen and Garnsey, p. 46), 'a plea for religious freedom [that is] the most elaborate and eloquent of its kind surviving from antiquity'. Its central message is that forbearance, not persecution, is the path to universal justice and to the re-establishment of Rome's ancient constitution.

Monotheism was, in Lactantius' formulation, superior to polytheism, and Constantine, long a monotheist, although not yet fully a Christian, was on the path to restoring truth and justice to Rome. Thus in 313–14 Lactantius retouched his work and dedicated it to the emperor with these words:

All fictions have now been laid to rest, most holy emperor, ever since God most high raised you up to restore the abode of justice and to protect the human race. Now that you are the ruler of the world of Rome we worshippers of God are no longer treated as criminals and villains . . . Nobody now flings the name of God at us in reproach, nobody any longer calls us irreligious . . . The providence of the most high godhead has promoted you to supreme power so that you may in the truth of your piety rescind the wicked decrees of others, correct error, provide for the safety of men in your paternal kindness, and finally remove from public life such evil men as God has ousted with his divine power and has put into your hands, so that all men should be clear on what comprises true majesty . . . They are paying, and have paid, the penalty for their wickedness; you are protected from all dangers by the powerful right hand of God . . . because you were the only one to demonstrate special qualities of virtue (*virtus*) and piety . . .

Lactantius' works had a profound effect upon Constantine. As Digeser has shown, the *Divine Institutes* swiftly became a source of language and ideas for the emperor, which he employed in his letters and orations. A telling insight into Constantine's Christian education, and into the influence of Lactantius, is offered by the emperor's own *Oration to the Saints*, a sermon that he delivered on a Good Friday of uncertain date. Its most recent translator assigns the sermon to the year 315 and suggests it was delivered to the citizens of Rome, but most others have favoured a later date, including 321, 324, 325 and 328. Whatever the exact date, and we shall return to this later, the oration was delivered when Constantine had progressed considerably with his Christian education, for it greatly resembled Lactantius' *Divine Institutes* in thought and terminology. The philosophical content of the emperor's sermon owed much also to a commentary on Plato's *Timaeus* which its author, Calcidius, had dedicated to Constantine's closest Christian adviser besides Lactantius, Ossius of Cordoba. Many attempts have been made to attribute the oration to Ossius or to Lactantius, rather than to the emperor himself. But this is a fruitless exercise, akin to arguing that modern statesmen do not compose their own speeches. The themes of the sermon, and the terms in which they were expressed, were the emperor's own, and these he had embraced by 315 and continued to refine over the following decade. Constantine concludes (*Oration* 26) with a telling observation: that the citizens of Rome have witnessed the triumph of the Christian god, still the grantor of victory, through Constantine, but they must continue to pray publicly and privately for his success:

They indeed have witnessed the battles and observed the war in which God's providence awarded victory to the people, and have seen God co-operating with our prayers. For righteous prayer is an invincible thing, and no-one who pays holy adoration is disappointed of his aim ... Those who pursue piety should confess their gratitude to the Saviour of all for our salvation and the good state of public affairs, and petition Christ for one another with holy prayers and litanies, that he may continue to benefit us. For he is an unconquerable ally and defender of the righteous, he himself is the best judge, the guide to immortality, the bestower of eternal life.

The setting Sun?

A third, short work by Lactantius, *On God's Anger*, written after both the *Divine Institutes* and *On the Deaths of the Persecutors*, describes the path that the convert to Christianity must take: the convert would understand and reject false religions; then he would perceive clearly the singular, greatest god; and third, he would recognize Jesus Christ as 'His Servant and Messenger Whom He sent to earth'. Constantine's Christian education led him along this path, providing an intellectual framework for his intuitions and shaping his policy. He advocated not the performance of state-mandated rituals, but rather the efficacy of prayer to the single 'greatest god'.

For the broadest audience Constantine had projected his devotion to the Sun god using the established language of late Roman imperial art. There were advantages in such a policy, where such an association advanced dynastic claims to sole rule. Sol had been the patron of Constantine's chosen forebear, Claudius Gothicus, and had dominated the imperial iconography of the sole emperors who had preceded the Tetrarchs, notably Aurelian and Probus (AD 276–82). Moreover, Sol was well established in the canon of appropriate symbols for the representation of the 'greatest god'. But Constantine also knew that to Christians

Christ was the true Sun, and his use of Sol sent a message about his divine patron that was acceptable to all; or rather, to all but Constantine himself, as his personal beliefs changed and his hold on power became ever firmer.

If Sol was Constantine's public patron, preserver and companion until 317, he was not the god Constantine now worshipped in private. Constantine had long given broad hints that his personal devotion was to the god whose symbol he sported, the chi-rho, which bore no association with Sol. Eusebius, in a passage of his *Life of Constantine* quoted in full below, claimed that Constantine had the chi-rho, his sign of victory, displayed on his helmet. The chi-rho does indeed feature prominently on the crest of the emperor's helmet on a silver medallion struck in Ticinum, probably in 315. The medallion was struck to mark Constantine's *decennalia*, for distribution among his more eminent followers, most likely army officers. The helmet itself is of a new type, with a high crest and cross bar, bedecked with jewels. It appears to have featured on bronze coins for the first time slightly earlier than on the silver medallions, and some of the coins show the chi-rho on the side rather than the crest of the helmet. The coins have always been controversial, and so it is of immense significance that a version of the very Christogram seen mounted on Constantine's helmet has very recently been discovered in the Netherlands. The location suggests strongly that it could not have belonged to Constantine himself, and one cannot be certain that it dates as early as his reign. It is most likely from the later fourth or early fifth century. But it is clear that the symbolism Constantine sought to propagate after the Milvian Bridge was later adopted on the arms and armour of his overtly Christian successors.

As Constantine began publicly to recognize Christ, so Sol gradually disappeared from his coins, first from his large issues in bronze, which followed fairly soon after the promotion on 1 March 317 of the new Caesars to the imperial college. Sol appeared only intermittently on gold issues, notably from mints at Ticinum in 320–1, Sirmium in 320–3 and Antioch in 325. Radiate crown obverses are limited to the junior emperors after 317–18 and disappear altogether after 324–6. The disappearance of Sol, therefore, was as gradual as Constantine's conversion, becoming absolute only in his last decade. Before then his agenda was to promote not Christianity but toleration.

Legislating toleration

All types of monotheists, the emperor included, prayed to the same 'greatest god', and this Constantine acknowledged when writing to Christians, whose priests he determined to afford the same privileges as those in other cults. This is clear in laws he issued, some of which have been preserved in two later Roman law compilations, the Theodosian Code (abbreviated below *CTh*) and the Justinianic Code. More than 300 entries in these codes are laws attributed to Constantine, all dating after 312, and three-quarters of those from before 324. The earliest, dating to 313 (*CTh* 16.2.1–2), exempt Christian clergy from compulsory public services so that they, like the priests of other religions, might devote their energies solely to the propagation of faith and to prayer. An important point to note in addressing these early laws is that they did not promote a peculiarly Christian agenda. Rather, they promoted particular Christians, clerics, who might then protect the interests of their communities. The rights of Christians were henceforth to be protected like those of other citizens, by powerful patrons who might interpret both existing law and new laws. Constantine legislated not Christianity but toleration. It was decreed that, pursuant to the edict of toleration issued from Milan in 313, bishops were to have the right to hear legal cases. Consequently, Christians would no longer be obliged to have their cases heard by those who had until recently enforced the persecution of their communities. In 318 it was determined that any Christian who so desired might have his case heard not by the civil judge, before whom it may have been instituted, but by an episcopal court (*CTh* 16.2.1). One might observe in this ruling a desire to protect those who were vulnerable to the whims of the powerful, and the jurisdiction of bishops was reiterated in 319, in response to a particular appeal to authority, in a decree addressed not generally but to Octavianus, an official in Lucania and Bruttium (modern Calabria) (*CTh* 16.2.2); and again in 321, in a decree to Bishop Ossius, Constantine's close associate, which permitted bishops the right, accorded to other magistrates, to manumit slaves in their churches (*CTh* 4.7.1).

It has often been written that laws introduced in 320, aimed at regulating marriage and celibacy, present clear evidence of a Christian legislative agenda. Certainly, Constantine was the first emperor to rescind aspects of the *lex Papia Poppaea*, enacted in AD 9 to further Augustus' moral agenda and to promote procreation among legally married couples. Constantine annulled penalties for childlessness and celibacy, so that celibates might 'live as though numbered among married men and supported by the bonds of matrimony' (*CTh* 8.16.1). But those penalties had not been particularly severe and must only very rarely have been applied. For example, a celibate might, after April 320, inherit property from those who were more distantly related to him or her than the sixth degree. Moreover, where a person was already married, then the existing law continued to apply. A married couple that was childless, Christian or not, did not benefit from Constantine's new law. Nonetheless, the law was praised by Eusebius (*VC* 4.26) and others who would promote celibacy as a boon to Christians, as was the measure to ban facial branding and tattooing (*CTh* 9.40.2):

If any person should be condemned to the arena or to the mines, in accordance with the nature of the crime in which he has been detected, he shall not be branded on his face, since the penalty of condemnation can be branded by one and the same mark on his hands and on the calves of his legs, so that the face, which has been made in the likeness of celestial beauty, may not be disfigured.

Those made in the likeness of celestial beauty would still face death as a gladiator or subterranean slave-labourer. A law banning crucifixion as a method of capital punishment has not survived, and we know that a pretender who set himself up as ruler of Cyprus in the 330s was crucified (see below, p. 249).

Constantine's legislation that may have been most clearly informed by his developing faith was devoted to children. Celibates enjoyed new rights, but those who married still did so to have children. A law of 315, attributed to both Constantine and Licinius, offered food and clothing to those in Italy who declared that they were too poor to raise their children (*CTh* 11.27.1), as did a second of 322 in Constantine's name, addressed to those who were tempted to sell their children (*CTh* 11.27.2). The laws' intention was to discourage the exposure or sale of infants, but it did not go so far as to ban such practices. Similarly, whoever had collected and raised an abandoned child with the consent of its father 'shall have the right to keep the said child . . . as his child or as a slave, whichever he should prefer' (*CTh* 5.9.1). This second provision was enacted in 331, some years after Constantine had engineered the death of his own child, no longer an infant.

A law of 323 on lustral (purificatory) sacrifices is of peculiar interest, for it suggests that those who were charged now with protecting Christians, their priests, were not themselves always safe from persecution (*CTh* 16.2.5). On 25 December 323 – the significance of the date will become still clearer – it was determined that Christian clerics were to be exempted from participation in traditional rites of purification. The decree is not a general ban on sacrifice, but rather is couched as a means to punish those who would persist in forcing clerics and others to participate in state *religio*. Under persecuting emperors sacrifice had been the litmus test of loyalty to the state, and it was compulsory participation, enforced by local magistrates, against which Constantine legislated. This was surely directed at those within Licinius' lands, and to these we shall turn shortly. Constantine enacted no ban on sacrifice, for this would have contradicted his mandate of toleration. Clearly, however, he wished to discourage sacrifice and to promote the power of prayer. He appears to have abstained from participation in blood sacrifice, and legislated against those who used magic. However, he ordered no general destruction of temples. Those three temples that we know to have been destroyed were remarkable. One stood on the site of Mamre, where tradition held that God had appeared to Abraham at an oak tree (or terebinth); a church would be placed there. A second temple had been at Aphaca in Phoenicia, a site dedicated to Aphrodite (Venus) where homosexual intercourse and ritualized prostitution were encouraged; the destruction of this temple can best be understood in the context of Constantine's moralizing legislation. A third temple was dedicated to Asclepius and, more problematically, to Apollonius of Tyana, a rival to Christ; this last was probably destroyed by angry

Christians without official sanction in the aftermath of Constantine's victory of 324. Eusebius was well informed on the church at Mamre, for he was one of the Palestinian bishops to receive a letter from the emperor ordering its construction. He exaggerates, however, when he proceeds to describe the 'destruction of idol temples and images everywhere' (*VC* 3.52–6). Libanius, a pagan, later observed with profound regret but accurately that temples survived but were starved of wealth. In 321 it was decreed that Christians might leave their property to the Church, and this they did in abundance (*CTh* 16.2.4).

The battle for toleration

In 313 Licinius had agreed with Constantine to follow the same policy of universal religious toleration, and for the most part he had done so. After the end of hostilities in 317, Licinius had recognized Constantine as senior Augustus and their pact held for some years, as is demonstrated by the emperors' mutual recognition of consuls. The honorary office of consul was rotated between combinations of Augusti and Caesars: in 318, Licinius and Crispus were consuls; in 319, Constantine and Licinianus; in 320, Constantine and Constantine II; and in the first months of 321, Licinius and Licinianus. Throughout this period, Licinius and his son maintained their devotion to Sol Invictus as a manifestation of the 'greatest god' that was acceptable to all. From an army camp at Salsovia an inscription has survived revealing that the emperors Licinius Augustus and Licinius Caesar (i.e. Licinianus) commanded that a statue of Sol be consecrated each year on the *dies Solis*, the 'Day of the Sun', which was 25 December. This was a parallel measure to the dedication of a new altar to Jupiter each January, as prescribed in the army *feriale* (religious calendar). However, Licinius did not agree that prayer was more powerful than correct ritual observance, and he renewed efforts to promote official *religio*. Jupiter reappeared on his coins as a divine protector and companion, coinciding with Sol's last major outing on Constantine's coins, and this heralded a second, decisive rupture between the two emperors. In 320 the obverses (fronts) of Constantine's gold coins had the familiar invocative inscriptions SOLI INVICTO COMITI, while Licinius favoured IOVI CONSERVATORI ('To Jupiter preserver [of Licinius])'. On the reverses the imperial rivals are portrayed being crowned by their rival gods.

Shortly afterwards, if we believe Constantine's propaganda, Licinius repudiated Constantine's demands for universal religious freedom and, proceeding in familiar fashion, began to expel Christians from his palace. In his *Life of Constantine*, Eusebius offers a series of additional vignettes that attest to the threat of renewed persecution: women and men were forbidden to worship together, and women were banned from receiving instruction from (male) priests or bishops; bishops were to stay in their own cities and were forbidden to gather for synods; the tax privileges and exemptions that Christian clergy had been granted were revoked. Most strikingly, in his *Proof of the Gospel*, a work completed between 320 and 324, Eusebius observed that magistrates once again were seen to punish those who believed in Christ and consequently refused to sacrifice. Licinius is shown to be following the path set by Diocletian, and Christians in his lands are alleged to have appealed for Constantine's intervention. This account seems highly suspect, offering a compelling justification for Constantine's decision to launch an offensive war against his colleague. If conditions were deteriorating for Christians, and it is by no means certain that they were, there were no new Christian martyrs made in Licinius' lands, as there were in Constantine's, who was at that time seeking to bring a Christian sect in North Africa into line (we shall return to this below; see p. 263).

On 25 December 323, the 'Day of the Sun' but also the day Constantine now identified as the *dies natalis* of Christ, he issued his law exempting all Christians from participation in lustral rites throughout the empire. 'Soon after that,' according to the *Origo*, 'war broke out again between Licinius and Constantine.' Constantine prepared for war at Salonica, which he had annexed from Licinius in 317. Formerly the capital of Galerius, it had an imperial residence and hippodrome for Constantine's immediate use. It also offered a splendid natural harbour, which Constantine augmented and where he constructed his fleet. The assault was to be by land and sea, for Licinius was now based on the Sea of Marmara, shuttling between Nicomedia and the city of Byzantium. While based at Salonica, Constantine dealt with an invasion across the Danube in spring 323 by an army of Sarmatians, led by one Rausimodus, who plundered Moesia and Thrace, taking many captives. Perhaps this was opportunism: Rausimodus may have known of the breach between the Augusti. Or perhaps Rausimodus had been made aware of the breach by Licinius' agents and encouraged to raid Constantine's territory. When Constantine marched to repel the invasion, he swiftly met and crushed the Sarmatians in battle at Campona in Pannonia. Rausimodus retreated back across the Danube, perhaps imagining that Constantine would return to Salonica. This was not the case, as Zosimus later related (II. 21):

When Constantine heard of this he set off in pursuit and crossed the Danube himself. As the barbarians were fleeing towards a thickly wooded hill he attacked them and killed many of them, including Rausimodus himself. He took many prisoners, accepted the surrender of the multitude of those remaining, and returned to his quarters with a throng of captives. After distributing these among many cities, he came to Salonica . . . where up to two hundred triremes were built, and more than two thousand transports, and where one hundred and twenty thousand infantry and ten thousand each of sailors and cavalry were assembled.

To mark his Sarmatian victory, Constantine took the title Sarmaticus Maximus and issued coins announcing SARMATIA DEVICTA, 'Sarmatia has been conquered'. Such coins were struck at Trier, Arles, Lyons and Sirmium, all mints under Constantine's control. None were struck by Licinius, who instead melted some down as a public statement, and asserted that in repelling the Sarmatians, Constantine had violated the border between their lands in Thrace. Licinius sent orders across the eastern Mediterranean that warships be sent to the Hellespont. By Zosimus' account, he assembled 350 triremes, as well as 150,000 infantry and 15,000 cavalry.

The climactic war between the two emperors took place in summer 324. In Constantine's lands the usual calumnies were spread in preparation: Licinius, like Maxentius and Maximinus Daia before him, was a tyrant; he wallowed in avarice, cruelty and lust, murdering rich men and seducing their wives; like them, too, he was a persecutor and deserving of divine punishment. Unlike on those earlier occasions, however, it was made clear that the divinity to issue that punishment, through his chosen vehicle Constantine, was the god worshipped by the emperor and his fellow Christians. The first engagement took place on 3–4 July 324, between Constantine's land troops and those Licinius had assembled at Adrianople in Thrace, his westernmost staging post. Zosimus offers an elaborate ruse as an explanation for Constantine's success, involving immense personal bravery from the emperor. Sending a large force up into the wooded hills above the river Hebrus, Constantine feigned an attack across the river, personally leading only twelve men. That this went unmentioned by anyone else leads one to favour the simpler explanation in the *Origo*, that 'Constantine was victorious due to the discipline of his troops in battle, although they had difficulty with the heights, and his own good fortune (*felicitas*).' Still, the mention of the heights, and the further information that Constantine was injured in the thigh, leave open the possibility that Zosimus has merely exaggerated, not invented, the emperor's role. He almost certainly exaggerated the figure for Licinius' losses: 34,000 men.

Licinius' remaining land forces withdrew in confusion towards Byzantium, while a second engagement took place at sea, in the narrow straits of the Hellespont (see map 6). Off the coast of Callipolis (modern Gallipoli), Constantine's ships commanded by his first son Crispus met those under Licinius' admiral Amandus (whom Zosimus calls Abantus). The narrowness of the strait persuaded Crispus to send forward only eighty ships, and in response, sensing a chance to surround and crush his enemy, Amandus sailed forth with two hundred. But with no room to manoeuvre, Amandus' triremes proved to be easy targets for Crispus. Many were wrecked, and the crews of others leapt overboard abandoning their vessels. On the following day, as the fleets re-engaged, Crispus sensed the favour of his father's patron. The prevailing wind changed from a steady northerly to a violent southerly, driving many of Licinius' ships against the Asian shore and others onto rocks. According to Zosimus, one hundred and twenty triremes were lost, and five thousand men, many being infantrymen who had retreated from Adrianople and were being ferried across the strait. This left Amandus only four ships with which to effect his own disgraceful flight. Licinius and his remaining troops shut themselves up in Byzantium, to face Constantine's siege. However, as Constantine's men raised a mound against the walls and rolled forward their siege engines, Licinius withdrew, sailing to Chalcedon (modern Kadıköy, an Asian suburb of Istanbul). There he secured the support of an army of Goths, led by one Alica, which joined his line. Despite his failure to hold Byzantium and his lost ships, the advantage was once again with the older Augustus.

Licinius arrayed his forces on the hills above Chalcedon and sent the captain of his court guard, Martinianus, to nearby Lampsakos to prevent Crispus' ships from ferrying Constantine's army across (Lampsakos, modern Lapseki, faces Callipolis at the narrowest stretch of the Dardanelles). To induce Martinianus to remain loyal, Licinius promoted him to the rank of Caesar, just as he had his expendable subordinate Valens in 316. Constantine avoided the trap by leaving his transport ships at Callipolis and swiftly building new skiffs and barges (or requisitioning those anchored nearby), which he sailed across the Hellespont at the mouth of the Black Sea to Hieron, the 'Sacred Promontory', two hundred Roman stades (approximately twenty-three miles) north of Chalcedon. Zosimus (II. 26) relates:

There he [Constantine] landed his army and went up to some hills from which he extended his battle line. Licinius saw that Bithynia was now in enemy hands, yet having been thoroughly tested in all dangers he recalled Martinianus from Lampsakos and encouraged his men by promising them solemnly that he would command them himself. He then drew up his army and advanced from Chalcedon to meet the waiting enemy. A sharp battle took place between Chalcedon and Hieron, which Constantine won convincingly, for he attacked the enemy vigorously and effected such carnage that barely thirty thousand escaped. And as soon as this was known to the inhabitants of the city of Byzantium, they threw open their gates to welcome Constantine, and the Chalcedonians did the same.

Licinius withdrew from the battlefield to Nicomedia with his remaining forces: those not killed in the several encounters, or taken captive, or who had not fled or deserted. Although Constantine proceeded to set a siege, the war had by now been won, at Chrysopolis, between Chalcedon and Hieron, on 18 September 324. Having too few men to resist, Licinius surrendered. He sent his wife, Constantine's half-sister Constantia, to beg for his life, and when that was granted he came in person to relinquish his purple cloak. Showing his usual ruthlessness, Constantine sent Licinius as a private citizen to Salonica and there had him murdered in the spring of 325. Loose ends were of course tied up. Martinianus was tracked down and killed in Cappadocia. Licinianus, Licinius' ten-year-old son with Constantia, was treated with remarkable clemency, for a short while. He was relieved of his imperial style and permitted to live, but only until 326, when he too was put to death. Constantia alone was allowed to live, and she died a Christian some years later, probably in 330.

Eusebius and the *labarum*

To mark his victory in a war he had fought, according to his propaganda, to restore toleration, Constantine issued a statement to his newest subjects, which has been preserved by Eusebius (*VC* II.56):

My own desire, for the common good of the world and the advantage of all mankind, is that your people should enjoy a life of peace and undisturbed concord. Let those, therefore, who still delight in error, be made welcome to the same degree of peace and tranquillity that is enjoyed by those who believe. For it may be that this restoration of equal privileges to all will prevail to lead them onto the straight path. Let no one molest another, but let everyone do as his soul desires. Only let men of sound judgment be assured of this, that those only can live a life of holiness and purity, whom you call to a reliance on your holy laws. With regard to those who will hold themselves aloof from us, let them have, if they please, their temples of lies: *we* have the glorious edifice of your truth, which you have given us as our native home. We pray, however, that they too may receive the same blessing, and thus experience that heartfelt joy which unity of sentiment inspires.

While recognizing the importance of this ultimate victory, Eusebius evinced little interest in the manner by which Constantine defeated Licinius. In the *Life of Constantine*, the entire campaign is presented as a mere pendant to the account of the victory at the Milvian Bridge a dozen years before. In place of Maxentius, Licinius is now referred to as 'Godhater' and, of course, 'tyrant'.

Thus one side advanced confident in the great throng of gods and with a large military force, protected by shapes of dead people in lifeless images. The other, meanwhile, girt with the armour of true religion, set up against the multitude of his enemies the saving and life-giving sign as a scarer and repellant of evils. For a while he exercised restraint . . . but when he saw his opponents persisting, already with sword in hand, the emperor became enraged and with one blow put to flight the whole opposing force, and won victories over enemies and demons alike.

The 'life-giving sign' Eusebius had introduced earlier, in describing the emperor's victory over Maxentius. It is, by his telling, the very sign that Constantine had observed. Eusebius states that his insights are guaranteed by his claim to special knowledge through his personal contacts with the emperor (*VC* I.28; II.8), but he met the emperor on just a few occasions, and largely observed him from Palestine, a great distance from the court at Constantinople. Moreover, Eusebius' purpose in composing the *Life* was didactic, so while historical detail had a role to play in his work, it was far from paramount. Rather, the *Life of Constantine* presents a distinctive vision of Constantine, drawing on various literary forms, especially imperial panegyric, and inventing aspects which were to become common in hagiography, written accounts of saints' lives. It is in this light that we must understand his reworked description of the vision of 312, and the subsequent fashioning of the imperial standard known as the *labarum*.

It is only now, therefore, a dozen years after the event it purports to describe, that we may turn to Eusebius' account of Constantine's vision (*VC* I.28–32):

About the time of the midday sun, when the day was just turning, [Constantine] said he saw with his own eyes, up in the sky and resting over the sun, a cross-shaped trophy formed from light, and a text attached to it which said, 'By this conquer'. Amazement at this spectacle seized him and the whole company of soldiers* that was then accompanying him on a campaign he was conducting somewhere, and witnessed the miracle. He was, he said, wondering to himself what the manifestation might mean; then, while he meditated, and thought long and hard, night overtook him. Thereupon, as he slept, the Christ of God

* We shall return to this statement below.

appeared to him with the sign which had appeared in the sky, and urged him to make a copy of the sign which had appeared in the sky, and to use this as protection against the attacks of the enemy. When the day came he arose and recounted the mysterious communication to his friends. Then he summoned goldsmiths and jewellers, sat down among them, and explained the shape of the sign, and gave them instructions about copying it in gold and precious stones . . . [They produced] a tall pole plated with gold that had a transverse bar forming the shape of a cross. Up at the extreme top a wreath woven of precious stones and gold had been fastened. On it two letters, intimating by its first characters the name 'Christ', formed the monogram of the Saviour's title, rho being intersected in the middle by chi. These letters the emperor also used to wear on his helmet in later times. From the transverse bar, which was bisected by the pole, hung suspended a cloth, and imperial tapestry covered with a pattern of precious stones fastened together, which glittered with shafts of light, and interwoven with much gold, producing an impression of indescribable beauty on those who saw it. This banner then . . . carried the golden head-and-shoulders portrait of the God-beloved emperor, and likewise of his sons. This saving sign was always used by the emperor for protection against every opposing and hostile force, and he commanded replicas of it to lead all his armies.

In this account of Constantine's vision, his subsequent dream, and the manufacture of the *labarum*, Eusebius collapses the developments of a decade or more into one episode, presenting a careful description of the device he can only have seen after 325. In this he emulates Constantine himself who, at the time he first met Eusebius in 325, saw his conversion not as a process over a decade, but rather as a moment of revelation on which he acted decisively. Eusebius displays no interest in the historical context of the vision, referring vaguely to 'a campaign he was conducting somewhere', nor does he express surprise that 'goldsmiths and jewellers' would be readily at hand among Constantine's small expeditionary force. In fact, he realizes that they were not, concluding that 'That was, however, somewhat later'. First, stunned by his vision, Constantine summoned experts to explain the sign to him, who said that 'the god was the Only-begotten Son of the one and only God, and the sign which appeared was a token of immortality, and was an abiding trophy of victory over death'. It is striking that the sign of the cross is described as a trophy, in Greek *tropaion* or Latin *tropaeum*, the term for the cruciform symbol of victory that was erected by Roman armies. Eusebius equates the Roman trophy with another Roman innovation, the crucifix. Once an instrument of torture, the crucifix had become for the Christians a symbol of Christ's victory over death. Eusebius now performed a further translation, imbuing another Roman symbol, the trophy, with a specifically Christian meaning. Eusebius claims that for Constantine his cruciform trophy was from the outset a manifestation of his conversion, a novelty of the highest order. But was it such an innovation?

The first certain depiction of the *labarum* can be dated quite precisely, for it is to be found with the caption SPES PUBLIC ('the hope of the people') on the reverse of an extremely rare bronze *follis* (coin) minted in Constantinople in 327 (fig. 41). Here, a staff is topped with the chi-rho, beneath which hangs a banner displaying three disks. The description offered by Eusebius identifies these as portraits of the Augustus and Caesars, and the presence of three disks/busts on the coin would be accurate in 327. The point at the base of the staff pierces a serpent, evidently intended to represent Licinius, but also perhaps an allusion to 'a dragon and a crooked serpent in the books of the prophets of God' (Isaiah 27:1). The coin design is a development of a far more common bronze type struck at Ticinum in 319–20, showing a *vexillum*, a military flag standard, planted between two bound captives, with the inscription VIRTUS EXERCIT ('the Valour of the Army'). The banner hanging from the *vexillum* offers VOTA XX (twenty prayers of thanks). If the *labarum* had existed in 319, one might expect it to appear on these coins or another of the hundreds of variants that were minted between 312 and 327. It does not, and where Constantine is shown holding a device it is not the *labarum*, but the *tropaeum* or *vexillum*.

A striking illustration of a victorious emperor bearing a trophy can be seen on the reverse of a four-and-a-half *solidus* gold multiple struck in 326 at Siscia (modern Sisak, Croatia). On the obverse of the coin is a bust of the emperor gazing heavenwards. There is no inscription. On the reverse, the emperor, in military uniform, tramples or kicks a defeated foe with his right foot, and with his left hand drags a captive by the hair. Over his left shoulder, from which his *paludamentum* (cloak) billows, he carries a *tropaeum*. On the first of three types the inscription reads GLORIA CONSTANTINI AUG, 'To the Glory of Constantine Augustus' (fig. 42). On a second type, the reverse reads GLORIA SECULI, 'To the Glory of the Ages'. The reverse inscription on the third type reads VIRTUS D[OMINI] N[OSTRI] CONSTANTINI AUG, identifying the cause of victory as the emperor's virtue. This draws on the imagery of an earlier gold medal, one-third the size, struck at Sirmium in 322–3, with the inscription VIRTUS AUG ET CAESS NN, 'To the Virtue of Our Augustus and Caesars'. There is a contemporary silver coin from Sirmium with the trophy on its reverse, with two spears and four shields at its base beneath VIRTUS AUG ET CAESS. A third version of the gold medallion, again of the smaller one-and-a-half *solidus* type, was struck in Nicomedia late in 324, with three notable innovations: the emperor holds not a spear but a *vexillum* in his left hand; he no longer holds the trophy over his shoulder but erects it; and at the base of the trophy sit two bound captives.

Although it is to some extent an argument from silence, still it seems safe to conclude that the *labarum* was produced as the imperial standard for the 'battle for toleration' against Licinius and no earlier. Subsequently, the *labarum* did not become a standard for the entire Roman army. Rather, it appears to have been made for those who had direct contact with the emperor, just as the chi-rho appears later on the shields of imperial bodyguards but not of regular rank-and-file troops. Eusebius can be forgiven for not knowing this, as he witnessed the drills in Constantinople where the emperor insisted that the *labarum* be carried. It was, therefore, a new standard for Constantine's *comitatus*, the emperor's personal guard which replaced the Praetorian Guard. As we noted in an earlier chapter, the Praetorians, by virtue of their special relationship with emperors, had placed his image on their regular standards. Other units had been content to place images of the emperor and his sons, the *imagines*, beside their regular standards. This practice continued, although others might also wish to march under the 'saving sign' and bear it alongside their established *signa*.

Evidently, reproductions of the *labarum* were used in battle by the imperial guard, while the original precious item was kept in reserve. This makes better sense of a later revelation (*VC* II.6–8 and 16–17) that the 'saving trophy' played a vital role in the victory over Licinius. Here, the power of the symbol was revealed when 'the soldier carrying the standard on his shoulder got into a panic and handed it over to another man, so that he could escape from the battle. As soon as . . . he withdrew from the protection of the standard, a flying javelin pierced his midriff and ended his life. Meanwhile . . . to the one who lifted up the saving trophy it became a life-saver; frequently the bearer was saved when javelins were aimed at him, and the staff of the trophy caught the missiles.' It is quite extraordinary that javelins would lodge in the narrow pole, particularly if this were the gold- and jewel-encrusted imperial standard. Indeed, although the story is clearly a pious fiction, one must imagine the emperor, in telling the story to Eusebius, had in mind a wooden-shafted replica rather than his personal standard.

It is wrong, of course, to interpret the role of the *labarum* too literally, for it served many symbolic functions in Eusebius' text. Most importantly, however, it indicated that Constantine's signal advantage over his enemies was his ability to recognize a powerful sign of divine favour and translate it to the profane world. Thus within a traditional Roman context he forged a material focus for his *virtus*, the 'military courage' or 'valour' that would be rewarded with success. In a Christian context, Constantine supplied a channel through which grace could operate: the imperial standard, or *labarum*, which Constantine had produced for his guards and replicated for his regular troops to carry alongside their standards. However, for Eusebius it was not enough that the troops followed such a blessed leader or marched under his new saving sign. They also had to share his vision.

A common vision?

It is clear from the passage quoted in full above (p. 183) that Eusebius (*VC* I.28), and following him the fifth-century Christian historians Sozomen (I.3) and Socrates Scholasticus (I.2), wished that Constantine's soldiers had shared his midday vision before the Battle of the Milvian Bridge, if not his subsequent nocturnal visit from Christ. Although no contemporary source suggests this, later representations of the vision, perhaps most famously Raphael's Vatican fresco, show emperor and troops gazing heavenwards, observing the sign of divine favour. Constantine's vision may very well have been a pious fiction, devised to demonstrate his suitability to rule alone and to authenticate his novel claims of descent. However, Peter Weiss has advanced a striking hypothesis, only hinted at by earlier commentators, that Constantine's vision was real, however it was interpreted and later reinterpreted. Weiss has argued that Constantine and his troops all witnessed a solar halo, on a spring afternoon in 310. 'Solar halos,' he notes, 'are created by sunlight refracted through ice crystals in the high levels of the atmosphere.' The less common variant of the solar halo (the 46° halo) manifests itself as two concentric circles of light around the sun. The outer circle is faint, but within the inner circle one sees three points of intensive light, one to each side and one above the sun. These, one might argue, could have been seen as the numerals XXX within a circle. But the halo also gives the impression of a single 'light cross', formed by a horizontal axis passing through a 'sun pillar'. The effect appears suddenly and lasts for up to two hours, before disappearing just as suddenly. It occurs mostly on afternoons in late winter and spring. According to Weiss, this vision was first interpreted as *vota*, prayers for a thirty-year reign, in a laurel wreath, but later a dream allowed Constantine to recall it as a 'cross formed of light'. This reinterpretation has misled many into believing the vision took place in 312 on the eve of Constantine's victory at Rome's Milvian Bridge. They trust later Christian commentators who attributed these successes to their god, and it is clear that Constantine himself came to see things their way.

If we are to follow Weiss's explanation, it is perfectly reasonable to assume that in 310 the whole army witnessed the 'cross of light' formed by a solar halo, and subsequently all were willing to embrace the explanation offered by their victorious *imperator*. But we need not follow Weiss to find a reason. Moreover, the Roman army comprised more than those troops who had accompanied Constantine in 310–12, and its transformation into a Christian force required more than a willingness to march beneath a new symbol, the *labarum*. The wielding of the *labarum* and the rhetoric employed by Eusebius have led many to call Constantine's struggle with Licinius a 'holy war'. Some have even referred to it as a 'crusade'. The latter definition is especially inaccurate, in a literal sense, as Constantine's troops fought not under a cross, from which word in Latin and French (*crux, croix*) we derive 'crusade', but rather under a chi-rho. Nor may 'crusade' be regarded simply as a synonym for 'holy war', of which there were many types. Crusaders in the twelfth century would be offered explicit spiritual rewards for fighting, ranging from the remission of their sins to the status of martyr. None of Constantine's soldiers received such promises. But they did know that to fight for the god-protected emperor, whose divine companion had delivered victory on every occasion since 306, was rewarding. His legions fought with discipline and bravery, defending the lives of comrades in arms and the reputation of their commander. All knew that fewer men died under Constantine's command than under that of his enemies, and that those who lived were paid handsomely and frequently. The imperial theology of victory showed him to be the rightful emperor, and while this interpretative framework would in time be surpassed by ideologies of holy war, from jihad to crusade, that time had not yet arrived. Constantine fought no crusades, but his wars did transform how Christians viewed war, and allowed the transformation of the Roman army into a Christian army in the century following Constantine's victory over Licinius. The first order of business was to celebrate that victory in stone.

8

Constantinople

Nikopolis: victory city – Location and foundation –
The monumental core – A Christian city? – A second senate –
A new Alexander, a new Moses

To mark his victory over Licinius, Constantine re-founded the city of Byzantium as 'the city of Constantine', in Greek *Konstantinoupolis*, or Constantinople. Unfortunately, the visitor to modern Istanbul sees little of Constantine's city. Much of the original construction was destroyed by fire in AD 532, during the infamous Nika riot, which was quelled only by the emperor Justinian's murder of 30,000 in the city's hippodrome. The Sphendone, the curved end of the hippodrome, survives today as it was in the early fourth century, although to access its substructure one requires a small boat to navigate its flooded vaults. Much around it was rebuilt by Justinian, whose majestic domed church dedicated to Holy Wisdom, Hagia Sophia, still stands with minarets added by Mehmet the Conqueror in 1453. "As one exits it to the east..." one may glance up and see a mosaic of the later tenth century, which depicts the Mother of God holding the infant Christ. To her right a youthful Justinian offers her the church, and to her left Constantine, almost identical to his pair, offers her the city represented by its walls (fig. 43).

The Church of the Holy Apostles, which incorporated Constantine's mausoleum, fared less well at Mehmet's hands than Hagia Sophia. Being sufficiently distant from the heart of the antique city, it had survived the Nika riot, but not Mehmet's determination to rid Constantinople of its imperial line of succession. The tombs of the Christian emperors were removed and the building razed, to be replaced by the Fatih Mosque, 'the mosque of the conqueror', which was also a mausoleum for the new rulers, the Ottoman Turks. Little of the imperial palace was known until recently, but now, in addition to those parts preserved in the Great

Palace Mosaic Museum,"one can see elements in the excavations at the site which incorporates the Four Seasons Hotel."

The sixth-century *Easter Chronicle* gives an interesting perspective on the foundation of Constantinople that deserves to be read in full:

Constantine . . . while staying at Nicomedia, metropolis of Bithynia, made visits for a long time to Byzantium. He renewed the first wall of the city of Byzas, and after making considerable extensions also to the same wall, he joined them to the ancient wall of the city and named it Constantinople. He also completed the hippodrome, adorning it with works of bronze and with every excellence, and made in it a box for imperial viewing in likeness of the one which is in Rome. And he made a great palace near the same hippodrome, and the ascent from the palace to the box in the hippodrome by way of the *Kochlis*, as it is called. And he also built a forum which was large and exceedingly fine; and he set in the middle a great porphyry column of Theban stone, worthy of admiration, and he set on the top of the same column a great statue of himself with rays of light on his head, a work in bronze which he had brought from Phrygia. The same emperor secretly took away from Rome the palladium, as it is called, and placed it in the forum he built, beneath the column of his monument, as certain of the Byzantines say who have heard it by tradition. And after making bloodless sacrifice, he named the Fortune of the city renewed by him Anthousa. The same emperor also built two fine porticoes from the entrance of the palace as far as the forum, adorned with statues and marbles, and he named the place of the porticoes Regia. Nearby he also built a basilica with an apse, and placed outside great columns; this he named the Senate, and he named the Augusteion because he had also set up opposite his own a monument of his mother, the lady Helena Augusta, on a porphyry column. Likewise too he completed the bath which is called the Zeuxippon, adorning it with columns and varied marbles and works of bronze.

We must be wary of trusting this later source in all its details, and we cannot attribute the design and decoration of the new city entirely to Constantine. But it is clear that he was closely involved in all aspects of the city's construction from foundation to dedication, through six years, and that the features identified in the chronicle were certainly in place during Constantine's reign.

Nikopolis: victory city

Constantine chose Byzantium as the location for his city because of its proximity to the battlefield of Chrysopolis. The city was given his name so that it might be an enduring witness to his most recent and splendid victory. Thus, it joined those other *nikopoleis*, 'victory cities', founded or re-founded by his forebears. Constantinople was also to become an imperial residence, with buildings more splendid than those at nearby Nicomedia, constructed by Diocletian with whom Constantine had resided twenty years before, and where he now dwelt as he oversaw the construction of his new city. It was easily to surpass Salonica, erected by Galerius, whither Licinius had been sent into captivity and where he was put to death. It was to be more splendid than Sirmium and Sardica, Trier and Arles, in all of which cities Constantine had resided and presided over games and government in hippodromes and palaces. Constantinople was to be compared only to Rome and was accordingly referred to as New Rome.

The motivation for the situation of the new city was not that of the old: trade. The Greek colonies north of the Black Sea, whose existence had given impetus to the rise of a trading colony on the site from the seventh century BC, had ceased to be of significance a century before Constantine. If the presence of Constantinople promoted a recovery in mercantile activity across the Black Sea, this was only some five centuries later. By then legend held that Constantine had first considered the site of Troy, known to him but not to us until its rediscovery by Frank Calvert, and later by Heinrich Schliemann, near modern Çannakale in Turkey. Troy was the chosen progenitor of Rome, and the story of the foundation had been retold and fixed in tradition by Virgil's *Aeneid*. Small wonder that the city of Constantine was to have returned to the source, in the tales of those who experienced its rise and wished to appropriate the common past of the two cities, Old and New Rome. But Constantine had a different idea in 324.

The victorious emperor had unified the Roman world and ruled as a single sovereign. His new city would straddle the divide between Europe and Asia. The city of Constantine was equidistant from the

Rhine and the Euphrates. It sat at the end of the Egnatian Way, the great land road across the Balkans, and of the military road east. But such strategic thinking was not unique to Constantine. It had long been apparent, and the city had suffered as a consequence. The walls of Byzantium and much within them had been razed by Septimius Severus in AD 196, as punishment for the inhabitants having supported the pretender Pescenius Niger. According to Cassius Dio, writing only six or seven years after the episode, the city had resisted a siege for three years. It did without land walls for as many decades afterwards. However, by the 320s much had been rebuilt, and a new hippodrome and bath complex supplied. Later legend assigned these to Septimius Severus, safely distant and already identified as the destroyer of much of the older city. But that contradicts the testimony of Herodian, an author of the third century, who saw the city's walls still in ruins in 240. Recently, it has been suggested that the hippodrome, at least, post-dates 260. Thus, Septimius Severus seems an unlikely re-founder. The most likely candidates are those who were based at nearby Nicomedia: Diocletian, Galerius and Licinius.

The best reason one can suggest for Constantine's choice of Byzantium as his 'victory city' is, therefore, tendentious but worthy of consideration: another Tetrarch had been there first. Given his actions in Rome, following the defeat of Maxentius, one might suppose that Licinius is the most likely candidate. Licinius, like Constantine, had reason not to remain in Diocletian's Nicomedia. He had placed a garrison in Byzantium to confront Maximinus Daia in 313. Constantine had expected Licinius to flee towards Byzantium in 317, following the battles at Cibalae and on the plain of Arda. And subsequently, when Licinius' only possession in Europe was Thrace, he travelled frequently to the western edge of his realm. When Constantine marched against him in 324, Licinius met him first in open battle at Adrianople, but then turned back to secure his position within Byzantium. It seems likely, therefore, that Licinius had spent much time in Byzantium, and consequently had made efforts to make it suitable for the imperial presence. But so successful was Constantine's effort to put his stamp on the city that no source mentions a role for Licinius. Constantine's effort to appropriate and recast Byzantium was still more effective than his eradication of Maxentius' scheme for Rome. The second great victory, unlike the first, was absolute.

Location and foundation

If Constantine's choice of Byzantium was, in the first instance, driven by a determination to obliterate the memory and legacy of Licinius, then his motivations changed. In developing the monumental core of Constantinople, he was inspired by a trip to Rome in 326 to celebrate his *vicennalia*, the anniversary of his twenty years in power. He had staged events with great success in Nicomedia to mark the start of the year, in July 325. Those he staged in Rome to mark the end of the year were less successful and marred by tragedy, the result of Constantine's own temper and ruthlessness. To this we shall return. As a consequence, the emperor would never again return to Rome and devoted himself more fully to the creation of his new city. But the site he had chosen enjoyed many natural disadvantages. It was the success of Constantinople, rather than its fortunate situation, that would alter trade patterns in the Mediterranean for centuries to come. Sitting far to the north of the regular routes, it pulled vessels through the Dardanelles despite the fact that in the summer sailing season the prevailing winds there were northerly and thus against the incoming fleet. Initially, it was the demands for building materials and provisions from the south, including the imperially mandated grain convoys from Egypt which ensured bread rations for the citizens, that made Constantinople and its hinterland an economic hot spot. That it endured as such was, however, quite surprising, as there was no reason to suppose that Constantine's heirs would all choose to remain in the city. Its location was far from ideal.

There was little enough fresh water to supply the population of the trading colony that preceded the megalopolis, and subsequent emperors strived to ensure that the city's vast baths and ever-flowing fountains were supplied, building a system of aqueducts and cisterns. One aqueduct had been provided by Hadrian, but Constantine undertook no further measures to supply the city, which as Cyril Mango has observed would have demanded perhaps five times more water than industrial Paris in 1900. The Roman thirst for water was extraordinary, perhaps half a million cubic metres per day for Constantinople at its height. One of Constantine's first acts was to rebuild the Baths of Zeuxippus, also called the Zeuxippon, whose origins legend attributed to Septimius Severus but which more likely had been the work of a rival Tetrarch. The Zeuxippon was opened on the very day the city was dedicated, and which henceforth would be its birthday: 11 May.

It is remarkable, therefore, that the three vast open-air cisterns that supplied the majority of the city's inhabitants were constructed only later, outside the walls established by Constantine but within those added by Theodosius in AD 413. Even the imperial palace did not acquire its famous underground cistern, today known as the Yerebatan Sarayı, until the sixth century. And since the city was surrounded on three sides by sea water, the freshwater supply came exclusively from the European hinterland, flowing from eighty miles away through aqueducts completed only in the reign of Valens (d. 378). While the empire's frontier lay at the Danube, this supply was simple to ensure. But Valens died at the hands of Goths at the Battle of Adrianople, fought in Constantinople's Thracian hinterland in 378. By then it was manifestly clear that Constantinople and its supply lines were acutely vulnerable. Although between the Danube and Constantinople lay the natural barrier of the Haemus, the Balkan mountains, once the Haemus passes had been breached, nothing stood between the mountains and the city. Elaborate long walls were later constructed, in large part to defend the city's water supply. But the agricultural hinterland of Thrace could not effectively be protected, and this exposed it to devastation and the city to the threat of siege.

Constantine took no measures to defend the supply lines of his new city, for he had no idea that the city would grow so rapidly, and his experience of Nicomedia, Trier and Sardica had given him no reason to expect such growth. But he undertook to fill the city with a population sufficient to magnify the emperor, to pack his hippodrome and forum, to line his porticoed streets when he processed by and fill the shops otherwise, and to enjoy his largesse in doles of grain and meat. From 332 measures were in place to ensure that sufficient grain was brought from Egypt to feed up to tens of thousands of citizens. Shipowners who signed on received tax exemptions, but no efforts were made to improve harbour facilities, nor to supply adequate granaries and warehouses. Sea walls were added only in the reign of Constantius II, and it was only in his reign that the land walls attributed to his father were completed.

It would be wrong to lambaste Constantine for not considering the possibility that Constantinople would have a population of (if we follow Cyril Mango) around 350,000 a century after his death. Nor should we fault him for not anticipating the possibility that barbarians would breach the empire's frontiers decades hence, although the dangers were manifestly clear within half a century of his death. Constantinople would prove more defensible than Salonica or Nicomedia, and indeed Milan and Rome, both of which Constantine had himself captured. But how a vast city might be fed and watered, or how it might survive an assault from without, were not pressing concerns in 324. At that time, Constantine was concerned principally with establishing an extensive ritual space, a city-sized stage upon which to act out his new majesty. No longer sharing the spotlight with a rival, for the first time in half a century a Roman emperor ruled alone, and Constantine would project that new sovereignty from his victorious foundation. Whereas Constantine had sought to place his own stamp on Maxentius' rebuilding of the city of Rome, Constantinople was of a quite different order. It was to shine brighter than Rome in having the best of all things from across the Roman world, the old integrated with the new.

The monumental core

What Constantine could do with his new city was restricted by what was there already and by his desire to have everything in place in time for the dedication of the city on 11 May 330. Garth Fowden has compellingly sketched the problems inherent in finding a column suitable to support the statue of the emperor which stood in his new forum, just outside the old line of the city's walls. Fowden noted that not a single suitable monolith was identified throughout the empire, or at least not such that it would reach Constantinople in time. Thus, the column is made up of porphyry, purple marble drums that have aged and worn terribly when compared to the Theodosian granite obelisk. This was apparent even before Istanbul's air and rain became far more polluted with rapid industrialization in the twentieth century (fig. 44). As early as the sixth century the column's drums were wrapped with iron bands. The city's main street, the Mese ('middle street'), had long ploughed a course through the middle of Byzantium to join the Egnatian Way (map 7). The roads that skirt the coast to the north and south, along the Sea of Marmara and the Golden Horn, were in place before Constantine's builders arrived. This much is clear from what came after, namely streets introduced between them on a grid, and these ran across the city's six hills or up their slopes, in which case steps were provided. The city of the mythical Byzas was concentrated on the acropolis, the elevated area between the Mese and Golden Horn, which is today occupied by the Ottoman Topkapi Palace. The hippodrome had been placed on largely empty ground, with a number of other structures and spaces that Constantine would develop as the core of his new city, the ceremonial stage where he would enact his new sovereignty.

At the heart of this ceremonial space was the imperial palace (map 8). From Constantine's foundation would grow a mighty complex that stretched from the hippodrome to the shores of the Sea of Marmara, but the original palace endured at its core. Nothing of the Daphne Palace (as it was known in the tenth century) has survived, but we can reconstruct it from a description contained in a tenth-century text, *The Book of Ceremonies*, compiled for the seventh emperor with the name Constantine. The Daphne was rather modest in size, comprising a southern courtyard enclosed by a porticoed villa in which the emperor's private apartments were situated, and a northern courtyard flanked by a reception hall (the Augusteus) to the east and a banquet hall (the Triklinos of the Nineteen Couches) to the west. The two were linked by passages which met at an octagonal hall, possibly a throne room or robing chamber – court ceremonial required frequent changes of costume. Separating the three halls from the open space beyond was a semicircular portico, which gave the courtyard the form of a horse-shoe and hence the name Onopodion. The Onopodion was enclosed to the north by a straight wall, in the middle of which stood a gateway, granting access to the palace from the Tribounalion (Tribunal), an open space to the north. In the centre of the outer wall was a gate, the Triple Door, and above this a gallery, the Heliakon, from which the emperor might address those gathered in the Tribunal. When larger crowds were to be addressed, the emperor proceeded along the Kochlis, a passageway from the southern courtyard ending at the Kathisma, which was both a room in the palace and the imperial box overlooking the hippodrome halfway down its south-eastern flank. The imperial palace complex abutted the hippodrome to the south-east, allowing the emperor direct and unmolested access to his people, but also offering the best view when he attended the games, as it was located just beyond the starting gates (*carceres*). The juxtaposition of the palace and hippodrome, and the orientation of both, were copied exactly from other Tetrarchic imperial residences. Indeed, the dimensions of the hippodrome correspond almost exactly to those of its counterpart in Salonica, being about 450 metres in total length.

North of the Tribunal were placed the grand imperial Baths of Zeuxippus, to which we shall return shortly. The northern entrance to the baths lay on the southern side of the Augusteion, a colonnaded square that was the point of transition from public to imperial space. From its south-western end ran the imperial road, the Regia, which terminated at the Chalke ('bronze') gates, later the entrance to the enlarged palace complex. From the north-western end of the Augusteion one entered the square known as the Basilika, home to schools attended by the likes of Julian, Constantine's nephew who would become the last pagan emperor of the Romans. In the centre of the square was a double-arch, or *tetrapylon*, known as the Milion. This marked the eastern end of the Mese, the grand colonnaded street through the city, and was the point from which all distances would later be measured.

Proceeding along the Mese, one reached the small Forum of Constantine, in the middle of which stood his statue on its porphyry column (map 7). This marked the point identified as the exact centre of the new city, and thus called in Greek *omphalos*, also the word for 'navel'. On the northern side of the forum was placed the Senate house, past which the Mese continued in a straight line to the Philadelphion, a plaza bedecked with statues honouring members of Constantine's family. A far later source, largely mythographical, noted among these a porphyry composition of four men embracing, which it identified as

Constantine and his sons. Could this be the location of the porphyry Tetrarchs, now in Venice, it was asked in the 1950s? The answer was provided rather dramatically by the discovery, during excavations at this very spot, before the Myrelaion church known today as the Bodrum Camii, of the missing foot of the fourth Tetrarch, wrenched off when the object was plundered by crusaders in 1204 (fig. 15).

At the Philadelphion the Mese bifurcated, with one branch following its established course to join the Egnatian Way, and a second now heading north-west towards Constantine's mausoleum, a rotunda like that of Galerius in Salonica (fig. 45), which later formed part of the Church of the Holy Apostles. Where the road split, there was a most striking building, the Capitol, which was by the end of the fourth century a place of Christian worship. However, given its name, it is hard to avoid the conclusion that the Capitol was conceived as a temple to Jupiter, and more particularly to the triad of Jupiter, Juno and Minerva, guardians of *romanitas* in the Second Rome.

Returning along the Mese to the Augusteion, one saw on its southern side the Baths of Zeuxippus, which were adorned with antique statues, numbering at least eighty gathered from across the Roman world. We know an extraordinary amount about them, for an Egyptian named Christodorus described them all in a poem later included in an anthology. Most of the statues were bronze, and most of famous men: politicians and rulers, orators and philosophers, poets and historians, even pugilists. But nine were of gods. Evidently, the Christian Constantine, while he may not have chosen them himself, expressed no concern at their inclusion in his baths. Nor was there any complaint that in the hippodrome there were statues of the divine twins Castor and Pollux, marking the site of their former temple, and tripods brought from the oracle at Delphi. Indeed, in the imperial palace, where at least for a while Constantine would have contemplated them himself, were deposited statues of the Muses, taken from Mount Helicon. These were later moved to the senate building, outside of which stood statues of Zeus and Athena.

On the opposite side of the street, on the right, was the newly completed hippodrome. Constantine's renovations had been extensive, adding mighty foundations to the southern end of the structure to support a large bend, the Sphendone. The formal dedication of the city involved circus games, which henceforth took place each year on 11 May to mark the city's foundation. According to Sozomen, writing at the start of the fifth century, Constantine 'made for himself a gilded monument of wood, bearing in its right hand a Fortune of the same city [Constantinople], itself also gilded, and commanded that on the same day of the anniversary chariot races [it] should enter, escorted by troops in mantles and slippers, all holding white candles; the carriage should proceed around the further turning-post, and come to the arena opposite the imperial box; and the emperor of the day should rise and do obeisance to the monument of the same emperor Constantine and this Fortune of the city.' Henceforth, all emperors were to bow down to the founder, who had provided them with such an imposing setting. Before that, whenever Constantine made his way to the hippodrome along the private corridor from his palace, emerging in the Kathisma, the assembled throng would cheer madly. Eunapius, a pagan author writing without such enthusiasm, complained that:

[Nothing] can suffice to satisfy the intoxicated multitude that Constantine transported to Byzantium by emptying other cities to establish them in his presence, for he loved to be applauded in the theatres by men so drunk they could not hold their liquor. For he desired to be praised by the unstable masses, and that his name should be in their mouths, though so stupid were they that they could barely pronounce it.

The hippodrome was adorned with victory monuments, which were more than allusions to the ephemeral victories of the charioteers. An ass and keeper, which commemorated Octavian's victory over Mark Antony at Actium, was transplanted from Nikopolis ('Victory City') in Epirus to the victorious heart of Constantine's new Victory City. Suetonius had earlier explained the significance of the composition: they were Eutyches (Prosper) and his donkey Nikon (Victory) who had wandered into Octavian's camp on the eve of battle. Beside this at the mid-point of the *spina*, the central spine or median of the hippodrome, stood one of the three statues to survive (partly) today, the serpent column. One of the three heads is in the nearby archaeological museum, the others are lost. It had once stood at Delphi, a symbol of the Greek victory over the Persians at Plataea in 479 BC. Beside this was a statue of Hercules, which perhaps requires little further explanation, and another of an eagle defeating a snake, which recalled the images Constantine circulated on his coins of his military standard, the *labarum*, piercing a snake. Licinius was the snake.

A Christian city?

The prevalence of antique statuary is a strong clue that Constantine did not conceive of his new city, as has so often been said, as a new Christian capital for the Roman empire. Temples were constructed for pagan citizens, notably to the Fortune of Rome, a partner for that dedicated to the new Fortune of Constantinople, Anthousa. Eusebius attempted to explain away these lapses: 'the city which bore his name was filled everywhere with bronze statues, which had been dedicated in every province and which the deluded victims of superstition had long vainly honoured as gods with numberless victims and burnt sacrifices, who now learnt to think correctly when the emperor held them up as play-things to be ridiculed.' But then what is one to make of the most obvious 'plaything' displayed atop a tall porphyry column in the new forum? There stood a statue of Constantine himself in the guise of Sol Invictus. He held a globe in his left hand, a spear in his right (until it fell down and was replaced by a sceptre in the sixth century), and on his head the radiate crown of the Sun god. The statue was believed to have come from Phrygia, and a tradition held that it was the work of Phidias, the great sculptor of the fifth century BC, suitably modified. Evidently, this offended nobody, for it stood in place for more than seven centuries until, in 1106, it was brought down by a fierce storm. Later attempts to purify the statue had Constantine insert a fragment of the True Cross within the globe. But the discovery of the True Cross by Constantine's mother, Helena, emerged as a legend only in the later years of the fourth century. Before that the message of the statue was mixed, and, as Garth Fowden has observed, this was quite deliberate, 'an intended polysemy'.

The structures most strikingly absent from the monumental core of Constantine's city are churches. The first known chapel in the palace complex, dedicated to St Stephen, was erected no earlier than AD 421, and little further provision was made for the city's growing population. No contemporary description of the city's development remains before a document called the *Notitia*, written in AD 425, which mentions fourteen churches. If the population at the time were in the region of 350,000, each would have needed to house a congregation of 25,000, and thus significantly outdo even the modern megachurches of Texas, for example the 16,000-seat Lakewood Church in Houston. This was not the case, and it raises a question that has been debated for centuries: was Constantinople a Christian foundation? Christian writers claimed, quite obviously, that it was, but they have much to explain away. It was manifestly not the case, as claimed by Sozomen, that 'this city . . . was not polluted by altars, Grecian temples, nor pagan sacrifices [but adorned . . .] with many and splendid houses of prayer, in which the Deity vouchsafed to bless the efforts of the Emperor by giving sensible manifestations of his presence.'

Of the fourteen churches that are known to have stood in 425, only three or four can be attributed with any conviction to Constantine. These do not include the first version of the cathedral church of Hagia Sophia, dedicated only in 360. Rather, one can best work by means of analogy with Rome, where Constantine provided a large episcopal structure, the Lateran Palace, later known as the Church of St John in Lateran, which became the seat of the bishop of Rome. There were also, somewhat later, several smaller but quite splendid churches dedicated to local Roman martyrs, as we saw above (p. 149). In Constantinople, therefore, it makes sense to credit him with the Church of St Eirene, the city's first episcopal church (although this may predate him), and with two large basilicas devoted to the local martyrs Acacius and Mocius. The Church of St Acacius is first attested in 359 but may well date from the 330s, as may the Church of St Mocius, which is first mentioned in 402.

These would be embraced within Eusebius' observation that Constantine, 'being fully resolved to distinguish the city which bore his name with especial honour . . . embellished it with numerous sacred edifices, both memorials of martyrs on the largest scale, and other buildings of the most splendid kind, not only within the city itself, but in its vicinity: and thus at the same time he rendered honour to the memory of the martyrs, and consecrated his city to the martyrs' God.' A further measure of the number of churches in the city, again provided by Eusebius, is the commission for 'fifty copies of the sacred scriptures' that Constantine placed with the bishop of Caesarea. Constantine imagined that this number of books would satisfy all current requirements, and indeed all its future needs once the number of churches had been increased. Eusebius was clearly rather partial in his judgement on the new city and the intentions of Constantine in its construction. One might suggest instead that the city was furnished with places of worship sufficient for a middling population to perform publicly a diversity of religious rites, although it does seem very likely that Constantine banned blood sacrifice in those edifices for which he was responsible or for which he provided financial support.

Among the most splendid of Constantine's structures was his own mausoleum, which he dedicated to the holy apostles. His son Constantius would later build a large cruciform church adjoining Constantine's original circular mausoleum, and this many have argued was Constantine's own work. However, it seems clear that the emperor's principal concern was not to establish a church, but rather to ensure that his mortal remains rested beside those of apostles of Christ, who had been brought to his city to rest beside his tomb, and also within a ring of statues of Christ's other apostles, such that in time Constantine would be recognized as their equal, *isoapostolos*. We shall return to this in our last chapter.

A second senate

Constantine's act, which set his new city apart from all other Tetrarchic capitals and established it as a 'Second Rome', was to institute a second senate. The Roman senate met, as a rule, only twice a month, and in the third century operated almost entirely without imperial oversight. As we saw in an earlier chapter, it played a constitutional role when a usurper wished to have his seizure of power ratified, but this was rarely a decisive factor. The senate's powers had long since been subordinated to the imperial will, as Fergus Millar demonstrates with a telling example. The city of Aphrodisias in Caria (Anatolia in modern Turkey) was granted freedom from taxation by Julius Caesar and Augustus, an immunity that was confirmed by a ruling of the senate (*senatus consultum*) in 39 BC. One hundred and sixty years later, the emperor Hadrian confirmed 'the freedom and autonomy and other privileges granted by the senate and the emperors before me'. However, when in AD 250 the matter came before Decius, he told the ambassadors from Aphrodisias 'we preserve your existing freedom and all other privileges which you have gained from emperors before us'. The *senatus consultum* was ignored; the imperial will was all. Yet men still clamoured to become senators, and 'new men' married into established families, projecting their lineage into Rome's glorious past. Had Constantine himself not invented a past more glorious than his imperial father could offer?

In AD 300 the Roman senate was a select group of intermarried and immensely wealthy families, whose political function was stagnant, but which remained essential to the structural needs of governance and to the ideological needs of the empire. We might usefully ask why Diocletian had not created a senate for Nicomedia, whence he had governed the eastern empire for decades. The simplest answer, and therefore perhaps the correct one, would appear to be that Diocletian, and after him Galerius, commanded the support and loyalty of the east and had no interest in promoting the interests of their wealthy subjects. One senate, at a distance, was sufficient. The Tetrarchs relied on the army and promoted the interests of the equestrian class, whose rights had never been hereditary. Equestrians now governed provinces and dioceses at the expense of senators, and owed all to the emperor. Constantine did not reverse this policy, but rather promoted those who followed him, or whom he wished to recruit to his cause, to the rank of senator. Constantine, on the other hand, did not simply inherit Constantius' position, but in competition with Maximian and Maxentius had struggled for two decades to establish his mastery of the west. In the oration of 321, by Nazarius, we learn that one facet of this effort was to expand the Roman senate and to award senatorial status to men from across the western provinces:

You felt at last, Rome, that you were the citadel of all nations and of all lands the queen, when you were promised the best men from every province for your curia [senate house], so that the dignity of the senate be no more illustrious in name than in fact, since it was composed of the flower of the whole world.

Constantine had now to ensure the loyalty of the east, and to do so overnight, having no subordinate to whom he could immediately entrust government and intending to remain there and not to return to the west. He could not remove the ruling stratum without creating a cohort of potential rebels. Still less could he kill the greatest of them and import men of his own, who would have no experience of the lands or peoples over which they might be placed. The most sensible policy, and the one that Constantine adopted, was to reward the men who had been loyal to his enemies, so that he might bind them to him and have them administer the eastern lands in his name. The *Origo Constantini* put it plainly: 'There [in Constantinople] he founded a senate of the second order, [whose members were] called *clari*.' That is, the members of the senate of Constantinople were initially to be addressed as *clari*, 'distinguished', rather than *clarissimi*, as the 'most distinguished' members of the senate of Rome were entitled. However, within a few decades this distinction was abolished, and all senators were *clarissimi*, affiliated according to whether they lived in the eastern or western part of the empire.

Loyalty in the east was purchased by spectacular largesse, which earned Constantine the opprobrium of some commentators. According to Zosimus (II.38.1), 'Constantine continued wasting revenue by unnecessary gifts to unworthy men.' His views reflect a pagan tradition that was well established by the later fourth century that Constantine had squandered money on the worst types and on his indulgent building projects, extracting that wealth from the cities of the east and their temples. Eusebius, as one might expect, treated the same matter with approbation (*VC* IV.1). He did not record the founding of a senate, but noted that 'some received gifts in money, others in land; some obtained the praetorian prefecture, others senatorial or consular rank . . . for the emperor devised new dignities that he might give as tokens of his favour to a larger number of people.' New senators benefited from a range of offices that the Tetrarchs had reserved for equestrians: they were governors of provinces, vicars of dioceses (not yet an ecclesiastical preserve), and Praetorian Prefects, or each in turn as they rose through the hierarchy. First among them, Licinius' Praetorian Prefect Julius Julianus became consul for 325. The consulate, the crowning glory of a senatorial career, was now entirely in the gift of the emperor.

As Constantine set out in a letter from the last months of his reign, preserved in an inscription from the Forum of Trajan, he regarded the members of both senates as his own men. In 337 they numbered perhaps 300 in Constantinople and more than 600 in Rome. Constantius II, Constantine's son, would expand this greatly to around 2000 in Constantinople alone, mostly to shore up his power and to provide for the increasing ceremonial needs of his court. It is a remarkable fact that the senate in Constantinople survived well into the Middle Ages, serving each emperor of the Romans, whom we now call Byzantines, until the fifteenth century. Every imperial entry into the city was met by a party of senators at an appropriate gate, for example the Golden Gate for an emperor returning in triumph. Each imperial coronation included an acclamation by the senate, and each imperial birth and death was attended by a senatorial act of rejoicing or mourning. Constantius' expanded senate attended upon him as angels served the godhead, praising him continually. But the pattern was established by Constantine, who built on the innovations by Diocletian that he had witnessed at first hand.

A new Alexander, a new Moses

Now sole ruler over the whole Roman world, Constantine rapidly overhauled the imperial style. Where collegiality had prevailed, now family was emphasized, and Constantine was himself the vehicle for divine grace. This development can be seen almost immediately on coins. In place of the radiate crown and laurel wreath, the nimbus (halo) appears for the first time. More common is the diadem, a new type of crown suggesting a new conception of sovereignty; this appears on gold coinage from 324–5 (fig. 42) and on bronze from 328–9. The emperor and his family, not the imperial college, are celebrated, indeed venerated. Imperial women appear: mother Helena wearing her own diadem and Fausta without a crown (fig. 52). The busts appear to be gazing heavenwards, reviving an established type of Hellenistic origin. The most famous example of the gaze is that of Constantine's colossal head in the Capitoline Museums in Rome, but an equally fine example graces the new Greek and Roman galleries at New York's Metropolitan Museum (fig. 46). This would appear to represent a youthful emperor, but the hair-style reveals him to be older, with his remaining locks brushed forward towards the centre of his forehead and depicted rather more thickly than some rude commentators thought accurate. Constantine was teased for the concern he showed for his receding hair-line, and some even suggested that he adopted the diadem to mask it. However, the model for Constantine's pose required that he have thick hair, a sign of virility. A further classic portrait is the bronze head in Rome's Capitoline Museums, once thought to be of Constantius II but now once again held to be his father, which has extremely thick hair (fig. 47).

Constantine's pose is not original, nor is it at all Christian in conception. One is struck by the consonance of Constantine's busts with similarly disembodied heads of Mithras, for example that in the Museum of Ancient Arles, or that discovered in London in 1954 at the site of a Mithraeum, now displayed in the Museum of London (fig. 48). Both of the early third century, each bust is of a youth in a Phrygian cap gazing to the heavens, perhaps towards Sol in his *quadriga*. The ultimate source was quite clearly the heavenward-gazing Alexander, who had become the Sun god. H. P. L'Orange wrote six decades ago:

As Alexander stands at the beginning of the ancient world dominion, so the Alexander-Helios type initiates the Hellenistic-Roman representation of the Sun ruler. Not only is the tradition of this statuary type initiated here, but the actual world of ideas embodied in such representations, the whole solar explanation of the world dominion, now becomes current among the peoples of classical antiquity.

Constantine had placed himself in this line of succession, and by his pose staked his claim to world dominion, granted to him by the divine patron towards whom he gazed. In contrast with Alexander, whose pose includes a backwards-tilted head, the whole face glancing up, only Constantine's eyes gazed up, and they were now portrayed larger than life-size. This last feature was his one major departure from third-century practice.

Septimius Severus had reintroduced the pose in the early years of the third century, but it had still earlier Roman precedents, on the coins of Nero, where the emperor also wore the crown of his Sun god, and on Republican coins struck for Pompey and Scipio Africanus. If a portrait bust of Philip the Arab, now in the Vatican Museum, has been used to support suggestions that he was a crypto-Christian, the same has not been said of Caracalla, who also favoured the pose. An excellent example of a heavenward-gazing Caracalla can be seen near Constantine at New York's Metropolitan Museum, where one might also turn to the oversize bronze of Gallus (fig. 12), to see the same upward gaze as that favoured by Constantine's portraitists. Even in Tetrarchic art, where one discerns a clear break in many other ways, emperors frequently gaze to the heavens.

Eusebius, as was his wont, ignored all other precedents and recognized Constantine's heavenward gaze as an attitude of Christian prayer. However, the general tone of imperial coinage after 324–5 suggests an aura of imperial divinity. No longer wearing the crown of his erstwhile patron Sol, Constantine shares the qualities and the insignia of a greater god. The message of the coins is, moreover, even more carefully monitored, since gold and silver were now produced only in Nicomedia and, from 330, Constantinople. The city's founding enjoys its own medallions, of course, where it is shown as the result of imperial victory, and established forms join new forms. On one issue the city's Fortune, Anthousa, offers the emperor a Victory on a globe even as he is being crowned by a second Victory. On another, a nine-*solidus* multiple, the nimbate emperor sits on his throne, sons on either side, beneath the inscription SALUS ET SPES REIPUBLICAE, 'Health and Hope of the Republic'.

Constantine's pagan subjects, particularly those in the east, saw him as a new Alexander, a demi-god gazing heavenwards with at least some flowing locks, who had brought a vast empire under his sole rule through his leadership in war. But to Christians like Eusebius, he was also the leader of the new elect, the new Israelites, a new Moses, and this view Constantine's propagandists also reinforced. Later sources record the transfer of the staff of Moses by Constantine to his new capital, where it was placed in a church of the *Theotokos tou rabdou*, 'the Mother of God of the Staff', and subsequently transferred to the imperial palace. According to Eusebius, Moses' life in three cycles of forty years is mirrored in Constantine's reign, broken up by his decennial celebrations. Porphyry had denied the antiquity of the Moses story and claimed him for the pagans, and perhaps Eusebius' earliest drafts of the *Life of Constantine*, in which the comparison between Moses and Constantine is most apparent as a structural device, were written against Porphyry and thus in line with Eusebius' earlier work, the *Praeparatio Evangelica*.

In this light, Eusebius' account of the manufacture of the *labarum* can be seen to echo that of the Ark of the Covenant (Exodus 25–7), while its use parallels that of Moses' staff (in Septuagint Greek, *rabdos*), the power of which was revealed to him by God (Exodus 4:2–6; 17:8–13). Similarly, the reworked version of Constantine's vision may be seen as a parallel to Moses' vision of the burning bush (Exodus 3). Elsewhere, Constantine's palace upbringing is compared to that of Moses, who was likewise destined to free his people (*VC* I.12), and when Constantine fled a secret plot hatched by Galerius, he was 'in this also preserving his likeness to the great prophet Moses' (*VC* I.20). The most sustained comparison comes when Eusebius recounts the downfall of Maxentius, who has been transformed into a tyrant who oppressed the people of Rome. Of course, this reflects the propaganda disseminated shortly after Constantine's victory at the Milvian Bridge in 312, prior to his entry into Rome as 'liberator'. But it also demonstrates Eusebius' mature reflection on the episode, casting Maxentius as pharaoh both in his revision of the *Ecclesiastical History* (*HE* IX.9) and in the *Life of Constantine* (*VC* I.38):

Accordingly, just as once in the time of Moses and the devout Hebrew tribe 'Pharaoh's chariots and his force he cast into the sea, and picked rider-captains he overwhelmed in the Red Sea' (Exodus 15.4), in the very same way Maxentius and the armed men and guards about him 'sank to the bottom like a stone' (Exodus 15.5), when, fleeing before the force that came from God with Constantine, he went to cross the river lying in his path . . . So even if not in words, yet surely in deeds, in the same way as those who accompanied the great servant Moses, these who won this victory from God might be thought to have raised the same hymn against the wicked tyrant.

Eusebius proceeds to describe the celebrations of, and monuments to, this victory (*VC* I. 39–41), expanding upon his account in the *Ecclesiastical History* (IX.9.11). The statue of Constantine now explicitly holds 'a tall pole in the shape of a cross', and Eusebius records the same inscription: 'By this saving sign. . . I have restored them to their ancient distinction and splendour.'

Most strikingly, between about 320 and 390 many sarcophagi, of which at least twenty-nine have survived in full or in fragments, were for the first time carved with the scene of the crossing of the Red Sea and the death of the pharaoh. The locations of these sarcophagi are important for their interpretation, with single examples found at Brescia, Metz, Pisa and Split, and eleven more found in Rome and fourteen in southern France (at Aix-en-Provence, Avignon, Carcassonne, Moustiers-St. Marie and Nîmes). Nine survived at Arles alone, one of which is now at Aix and another at Bellegarde du Garde. Sarcophagi survive in abundance at Arles, most strikingly along the cobbled path known as Alyscamps, which is lined with hundreds (fig. 49). These attest to four centuries of Roman burial, from Julius Caesar to Constantine, that included few Christians. The vast majority of sarcophagi bear simple designs and inscriptions. Only a handful, several now gathered in the Museum of Ancient Arles, feature sculptural reliefs, for example the third-century depiction of Phaedra and Hippolytus (whose story we shall recount below; see p. 222), which was produced in Greece and transported to Gaul to be completed. A second-century representation of Psyche reflects local production. In comparison, the number and quality of fourth-century sculpted sarcophagi are remarkable, as is the ubiquity of scenes from the Old Testament, often juxtaposed with those of the New Testament. Particularly striking is the so-called Sarcophagus of the Trinity, which features sculpture in three registers: Old Testament in the uppermost and miracles of Christ in the lower, between which is a medallion featuring portraits of the departed couple. The sarcophagus of Marcia Romania Celsa shows the youths in the fiery furnace, from the Book of Daniel, balanced by the New Testament's Adoration of the Magi. The Red Sea sarcophagi are different. These feature a single narrative scene of a dramatic episode from Exodus. Of the nine discovered at Arles, two are displayed in the Museum of Ancient Arles: one a complete sarcophagus (fig. 50), the other a relief panel mounted on a wall (fig. 51). There is a striking parallel between the depiction of Pharaoh (Maxentius) and the portrayal of the bare-headed emperors of the third-century, seen on the Ludovisi Sarcophagus (fig. 11) and in the defeat of the Persians on the Arch of Galerius (fig. 18). One might consider this an inversion of the traditional symbolism.

It is worth elaborating on Constantine's particular connection with Arles. In the years after his victory over Maxentius, Constantine spent as much time in Arles as at Trier. In April or May 313 he transferred a mint there from Ostia, surely to pay his troops, and he convened his first church council there on 1 August 314. On 7 August 316, Constantine's wife Fausta gave birth to his second son and namesake in Arles, and in 328 the city was renamed Constantina, to mark this occurrence. Both occasions were marked by games in the splendid amphitheatre. Besides these facts, one might note the compelling suggestion in a late legendary account that Constantine had his vision near Arles. Placed beside these observations, the association between the imagery of the sarcophagi and Constantine's victory at the Milvian Bridge is highly suggestive. Might one conclude that wealthy supporters of Constantine, perhaps even officers in his Gallic army, chose to have themselves interred in a monument to Constantine's first decisive victory, at the same time demonstrating that they too were now Christians? It is to these Christian soldiers that we shall turn in the next chapter, but also we shall see how Constantine – the new Alexander, the new Moses – took a new first name, a Christian name: Victor.

PART III

Victor Constantine

✠

9

Victor Constantine

Victor eris – The new Flavians and the Great Cameo –
The deaths of Crispus and Fausta – Goths and Sarmatians
– Christian soldiers? – The Greatest Victor

To mark his victory in the civil wars that ended the Roman Republic and to distinguish himself from the many generals who had so recently claimed power, Octavian dispensed with the name he had taken upon entering public life. No longer Gaius Julius Caesar Octavianus, which drew attention to his adoption by Julius Caesar, he became Augustus, a name redolent of piety and authority. But Augustus was not his first name. His official title was now Imperator Caesar Augustus, with emphasis placed first on the title by which he had been acclaimed by his troops. It is from *imperator* that we derive the English title emperor, where Germans have preferred a derivative of Caesar. The so-called *praenomen imperatoris* was not taken by Augustus' immediate successors, but in a later period of civil war, AD 68–9, it became standard for pretenders. The title was a mark of victory, and each acclamation would follow an imperial success which was almost never won by the emperor himself. From the time of Vespasian, emperors received the acclamation not only for victories won on their behalf, but also to mark each year in power, and this practice continued into the reign of the Tetrarchs. Constantine had been acclaimed *imperator* and Augustus by his father's troops at York in 306. In the following years he would be acclaimed another thirty-one times, the most of any Roman emperor. He also adopted a new name, a mark of victory akin to Augustus' first use of the *praenomen imperatoris*. Constantine took as his first name, his Christian name, Victor.

Victor eris

After 324 Constantine was closer to divinity and considered himself a divine vehicle and channel for grace. In a letter to the provincials of Palestine, he observed that 'those who embark with righteous purpose on certain actions and continually keep in mind fear of the greatest god, holding firm their faith in him' have triumphed over those 'who flagrantly subjected to outrages and savage punishments' fellow believers. That is to say, Constantine's enemies' armies 'have fallen, many have been turned in flight, and their whole military organization has collapsed in shame and defeat'. Summarizing his rise to power, Constantine relates that the greatest god 'Examined my service and approved it as fit for his purposes; and I, beginning from the sea beside the Britons and the parts where . . . the sun should set, have repelled and scattered the horrors that held everything in subjection' (*VC* II.28). This imperial document, like all the others composed after the Battle of Chrysopolis, was issued in the name of Victor Constantinus Maximus Augustus. The emperor was no longer Invictus Constantinus Maximus Augustus, which surely was held too closely to echo the name of Sol Invictus. As Eusebius explained, 'he created this title personally for himself as his most appropriate epithet because of the victory God had given him over all his enemies and foes' (*VC* II.19).

Taking the name 'Victor' appears to have been a rather literal fulfilment of the exhortation *hoc signo victor eris*, which means 'By this sign you shall become victor.'* One can only guess that the phrase was revealed to Eusebius in Constantine's native Latin, when the two met for the first time more than a dozen years after the episode of 312, thus at exactly the time Constantine became Victor. Eusebius recorded the exhortation in Greek rather less literally as *touto nika*, 'By this you shall conquer', and he invented the notion that it was seen as a text attached to the 'cross-shaped trophy formed from light'. We have noted that in

---

* This phrase is distinct from the more familiar – insofar as any Latin phrase is now familiar – *in hoc signo vinces*. This variant was employed by Rufinus in his translation back into Latin from Eusebius' Greek, so is no earlier than AD 400. We shall return to Rufinus later in this chapter. The first, correct version appeared in extant form on coins struck by the usurper Vetranio in 350 (fig. 59), some fifty years before Rufinus' text.

Lactantius' account the exhortation to 'mark the heavenly sign of God (*caeleste signum dei*) on the shields of his soldiers and then engage in battle' comes in the dream, rather than as part of the vision, and no wording is offered. One might suggest, therefore, that to Constantine in 324 the phrase *hoc signo victor eris* was not a general exhortation, but rather a direct instruction to 'become Victor'.

The new Flavians and the Great Cameo

The victorious emperor now ruled free of interference from competitors; but he did not rule alone, for he took measures to promote the interests of his family, the new Flavian dynasty. After Chrysopolis, he granted both his mother Helena and his wife Fausta the title Augusta, and struck gold coins showing their busts, not his own (fig. 52). Helena was entitled to wear the imperial diadem, whereas Fausta, the junior Augusta, was not. Constantine's four sons, Crispus, Constantine, Constantius and Constans, were all to be emperors. Crispus and Constantine had already been promoted to the rank of Caesar; Constans, only an infant, would eventually follow in 333. In November 324 Constantius was raised to that rank, and a remarkable cameo was produced to mark the occasion, perhaps the same date that both Helena and Fausta were named Augustae. It demonstrates clearly the new emphasis on the emperor's victorious nature, his divinity, and most importantly the imperial family.

The Great Cameo (fig. 53), formerly in the collection of Rubens and now held by the Geld en Bankmuseum, Utrecht, depicts the emperor joined on a chariot by his wife Fausta, his young son and his mother Helena. A *cantharus* (urn) turned on its side rests under the chariot, suggesting that Constantine is Dionysus (Bacchus), to whom the vessel was sacred. Similarly, the chariot is pulled not by tigers, panthers or leopards (fig. 6), but by two centaurs, both rearing up (compare with fig. 7). This iconography is familiar from Dionysiac sarcophagi of the Antonine era. The leading centaur bears an elegant 'trophy' on his left shoulder and tramples two defeated enemies dressed as Romans, the followers of Licinius. The victory thus marked, Constantine is offered a laurel wreath by Victoria, who flies over the centaurs towards the chariot. But Constantine is not only Bacchus, for in his right hand he holds a thunderbolt, evoking Jupiter.

Constantine wears a laurel wreath, his wife a veil, perhaps in the guise of Ceres, as she holds an ear of corn in her left hand. Her right hand cannot be seen, but presumably she embraces Constantine as he does her. Husband and wife face each other, Constantine looking to the front of the chariot but not at his wife. Rather, he gazes to the heavens, his left arm resting on her shoulders. The shoulder-clasp is reminiscent of the embrace of the porphyry Tetrarchs (fig. 15), but here the four colleagues have been replaced by four family members. Over Constantine's right shoulder stands Helena, who points under the emperor's raised right arm to his son, who is wearing cuirass, helmet and sword. Fausta also points to her son. The young boy could be any one of Constantine's sons by Fausta, but is surely Constantius, who was born in 317 and was named Caesar a month after the Battle of Chrysopolis. This is the context for the production of the cameo, erroneously dated by others to the years after Milvian Bridge. The heavenward gaze and the focus on family which is driven home by the presence of the matriarchs are suggestive of the new imperial style, but their pointing fingers identify clearly the boy whose promotion marked his father's ultimate triumph and the end of the Dyarchy with Licinius. The cameo can, therefore, be dated rather precisely to within two years of November 324, for by the end of 326 Fausta was dead.

Looking at the Great Cameo, one might wonder at the nature of Constantine's Christianity. Was it not as yet incompletely conceived, laced with pagan sensibilities, offering no sanction for extreme violence? Here one might consider observations by Peter Brown on a slightly later work, the illustrated Calendar of 354. 'The more we look at such art,' Brown opined, 'the more we are impressed by the way in which the parts that we tend to keep in separate compartments, by labelling them "classical", even "pagan", as distinct from "Christian", form a coherent whole; they sidle up to each other, under the subterranean attraction of deep homologies. The classical and Christian elements are not simply incompatible . . . Rather, the classical elements have been redeployed. They are often grouped in such a way as to convey, if anything, an even heavier charge of meaning. The gods make their appearance, now, as imposing elements of power and prosperity. . . they add a numinous third dimension to the solidity of a *saeculum* restored to order by Constantine.' In simpler terms, how else was an emperor to display his conception of power than in the language of images with which all Romans were familiar, whether they were pagans or Christians? There were more overtly Christian models, for example that of Moses and the drowning of Pharaoh, but these were only now emerging and had never been a feature of imperial art and the language of power.

The deaths of Crispus and Fausta

Constantine's restoration was not yet complete, his world not fully ordered. The emperor's god was Moses' God, a vengeful god, swift to anger like the emperor himself, prone to Bacchic excess. So it came to pass that in 326, as the emperor celebrated his twentieth year in power, and even as he sought to forge the image of a new ruling dynasty, he murdered his first-born son Crispus and his wife Fausta, the mother of his three younger sons and two daughters. Crispus was now in his early twenties, a Caesar for almost a decade, and an accomplished leader. He had defended the western frontier from his base at Trier and commanded, in name or in fact, campaigns against the Franks in 320. Coins were struck to mark his victory, and in 321 Nazarius praised him thus:

Those very Franks . . . were felled under your arms [Constantine] in such numbers that they could have been utterly eradicated, if you had not, with the divine inspiration with which you manage everything, reserved for your son [Crispus] the destruction of those whom you had broken. For your glory, however, that nation which is fecund to its own detriment grew up so rapidly and was so stoutly restored that it gave the most valiant Caesar the first fruits of an enormous victory.

In the same year, as we have seen, Crispus was married to a girl named Helena, and by her he had recently had a son, Constantine's first grandchild. In 323 Crispus won a further victory over the Alemans, surely now commanding in person. And in 324 he made his way from Trier to the east, where he commanded his father's fleet in the sigma victory over Licinius. His great potential fulfilled, Crispus could look forward

CONSTANTINE

to his *decennalia* as Caesar and to the day when he would succeed his father as Augustus. Perhaps he anticipated it too keenly, and shared that desire with his father's wife, his stepmother Fausta.

No contemporary source records how first Crispus and then Fausta were killed, so effective was the emperor's campaign to damn their memories. Nothing is known of the fate of Crispus' young wife and son, but one must imagine they were disposed of as ruthlessly. Eusebius, ever the sycophant, mentions neither Crispus nor Fausta in his *Life of Constantine*, and even wrote Crispus out of the final version of his *Ecclesiastical History* (*HE* X.9.4), where he had appeared in an earlier version as 'an emperor most dear to God and in every way resembling his father'. Indeed, in characterizing their victory over Licinius, Eusebius had compared the relationship between father and son to that between 'God, the universal king, and the Son of God, the saviour of all men', proceeding further than one might expect of a bishop in his desire to flatter, and reminding some members of his audience, perhaps, of the relationship the Herculian Tetrarchs once enjoyed with the Jovians. We must wait until the later fourth century, therefore, to discover the first terse references to the murder. A passing mention by Ammianus Marcellinus reveals that the deed took place at Pola in Istria, an odd place that suggests Crispus may have died having recently been sent into exile. Writing around the same time, Aurelius Victor states that Crispus died at the command of his father but for no known reason, and Eutropius in his brief history offers a generic reason: 'the pride of prosperity caused Constantine greatly to depart from his former agreeable mildness of temper. Falling first upon his own relatives, he put to death his son, an excellent man; his sister's son, a youth of amiable disposition; soon afterwards his wife, and subsequently many of his friends.' Sidonius Apollinaris, a Latin author of the fifth century, offered a pithier statement: the wife was killed in a hot bath, the son by cold poison.

How were the two deaths linked, as surely they were? There are two distinct traditions. The first sets Fausta against Crispus, for example as recorded by the anonymous author of the *Epitome de Caesaribus* (41.11–12):

But when Constantine had obtained control of the whole Roman Empire by means of his wondrous success in battle, he ordered his son Crispus to be put to death, at the suggestion of his wife Fausta, so they say. Then he killed his wife Fausta by hurling her into boiling baths when his mother Helena rebuked him with excessive grief for her grandson.

According to this tradition, Fausta was jealous of Crispus' successes and desperate to secure the succession of her own sons. She concocted a tale of treachery knowing that her husband was swift to anger and to judgement. Helena, Constantine's mother, jealous of Fausta's influence over her son and enraged by the death of her first-born grandson whom she had raised, exacted her revenge, persuading Constantine in his remorse to compound his crime. However, the story does not hang together well, for if Constantine did indeed regret his rush to judgement, one would expect Crispus' memory to have been redeemed. It was not. Moreover, in a variant of the story related by Philostorgius in about AD 425, Fausta's death was the result of her adultery with a servant after she had effected Crispus' death, and the latter crime was detected by Constantine himself, not Helena.

John Chrysostomos, a Christian bishop and theologian renowned for his 'golden mouth', conjured for Fausta a death worthy of Prometheus who defied Zeus: 'suspecting his wife of adultery, the emperor bound her naked to the mountains and exposed her to the wild beasts when she had born him many royal children . . . The same man also murdered his son.' This would appear to verify Philostorgius' account, but it may also imply that Crispus was Fausta's adulterous lover. She was closer in age to her stepson than her husband, and they had grown up together for at least some years in Trier. This is spelt out by Zosimus (II.29), following Eunapius, who was unremittingly hostile to Constantine:

Without any consideration for natural law he [Constantine] killed his son Crispus . . . on suspicion of having had intercourse with his stepmother, Fausta. And when Constantine's mother, Helena, was saddened by this atrocity and was inconsolable at the young man's death, Constantine, as if to comfort her, applied a remedy worse than the disease: he ordered a bath to be over-heated and shut Fausta up in it until she was dead.

By the later twelfth century, the Greek historian Zonaras, drawing on these accounts but also on a rich vein now lost to us, sketched a vignette that combined the two tales. It is worthy of Euripides, in whose *Hippolytus* the tragic heroine Phaedra is compelled by Aphrodite, goddess of love, to desire her stepson, the eponymous hero. But whereas Phaedra hanged herself in shame, Fausta, 'who was madly in love with [Crispus] but could not get him to succumb' accordingly . . .

announced to his father that he [Crispus] loved her and had often attempted to do violence to her. Therefore Crispus was condemned to death by his father, who believed his wife. But when the emperor later realized the truth he punished his wife too, on account of her wantonness and for the death of his son. Fausta was thrown in a super-heated bath and there met a violent end.

This version, rather than resolving the tensions between the two traditions, suffers from the problems of both and from its close adherence to the conventions of classical literature. Would Fausta truly have acted solely through lust, a *topos* in classical literature that obscures rather than explains reasons for the behaviour of women? If Constantine felt duped and regretted his tragic rush to judgement, why did he not restore honour to his son's memory? And why did Fausta die in a hot bath? Was her death an accident, suicide or punishment?

David Woods has offered a further interpretation that merits close consideration. Since 'death by hot bath' is not a punishment known hitherto in the Roman world, it would be a bizarre and cruel invention by Constantine, unless one can suggest an alternative explanation. And Woods does: hot baths were considered essential to inducing miscarriage. The second-century physician Soranus, in his *Gynaecology*, sets out the following (adapted slightly from Woods' translation):

For a woman who intends to have an abortion, it is necessary for two or three days beforehand to take protracted baths, little food and to use softening vaginal pessaries . . . But if a woman reacts unfavourably to phlebotomy and is languid, one must first relax the parts by means of sitz-baths, full baths, softening vaginal pessaries . . . And she who intends to apply these things should be bathed beforehand or made to relax by sitz-baths; and if after some time she brings forth nothing, she should again be relaxed by sitz-baths and for the second time a pessary should be applied.

Fausta would not, of course, have wished to abort a legitimate child, so it could not have been Constantine's. Her impregnation must have taken place, therefore, while she was apart from Constantine for some time. Perhaps she had fallen pregnant by a lover, maybe her servant, as Philostorgius alleged. Perhaps Crispus was her lover, as Zosimus would have it, or perhaps he had forced himself upon her, as would be allowed by Zonaras' account. However she came to be pregnant, Fausta's attempt to abort the foetus led to her death in a hot bath. If Constantine learnt of this, one can be sure that shame would ensure his silence, and that of everyone else, on the matter. This would be the case especially had his wife been raped, although that seems the least likely scenario. Whatever the truth of this episode, it ended in Rome in 326, the year and location of Constantine's *vicennalia* celebrations. Constantine's new Flavian dynasty, which he projected as a replacement for the messy meritocracy of the Tetrarchy and whose unity was so recently carved into the Great Cameo, was shattered. Shortly afterwards, the imperial residence in Trier was razed and a double church constructed on its site. It is likely that this was part of the *damnatio memoriae*, razing Crispus' imperial residence and placing Constantine's own mark on the site. Although damning the memory of his son would appear to display the opposite of contrition, a pagan tradition would associate this act with Constantine's desire to atone for his most heinous crime.

Goths and Sarmatians

Zosimus, following his fourth-century source Eunapius, observed that after the deaths of Fausta and Crispus Constantine did three things: he became a Christian, seeking absolution for his greatest sin; consequently, he refused to sacrifice, and so earned 'the hatred of the senate and people' of Rome and fled east to found Constantinople; and he 'fought no more successful battles'. On the conversion, he spins a fanciful tale:

Since he was himself aware of his guilt and of his disregard for oaths as well, Constantine approached the pagan priests seeking absolution, but they said that there was no kind of redemption known that could absolve him of such impieties. A certain Egyptian, who had come from Spain to Rome and was intimate with the ladies of the court, met Constantine and assured him that the Christian religion was able to absolve him from guilt and it promised every wicked man who converted to it immediate remission of all sin. Constantine readily believed what he was told and, abandoning his ancestral religion, embraced the one the Egyptian offered.

This story was refuted early in the fifth century by Sozomen (I.5). It omits the fact that in 326 Constantine had long associated with Christian bishops, including the Egyptian mentioned here who travelled from Spain to Rome, namely Ossius, bishop of Cordoba. More credence has been given to the claims that Constantine earned the opprobrium of the citizens of Rome, for he never returned to the city after 326, and that he fought no more successful wars, although neither is true.

In the later 320s Constantine was in his fifties. He was approaching the age at which his father had died, still campaigning in Britain, and Zosimus, and his source Eunapius, paint a picture of a weak and foolish old man, whose powers had waned. Julian would also recall his great uncle's deterioration, although since he was just six when Constantine died, it is hardly surprising that the Augustus, within a year or two of death, appeared aged to him. By then Constantine may indeed have felt that he had earned his leisure, or at least the pampering of life at court, to balance the years in the saddle and the tent, albeit one as well appointed as the imperial tent. But in the decade before that Constantine won his greatest victories over foreign enemies. Thus, when the pagan orator Libanius delivered in 344 or 345 a speech in praise of Constantine's sons, Constantius and Constans, he singled out the wars against the Goths and Sarmatians that were fought between 328 and 334.

In summer 328 Constantine was campaigning against the Goths at the Danube. He won some minor skirmishes, for which he took the title Gothicus Maximus for the first time, emulating his chosen forebear Claudius Gothicus. He founded a fortress on the left (northern) bank of the Danube called Daphne, across from the established fortress at Transmarisca (see map 1). Still more impressively, Constantine built the first stone bridge across the Danube to the Gothic shore (the so-called *ripa Gothica*), from Oescus to Sucidava, which was indeed the longest stone bridge ever built by the Romans. The intention was to open the way into Gothic territory, to effect their submission, and milestones lined the route into barbarian lands as far as Romula. Constantine then proceeded to Trier, where three laws were issued that have been preserved in the Theodosian Code, and gold coins were struck at the local mint, suggesting his presence in September and December 328 and in early 329. He may have campaigned in familiar territory, along the Rhine, in October 328. By 9 March 329 he was back at Sirmium again issuing laws, before heading south along the rivers Sava and Velika Morava to Naissus, his birthplace, where his presence is recorded on 13 May. Two weeks later he was at his sometime capital Sardica, where he was based for some months. On 3 August, and again on 25 October, he was at Heraclea in Thrace, where a mint continued to produce a small supply of gold and silver coins. However, he wintered in Sardica, departing some time after 5 February 330, bound for Constantinople and its formal dedication on 11 May. At some point in this ill-documented tour, the emperor was taken by surprise when 'the Thaiphali, a Scythian people [in fact Goths], attacked him with five hundred horse', and according to Zosimus (Eunapius), 'not only did he not oppose them, but when he had lost most of his army and saw them plundering as far as his fortified camp, he was glad to save himself with flight'. The people of this region generally known as Goths were in fact a number of smaller groupings, among them the Thaiphali, who appear to have been subordinate to the Tervingi. It may have been the depredations of the Tervingi that forced the Thaiphali to move south across the Danube and to violate Roman territory.

Constantine shuttled between Constantinople and its Bithynian hinterland in 330 and 331, but in April 332 his attention was once again drawn north. The ruler of the Gothic Tervingi had sought to expand his territory once again, now at the expense of his Sarmatian neighbours further to the west. The Sarmatians appealed to Constantine, who marched north to Marcianopolis (modern Devnya in Bulgaria), the provincial capital of Moesia Secunda, and a short way inland from the Black Sea port of Odessos (Varna). He appears to have dwelt there while his eldest son Constantine Caesar was summoned from Gaul, to lead the army against the Goths. No reliable information on the campaign has survived, but it was clearly a mighty victory for the Romans. Rumours circulated that

100,000 Goths were driven into a freezing wilderness to die of hunger and cold. The emperor took the title Gothicus Maximus II, for this was his second victory over the Goths. Gold medallions showed the emperor as DEBELLATOR GENTIUM BARBARUM, 'conqueror of the barbarian peoples', dragging by the hair a captive identified as GOTHIA. Copious copper coins were struck for distribution to the victorious troops, declaring GLORIA EXERCITUS, 'the glory of the army'.

A peace treaty was concluded, and guaranteed by the departure of the son of the ruler of the Tervingi, Ariaric. He was well treated, of course, and at some point a statue of him was erected behind the senate house, to remind all of the emperor's great victory. In the course of the wars Constantine had strung along the Danube many small but powerful fortresses, called *quadriburgia* after their four turreted corners and celebrated in his many coin issues featuring camp gates. However, as a consequence of the treaty of 332, the whole length of the frontier between Romans and Goths was open to trade. Indeed, there was now a broad frontier zone where Roman coins and barbarian imitations circulated freely to facilitate exchange; they were pumped into the region to pay the troops who manned the fortresses. Many thousands of the copper coins were dropped and have been found by chance or in excavations within the lands bordering the Danube. Gold and silver coins were not frequently dropped, or at least were not left where they were dropped unless for an extremely good reason (death or something like it). However, some small hoards have been found, most likely attesting to gifts and tribute payments that Constantine's heirs continued to send north, intended to ensure the loyalty of the Tervingi but also to reward the families of those who now served in the Roman army. Moreover, in 336 a bishop was consecrated for the Goths, a certain Ulfilas, who was invested with his office at Constantine's command by Eusebius, metropolitan bishop of Nicomedia, a man of whom we shall learn far more in the following chapters. The peace with the Goths lasted thirty years.

'When peace with the Goths had thus been secured,' the *Origo Constantini* records, 'Constantine turned against the Sarmatians, who were showing themselves to be of doubtful loyalty.' In fact, a huge wave of them was pushed across the Danube by further fluctuations to the north. Constantine returned to the Danube to settle affairs, and is recorded at Singidunum (modern Belgrade, in Serbia) on 5 July 334 and for the last time at his birthplace, Naissus, on 25 August. At that time, gold coins were struck at Siscia for the first time in seven or eight years, bearing the legend VICTORIA CONSTANTINI AUG. The Augustus was campaigning in that region once again, and was for the last time victorious. The *Origo Constantini* rather improbably suggests that he rounded up and resettled 300,000 Sarmatians within the empire, to cultivate empty fields and to contribute troops thereafter to the army. The emperor took the title Sarmaticus Maximus II. In addition, coins were minted throughout the empire declaring the emperor VICTOR OMNIUM GENTIUM, 'Victor over all peoples'. The last gold coin issued by Constantine at Trier, where he had established his military reputation, bore that legend.

An imperial palace remained on the Danube through the fourth century, at Sirmium. Recent excavations have turned up a fourth-century head of the Fortune of Sirmium, a parallel for Anthousa, the patron goddess of Constantine's Constantinople. Only later would Mary, the God-bearer (*Theotokos*) and Virgin (*Parthenos*), usurp Anthousa in her principal function as the good fortune and defender of the city, defending the defenders of the Christian people. Contemporary with the head, a fragment of a large oval sardonyx cameo (fig. 54), now to be found in the National Museum in Belgrade, appears to capture the imperial victories won over several years in the lands bordering the Danube, against both Goths and Sarmatians. A rider, certainly a general, surely an emperor, perhaps even Constantine himself, sits astride a rearing white horse, his left hand grasping the reins, his right holding a spear above his head, aimed at a figure now lost. The eyes of the rider point in the same direction but appear to be inclined upwards, perhaps to the divinity ensuring his victory. Remarkably, the eyes of his horse also appear to look heavenwards. The rider wears a cuirass, but one can pick out the pleats of the military tunic that protrude from it to cover his upper thighs and upper arms, and a military belt (*cingulum*) around his waist from which dangle two studded leather straps. His *paluda-mentum*, the cape that distinguishes him as a commander, is tossed over his left shoulder. It flies out behind him, indicating motion, and the natural colour of the sardonyx, blood-red, indicates the crimson of an emperor. His mid-calf-length boots, *cothurni*, are those of a general, and the elaborate lacing can be seen. The broken, twisted body of a barbarian lies beneath the horse's rear legs, and another between the front legs, although the upper torso of the second barbarian is now lost. Beneath the horse's tail, the hands of a barbarian, shirtless, muscular and bearded, are bound behind his back by a Roman legionary, who is identified by his uniform and helmet. The rider, however, wears no helmet; his head is adorned only with thick tousled hair and a ribbon. Like the central figure of the Ludovisi Sarcophagus, he needs no such protection, for he is divinely guarded, and his awareness of that fact is manifested in the look of hieratic calm on his face.

Christian soldiers?

What of the soldiers of Constantine Victor? Were they now to share the emperor's faith even as they marched under his banner? Were they to fight as Christians against pagan barbarians? There is no evidence that Constantine interfered with private worship within the army, nor that he mandated private devotion to his chosen god. Rather, he inserted due reverence to his patron god within the first category of worship we identified earlier (p. 14), and even then avoided insulting his followers by obliging them to utter the name of that god. Troops were ordered to pray to the greatest god who favoured their commander but did so in neutral terms. This is clear from the words of a prayer preserved by Eusebius (*VC* IV.20):

> You alone we know as god,
> You are the king we acknowledge,
> You are the help we summon.
> By you we have won victories,
> Through you we have overcome our enemies.
> To you we render thanks for good things past,
> You also we hope for as giver of those to come.
> To you we all come to supplicate for our emperor
> Constantine and his god-beloved sons:

That he may be kept safe and victorious for us in long,
  long life, we plead.

Nor was the second category of worship, which built unit cohesion,
overturned. There is no indication that in camp or on campaign the
army abandoned any of its regular battle standards, although Eusebius
notes that when they were performing drills for the emperor, 'he had
the sign of the cross marked on their shields, and had the army led on
parade not by any of the golden images, as had been their past practice,
but by the saving trophy alone' (VC IV.21). This is a reference to the
labarum, the perfect composite battle standard and a focus for veneration of a new god of victory, but it took its place alongside the eagles
(*aquilae*) and flag standards (*vexilla*) of an earlier age.

While wielding no stick to enforce conversion, Constantine did offer
his troops carrots. Eusebius relates (VC IV.18–19) that Constantine
'taught all the military to revere' Sunday, the Christian Sabbath, which
was also the 'Day of the Sun'. And 'to those who shared the divinely
given faith he allowed free time to attend unhindered the church of
God, on the assumption that with all impediment removed they would
join in the prayers.' As well as the offer – for the first time one must
emphasize – of a day off once a week, there were numerous additional
incentives to convert to Christianity that required no legislation.
Patronage operated as well as ever it had in the Roman hierarchy, and
Constantine promoted Christians to positions of command. It made
sense to those aspiring to high rank to emulate the emperor, and this
had a trickle-down effect. The example of senior officers had always
inspired, or indeed compelled, junior ranks to enrol in specific cultic
groups, for example the mysteries of Mithras. If one can identify a
clearer dynamic for the rapid adoption of Christianity by officers in
Constantine's army than patronage and 'peer pressure', it was the regular 'combination of browbeating and cajolery' that Peter Brown has
identified as the motor for Christianization of the Roman aristocracy.
Among the rank and file many would seek the approval of officers
through emulation, and none would wish to stand out as a dissenter.
Within units, the natural arena for the 'recurrent *obbligato* of ceremo-
nious bullying', an ethos would rapidly have been established that

rendered devotion to the god of the Christians integral to devotion to the common good.

So much might be expected even if worshipping the god in question were of questionable utility. But through Constantine's success, the god of the Christians had clearly emerged as a god of victory. Who, therefore, would wish to worship a lesser god, whose patronage might be inadequate to protect the devotee from the wrath of the neglected Christian deity? Even if one continued to worship Jupiter Dolichenus or Sol Invictus, surely it could not hurt also to venerate the latest manifestation of the greatest god? Such calculations were at the root of many early 'conversions' within the army, particularly since the brand of Christianity that Constantine espoused did not preclude participation in regular public rituals. Constantine notoriously remained *pontifex maximus*, head of the Roman colleges of priests, throughout his life, although by 315 he had refused to participate in sacrifices. Eusebius claims that Constantine issued legislation banning sacrifice altogether, but it is far more likely that he banned sacrifices associated with the imperial cult, which was permitted to continue with Constantine's Flavian dynasty (*gens Flavia*) as its new focus. Constantine continued to receive traditional acclamations from his troops, who invoked more than one divinity on his behalf. Nor was military discipline to be affected by notions of Christian charity. Punishment meted out for transgressions by officers, Christians or not, remained severe, for example death for granting leave to soldiers who were then absent during an attack, or being burnt alive for allowing barbarians to plunder Romans or share in the spoils of victory. Imperial Christianity was not a religion of peace and forgiveness.

The emperor's ability to ensure that his troops worshipped his chosen deity was greatly enhanced by radical changes in the structure of the army. By 325, according to an entry preserved in the Theodosian Code (*CTh* 7.20.4), a distinction had been drawn between the lesser frontier army (*ripenses*) and the field army (*comitatenses*). The first of the Tetrarchs, Diocletian, had certainly led a retinue or *comitatus*, which scholars have identified both as a central reserve army and as a personal bodyguard. All agree, however, that Constantine's mobile field army, the *comitatenses*, which was formed around the expeditionary force he had led into Italy in 312, was substantially larger and more stable than any *comitatus* Diocletian had fielded. It was to be distinguished from Constantine's personal bodyguard, the *scholae palatini*, which was created in the aftermath of the Battle of the Milvian Bridge, when the Praetorian Guard that had fought for Maxentius was first routed, then dissolved. The *comitatenses* were divided into infantry and cavalry units, the former under the command of a Master of the Foot (*magister peditum*), the latter under a Master of the Horse (*magister equitum*). At Chrysopolis the force numbered up to 120,000 infantry and 10,000 cavalry. These rather exact, and probably exaggerated, figures are supplied by Zosimus. However many men there were, all had reason to accept Constantine's god of victory as their own. The whole force cohered around the emperor, its rituals were those that he prescribed, and its beliefs, when overtly expressed, were those that he espoused.

This process was surely helped by the fact that, when not on campaign, these troops were no longer stationed in permanent *castra* (camps), where they might observe the regular ceremonies and rigours of camp life. Instead, when the campaigning season was done and the emperor retired to one of his courts, the soldiers of the *comitatenses* were billeted nearby within a town or its vicinity, while the barracks for the bodyguard (*scholae*) were within the palace complex at Constantinople (map 8). The communal prayer that Constantine had his troops intone took place at the parade grounds outside the walls of Constantinople, where they would assemble for that reason on Sunday, and on other days to drill. Otherwise they might spend their time, notably their evenings, in the city. Legislation in the Theodosian Code, the earliest of which dates from 340, suggests that trouble arose frequently, not least extortion and abuse of those obliged to house and feed soldiers. Evidently, billeting eroded discipline and other factors which were reinforced and renewed constantly by the rhythms and rituals of the camps. Yet it will also have removed those barriers to new practices and observations that the camp system would have erected, and thus may have allowed for the more rapid expansion of Christian worship, notably in Constantinople's growing number of churches.

Imperial Christianity may have taken longer to permeate the frontier legions, which had little direct contact with the emperor or his entourage. However, they too were no longer concentrated in large camps from which they would march out on campaign. Instead, and in keeping with the empire's more defensive stance, legions were broken up into smaller units with uncertain names. These units were not the legionary cohorts of an earlier age, consisting of centuries and maniples, which all seem to have disappeared. And if legionary cohorts once possessed their own standards beyond those of the legion, they too were gone. Diverse groups might then be united into vexillations, scratch units put together for specific campaigns. The basic structure of the army in its high imperial phase thus gave way to ad hoc formulations. The ethos of a unitary legion, its essential *esprit de corps*, could hardly survive such a fate, and no longer would the legionary *signa*, least of all the eagles, play a role in the daily ceremony of a frontier soldier. In their place one might expect to find the faith of the emperor making ground.

Christianization was a protracted process and one might cite many examples which attest to the continued vitality of non-Christian cults. The worship of Mithras had lost much of its vigour by the later third century, but a small Mithraeum outside Prutting near the river Inn continued in use until the end of the fourth century. New frontier fortresses built by Constantine and his successors contained no obvious spaces for Christian worship. For example, Deutz (Divitia) opposite Cologne has no Christian chapel, even though it was built between 312 and 315 by the Twenty-second Legion C[onstantiniana] V[ictrix], a legion formerly known as Primigenia after the goddess Fortuna. This need not surprise us, as private devotion was always conducted beyond the walls of the camp. Yet the spread of Christianity among the *ripenses* can be detected in the archaeological record. Some frontier fortresses were modified before *c.*400 to facilitate Christian worship and, notably, the baptism of soldiers. The British outpost of Richborough (Rutupiae) in Kent, the last base of the Second Legion Augusta, included a chapel with a baptismal font. Three forts on the Rhine frontier, at Boppard, Kaiseraugst and Zurzach, all incorporated small chapels with fonts. On the middle Danube several sites, including Saldum and Zanes, may have been given rectangular chapel towers. Such construction within the walls of the camp was a marked change from earlier practice. Before such permanent installations were constructed, baptism would have been carried out in portable lead tanks, decorated with suitable scenes. Twenty-one of these have survived from the frontier province of Britannia, nine of which are marked with the chi-rho. Two fine examples found at Walesby in Lincolnshire and Flawborough in Nottinghamshire feature the chi-rho among other Christian iconography. The former is decorated near its rim with pictures of catechumens, candidates for baptism, above a simple six-pointed star (fig. 55); the latter has the invocation VTERE FELIX ('use happy', or better, 'good luck') next to *orantes*, figures holding their hands to the sky in prayer.

If these few archaeological observations tell us very little with certainty, they support the notion that the introduction of Christianity along the frontiers was slow, but that the process of Christian baptism took place with increasing regularity in military districts and army camps through the fourth century. Reasons for this might be found in the changing make-up of the later Roman army, notably in the recruitment of large numbers of barbarians. The names of several new units of auxiliaries raised by Constantine are known from the *Notitia Dignitatum*, dating from the late fourth century. Although recently scholars have emphasized the rhetorical qualities of this text, undermining its use as a means to reconstruct administrative and military realities for the western empire, the clues it provides are supported by allusions in earlier sources. It is clear that certain units were recruited in eastern Gaul and Germany, as they bear local tribal names like Batavi, Celtae, Heruli, Salii and Tubantes. Although the exact areas of recruitment cannot be ascertained, a few sources help. Socrates Scholasticus, writing of Constantine's accession, claimed that 'it was then no easy matter to dwell . . . in Britain, or in the neighbouring countries, in which it is universally admitted Constantine embraced the religion of the Christians, before his war with Maxentius, and prior to his return to Rome and Italy'. He meant that there were few Christians in those regions. However, as Zosimus later noted, Britons made up the bulk of Constantine's field army before he recruited Germans and Gauls. In a panegyric in honour of Constantius, which the future emperor Julian delivered in 355, he refers to the usurper Magnentius' use of troops raised by earlier emperors, notably 'Celts and Galatians [Gauls] who had seemed invincible even to our ancestors . . . [who] had been enrolled in the ranks of our armies and furnished levies that won a brilliant reputation, being enlisted by your ancestors, and later by your father [Constantine]'. This was the same army 'that had always proved itself invincible, and ... conquered a miserable old man [Maxentius]'. The Cornuti and Bracchiati have earned special attention from scholars, because of their eponymous horned helmets and armbands and because they seem to have played a decisive role in Constantine's Italian campaign of 312. The Cornuti are clearly depicted on the Arch of Constantine wearing their horned helmets and carrying shields depicting their emblem, two confronted goats' heads. While there is no reason to assert, as have some scholars, that the Roman army was barbarized in the fourth century, still there were clearly far greater numbers being recruited from among Germanic peoples settled both within and beyond the empire's borders.

Here, then, is a fine reason for the promotion of Christianity among recruits, beyond Constantine's desire to preserve the support of the greatest god for his endeavours. Christianity provided a coherent moral framework during times of peace, and in times of war it built morale in an increasingly fragmented force where ethnic units might otherwise fight or flee separately. Men would always fight more aggressively for comrades than for an idea, but Christianity as a common faith was a better means to bind men together than the diluted notion of Rome, the grandeur of which most soldiers would never see and whose patron gods could no longer be held to stay an enemy's hand or to deflect his sword. Men would fight to the death with greater confidence if they believed that they were watched over by the emperor's god of victory. A century after Constantine, Prosper of Aquitaine could note with conviction that the Roman army took in barbarians and sent home Christians.

The Greatest Victor

In his last years as emperor, as in his earliest, Constantine placed his victories in war above all other achievements. His official imperial titles reflected this, employing both the *praenomen imperatoris* and the additional phrase Maximus Victor ac Triumfator, 'greatest victor and winner of triumphs'. These titles were followed by four campaign-specific surnames (*cognomina*): Germanicus, Sarmaticus, Gothicus and Dacicus, 'conqueror of the Germans, Sarmatians, Goths and Dacians'. A letter despatched by Constantine to consuls, praetors, tribunes and senators in February 337 presents his imperial titulature in full: Imperator Caesar Flavius Constantinus Pius Felix Victor ac Triumfator Pontifex Maximus Germanicus Maximus IIII Sarmaticus Maximus II Gothicus Maximus II Dacicus Maximus Tribunicia Potestate XXXIII Consul VIII Imperator XXXII Pater Patriae Proconsul. As he approached death, Constantine wished to be addressed by the list of barbarian peoples he had defeated in battle, and where they had lost more than once to him, this too was emphasized. He had only lately won his second victories over the Goths and Sarmatians.

Constantine placed emphasis only on those victories he had won personally, reflecting the divine favour that had attended his campaigns and no others. He did not even claim those victories won in his name by his own sons when he did not accompany them. Thus he reversed a trend that had been established a century and a half earlier in the joint reign of Marcus Aurelius and Lucius Verus (AD 161–9), who had first taken *cognomina* to celebrate each other's victories. Marcus Aurelius was the first emperor to hold five *cognomina*, although he never took part in a battle, and for the first time *maximus*, 'the greatest', appeared beside the name of the conquered people. But even as the rhetoric of the singular sovereign and victor reached its crescendo, Constantine devolved power to seasoned administrators, and ultimately divided the empire in a fashion that recalled the Tetrarchy.

10

Constantine Maximus Augustus

Government – Life at court – Pentarchy – Persia –
The Holy Places

In 326 Constantine's new mint in Constantinople struck coins that proclaimed him as Augustus, the only emperor now to hold that title. On the reverses of both the silver and the gold issues the goddess Victory is depicted advancing to the left, bearing in her right hand a laurel wreath to crown the emperor. But on the obverse of the silver coin, though not yet the gold, the emperor is hailed as CONSTANTINUS MAXIMUS AUGUSTUS, 'Constantine the Greatest Augustus'. From 327 all coins, in gold, silver and bronze, struck in his name at Constantinople bore that legend, to celebrate the sovereign of the whole Roman world. Constantine reigned alone from Hadrian's Wall to the fringes of Mesopotamia, but between 330 and 337 he spent more time than ever, perhaps the majority of his time, in his palace at Constantinople.

Government

Constantinople was the new cog in a complex machine, and one with which most levers of government had hitherto had no connection. Constantine would build those connections rapidly, forging a far more centralized system than had existed for more than a century. But still, especially in the heavily urbanized east, his subjects dealt primarily with municipal leaders (traditionally *curiales*) and, increasingly, with bishops. In provincial administration, Constantine did not radically alter the reforms Diocletian had introduced two decades earlier, the bare bones of which are preserved in the *Verona List*, a document produced around AD 314. The empire was by then divided into twelve dioceses, each of which comprised a number of provinces that totalled a hundred or more. If one were to travel through the empire from one Pillar of Hercules to the other by land, one could circle the Mediterranean and pass through all twelve dioceses without ever crossing the sea except at the Bosphorus and the English Channel. Starting at Tingi (modern Tangier) in the diocese of Hispaniae, one would pass through: Africa, Oriens, Pontica, Asiana, Thracia, Moesiae, Pannoniae, Italia, Galliae, Britanniae, Viennensis and back into Hispaniae (see map 3).* Each diocese was under the care of a *vicarius*, which we might translate as 'vicar'. All provincial governors answered to a vicar, and the rulings of governors could be appealed by subjects to the appropriate vicar. Britannia, the most distant and least developed diocese, contained four provinces; Thracia, the smallest diocese in area, contained six provinces; Oriens, by far the largest, contained sixteen, later seventeen provinces.

Each vicar answered to a Praetorian Prefect. In 314 there were four Praetorian Prefectures, each containing three dioceses. Constantine expanded this to five, granting Africa alone to a Praetorian Prefect. The title Praetorian Prefect had until recently designated the commander of the Praetorian Guard, the imperial regiment based in Rome, or the military officer immediately subordinate to an emperor. Now, in a radical change, the office became entirely civilian. It was, indeed, the most important civilian office in the empire, and under the Tetrarchy, while each emperor had focused on campaigning, his Praetorian Prefect enjoyed overall responsibility for government, most significantly in financial matters and the levying of taxes. He also presided over the final court of appeal in each region. After 326, when only one Augustus reigned, the Praetorian Prefects attained still greater prestige. Indeed, this escalation is reflected in the appointment of ordinary consuls during the last decade of Constantine's reign. Consul was the most prestigious title one could hold in the Roman system, and – since counting in *Anni Domini* was not yet used – each year was entered in the rolls under the names of the two men thus honoured. When Tetrarchs went to war, a clear

---

* The ending -ae, as in Galliae, Pannoniae or Moesiae, is a plural, to indicate that there were several provinces in the diocese. These are also seen in the singular forms: Gallia, Pannonia, Moesia, etc.

sign of their mutual hostility was the refusal to recognize the same consuls; instead, each appointed his own favourites. In the later 310s and early 320s, as Constantine and Licinius worked out their differences, the consuls were the two Augusti and their sons and relatives. For example, in 321 the consuls were recognized either as Crispus and Constantine, sons of Constantine; or as Licinius and his son Licinianus. Now, as Constantine ruled alone, Praetorian Prefects took their places alongside emperors, and then replaced them as ordinary consuls. A list may serve to illustrate:

326 Constantine (for the seventh time), Constantius (for the first time)
327 Flavius Constantius [PP], Valerius Maximus [PP]
328 Flavius Januarius, Vettius Justus
329 Constantine (for the eighth time), Constantine (his eldest son, for the fourth)
330 Flavius Gallicanus, Aurelius Valerius Tullianus Symmachus Phosphorius
331 Junius Bassus [PP], Flavius Ablabius [PP]
332 Papius Pacatianus [PP], Mecilius Hilarianus
333 Flavius Dalmatius, Domitius Zenophilus
334 Flavius Optatus, Anicius Paulinus Iunior
335 Julius Constantius, Rufius Albinus
336 Virius Nepotianus, Tettius Facundus
337 Flavius Felicianus, Fabius Titianus

At least five of these men are known to have been Praetorian Prefects (marked PP) in the same year that they held the title consul. Only Constantine's relatives were so frequently honoured as consuls: Flavius Dalmatius and Julius Constantius were Constantine's half-brothers, and Virius Nepotianus was probably the husband of his half-sister Eutropia. Others may have been related to the emperor in ways we can no longer ascertain.

If the office of ordinary consul carried no power, it was accorded only to powerful men, and none were more powerful than the Praetorian Prefects. According to a law issued in 331 (*CTh* 11.30.16), judgements rendered by vicars might be referred to the imperial court, but those of Praetorians could not be appealed, since they 'alone may truly be said to judge in place of the emperor'. It might legitimately be stated that even as he ruled alone, Constantine ruled with four colleagues, foreshadowing a pentarchy. Indeed, such was the division of powers that, although the emperor might reverse any matter of his choosing and remove any Praetorian at will, still it would be fair to say that he retained exclusive authority only in two areas: in the realm of religion, as *pontifex maximus*, and in the realm of war as commander-in-chief of the army. In those areas the Praetorians had no involvement, particularly in military affairs, for here Constantine created the offices of the Master of the Foot (*magister peditum*) and the Master of the Horse (*magister equitum*) (see above, p. 231). The Praetorians' authority in civil matters was, however, circumscribed by the creation of offices attached to the person of the emperor or within his palace administration.

In charge of the palatine administration was the Master of Offices (*magister officiorum*), who might best be described as the emperor's chief-of-staff. His only equal was the Quaestor, who drafted imperial legislation and replied to letters and petitions. He was, in effect, the emperor's principal private secretary. If the Praetorians between them controlled justice, foreign affairs, home affairs, the levying of taxes and the distribution of provisions, their activities and those of their subordinates were monitored by officials working under the Master of Offices and the Quaestor on behalf of the emperor. Thus we see alongside vicars in their dioceses men known as *comites provinciarum*, 'counts of the provinces'. There is no indication whether this was a permanent post, or whether the counts roved widely, ensuring that the emperor's interests were served. 'Count' might more correctly be translated as 'companion' (sing. *comes*, pl. *comites*), for these men were regarded as, and in many cases were, the emperor's close companions and most senior advisers. Thus, in 330 he sent two counts to Antioch to resolve a dispute in its church, to which we shall turn in the following chapter. Their names were Acacius, who had earlier been despatched to destroy a temple at Mamre, and Strategius, who would later become a Praetorian Prefect. To Strategius Constantine had given the nickname 'Musonianus', after the first-century Stoic philosopher Musonius Rufus.* A still higher rank was introduced by Constantine, when he co-opted the ancient Roman designation of 'patrician' (*patricius*) and applied it to a very few men, perhaps those whom he entrusted with particularly sensitive tasks. It may have been a rank reserved for his relatives, if one accepts the kinship of Flavius Optatus, who had earlier served as an adviser to Licinius and tutor to his son and who was consul in 334. It has been suggested that Optatus, or his wife, was related to Helena, Constantine's mother.

The Masters of the Foot and of the Horse were both counts, as was the Master of Offices. In addition, two counts, as permanent senior staff, ran departments in the imperial treasury, one administering the imperial estates and properties, the other the collection of indirect taxes (e.g. customs duties) and, significantly, the distribution of donatives to the army. Beneath the ranks of patrician and count were numerous palatine administrators of great importance. The Master of Offices administered three secretariats (*scrinia*), dealing with petitions, reports and the requests of embassies. The Quaestor drew his principal subordinates in the emperor's private office from these offices. The Master of Offices also handled a cadre of roving 'agents' (*agentes in rebus*), whose tasks were ill defined but included oversight of the imperial postal system (*cursus publicus*), ensuring coordination between dioceses in adjoining prefectures. There was here duplication of responsibility, which was intended to provide oversight but may also have layered bureaucracy and increased inefficiency. The system would, over time, acquire ever more layers, with new offices created to perform established tasks, and surviving offices performing new tasks. Indeed, the tendency not to disband bureaux, but simply to duplicate and allow the older office to wither, led to the bureaucratic system that we call 'Byzantine'. A good reason for this inertia and complexity was the fact that employment in the palatine administration conferred substantial benefits. Bureaucrats, and their sons, and their grandsons, were exempted from serving as municipal officers in their home towns or cities, and might not be required

---

* It is unfortunate that we do not know more about the emperor's habits, for example whether he regularly doled out nicknames to 'name and tame' those around him, or to bring the ethos of the camp into the court.

to billet troops, nor to supply materials or labour for public works. Consequently, for three generations, palatine bureaucrats were freed from substantial financial burdens. Similar exemptions would be afforded to bishops.

The system was not born a behemoth, but still Constantine was condemned for his largesse by those who did not benefit or no longer benefited from his innovations, and he was berated by those who bore the burden of financing it through increased taxes and extraordinary levies. The burden of feeding the bureaucracy of Constantinople fell on the same subjects who were now asked to feed and entertain the tens, later hundreds of thousands of citizens who flocked to the new capital and who received the grain dole and attended the games. Meanwhile, within the palace, banquets and entertainment were provided on the grandest scale, and embassies from the furthest reaches were received.

Life at court

Constantine spent most of his time between 330 and 337 at Constantinople. On the few occasions that he found himself there, Eusebius, playing the role of courtier, observed embassies from every known continent (*VC* IV.7):

There were constant diplomatic visitors who brought valuable gifts from their homelands . . . we saw before the outer palace gates waiting in a line remarkable figures of barbarians, the quite singular cut of hair and beard; the appearance of their hairy faces was outlandish and astounding, their bodily height exceptional. The faces of some were red, of others whiter than snow, of others blacker than ebony or pitch, and others had a mixed colour in between . . . Each of these in turn, as in a picture, brought their particular treasures to the emperor, some of them golden crowns, some diadems of precious stones, others fair-haired children, others foreign cloths woven with gold and bright colours, others horses, others shields and long spears and javelins and bows, showing that they were offering service and alliance with these things . . . [The emperor] responded with equal gifts so as to make the bearers rich all at once. He honoured the most distinguished of them also with Roman titles, so that very many now longed to remain here, forgetting any thought of returning to their homes.

The palace complex in Constantinople had been established with ceremonies in mind (map 8). Ambassadors, as Eusebius noted, gathered outside the palace's outer gate, jockeying for position, to be ushered into the complex and brought gradually, through hallways and transitional rooms, before the emperor's chamberlains. They would have passed from the Augusteion into the Tribounalion and through the horseshoe-shaped Onopodion. Ultimately the most favoured would have seen the emperor himself, wearing his diadem and dressed in purple and gold-trimmed silks, perhaps brought by earlier guests, since the secrets of silk production did not reach Constantinople from China until the sixth century. The emperor had emerged from the Octagon, his robing chamber, into his reception room, the Augusteus, where he would be found seated high on his throne. Perhaps later the ambassadors might have dined in the Triklinos of the Nineteen Couches, in the emperor's presence.

In 335–6 ambassadors from the Indians, 'who live near the rising sun,' presented themselves bearing gifts. These were all sorts of sparkling jewels, and animals of breeds differing from those known among us . . . So when [Constantine] began his reign the first to be subjected to him were the Britons near where the sun sets in the Ocean, and now it was the Indians, whose land lies near the sunrise.' One must imagine the ambassadors brought rubies and sapphires, and of semi-precious stones certainly carnelians and agates, which they had supplied to Roman engravers for centuries. There may even have been diamonds, which were hitherto barely known in the classical world (although Pliny the Elder knew of them and that they were from India). Of beasts, one would like to imagine there was a single-horned rhinoceros, but there is no suggestion that this was known to Romans after the reign of Vespasian, although one may be depicted on a medallion of Caracalla. Surely there would have been Indian elephants and tigers, such as those first brought by Indian ambassadors to the empire in 19–20 BC and first displayed to the citizens of the older Rome by Claudius in c.AD 50. Elagabalus is alleged to have killed fifty-one tigers in the Roman hippodrome, but there is no indication that any gifted to Constantine met the same fate in Constantinople. On the Barberini Diptych, a carved ivory plaque now attributed to the reign of Justinian, an Indian embassy is depicted in its lowest register, where two men, nude from the waist up and wearing turbans, bow low to the emperor and offer him a tiger and a rather small elephant (fig. 56). One man is weighed down by an enormous tusk, reminding us that the Romans relied on such imports and gifts for the production of the very item we behold. The tiger symbolized strength and ferocity, of course, and the Indian ambassadors knew that Roman emperors conceived of wild beasts as akin to the barbarians they defeated in war. But more especially for Constantine, the new Alexander, the tiger suggested that his dominion reached as far as Alexander had travelled. And it represented victory, for tigers, like leopards, panthers and centaurs, are commonly shown in Roman art pulling the chariot of Dionysus (figs. 6, 7, 53).

When not entertaining barbarians, Constantine was entertained by the most refined of his coterie, who offered their latest philosophical or historical insights. As bitterly as the Augustus now looked back on his time at Diocletian's court in Nicomedia, he certainly recalled the intellectual energy generated by Porphyry's lectures. He heard often from panegyrists, of course, on large public occasions, and even in his salon he was offered flattering prose by those who had more or less time to devote to literature. Flavius Ablabius, while serving as Praetorian Prefect after 329, was perhaps an historian of the Goths, writing to celebrate Constantine's victories. Certainly, an Ablabius was cited later as a source by Cassiodorus and Jordanes. Ablabius was also a poet, or at least an aphorist, for Sidonius Apollinaris, in 477, attributed to him a stinging rebuke of Constantine at the time of the deaths of Crispus and Fausta. 'Who wants back Saturn and his golden age? We have the diamond age – of Nero.' The satirist Ablabius did not attack only with his words, for he engineered the demise of another doyen of the salon, Sopater, an orator and Neoplatonist philosopher, who had moved to Constantinople from Apamea, near Antioch, upon the death of his teacher Iamblichus. Swiftly, Sopater had become a favourite of Constantine and a frequent dining partner, but he would fall victim to Ablabius. A fanciful story is recounted by Eunapius:

It happens, moreover, that the site of Byzantium is not adapted for the approach of ships that touch there, except when a strong wind is blowing due from the south. At that time, then, there happened what often used to happen according to the nature of the seasons; and the citizens were assembled in the theatre, worn out by hunger. The applause from the drunken populace was scanty, and the emperor was greatly discouraged. Then those who had long been envious thought that they had found an excellent occasion, and said: 'It is Sopater, he whom you honour, who has fettered the winds by that excessive cleverness which you yourself praise, and through which he even sits on the Imperial throne.' When Constantine heard this he was won over, and ordered Sopater's head to be cut off; and those envious persons took care that this was no sooner said than done. Ablabius was responsible for all these evils, for, though he was Praetorian Prefect, he felt stifled with envy of Sopater, who received more consideration than himself.

The tale is hardly credible, but the death of Sopater does coincide with troubles in Alexandria and also with disruption in grain supplies to Constantinople associated with a period of famine in the east. Perhaps Sopater served as a prominent scapegoat, whose licence at court had expired. Constantine was also at this time, as we shall see, striving to settle the matter of Arius, the heresiarch whom he only then condemned as no better than Porphyry. Evidently, Neoplatonism was not at that moment a favoured philosophy in Constantinople.

Into this world of orators and philosophers wandered bishops from the provinces. It was imperative, in order to make an impression, that they were as eloquent and skilled as non-Christians. The bishop considered the most educated and able by many including himself, Eusebius of Caesarea, found himself only occasionally in the emperor's presence, although he is very successful in obscuring that fact in his works and has ever since served as the principal witness of Constantine's reign. Others who knew the emperor better were, earlier in his reign, Lactantius and Ossius, bishop of Cordoba, and later, Eustathius of Nicomedia. There were many others who benefited from Constantine's interest and patronage, as we shall see, but it is as well here to note that the bishops were but one group, and certainly not a united group, seeking to influence and impress the sovereign.

Pentarchy

The height of imperial majesty was achieved in Constantine's thirtieth year of power, which commenced in September 335. In that month the great church complex at the Holy Sepulchre in Jerusalem was dedicated, and the empire's Christian bishops were summoned from a council in Tyre to attend at imperial expense. We shall turn to these matters shortly. But Constantine did not travel to Jerusalem, nor did he visit Rome, as he had for his *decennalia* and *vicennalia*. Instead, he spent the year mostly in Constantinople in celebration. The coins he issued offered prayers for his thirty years and expressed the hope that he would reach forty, but the aging emperor was not confident that he would. He was now approaching sixty, already older than his father at his death, and he relied increasingly on others. Although there are no clear indications in the historical record that his authority was undermined, some big beasts prowled around, most threateningly two of his half-brothers, Julius Constantius and Flavius Dalmatius, the sons of Constantius Chlorus and grandsons of Maximian. The brothers were at first despatched far from court, to Toulouse. They may also have spent some time in Rome and elsewhere in Italy, always carefully watched. However, by the time the court moved to Constantinople, they had been brought back from exile, the easier to monitor their actions and intentions. If they were not trusted, still they were assigned important ranks. Dalmatius was appointed censor in 333, by now an honorific title but perhaps associated with Constantine's moral agenda, for traditionally censors monitored the public morals. It seems certain that he also held the rank of patrician, to which Julius was promoted in 335. They in turn used their access and prestige, and perhaps even veiled threats, to press the interests of their own sons, Constantine's nephews. Moreover, as part of his tricennial celebrations, Constantine married his second son, Constantius, now aged nineteen, to the daughter of Julius Constantius and acted as the groom's 'best man' and as the host of banquets and receptions.

A statue base from Antioch, inscribed in 336, reveals that in his tricennial year Constantine was supported by five Praetorian Prefects: Papius Pacatianus, Flavius Ablabius, Valerius Felix, Annius Tiberianus, and Nestorius Timonianus. It does not reveal that at this time the Prefects had become associated with junior emperors, forming a Pentarchy. Constantine had long realized the value of shared command, but rejected the premise of the Tetrarchy that this should not take account of blood.

Once he had established himself as the sole Augustus, he began to associate his sons and also his nephews with established Praetorian Prefects, anticipating that they might thereby learn how to govern. They occupied the imperial buildings in capitals established for earlier Tetrarchs, at Milan and Trier, Sirmium and Antioch, and enjoyed their own palatine staffs, although these were considerably smaller than that attached to the Augustus.

We have so far met only two Caesars, Constantine's sons Constantine and Constantius, elevated in 317 and 324. The youngest son, Constans, became a Caesar in 333, and Aurelius Victor records that his promotion was followed by ominous portents in the sky. One might suppose that the appearance of a comet would be interpreted as a good sign by those who supported the promotion, although Victor records the sentiments of those who held the opposite viewpoint and who proved to be correct, at least within five years. In 335 Constantine also elevated to the rank of Caesar his nephew, Flavius Dalmatius, son of his half-brother of the same name. Aurelius Victor records the promotion tersely: 'About two years after this [the promotion of Constans in 333], he [Constantine] designated as Caesar his brother's son, who was named Dalmatius after his father, even though the soldiers vigorously objected.' It was around the same time that Dalmatius' second son, Hannibalianus, was given the title 'King of Kings and of the Pontians'. Only the sons of Julius were neglected at this time; their names were Gallus and Julian.

Constantine II, the oldest surviving son, received what one might call the patrimony: he settled in his father's palace at Trier in the diocese of Galliae, and governed as well Viennensis (with Arles), Britannia, where his father had been acclaimed, and Hispaniae; his Praetorian Prefect was Annius Tiberianus. Constans, the youngest son, received the spoils of Constantine's first great victories, in Italy and Pannoniae, with the cities of Rome, Milan and Sirmium; his Praetorian was Papius Pacatianus. Flavius Dalmatius was granted Moesiae and Thracia, along with the Prefect Valerius Felix and Naissus, Constantine's birthplace. Constantius II was to administer the mighty diocese of Oriens with the guidance of Nestorius Timonianus, and he was to do so from the imperial palace at Antioch. Constantine kept for himself his most trusted adviser and senior Praetorian, Flavius Ablabius. According to Eunapius,

Ablabius, born humbly in Crete, 'proved to be so much the darling of Fortune who delights in novelties, that he became even more powerful than the emperor'. It seems likely that Ablabius engineered the division of empire during his tenure in Constantinople, and this was intended in part to ensure his own continuing good fortune, for he had managed to have his daughter Olympias betrothed to Constans. There is no indication that the young girl accompanied Constans when he was shipped off to Italy, initially to Milan, and travelled from there to Rome and also to Hispellum, a city in Umbria, the region from which the original Flavian dynasty emerged. At the request of the citizens, Hispellum was formally renamed Flavia Constans, and a temple, not a church, was erected and a priest appointed to administer the cult of the Flavian dynasty.

Eusebius, in his *Tricennial Oration* (3.2), delivered shortly after the promotion of the fourth Caesar, said of Constantine that 'having yoked the four valiant Caesars like colts beneath the single yoke of the imperial chariot, he controls them with the reins of holy harmony and concord'. Eusebius considered the appointment of four Caesars to be the fulfilment of the prophecy in the Book of Daniel (7.27), where the 'four living things' (or 'four beasts') would herald the coming of the 'Ancient of days' to render 'judgement on the saints of Most High: and the time came on and the saints possessed the kingdom'. There were, however, pressing practical reasons to appoint the Caesars to high command. Besides neutralizing his half-brothers, Constantine would also placate his older surviving sons. They had reached ages where they might expect greater authority and even contemplate challenging their father if denied, doubtless supported by the disappointed or disaffected that every regime generates. There were many such men despite Constantine's willingness and ability to suppress and eliminate dissent. For dynastic reasons, moreover, Constantine would have wished to effect a settlement while he could still enforce his will and to place his sons in positions of authority from which they might resist challenges more effectively. To have earned the trust and loyalty of the regional armies was the greatest gift he could bestow. Thirdly, to have effected a territorial division equitably and in advance would provide some, if not great, hope that the sons would accept the father's disposition, and perhaps accept a junior role for their cousins. The alternative was civil war, which the empire could not afford, for a new threat had emerged. For the first time in almost four decades war with Persia loomed.

Persia

Throughout his later campaigns against the Goths and Sarmatians, Constantine retained faith in the power of his saving trophy, the *labarum*. He knew that his god would support him against enemies of the chosen people, the Romans, and he had made this plain in a letter to Shapur II, ruler of the Persians (*VC* IV.8–13). Shapur's ancestor and namesake, Constantine observed, had been a mere agent of the wrathful Christian god when capturing the Roman emperor Valerian (d. AD 260), a persecutor of Christians. 'This God I serve,' he continued, 'Whose sign my army, dedicated to God, bears on its shoulders; to whatever task the word of justice calls it that army marches . . . and I receive His grace in manifest trophies of victory.' Many have regarded this, unlike other letters preserved by Eusebius, as a pious fiction. However, it may well reflect Constantine's response to an embassy, despatched by Shapur to the new emperor in the east, following his victory over Licinius, where the *labarum* and the rhetoric of Christian victory were so prominent. Formally, Rome had been at peace with Persia since Galerius' great campaigns of the 290s in which the young Constantine had participated, and the Persian embassy reaffirmed that status. However, in the years between, an episode of the greatest importance had occurred: the conversion of the kingdom of Armenia to Christianity, traditionally attributed to the influence of a bishop from Cappadocia, Gregory the Illuminator. And in around 330, the rulers of Caucasian Iberia, roughly corresponding to the eastern part of modern Georgia, adopted Christianity. These were not inconsiderable lands that lay between the vast empires of Rome and Persia, subject at various times to one or other of them, and contained large numbers of Zoroastrians.

These sweeping religious and cultural changes took place at a time of great unrest, for famine and plague had swept through the east between 330 and 333. An account is preserved in the ninth-century Chronicle of Theophanes Confessor, under the year 331–2:

In this year, when the seventh indiction was about to follow, a famine occurred in the east which was so extremely severe that villagers gathered together in great throngs in the territory of the Antiochenes and of Cyrus and assailed each other and stole food in attacks by night, and finally, even in daylight they would break into the granaries, looting and stealing everything in the store-houses before they departed. A *modius* of corn cost 400 pieces of silver.

To alleviate the situation, Constantine diverted grain ships to Antioch. The Church was supplied with 36,000 *modii* – the exact weight varied, but a *modius* can be taken to be between eight and nine kilos, and the total amount of grain to be somewhat more than 300 tonnes – for distribution.

Around the same time a huge earthquake destroyed Salamis on Cyprus, a city of more than 30,000, sending tremors extending thousands of miles. In the aftermath, a pretender rose up, named Calocerus, who was able to establish control over the island, a province in the diocese of Oriens. Constantine sent his half-brother Flavius Dalmatius to over-see the situation in Antioch and to crush the pretender in Cyprus. This he did with ominous efficiency, and it was surely as a challenge to Constantine that, in violation of recent legislation forbidding the prac-tice, he put Calocerus to death by crucifixion. Rumours will have circulated that Dalmatius was not truly a Christian, and this much is reflected by Eusebius later. The historical record would also be altered to mask Dalmatius' rebuke: Calocerus was said to have been burnt alive, in Tarsus, a demise which would offend fewer Christians.

The Persians were also deeply affected by the pestilence and famine. Were these signs of divine displeasure? Shapur may have wondered, since so many were turning away from his faith and that of his ancestors, Zoroastrianism. In 334 Shapur sent his troops to remove and blind the Christian king of Armenia and to install a Zoroastrian of his choosing. He also began to persecute Christians living in Persian lands. A Christian witness to the Persian persecution, Aphrahat of Mosul, turned to his Old Testament, where the Book of Daniel revealed to him that the Persians would be cast down by the Romans, whose empire would persist until the end times, when its powers would be surrendered to Christ. Aphrahat anticipated that Constantine would march against Persia and that he would be victorious. Constantine drew the same conclusion. He named his nephew Hannibalianus 'King of Kings' of Armenia and the other Pontic peoples and, perhaps now wary of trusting his half-brother, sent his son Constantius and his most senior Praetorian Prefect Flavius Ablabius to Antioch to prepare for war.

Constantine was anxious for war and to take the path of Alexander into Mesopotamia. The title Persicus Maximus would be his, he was convinced, and at least according to Socrates Scholasticus a century later, Constantine 'constructed a tent of embroidered linen on the model of a church, just as Moses had done in the wilderness. It was designed to be carried about so he might have a house of prayer ready even in the extreme deserts.' He was still both new Alexander and new Moses.

As these preparations continued, a Persian embassy arrived at Constantine's court. The section of Eusebius' *Life of Constantine* that would relate this episode has been lost, perhaps deliberately excised, but a version of the encounter has been preserved in an Oration (59) by Libanius, delivered a decade later. Libanius explains that the Persians had long desired iron ore, which they needed to manufacture weapons and armour, but which could not be obtained in abundance except from within Roman territory. Constantine had earlier, in 324, presumably following Licinius' example, granted permission for iron ore to be exported, and was persuaded that the Persians needed it to fight their barbarian neighbours. But when Shapur's true intentions, to reverse the defeat and losses of 298–9, became plain, and Constantine saw the formidable force of heavily armed and chain-mailed cavalry the Persians had constructed, he saw no alternative to war. The embassy was dismissed out of hand.

Libanius' oration was addressed to Constantine's sons, Constantius and Constans, in 344–5. Constantius had been with his father at the start of the conflict with Persia and pressed the war even as Libanius spoke. Indeed, the war with the Persians dragged on for half a century with no substantial advantage to the Romans, and it was tempting to blame the father for the son's woes. Libanius does just that, reminding his audience that 'Should any knowledgeable person examine the dates, he will find that the beginnings of the war preceded Constantine's death so that, although the war was commenced against him, the labour of the war fell on his son.' Constantine would never make it to the Persian front and hence never confront Shapur. Later legendary sources would make allowance for this ultimate failure, awarding the saintly emperor not one but two victories over the Persians.

War with Persia would have appeared inevitable when Eusebius delivered his *Tricennial Oration* in praise of Constantine, probably at the end of that anniversary year, on 25 July 336. The orator placed sustained emphasis on Constantine as Victor and the efficacy of his 'saving sign'. The speech is in twenty chapters, and in chapter 3 the orator reminds us that neither Constantine nor the senate accorded him the title 'Victor', but God: 'He Himself makes possible this celebration, since He has designated him Victor over all rivals and foreign foes, and thus revealed a model of piety and truth to all the earth.' In chapters 5 and 6, Constantine is a 'Victor over the passions that have overcome mankind', and as a reward has obtained victory not only over all 'impious and savage foes, but over equally barbarous adversaries, the evil spirits themselves'. Chapter 7 concludes with the observation that 'As Victor in truth, [Constantine] conquered that two-fold barbarian race, taming the wild breeds of barbarian men . . . and proving by his very acts that the rough and brutalized race of invisible demons had been conquered long ago by the Higher Power'. The spoils here are spiritual, distributed among Christians, or the 'soldiers of the Victor'. But real soldiers are the concern of chapters 9 and 10, which offer reflection on how, through righteous war, God's vehicle brought low tyrannical worshippers of demons and established peace for his Church. 'Those mad enough' to oppose him met an awful end. 'But he who triumphed under the saving trophy, one man all by himself (though not really alone because allied to and cooperating with him was The One)' enhanced his victory by the construction of churches throughout the empire. Most ostentatiously, he built throughout the Holy Places in Palestine, and these structures, not victory over Persia, would be Constantine's enduring legacy in Oriens.

The Holy Places

Shortly after the deaths of Fausta and Crispus in 326, and just before her own death, Constantine's mother Helena undertook a trip to the Holy Places in Palestine. Pilgrimage was certainly not a popular enterprise at this time, and one cannot but wonder whether this was intended in some way as an act of expiation for involvement in the deaths, notably of her daughter-in-law, who had challenged her for her son's affections and with whom she was obliged to share the title Augusta. According to Eusebius, Helena had travelled 'to complete in prayers her thank-offerings to her son, so great an emperor, and to his sons the most God-beloved Caesars, her grandsons'. No mention is made of the recent death of her eldest grandson, also a Caesar.

On her travels the empress, now acclaimed by citizens and soldiers as Augusta Imperatrix, distributed largesse in abundance. According to Eusebius, she was responsible for the construction or decoration of two churches, the Church of the Nativity and the Church on the Mount of Olives, at the sites of Christ's birth and of his ascension. Both attributions must be treated as figurative rather than as strictly true. Helena had similarly given birth to a blessed son, and accordingly 'beautified the God-bearer's pregnancy with wonderful monuments, in various ways embellishing the sacred cave there' in Bethlehem. Her role in founding the church devoted to Christ's ascension was similarly emblematic of her own imminent 'journey into heaven'. If Helena had little direct involvement in the construction of these two churches, it is clear that Constantine took a very close interest in them, and still more so in the complex he sponsored at the site of Christ's tomb, the Holy Sepulchre. The location of the tomb had been known for some time, according to local legend, and for many years it was the site of a temple dedicated, according to conflicting accounts, to Venus (Aphrodite) or to Jupiter. On the emperor's instruction, this was to be cleared and the rubble carried far away 'because it was stained with demonic blood' from sacrifices. The instruction was not, however, taken literally, as the reuse of ancient columns, surely from the temple, demonstrates. As the excavation went deeper, a cave was revealed, identified as the tomb of

Christ, which was to be the focus of a new ecclesiastical complex. By the middle of the fourth century the tomb was enclosed by a separate church, a rotunda familiar from several images and a detailed report by a seventh-century pilgrim named Arculf. However, originally the tomb lay at the western end of an open colonnaded courtyard. Pilgrims' tokens suggest that the entrance to the cave was blocked off by a grille. Within the cave were installed 'superb columns and full ornamentation'.

Facing the tomb across the courtyard Constantine erected a grand basilica. In a letter to Macarius, bishop of Jerusalem, preserved by Eusebius (*VC* III.31), the emperor goes into the details of construction of the basilica, down to the decoration of the recessed ceiling panels, and its official oversight:

As to building and decoration of the walls, be advised that our friend Dracillianus, who exercises his office among the *praefecti illustri*, and he who is governor of the province have been entrusted by us with its care. For my Religious Care has ordered that craftsmen and labourers and everything they may learn from your Good Sense to be needed for the building work should forthwith be supplied by their provision. As to the columns or marble, you should after a survey yourself write promptly to us about whatever you consider to be of most value and use . . . As to the vault of the basilica, whether you decide it should be coffered or in another style of construction I would wish to learn from you. If it were to be coffered, it might also be decorated with gold.

Unlike the cedar used for the panelled ceiling, marble could not be supplied locally, but the levers of government were in motion to ensure Macarius received whatever he desired for this holiest of undertakings. Dracillianus was no minor apparatchik, but vicar of the whole eastern diocese comprising several provinces including Palestine, the governor of which is not named. Eusebius also provides a description of the completed complex, which he visited upon its dedication. One's eye is drawn to his noting the twelve columns tipped with silver, symbolizing Christ's apostles, which foreshadow Constantine's own tomb.

Legend adhered to Helena's pilgrimage such that few historical details survive scrutiny. Most notoriously, she is alleged to have discovered the True Cross, the crucifix of Christ. This is related by Ambrose of Milan, in an oration *On the Death of Theodosius*, the emperor who died in 395, and at greater length by Rufinus, who translated Eusebius' *Ecclesiastical History* into Latin. It was Rufinus who, translating from Eusebius' Greek, first attached to Constantine's vision the erroneous phrase *in hoc signo vinces*. In the first of two books that he appended to this translation, in a section not drawn from Eusebius, Rufinus dwelt on the visit of Helena to Jerusalem, where he had himself spent a decade:

She asked the inhabitants where the place was where the sacred body of Christ had hung fastened to the gibbet. It was hard to find because an image of Venus had been fixed there by the persecutors of old, so that if any Christian wished to worship Christ in that place then he would seem to be worshipping Venus . . . But when the pious woman had hastened to the place indicated to her by a sign from heaven, and had pulled away everything profane and defiled, when the rubble had been cleared away she found deep down three crosses jumbled together.

There was also the *titulus*, the sign Pilate had made with the mocking title, in Greek, Latin and Hebrew, 'Jesus of Nazareth, King of the Jews'. In order to determine which of the three crosses was related to the *titulus* and hence was indeed the True Cross, all the pieces were taken to the house of a mortally ill woman. The bishop of Jerusalem, Macarius, touched the woman with each cross in turn, and after two failures, the True Cross revealed itself by curing the invalid. 'The empress then, having been granted her prayer with such a clear token, poured her imperial ambition into the construction of a wondrous temple on the site where she had found the cross.' For good measure, she sent a fragment to her son, as well as the nails which he incorporated into his helmet and his horse's bridle.

None of this is true, nor are these Rufinus' own recollections. It is now clear that Rufinus was again simply translating from Greek into Latin, but now not from Eusebius' *Ecclesiastical History* but rather from a parallel work by one Gelasius of Caesarea. Gelasius' history has been lost, but parts of it have been preserved in works of the fifth century, including that by Socrates Scholasticus, which we have had cause to cite before. A substantial portion is preserved in the first fifteen chapters of Rufinus' tenth book, which includes the legend of the discovery of the True Cross (X.7–8). When did this legend emerge? Evidently, it was in circulation before Gelasius wrote his work, in response to a deathbed request by Cyril, bishop of Jerusalem (d. 387). This is peculiarly significant, as Cyril was the most vigorous advocate for Jerusalem through the later fourth century, promoting its interests from the 350s and placing the cross at the heart of his campaign (see below, p. 296).

In 381–4 a pilgrim named Egeria visited the Holy Places, where she wondered at the Holy Sepulchre as well as the churches of the Nativity and Ascension called Eleona, and at the many services that took place within and between them at Easter. On Good Friday, she observed that the colonnaded courtyard before the sepulchre was so full that one could not enter. At various times it was filled with pilgrims, resting and washing their feet before proceeding further, or with catechumens listening to sermons. At Tyre, it is explicitly stated that the large courtyard was intended for catechumens, where they might receive instruction before entering the church. Within the church itself there were further dividers that separated the baptized from the ordained. The altar was fenced off within the sanctuary, the holy of holies, where only those ordained might enter. This graduated architecture created degrees of sacred space that mirrored the progression of a Christian's education. Most went only so far, but others might go a little further. The emperor, notably, was permitted to pass between the realms of the secular and the sacred. In later centuries, when the Byzantine emperor entered the cathedral church of Hagia Sophia in Constantinople on the major feasts of the Christian calendar, he removed his crown, signifying his earthly dominion. Once and briefly during the liturgical entrance, unlike any other layman, the emperor was permitted to enter the sanctuary, led by the patriarch, to kiss the altar cloth. Afterwards, this area was off limits to him, and he conducted his role in proceedings from behind the chancel barrier. However, the initial entry into the holy of holies was understood by emperors to signify their quasi-priestly status, a conception that is founded in Constantine's last decade in power. Strikingly, however, this was not something Constantine could achieve himself, for throughout his life until his final days he was not baptized, and therefore was not admitted into churches to witness the Christian liturgy.

11

Constantine and the Bishops

*Constantine the universal bishop – The Donatist schism
and the Council of Arles – The Arians and the Council of Nicaea
– The Christian emperor after Nicaea – The Church
after Constantine*

When I was a boy, the ruler who had enjoyed a reign of terror in Rome was brought down by the leader of an army of Gauls, who attacked the gods to whom they had prayed just before. Having defeated the person who had allowed the cities to prosper, and thinking it to his own advantage to recognize some other as god, he, on the one hand, used the sacred treasures to build the city upon which his heart was set, but on the other made absolutely no alteration in the traditional forms of worship; though poverty reigned in the temples, one could see all the rest of the rituals being fulfilled.

This was the recollection of the aged Libanius, delivered in a speech in around AD 390. The pagan orator was no fan of Constantine, but he wished to remind the reigning emperor Theodosius that his predecessor, the first Christian emperor, had insisted on toleration of all faiths, even if he had not spent lavishly on the temples as he did in his later years on churches. Theodosius was unmoved. He declared Christianity the religion of state and shut down temples across the empire.

Constantine's interest was not to effect the triumph of Christianity throughout his lands, but rather to appease the god who had granted him victory. He would give that deity no cause to withdraw favour, and so allowed worship to continue in all its forms. The pagan cults caused him little concern in that regard, and he merely curtailed those excesses that he personally considered particularly foul, for example ritualized prostitution and homosexuality in some temples dedicated to Aphrodite (Venus). However, the Christian Church was another matter, for it was riven with deep cracks. From shortly after the Battle of the Milvian Bridge Constantine was adamant that unity should be established among the Christians. But his desire could not be effected on the battlefield, and his interlocutors were not his lieutenants who owed him absolute obedience. They were bishops, and to corral them Constantine required a range of skills he only weakly possessed: patience not action, persuasion not force, compromise not diktat. He would attempt to deal with the bishops as a bishop, a 'first among equals', mixing flattery with firmness. However, the general was never far from the scene.

Constantine the universal bishop

As Claudia Rapp has recently shown, the authority of the fourth-century bishop was tripartite: spiritual, ascetic and pragmatic. But this was not a stool resting equally upon all three legs. Spiritual authority was the foundation of all, a divine gift that existed independent of its recognition by others. Those to be endowed with spiritual authority prepared themselves through pious practice, acts of discipline and asceticism, the latter most obviously derived from the broader Greek term for this type of behaviour, *askesis*. Those endowed with spiritual authority need not stand for decades atop pillars or confine themselves to the desert, but some did, and such ascetic behaviour was recognized by others as holy. It conferred ascetic authority, which might further be translated into pragmatic authority, when leadership roles were assigned to men who had demonstrated their piety, often through long years. Pragmatic authority, as wielded by bishops, was dependent upon spiritual authority; it was earthly recognition that one possessed a divine gift, and that this had been demonstrated through ascetic practice. Constantine knew that he too enjoyed spiritual authority, a divine gift, and that his acts of war were his *askesis*, from which his pragmatic authority derived. He also knew that in all categories his authority surpassed that of any single bishop, or indeed of them all combined. If bishops were successors to the apostles, and by virtue of their ordination received the same Holy Spirit as had the apostles from Christ, Constantine came to consider himself a second Christ.

Progression from spiritual awakening through ascetic practice to pragmatic authority can be identified in the lives of many devout bishops – for such lives, increasingly, were written by their disciples in emulation of the Evangelists – and the most renowned of the fourth century devoted themselves in turn to education, contemplation and ministry. Their lives, recorded in three stages, replicated that of Moses, who was recognized as the prototypical episcopal leader. Moses was also, as we have seen, the model that Eusebius of Caesarea, a bishop, chose for the emperor in his *Life of Constantine*. And in the same work, Eusebius reported that:

On one occasion, when entertaining the bishops to dinner, [Constantine] let slip the remark . . . 'You are bishops of those within the Church, but I am perhaps a bishop appointed by God over those outside.' In accordance with this saying, he exercised a bishop's supervision over all his subjects, and pressed them all, as far as lay in his power, to lead the godly life.

Scholars have forced this saying to do some rather heavy lifting, attaching to it the notion that the later Roman and Byzantine state conceived of no distinction between church and state authority, and established an ideology of rulership known as 'caesaropapism'. We need not become enmeshed in that discussion, for it is perfectly clear that Constantine was simply flattering his guests, suggesting a comparison with his majesty. Moreover, what he said was literally true: Constantine retained the title *pontifex maximus*, in which capacity he was chief priest presiding over the leaders of all recognized Roman cults, including now the cult of the Christian god, although he was not a devotee of all cults. Since he was not yet baptized, Constantine still stood outside the Christian Church. The emperor was, in a very real sense, a 'bishop . . . over those outside' and a 'universal bishop', a style accorded to him in Greek (*koinos episkopos*).

Constantine considered the bishops another group of subordinates, whose spiritual and pragmatic authority was not qualitatively different to his own, just less abundant. As a general, not a bishop, Constantine understood that loyalty to the commander-in-chief was achieved not through consultation but through the chain of command. His generals and their subordinate officers, so long as they were loyal, guaranteed the efficacy of the fighting force and its devotion to the emperor and his goals. So it would be with the Christian Church and its generals, the bishops, who were his imperial subjects. Thus, 'like a universal bishop appointed by God he convoked councils of the ministers of God' (*VC* I.44), the first being at Arles in 314.

The Donatist schism and the Council of Arles

In the aftermath of the Battle of the Milvian Bridge Constantine was confronted for the first time with the problems of internecine strife within the Christian Church. When he secured control of Maxentius' dominions in 312, Constantine distributed donatives to the various religious communities in Italy and North Africa now under his jurisdiction, notably in Rome and Carthage. When the severed head of Maxentius was sent across the Mediterranean to confirm Constantine's victory, a substantial cash sum went with it, to be distributed among his most favoured subjects. Eusebius purports to record the letter sent to the bishop of Carthage, one Caecilian, explaining how he will receive a cut (*HE* X.6):

Inasmuch as I have resolved that in all provinces, namely Africa, Numidia and Mauretania, certain named ministers of the holy Catholic religion should receive some contribution towards expenses, I have sent a letter to Ursus, the eminent finance officer of Africa, informing him that he must arrange a transfer to your steadfastness of 3000 *folles* in cash. Your task upon receipt of this sum is to see that it is distributed among all the persons named above according to the schedule supplied to you by Ossius [of Cordoba].

The distribution list has not been preserved, but one can be certain that those whom Ossius favoured with the emperor's largesse did not include the Christian faction who demanded the removal of Caecilian and the recognition of their own candidate, Donatus, as bishop of Carthage. In spring 313, having left Rome, Constantine received a petition from these Christians seeking his intervention in their dispute.

The reason for the dispute lay in the unhappiest of circumstances: during the Great Persecution, certain North African priests had succumbed to the persecutors and handed over sacred vessels and scripture. These were called *traditores*, literally 'handers-over', from which of course we derive the term 'traitors'. It was universally recognized that 'traitors' should no longer administer the sacraments, but the North African community was divided on whether this was to be enforced retrospectively. Since all 'traitors' had continued to administer the sacraments between their 'handing over' and their dismissals, were these ritual acts all polluted? More pressingly, was the sacrament of baptism administered by 'traitors' invalid, and must all recent catechumens be baptized anew by recognized priests? Still worse, were those Christians who had received the sacrament of last rites from a 'traitor' condemned for eternity? The followers of Donatus, called Donatists, insisted so; the followers of Caecilian insisted not.

The larger matter was for practical purposes reduced to whether Donatus or Caecilian was the legitimate bishop of Carthage, and this was referred to Constantine by the Donatists not because Constantine was a Christian – for as we have seen, that was not yet wholly apparent nor publicly acknowledged – but because Constantine had declared universal toleration and demonstrated his desire to enforce it. Consequently, the North Africans felt secure enough to refer their case to the emperor, who was the son of an emperor who had not enforced the persecution in Gaul and Britannia. They did so, moreover, knowing that they had little support within the loose confederation of Christian congregations that circled the Mediterranean, where the persecution had been enforced. Lacking allies in their broader community, they surely considered an imperial judgement their best hope of success. This was not the first time a Christian congregation had turned to an emperor in this fashion. An appeal had been made to Aurelian, certainly not a Christian, by a group of eastern bishops seeking to oust the bishop of Antioch, Paul of Samosata. Paul had secured the patronage of Zenobia, the Palmyrene empress, and resisted the judgement of a church council for three years until Aurelian's victory of 272 (see above, p. 80). Still, Aurelian did not pass judgement, but referred the case to the bishop of Rome, whose verdict he undertook to uphold. Constantine followed this precedent.

Constantine ordered the institution of a panel to arbitrate the dispute, to be chaired by the bishop of Rome, Miltiades. The emperor acceded to the Donatist request that it comprise bishops from Gaul, where the absence of persecution had produced no 'traitors', and summoned three with whom he would have been familiar, from Autun, Cologne and

Arles: all towns Constantine had visited in recent years. However, Miltiades took it upon himself to pack the committee also with fifteen Italian bishops. For more than half a century Italian bishops had refused to allow rebaptism – they had endured their own, unrelated rebaptism controversy in the third century – and hence would be predisposed against the Donatists. Moreover, Miltiades mandated that the petitioners mount a full legal case, when they were prepared only to submit to arbitration. With the Donatists wrong-footed and unprepared, the council ruled in favour of Caecilian by default.

The Donatists appealed Miltiades' decision, claiming that 'the whole case had not been heard, and that the same bishops had . . . reached the verdict most amenable to themselves'. Constantine, surely angered by Miltiades' ploy and still desirous of unity, ordered that all bishops from the lands under his jurisdiction attend a council, to be held in Arles in 314. Letters were sent to provincial functionaries to ensure that the bishops obeyed the summons, and 'several modes of transport' were provided to ensure that they arrived before 1 August. Mail carriages and horses of the *cursus publicus* (imperial postal system) were made available to the summoned bishops, each of whom was entitled to bring two priests and three servants. This action had no precedent, and it effectively excluded the bishop of Rome, who in order to defend his claims to primacy did not attend councils held elsewhere. Miltiades would die shortly afterwards and his successor, Silvester, received a polite note from the council explaining all they had determined in his absence: 'And we wish, most beloved brother, that you had thought so important a spectacle as this significant enough to attend.' Ossius of Cordoba was also kept from the proceedings, for his opinion had been made plain in the initial distribution of largesse, and Constantine would not wish to show his hand. However, more than thirty others attended at the emperor's pleasure and expense, and it is hardly surprising, therefore, that they ruled on several matters in a manner favourable to their new patron, including a prohibition on Christian soldiers casting aside their weapons in peacetime. In the matter of greatest concern, the Donatists were once again ordered to relent, which was certainly the emperor's preferred outcome.

Above all else, Constantine demanded unity within the church, so that efficacious prayers might be offered to the 'greatest god'. His wars were far from over in 314, as we have seen at length. In his letter to Aelafius, vicar of Africa, Constantine had revealed his hand:

For since I am informed that you too are a worshipper of the highest god (*summus deus*), I confess to your dignity that it is not right at all that contentions and disputes of this kind be ignored by us, by which perhaps the highest god may be moved to wrath not only against the human race, but against me, to whose care by his celestial will he has committed the management of all earthly affairs, and might decree something different if he is so provoked. For only then shall true and full security be possible for me.

The Donatists were rigorists, having no truck with Christians who would compromise or, as Constantine saw it, tolerate others. They sowed dissension and were, therefore, to be brought into line. The verdict of the Council of Arles was intended to put an end to their recalcitrance. It did not: the Donatists complained once again, as Constantine revealed in a highly rhetorical letter to the bishops, his 'beloved brethren', whom he had only recently released from his care in Arles. He wrote, again mitigating his firmness with flattery:

So great a madness persists in [the Donatists] that with incredible arrogance they . . . repudiate the equitable judgement that has been given, so that, by the will of heaven, I have learnt that they demand my own judgement . . . They demand my judgement when I myself await the judgement of Christ. For I tell you, as it is the truth, that the judgement of the priests should be regarded as if God himself were in the judge's seat. For they have no power either to think or to judge except as they are instructed by Christ's teaching.

Constantine's evaluation of the limitations of the bishops is thus revealed: certainly, they are competent to render judgement on fellow Christians, insofar as they are imbued with divine wisdom and follow Christ's teaching; but power must be recognized, and where theirs is not, none would deny his own. Caecilian and Donatus were summoned once again to court, where Constantine would decide. Neither came, instead slipping away to rejoin their communities, which would remain in schism throughout the fourth century.

It is clear that the bishops were, to Constantine in 314, a means to

41. An extremely rare bronze *follis* minted in Constantinople in 327. The staff topped with the chi-rho beneath which hangs a banner displaying three disks is evidently the *labarum*. The point at the base of the staff pierces a serpent, intended to represent Licinius (and perhaps Satan). (The Trustees of the British Museum)

42. A four-and-a-half *solidus* gold multiple, minted at Siscia (modern Sisak, Croatia) in 326. On the obverse of the coin is a bust of the emperor gazing heavenwards. There is no inscription. On the reverse, the emperor, in military uniform, tramples or kicks a defeated foe with his left foot, and with his right hand drags a captive by the hair. Over his left shoulder, from which billows his *paludamentum*, he carries a *tropaeum*. (The Trustees of the British Museum)

43. Mosaic of the Theotokos (Mother of God), above the eastern entrance to Hagia Sophia in Istanbul. She is shown receiving the Church of Holy Wisdom from Justinian and the city of Constantinople from Constantine. (akg-images/ Erich Lessing)

44. Porphyry column atop which once stood the statue of Constantine, now known as Çemberlitaş, 'the burnt column', Istanbul. (Roger Viollet/TopFoto)

45. Rotunda of Galerius, Salonica (modern Thessaloniki), near the Arch of Galerius. (Author)

46. Bust of Constantine, sculpted after 325, now at the Metropolitan Museum of Art, New York. (Scala/Metropolitan Museum of Art/Art Resource)

47. Bronze bust of Constantine, formerly believed to represent Constantius II, in the Capitoline Museums, Rome. (Author)

48. Head of Mithras, to be found in the Museum of London. (Museum of London/HIP/TopFoto)

49. Path lined with Roman sarcophagi, Alyscamps, Arles. (Author)

50. Red Sea sarcophagus, depicting Moses and the Israelites and the drowning of Pharaoh, in the Museum of Ancient Arles. (Author)

51. Carved relief panel from a second Red Sea sarcophagus, Museum of Ancient Arles. (Author)

52. A gold coin struck for Fausta early in 326, now in the Münzkabinett, Staatliche Museen zu Berlin, Germany. The inscription reads FLAVIA MAXIMA FAUSTA AUGUSTA. (Scala/ BPK, Bildagentur fuer Kunst, Kultur and Geschichte, Berlin)

53. The Great Cameo, to be found in the Geld en Bankmuseum, Utrecht, which depicts Constantine and his family upon a chariot in a Dionysiac scene. The chariot is pulled by centaurs, and Victory hovers, crowning the emperor. (Utrecht Geldmuseum Collections)

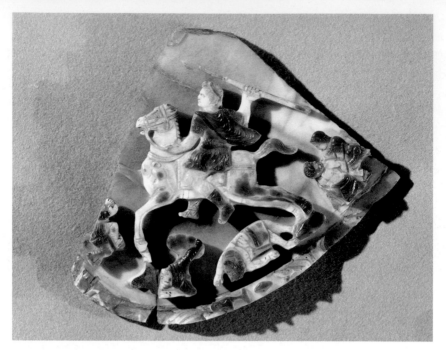

54. The Belgrade Rider, a sardonyx cameo found in Serbia, which may depict Constantine. It is now in the National Museum, Belgrade. (Narodni Muzej, Belgrade/Lauros/Giraudon/Bridgeman Art Library)

55. A portable lead baptismal font found at Walesby in Lincolnshire, showing catechumens preparing for baptism and a simple six-pointed star. (The Collection, Art and Archaeology in Lincolnshire)

56. The victorious emperor defeating his enemies. Central section of the so-called Barberini Diptych, an ivory now generally dated to the sixth century, to be found in the Louvre, Paris. (Scala/Louvre)

57. *Consecratio* coin struck to mark the death and apotheosis of Constantine. This example is to be found in the British Museum, London. (The Trustees of the British Museum)

58. Helena's sarcophagus. It was originally carved in porphyry for the body of Constantine, but remained in Rome, where it is now to be found in the Vatican Museums. (akg-images/Nimatallah)

59. Coin of the usurper Vetranio, who challenged Constantine's sons for the throne, with the legend HOC SIGNO VICTOR ERIS, 'By this sign you shall become Victor'. (Classical Numismatic Group)

60. Silver *largitio* dish depicting Constantius II mounted beside a guardsman bearing a shield marked with the chi-rho. It is now in the Hermitage Museum, St Petersburg. (The State Hermitage Museum, St Petersburg)

an end. He did not recognize their claims to a greater authority than his own in any matter concerning his Christian subjects, but was willing to delegate his authority where there were mechanisms in place and where a verdict would be recognized. When Miltiades overstepped, he brought the matter to Arles, better to control its resolution. And when it was clear that the council had not achieved that resolution, Constantine reverted to his tried methods: summary judgement, autocracy and force. In spring 315, in a letter to Celsus, his new vicar of Africa, Constantine reveals how close he had now come to instituting persecution:

When I come to Africa, I shall by reading a very plain verdict fully demonstrate to all . . . what sort of devotion should be paid to the greatest god and in what kind of cult he would appear to delight . . . Those who incite and do things so that the greatest god is not worshipped with the requisite devotion, I shall destroy and scatter. And as it is sufficiently apparent that no-one can obtain the blessings of martyrdom in a manner that is seen to be foreign and incompatible with religious truth, those whom I find to be opposed to right and religion itself, and apprehend in violation of the due form of worship, then these without doubt I shall cause to suffer the due penalties of their madness and their reckless obstinacy.

Fortunately for the Donatists, Constantine never embarked on this trip to Africa. However, he did follow Diocletian's example and insist that all Christians worship in the fashion he had determined, on pain of death. And he went further than the Tetrarchs in arrogating to himself the right to determine what was, and what was not, martyrdom. The natural response to Constantine's suppression of the Donatists, even as he pressed for toleration of all faiths, was the formulation and circulation of new tales of martyrdom. Between 317 and 321, according to these tales, imperial officers colluded with Caecilian's followers to torture and execute the faithful. In the *Sermon on the Passions of Saints Donatus and Advocatus*, attributed to Donatus himself, imperial soldiers herded Donatists into a church in Carthage and slaughtered them all, hacking them to pieces that only later family members would reassemble. The tales may well be grisly and pious fictions, intended to fan the flame of dissidence in Donatist communities so that they might better resist the pressure to conform. But utter lies do not convince, and Constantine's ire, which only subsided when his attention was drawn wholly to the east and to Licinius, suggests that his mandate of toleration did not extend to those he condemned as schismatics. The same intolerance would also be shown to those condemned as heretics – those who not only refused to acknowledge correct authority but also resisted correct belief.

The Arians and the Council of Nicaea

Even as the Donatist problem persisted, a second rift opened within the Christian Church of North Africa, beginning in Alexandria, a more important bishopric than Carthage and one which claimed apostolic foundation. A dispute had arisen between the bishop of Alexandria, Alexander, and one of his priests, Arius, who was a popular preacher. Arius earned the censure of his bishop for suggesting that God the Father preceded the Son and had created the Son from matter, which contradicted Alexander's understanding of the relationship. This was in origin not an abstruse point of theology, however, as Alexander feared the challenge to his authority and to his right to determine correct belief for his flock. Many were turning to Arius, who found supporters particularly among other intellectuals. Arius' greatest ally was a certain Eusebius – named surely to frustrate historians and those interested in clarity, for this was not Constantine's biographer, by now bishop of Caesarea. This second Eusebius had been, with Arius, a pupil of Lucian of Antioch (murdered in the Great Persecution), and latterly was the bishop of Berytus (modern Beirut). In 318, against the rulings of several church councils (including Arles) which required bishops once appointed to shun promotion and remain in one place, Eusebius accepted a more senior posting and moved to Nicomedia in Bithynia. He is known to history, therefore, as Eusebius of Nicomedia.

Alexander of Alexandria convened, in around 319, a council of his subordinate priests (thirty-six) and deacons (forty-four), and announced its ruling in a letter despatched to leaders of other churches. 'I wished indeed to consign this disorder to silence,' he began, and had hoped that it would not spread to other regions 'and contaminate the ears of the simple.' But since 'Eusebius, now in Nicomedia, thinks that the affairs of the Church are under his control because he deserted his charge at Berytus . . . and has sent commendatory letters everywhere', Alexander issued a riposte, naming and shaming those he branded 'apostates' and 'heretics'. The exact views that Arius and Eusebius shared have been obfuscated by the rhetoric of their detractors, who liked to reduce them to 'sound bites'. Thus, Arius is most frequently said to have declared 'There was when he was not', referring to the existence of time and matter before the creation of the Son by the Father. The elegant apophthegm does not appear in the statement of faith in verse, the *Thalia*, that Arius produced, presumably to appeal to the 'ears of the simple'. Numerous additional councils were convened and sides were taken before, perhaps disturbed by the unruliness of Christians under his jurisdiction, Licinius banned further convocations. This ruling was portrayed by Constantine's propagandists as part of the tyrant's renewed persecution, and so, upon achieving his victory at Chrysopolis, Constantine was obliged to turn rather quickly to the matter.

In 324 Constantine despatched Ossius of Cordoba to mediate between the parties at Antioch. He bore a letter that set out the emperor's thoughts in all their simplicity. The letter has been preserved (*VC* II.64–72):

Victor Constantinus Maximus Augustus to Alexander and Arius

I call upon God himself to witness, as I should, the helper in my undertakings and Saviour of the Universe, that a two-fold purpose impelled me to undertake the duty which I have performed. My first concern was that the attitude towards the Divinity of all the provinces should be united in one consistent view, and my second that I might restore and heal the body of the republic which lay severely wounded. In making provision for these objects, I began to think out the former with the hidden eye of reason, and I tried to rectify the latter by the power of the military arm. I knew that if I were to establish a general concord among the servants of God in accordance with my prayers, the course of public affairs would also enjoy the change consonant with the pious desires of all.

Evidently, the emperor's theology had not developed profoundly since the Council of Arles, and he proceeded to outline how the same concern had occupied him when dealing with the Donatists. This latest dispute was still more grievous, he opined, but 'the cause was exposed as extremely trivial and quite unworthy of such controversy'. Those on both sides of the argument surely felt otherwise, since for them the nature of Christ affected the salvation of all for whom he died. To those opposed to Arius, he was a heretic who claimed that the Son was less than fully God, denied the divinity of his sacrifice, and hence barred the possibility of *theosis*, the deification of mankind. To Arius, those who maintained that the Father and the Son were equally eternal (coeternal) and of the same substance (consubstantial) were misleading their congregations into an earlier heresy, that of Sabellianism, which treated the Godhead as unitary and the Son and Holy Spirit as aspects of divinity. Salvation could only be guaranteed by correct belief, in Greek *orthodoxia*. Orthodoxy and the issue of salvation were not, to either party, trivial matters, and thus neither was likely to favour Constantine's offer to act as 'a peaceful arbitrator between you in your dispute', even as he reiterated how 'the matter is small and utterly trivial', arising from a debate that should not have been aired. 'It was neither right to ask about such things, nor to answer when asked.'

Constantine's policy of least said, soonest mended was remarkably similar to Licinius'. But whereas the latter banned further discussion, Constantine assented to even more. When Ossius achieved no consensus in Alexandria, he moved on to preside at a council in Antioch, where the recent death of the bishop had led to a disputed election. A certain Eustathius had been installed, but Arians in the see had expressed their preference for another, the bishop of Caesarea whom we know as Eusebius, Constantine's biographer. Ossius confirmed the selection of Eustathius, and the council provisionally excommunicated Eusebius of Caesarea and two other bishops. They were invited to attend a further council, to be held in Ancyra (modern Ankara), to confirm their acceptance of the majority view. This did not suit the emperor, however, who had witnessed the problems that arose when a council was left to its bishops to run. To guarantee a solution that would suit him, Constantine determined that all must once again come to him. He sent a letter summoning bishops not to Ancyra, but to Nicaea, 'a city in Bithynia, both because the bishops from Italy [the bishop of Rome not among them] and the rest of the countries of Europe are coming, and because of the excellent temperature of the air, and in order that I may be present as a spectator and participant in those things that will be done'.

The only eyewitness account of the Council of Nicaea, which was only later called the first ecumenical council of the Church, was written by Eusebius of Caesarea around a decade afterwards. It was at the council that Eusebius met Constantine for the first time, and he was evidently impressed by the pomp and ceremony that surrounded the imperial person. That is to say, he elected to describe the emperor's demeanour and majesty in handling the querulous bishops rather than the deliberations of the synod, which was quite correct given the nature of the work, the panegyrical *Life of Constantine* (*VC* III.4–24), and quite in keeping also with our interests. Nonetheless, his account became the basis for all later descriptions of the council, and consequently for the role Constantine played to be magnified. We can say little more than that Constantine gave a speech of welcome in Latin to the more than 250 bishops – later tradition holds there were 318, corresponding to the number of Abraham's servants at Genesis 14 – mostly Greek-speakers, who attended at his expense, and that he acted on occasion as a mediator between controversialists, 'and by speaking Greek, for he was not ignorant of that language either, he made himself pleasant and agreeable, persuading some and shaming others with his words', urging unity at all times. Just as Constantius Chlorus was credited by panegyrists for recovering Britain in 296, although he failed to make it across the English Channel (see above, p. 94), so his son 'presided' over the Council of Nicaea. It seems certain, however, that Ossius of Cordoba played the role of Asclepiodotus, the unmentioned underling who took charge, in this case chairing sessions and controlling theological disputation. Constantine attended sessions and flattered many participants with his attentions, notably kissing the empty eye-sockets of one Paphnutius who had been blinded in the Great Persecution. However, it would later be charged that Constantine, or Ossius, shut down all intellectual exchange, imposing instead a solution based on the use of the term 'consubstantial' (*homoousios*). By using the very term that Arius rejected as the root of the heresy of Sabellianism, the fate of the preacher was sealed. He was condemned and exiled with two bishops who refused with him to agree to the statement of faith, which came to be known as the Nicene Creed. The method for determining the date for Easter, which all must observe, was also agreed, and Constantine undertook to enforce universal observance of orthodoxy, or 'correct belief'.

The end of the council coincided, surely not by chance, with the end of Constantine's *vicennalia*, and so the bishops were invited to the imperial palace in nearby Nicomedia – in 325 Constantinople was not yet complete – to dine and celebrate the emperor's twentieth year in power. They were sent away with gifts and large cash donations for their churches. Besides praising his protagonist, Eusebius of Caesarea had further reasons to remain opaque on what took place at Nicaea, for his own role in the proceedings was hardly less controversial than that of his namesake, the bishop of Nicomedia. Constantine's biographer had been named in letters that circulated prior to Nicaea as one sympathetic to the teachings of Arius, and had been excommunicated provisionally by the Council of Antioch. At Nicaea he advanced his own statement of faith, setting out how he understood the Trinity. His was not the same creed as that adopted by the council: notably it omitted the term 'consubstantial'. However, he agreed to the Nicene version and returned to his see in full communion. Eusebius of Nicomedia also signed the creed, but did not agree to the exile of Arius. Shortly afterwards, he was charged with corresponding with Arius and also exiled by order of the emperor. This was a striking turn of events, for Nicomedia was still Constantine's imperial capital.

To explain his actions, Constantine sent a letter to the Christians in the city denouncing their deposed leader. Eusebius of Nicomedia, Constantine charged, had supported the 'tyrant' Licinius. The accusation must be understood in the context of Constantine's programme to condemn the memory of Licinius, as he had Maxentius before and Maximian still earlier, but also as an attempt to obscure the favour the emperor had previously shown the bishop. It is likely that the council had been moved to Nicaea at Eusebius' request, and that as metropolitan bishop in Bithynia, in which Nicaea was situated, he was allowed to address the council before any but Constantine. So we read in the letter that, as battle loomed at Chrysopolis in 324, Constantine had arrested as spies the priests and deacons who had accompanied Eusebius to the scene of battle. It is hardly surprising that the bishop and his entourage had made contact with the emperor and his invading army at Chrysopolis, which fell within Eusebius' jurisdiction on the Asian side of the Bosphorus. Moreover, the suggestion that they were agents of Licinius seems to contradict the notion that Licinius had turned to persecuting Christians, unless Constantine is now suggesting rather ludicrously that his rival made exceptions. In short, we have another example of Constantine's predilection to shape the past to suit present circumstances. In the immediate aftermath of Nicaea, Arians were out of luck and 'Catholics', adherents of the universal and orthodox Church, were in favour. Consequently, the former were portrayed as colluders with a persecuting tyrant. The congregation at Nicomedia was to 'act so that we may rejoice in the possession of holy, orthodox and philan-thropic bishops. And if anyone dares inconsiderately to be roused to remembrance or praise of those corrupters, he will be restrained from his daring by the action of the servant of God, namely myself. God guard you, beloved brethren.'

The Christian emperor after Nicaea

Little, then, had been changed in Constantine's attitude by his failure to suppress the Donatists by force, and once again he saw the threat of violence as a solution to the recalcitrance of fellow Christians, his 'beloved brethren', who had so recently enjoyed similar treatment from Diocletian, at whose court in Nicomedia Constantine had resided during that very period. Here we might recall Constantine's own *Oration to the Saints*, a speech to assembled bishops, delivered most likely in Nicomedia. It has been suggested that the oration was given as early as 315, but a later date seems more likely, and one might dwell on the claims to Christian leadership Constantine advances therein. A key element of the speech was to convince the bishops in his own words, and not only in those of Lactantius and Ossius, that he was not responsible for persecutions of Christians. To that end, Constantine emphasized that he was not raised a Christian and had come to his faith through grace. Eusebius of Caesarea embraced that message and disseminated it, crediting Constantine with converting his mother Helena, for to suggest that she had raised her son to venerate the Christian god would open him to charges of apostasy and inconstancy. Indeed, one might begin to see in his virulent attacks on the Donatists an attempt to protect himself from the charges they levelled at less rigorous Christians who had not embraced martyrdom during the persecution, and similar self-serving tactics in his threats to the various groups of heretics. It is especially noteworthy that the emperor felt entitled to threaten the Christians of Nicomedia, who would have observed Constantine at Diocletian's palace listening to the lectures by Porphyry and Sossianus Hierocles, and would perhaps have seen his acquiescence when the first of their community, and Lucian of Antioch, were executed. To cover his tracks, Constantine now ordered that all copies of Porphyry's *Against the Christians* be burnt and that the same fate be afforded anyone found in possession of a copy.

For good measure, Constantine issued a threatening letter addressed to every other group of heretics and schismatics known to him. It has been preserved by Eusebius (*VC* III. 63–6):

Be it known to you by this present decree, you Novatians, Valentinians, Marcionites, Paulians and those called Cataphrygians, all in short who constitute the heresies by your private assemblies, how many are the falsehoods in which your idle folly is entangled and how venomous the poisons with which your teaching is involved, so that the healthy are brought to sickness and the living to everlasting death through you . . . Accordingly, since it is no longer possible to tolerate the pernicious effect of your destructiveness, by this decree we publicly command that none of you henceforth shall dare to assemble. Therefore, we have also given order that all your buildings are to be confiscated, the purport of this extending so far as to prohibit the gathering of assemblies of your superstitious folly not only in public but also in the houses of individuals or other private places . . . let [these places] be confiscated and handed over incontestably and without delay to the Catholic church, and let other sites become public property.

The date of this decree has been much debated, since Eusebius places it after the Council of Nicaea, although at that council the Novatianists were shown some sympathy. A date after Nicaea seems very likely, as Constantine no longer regards alternative doctrines as 'trivial', but rather stresses that those led astray by heretic priests surrender salvation and face 'everlasting death'. So it may be that Eusebius displays his own prejudice against the Novatianists by inserting them at the start of the list of those condemned to lose their property. Constantine's policy is evidently an extension of his failed suppression of the Donatists, the object now being to dispossess all those whose doctrines or leaders were not currently recognized as 'Catholic'. The emperor had taken the lead in enforcing correct worship in a manner Diocletian and Galerius would have recognized, and by his actions one group of Christians benefited materially.

Constantine's professed policy of toleration for all faiths, for which he had fought his last great war against Licinius, foundered on the diversity of Christian doctrine and practice. In the name of unity he persecuted those whose beliefs were now far closer to his own than those held by worshippers of Sol Invictus, and still more than those of devotees of Dionysus or Asclepius. Whereas those who had not yet found the Christian god should be led in that direction by moderation, those who had done so but rejected correct authority (schismatics) or correct belief (heretics) were to be pressured equally, and punished if they failed to relent. The diminished status of schismatics and heretics was confirmed in laws issued in 326 (*CTh* 16.4.5; 16.5.1), and it is in the Theodosian Code that we observe how this was subsequently reinforced through the following century. Numerous chapters are devoted to heretics and schismatics, where punishments are far harsher than those meted out to pagans, who were as yet children and not threats to the unity of the true faith. During Constantine's reign, heretics and schismatics were not to share in the bounty that accrued to the true 'Catholic' faith, until the emperor changed his mind. Constantine changed his mind frequently.

In 327 Constantine, the champion of orthodoxy and benefactor of the Catholic Church, had no compunction about repealing the exile of Arius, and shortly afterwards of Eusebius of Nicomedia. In a letter of eloquence and guile that struck just the right note with Constantine, Arius promised to pray for the emperor and his family from the bosom of the peaceful and unified Church. Eusebius' letter was rather more procedural, observing the oddity that he would still be exiled when the man with whom he had corresponded was not. Both matters were put before another great council, recorded rather briefly in the *Life of Constantine* (*VC* III.23). Attended once again by more than 250 bishops, the council held in Nicomedia in December 327 was hardly noted by later historians such as Socrates Scholasticus and Sozomen. A notable exception is Philostorgius (II.7), who records that the Arians also circulated a revised creed at this meeting. The council reversed the decisions of Nicaea: Eusebius of Nicomedia was recalled and lost no time in returning to his church and fomenting trouble for his opponents; Alexander of Alexandria was ordered to receive Arius back into his see, but refused. Alexander died shortly afterwards, in April 328, which proved to be to the detriment of the Arians, as it brought to the fore a young and brilliant new bishop of Alexandria named Athanasius.

The emperor's actions in the years after Nicaea were inconsistent, although his purpose was consistent: he remained committed to the unity of faith and worship of the greatest god, but lacked a clear idea of how to achieve it. No longer was there a dominant voice at court, for by the end of 326 Ossius of Cordoba had departed for Spain. Constantine's Christian adviser for more than a dozen years, he was recognized at Nicaea as 'the most famous one', and remained an implacable opponent of Arianism in his diocese. Why Ossius left is a mystery, but perhaps not a great one: he may simply have wished to leave the limelight and serve his parishioners. However, his willingness to cast aside such influence at this crucial juncture lends itself to further conjecture, and perhaps one might link Ossius' departure to the murders of Crispus and Fausta. Was the bishop unable to prevent the episodes, unable to offer Constantine the forgiveness he sought, or perhaps both? We might recall from an earlier chapter that Zosimus, a pagan author of the sixth century, referred in his tale of Constantine's conversion to 'a certain Egyptian, who had come from Spain to Rome', who is portrayed as the emperor's means to secure absolution for the murders. Without Ossius' guidance, Constantine floundered from council to council, accepting and rejecting suggestions from those who wished him to coerce opponents. For some time, and rather shockingly for the Catholics, the emperor fell under the spell of a man he had previously condemned but who now was once again his local bishop, Eusebius of Nicomedia.

The politicking and chicanery of the following years cannot be explored in detail here, since our interest is not ecclesiastical politics.

Instead we shall consider what Constantine's actions and rulings tell us, if anything, of his mind and demeanour in his last decade. In 328 Athanasius was ordered, like Alexander before him, to accept the ruling of the Council of Nicomedia and restore Arius and his followers to full communion with the Alexandrian church. He resisted this order from his base in Egypt, frequently fleeing Alexandria into the Upper Thebaid, that is the desert, to live among the monks and avoid the officers sent to enforce the emperor's will. Athanasius even challenged the emperor's monopoly of legitimate violence, sacking rival churches, upending altars and destroying liturgical vessels, or so it was charged by his bitter rivals. In 332, facing such serious accusations, Athanasius was obliged finally to present himself to the emperor and defend the charges, at a trial engineered by Eusebius of Nicomedia. Evidently, the latter's influence had waned since Constantine's move to Constantinople, for Athanasius was acquitted. He returned victoriously to Alexandria and turned shortly afterwards to Libya, where Arius and his community were living, to assert his authority over suffragan bishoprics and to ensure the rejection of Arian candidates. Arius responded angrily in a letter to Constantine, and that was his undoing.

Constantine, although he now devoted more of his energy to the Christian Church, remained a military man, who took counsel from his subordinates but made the decisions himself and gave orders that none were permitted to countermand. Military discipline was predicated on recognition of the commander's absolute authority, which was reinforced by codified acts of violence. Ultimately, acts of insubordination, if sufficiently egregious, were punishable by death. A similar code of conduct did not apply in Constantine's dealings with the bishops, although on many occasions he assumed that it did. When persuasion and flattery failed to achieve the emperor's desired end, he might try again. When frequent attempts failed, he would resort to threats and to acts of violence. This was the case with the Donatists and with other groups of schismatics, and it was his last resort with Arius. In 332 Arius wrote to insist that the emperor move against Athanasius to ensure that he, Arius, and his many followers were readmitted to the Alexandrian church. One did not insist when dealing with the emperor, still less threaten, as did Arius, to establish his own separate church. Two letters were despatched from Constantine: the first, to Arius personally, called him the mouth-piece of Satan and much else besides; the second informed everyone else of Arius' fate and that of his writings:

Since Arius has imitated wicked and impious people, it is just that he should undergo similar ignominy. Therefore, just as Porphyry, that enemy of piety, for having composed licentious treatises against religion, found suitable compensation when he was branded with infamy, overwhelmed with reproach, and his blasphemous writings were destroyed; so it shall be with Arius, and those who share his sentiments shall be called Porphyrians, that they may hold the appellation of those whose conduct they have imitated. And in addition to this, let any treatise composed by Arius be consumed by flames, so that not only will his depraved doctrine be suppressed, but also so that no memorial of any kind will be left for him.

Those concealing books by Arius, like Porphyry before him, were to be executed if they did not immediately burn them. Priests who refused to submit to the authority of a Catholic bishop were to pay additional taxes and were no longer exempt from state liturgies; that is, they must pay for local amenities and services in the manner of other notables. Arius was to present himself to the emperor for final judgement. His fate was sealed, it seemed. And yet on the next occasion that we meet Arius, in 335, he is on his way to the Holy Places, where a council of bishops is convening at Tyre to judge Athanasius. Once again charged with egregious offences, the bishop of Alexandria had already demonstrated that he was innocent of the murder of one Arsenius, countering the production of a severed limb by his accusers with the intact, and living, body of his alleged victim. But again, in 335, Eusebius of Nicomedia constructed an alliance of those opposed to Athanasius, who brought charges of violence and contumacy against him, and once again the emperor responded by summoning a council under the usual conditions: all expenses were to be paid, and all were obliged to attend.

Constantine tasked the Council of Tyre with a rather familiar duty, to restore unity to the Church. This was now a rather feeble refrain, and the bishops conducted their own business, blithely ignored by Eusebius of Caesarea (*VC* IV. 41–2), who presents the affair simply as a prelude to the emperor's *tricennalia* celebrations and the dedication of the Church of the Holy Sepulchre in Jerusalem, where he delivered his oration in praise of the building and its patron. Shortly thereafter, Eusebius travelled to Constantinople with Eusebius of Nicomedia and others to ensure that the decision of the council was enforced and that Athanasius was sent into exile. Athanasius beat them to court, but after yet another audience with the emperor and yet another change of heart, Constantine first sided with Athanasius, then sent him into exile at Trier. But when Arius returned to Alexandria, those loyal to Athanasius refused to accept him. He returned, once again, to Constantinople and to another council under Constantine's gaze. There it was determined that Arius would be brought into full communion by the bishop of Constantinople, who then refused, revealing himself to be a supporter of Athanasius. Under imperial instruction, Arius was to be marched into church and admitted into full communion, but he never made it. Tradition holds that he died on the way, a hideous death reminiscent of Galerius', which in Lactantius' account drew heavily upon the death of Antiochus, persecutor of the Jews in 2 Maccabees. Arius' demise demonstrated that God's judgement on the matter of His own nature and substance ultimately differed from Constantine's.

The Church after Constantine

As Constantine had reminded his bishops after Arles, 'the judgement of the priests should be regarded as if God himself were in the judge's seat', but when it was not, then he, Constantine, took that seat. The final right of appeal was to him alone, for the Holy Spirit had entered him as it did a bishop at ordination, and worked through him as it did a bishop when he administered the sacraments. And if Constantine's right to preside over all Christians had been established at Arles, his ability to do so was shown at Nicaea. His knowledge of the Christian faith developed as he attended councils and his legislation was formulated through decades in consultation with bishops; and bishops now turned to him as a matter of course as the final arbiter in their disputes and as the enforcer of their decisions. Consequently, for a decade after Nicaea, if we follow our principal sources, Constantine appears to have devoted extraordinary time and energy to the Christian Church and its bitter disputes. And in those disputes he appears to have followed no consistent line, veering between sides rather suddenly and without adequate explanation. His ostentatious displays of tolerance, calling council after council, were punctuated by violent outbursts and threats of persecution, all in the name of a unity that he never achieved.

We must be wary of this picture for two reasons. First, Constantine is presented to us primarily by Eusebius of Caesarea, who was deeply enmeshed in the affairs he describes, and by various Christians at the time and later – Catholics, Arians, Donatists and others. Constantine's views, expressed in his letters, are not presented except where they can be shown to conform to one viewpoint or another. Second, and more significantly, all sides in the discussions were interested in the emperor only insofar as he played a role in their own lives and disputes. Eusebius is perfectly open in this regard: he tells us (*VC* I.11) that he will not devote space to wars or peacetime decrees – although of course he frequently does – but 'will put into words and write down only what relates to the life which is dear to God'. That is, he is concerned exclusively with Constantine's relationship with the Christian Church. So it is also with Eusebius' *Ecclesiastical History*, and the continuations of that work by others, including Socrates Scholasticus and Sozomen. It may be, therefore, that Constantine devoted rather little time and energy to the affairs of the Church over the last decade of his life, albeit relatively far more than at any other period. So much would appear to be the case if we relied only on the *Origo Constantini*, or perhaps also on Zosimus and Eunapius, which are far shorter accounts and not by eyewitnesses. We have only terse comments on, for example, the emperor's close relationship with the Neoplatonist philosopher Sopater, formerly a courtier of Licinius, but would love to know more about his patronage of the literary arts and oratory. If we had an account of the emperor's last years penned by one of Constantinople's new senators, one suspects he would have been a sedulous attendee of debates and the greatest patron of municipalities and their public works.

For all the hyperbole of our skewed sources, it is clear that Constantine's interventions had a profound effect upon the Church. It was not in spite of Constantine's conversion and patronage of the Church that disputes became more frequent and more pronounced, but rather because of them. Indeed, it is because of Constantine's actions that we have begun to speak of *the* Church, still rather incongruously. For that reason it may be useful to take a step backwards and indulge very briefly in some jargon-laden theorizing. Sociologists of religion would consider Christianity after Constantine's reign to be a cult in a state of 'reduced tension' with state and society. It was, therefore, a breeding ground for the formation of splinter groups or sects. One can distinguish between cults and sects rather simplistically: a cult is characterized by the willingness of its members to embrace new ideas, whereas a sect is distinguished by its members' resistance to new ideas. Cults tend to attract those who are not strongly attached to another faith and who are generally better educated and wealthier. Sects fragment from established cults and tend to consist of those who have benefited least in material terms from association with the cult, and for whom increased secularization (contact with 'the world') seems to diminish the spiritual elements of the faith. In other words – and they are surely necessary – the more worldly the Christian Church became, the more likely it was that sects would develop that rejected worldliness and turned away.

Christianity, as we have seen, was a cult that had been arranged rather loosely across a vast region for three centuries. It was based on open networks that after a long period of being closed off from secular power structures were now increasingly folded into them. The cult had endured frequent fragmentation through its first three centuries, when sects turned away from it and its looser connections to state and society. This became much more frequent as the Christian cult became favoured by the emperor and attained its most tainted state. And yet, as we have seen, many of those sects made appeals (at least initially) to the emperor, to the worldly centre, for judgement, even if they rejected that judgement when it went against them. Centripetal forces were stronger than centrifugal ones, and this bolstered the status of bishops, who were the link between centre and periphery. Having been, to a great extent, distinct from each other, diverse communities of the faithful were now bound together through imperial legislation and patronage, and by councils attended by their bishops.

The view that the Church was corrupted by its encounter with Constantine, replacing martyrs and pacifists with patriarchs and militants, was thus forged in his own era, and it has retained its vigour into the modern period. Many have argued that the Church became an instrument of the state and that the original message of Christianity was lost. Bishops were at the forefront of this deterioration, no longer spiritual leaders but instead provincial factotums, representatives of a new state-centred ecclesiastical structure with duties and interests that intersected with the civilian and military administrations. Although bishops were never brought fully into the imperial administration and continued to derive their status from recognition of their spiritual authority as demonstrated by ascetic behaviour, still they were increasingly required to write letters of petition, or to travel to the residence of a provincial governor or even to the imperial court to petition in person. So frequently indeed did bishops afford themselves of this opportunity to travel, that restrictions were introduced at two church councils in the 340s. With a duty to advocate, bishops were now mostly among the best educated and best connected people in each community – if not always born into wealth, then certainly able to attain it with high social standing. They were afforded titles as splendid as those attached to senators, 'the most glorious' (*gloriosissimus*) or illustrious (*illustris*). Indeed, bishops were drawn increasingly from the senatorial aristocracy. An apt phrase developed to describe these patrician bishop advocates: 'noble by birth, still nobler through religion'.

Constantine's reign was, therefore, a watershed for episcopal authority, even if it did not utterly change the nature of the office. The same can be said for its impact on the Church's stance on war and violence. As we have seen, there were many Christian attitudes to war and violence, and pacifism was certainly strongly represented among them. This remained the case after Constantine. But as a consequence of his conversion and the consistent message disseminated from his court that the 'greatest god' was his patron, Constantine established Christianity as the religion of victory within the army. The remarkable efforts of certain apologists, notably Lactantius and Eusebius, enabled those who had already converted to share the Good News: Christianity was on the march.

12

Death and Succession

Constantine's death – Apotheosis – Constantine as Christ – The
succession – Constantius Victor – Christian victory

In January 328 Constantine renamed Drepanum in Bithynia, the city of his mother's birth, Helenopolis, 'city of Helena'. The remains of her favourite martyr, Lucian of Antioch, were transferred there and installed in a martyrium for pilgrims to visit. Lucian had been killed during Constantine's youthful residency at Nicomedia, and he had a second legacy as the teacher of a young man named Arius. Setting out from Constantinople in spring of 337, Constantine put in at Helenopolis. He was feeling ill, but determined to travel on to Nicomedia with his entourage and full military retinue. He stopped at an imperial villa just outside Nicomedia, which appears rather inelegantly to have been called 'the Chaff-House' (*Achyron*). This allowed his troops to encamp nearby, and saved him from the rigours of a formal arrival in the city. Still, he was visited by the local notables, including Eusebius, the bishop of Nicomedia, and other local bishops and priests. Such a visit was required when the emperor was nearby. Exceptionally, however, Constantine informed the assembled clerics that he intended to receive baptism. Eusebius of Caesarea provides the words of a speech he cannot have heard from the emperor's lips (*VC* IV.62):

This is the moment I have long hoped for, as I thirsted and yearned to win salvation in God. It is our time to enjoy the seal that brings immortality, time to enjoy the sealing that gives salvation, which I once intended to receive at the streams of the River Jordan, where our Saviour is reported also to have received the bath as an example to us. But God who knows what is good for us judges us worthy of these things here and now.

Constantine's death

In the early fourth century baptism was not performed on children. For a normal catechumen – one who wished to become a member of the Christian Church – the sacrament of baptism was the culmination of a course of instruction lasting up to three years. Origen, we may recall, was an instructor of catechumens, and he and others employed the prescriptions of the church orders to determine who might and who might not receive baptism. In several versions of the *Apostolic Tradition*, those who held public office, administered justice or were officers in the army were – like gladiators and prostitutes – expressly forbidden from receiving baptism, since their professions involved them in activities that were impermissible for Christians. Constantine, as commander-in-chief of the army, the empire's highest justice and its chief priest (*pontifex maximus*), was disqualified from baptism on many counts, at least until he confessed his sins and promised to live according to Christian precepts. Confession to a priest was not, as it would later become, a regular feature of the life of a Catholic Christian, associated with penitential acts to atone for sins. Rather, it was a sacrament performed once in a lifetime, and since it could not be repeated, it always signalled death, at least of a former self. It would become repeatable within half a century of Constantine's death, and then it also became standard to offer confession in order to take monastic vows. But still confession was not undertaken lightly or regularly. Constantine confessed because he anticipated death, but according to Eusebius, he hedged so far as he was able, announcing: 'If the Lord of life and death should wish [him] to live again', he would do so according to new rules 'which befit God'. In any event, he made plain to the bishops that he had already given his confession, at the martyrium of Lucian, and therefore required only that they perform for him the necessary rites in the imperial villa.

Intensive preparation during Lent was afforded to those who would be received into the Church, and the initiation ceremony took place at the end of the Easter vigil on Holy Saturday. In 337 Holy Saturday fell on 2 April, and it had passed before Constantine left Constantinople. But the emperor was no ordinary catechumen, and his progression was expedited. The awesome mysteries that attended those admitted into the Christian cult were performed by Eusebius of Nicomedia: exorcism, the triple immersion in water, the laying-on of hands. Reborn, the emperor cast aside his purple and crimson garments, the colour of power but also of blood, and henceforth wore only pure white robes. He was reborn so that he might die and live forever. 'When the tribunes and senior officers of the armies filed in and lamented, bewailing their own imminent bereavement and wishing him longer life, he answered them too by saying he enjoyed true life now, and only he knew the good things he had received.' It is at this point in Eusebius' narrative, the only contemporary account of Constantine's final journey, that we realize that the emperor is on campaign, bound for Persia. Eusebius and those who followed him obscured this fact, to dwell on the culmination of Constantine's spiritual journey. Constantine died on 22 May 337.

As Constantine attended to these final matters, word of his illness was sent to Antioch. The news was sent to Constantius, the second son who now resided there, but also to Flavius Ablabius, who was Constantine's trusted adviser and most powerful subordinate. Praetorian Prefect since 329, Ablabius had run Constantine's government from Constantinople for most of the period since. In 336 he had been despatched with Constantius to Antioch, not as a demotion but rather to oversee Constantine's most important undertaking, the preparations for war with Persia. It is clear from his subsequent actions that Constantius bridled at Ablabius' direction, but so long as his father was alive, he had no independence of action. Constantius and Ablabius received news of the emperor's illness and departed forthwith, although neither of the other sons had yet been informed. Constantine II received news of his father's death at Trier shortly before 17 June. One must imagine Constans at Milan or Aquileia was informed a few days earlier than that, as a consequence of the workings of the *cursus publicus*, the imperial message service.

Constantine died before the news of his illness could have reached Antioch. By the *cursus publicus*, messages were transferred through stations eight to ten miles apart, at each of which up to forty fresh horses were kept by grooms. Every third station was more substantial, an inn (*mansio*) providing overnight accommodation not only for the horses' grooms and the couriers but also for other travellers. A courier would regularly travel for up to ten hours a day, averaging five or six Roman miles per hour. It was not Roman practice to employ relays, so there were no spare couriers waiting at stations to take over when a messenger tired. A single courier would carry each message to its destination, and he would travel in a carriage, not on horseback. Consequently, even if one travelled at full speed taking new horses at every station, for as long as there was daylight and by moonlight where possible, an urgent message would travel at most seventy to eighty Roman miles per day.*

According to the *Antonine Itinerary*, a document that lists two hundred and twenty-five routes along Roman roads and their stages across the empire, the distance from Nicomedia to Antioch was 747 Roman miles, but it was a hard route in places. The road passed first through Nicaea and Iuliopolis along the valley of the Sangarius river as far as Ancyra (modern Ankara). From there it headed south through Archelais and Tyana, and then through the Cilician gates, a pass in the high Taurus mountains, to reach Tarsus. South of Tarsus the road passed beside the plain of the Issus and across the Amanus mountains to Antioch. A pilgrim from Bordeaux, who set out for the Holy Land in 333, stopped at many stages along the route, counting the miles between them: from Nicomedia to Ancyra, 258 miles; from Ancyra to Tarsus, 343 miles; from Tarsus to Antioch, 141 miles; giving a total of 742 miles.

We cannot know for sure when news of Constantine's illness was sent out from Nicomedia, although Malalas in the sixth century states

---

* In this way, in April 193, news of the death of Pertinax in Rome reached Septimius Severus, 735 Roman miles away at Carnuntum, after eleven days. Terrain has to be taken into account, of course, and the route north from Rome was extremely hilly. It was once believed that the journey from Constantinople to Antioch took only three or four days, and still it is often imagined that a relay of riders with an urgent message might cover vast distances mounted on horses ridden at full gallop (30 mph or more). Even Procopius (*Secret History*, 30) claimed that the public post once covered ten times the distance of a single traveller in any given day, which might mean up to 250 miles, although at that point he is exaggerating to emphasize how Justinian had allowed the service to decline. Roman roads were intended for infantry: they were paved with stones which were hard on hooves in an age before horses were shod in iron, and could be slippery, especially for a rider without stirrups (introduced to the Romans only two centuries after Constantine). Consequently, those on horseback travelled along dirt tracks beside the roads, certainly not at full gallop. The only comparable modern service, the short-lived Pony Express, had stations every ten miles and averaged ten miles per hour across the western states of the USA. The riders, on horseback, not in carriages, and weighing no more than 125 pounds, carried up to forty pounds of mail and provisions in a pannier.

that the emperor died after six days. There was a new moon over Nicomedia on 16 May 337, so conditions for night travel were at their poorest. However, there would have been around fourteen and a half hours of daylight, so a courier might have achieved around eighty miles each day if the weather was good and the journey without mishaps. The journey between Nicomedia and Antioch, which was approximately 750 Roman miles and crossed several mountain ranges, would normally have taken fifteen days, but might be covered in a little under ten by a courier travelling in optimum conditions.

Armies travelled far more slowly, with infantry covering three miles per hour on good roads, so at most between twenty and twenty-five Roman miles per day. An aged emperor who was heading to war but could no longer ride comfortably for long distances would have been carried in a litter by slaves. He would not have been drawn in a carriage by horses, for that would have had no springs and its wooden wheels wrapped in iron would have conveyed every bump in the road into his tired bones. Add to this the mighty baggage train, and one must anticipate that Constantine's cortege was not expected in Antioch until at least five weeks after his departure from Constantinople, hence towards the middle of June. The news of his illness would have reached Antioch far sooner than that, on around 26 May. Still, Constantius' officers and retinue would already have been assembled, and the imperial tent and baggage train were perhaps compiled for the journey into Mesopotamia. If Ablabius and Constantius had set off immediately and on horseback with only a skeleton staff and essentials, they might have reached Nicomedia in a little over two weeks. If we estimate that the message took ten days to arrive in Antioch and that Ablabius and Constantius left within two days and travelled for sixteen, they would have arrived four weeks after the news of Constantine's illness was sent, and three weeks after his death. The tale of Constantius' journey was never rewritten to echo Constantine's own mad, successful, fictional dash to his father's deathbed. The closest one finds is a panegyrical treatment by Libanius (Oration 59):

For on the one side his father's funeral drew his attention and on the other the din of the Persian assault. He was obliged either to meet the enemy and neglect the funeral rites or to observe the rites and lay the empire open to the enemy. What did he do? He did not consider advantage more highly than rites, but rather both duties were successfully combined and the secondary purpose of the journey was more honourable than any deed. For he himself hastened energetically to the burial, while fear held the Persians back in their own land. Whether they received their fright from heaven and were restrained or whether it was through not knowing anything of his withdrawal but thinking they would encounter the emperor's right hand, either explanation is equally sufficient for a eulogy.

Apotheosis

In Nicomedia matters were controlled entirely by the army until the arrival of Ablabius and Constantius, and perhaps even afterwards. It must be remembered that by the 330s the office of Praetorian Prefect was entirely a civilian post, and therefore that Ablabius' interests and those of Constantine's generals cannot be considered as identical. There was another Praetorian Prefect with a hand in the game, Evagrius, who was as senior as Ablabius and had substituted for him in Constantinople. Christian writers would later introduce the notion that Constantine turned to the division of the empire only in his last days and that he set out his wishes in a last will and testament that he entrusted to an unnamed presbyter, according to Socrates Scholasticus, or to Eusebius of Nicomedia, according to Philostorgius. But the Praetorian Prefects and palatine mandarins, not the bishops, administered affairs of state, and in the current climate their actions were closely monitored by the generals. Meanwhile, the Augustus would continue to rule even in death. Constantine's body was stripped of its white robes and dressed once again in purple and gold. His corpse was transported in a gilded coffin to Constantinople, and there it lay in state in the imperial palace, wearing a diadem, to receive clients who came, as in life, every morning to pay their respects to the most powerful patron in the Roman world. As Eusebius notes, 'this continued for a long time, the military having decided that the remains should stay there and be watched until his sons should arrive and pay respects to their father by personally attending to the rites.' Indeed, laws continued to be issued in Constantine's name until August 337, three months after his death.

Clues in sources concerning earlier emperors' lying-in-state suggest that the emperor's body was not kept in public view for very long, but rather that a waxwork figure was made. So it had been for Pertinax, whose effigy, according to Cassius Dio, was attended by a boy who swished peacock feathers, which were symbols of immortality but also kept flies off the model 'as if it were really a person sleeping'. The effigy had a further important role to play. Another third-century historian not unfamiliar to us, Herodian (IV.2), described the funeral of Pertinax's successor, Septimius Severus, in 211. He wrote in general terms:

It is normal practice to deify emperors who die leaving behind children to succeed them. The name given to this ceremony is apotheosis . . . After a costly funeral, the body of the dead emperor is buried in the normal human fashion. But then a wax model is fashioned in the exact likeness of the corpse and placed on a large high couch of ivory draped in coverings embroidered with gold. This wax figure lies on the couch like a sick man, pale and wan.

Various charades and ceremonies take place for a week, as a doctor visits daily to announce that the patient is getting worse. Eventually, the emperor is pronounced dead and carried out still on the ivory couch, which is placed on a pyre constructed in the form of a lighthouse, in four storeys. The couch is placed on the second storey, while the first and third are filled with piles of aromatics. The fourth storey houses a caged eagle which is released when the pyre is set alight. 'The eagle flies forth, soaring with the flames into the sky; the Romans believe that this eagle carries the soul of the emperor from the earth up to heaven. Thereafter the emperor is worshipped with the rest of the gods.'

Eusebius provides the only account of Constantine's funeral, and he does his very best to make it appear Christian. However, he provides very clear clues that a ceremony of apotheosis was performed, protesting: 'He is not like the Egyptian bird, which they say has a unique nature, and dies among aromatic herbs, making itself its own sacrifice, then revives from the ash and, as it flies up, turns into what it was before.' Neither phoenix nor eagle, Constantine's soul was borne to heaven by other means. 'At the same time coins were struck portraying the blessed one on the obverse in the form of one with his head veiled, on the reverse like a charioteer on a *quadriga*, being taken up by a right hand stretched out to him from above.' The *quadriga*, long associated with the worship of Mithras and with Sol Invictus, was an acceptable metaphor for the emperor's translation to heaven, beckoned by the Hand of God and rising like Elijah in his chariot. Many of these coins have survived (fig. 57).

The bishops would have had no control over how the army honoured its dead Augustus, so Eusebius explained away the rites, witnessed by thousands, which might have troubled Christians. However, he rejoiced in the fact that Constantine had already received a Christian burial, observing that the ceremony was performed only once Constantius and the military officers had withdrawn. It is not striking that Constantius did not participate in the Christian rites, for he was not yet baptized. Moreover, emperors were discouraged from contact with the dead. Constantine 'was accorded the place he earnestly desired alongside the monument to the apostles'. That is, he was buried in a mausoleum he had prepared for himself in Constantinople, and of which Eusebius had earlier provided a description, presumably from personal experience (*VC* IV.58):

He built up the shrine to an unimaginable height, and made it glint with stones of every kind, facing it from the ground to the roof. He divided the ceiling into delicate coffers and covered them with gold. Above this on the roof he provided copper instead of tiles to protect the building securely against rain. Round this too glittered much gold, so that by reflecting back the rays of the sun it sent dazzling light to those who gazed from afar . . . round it was a huge uncovered courtyard, open to the fresh air, surrounded by porticoes on four sides, which encompassed the court as well as the shrine itself.

The techniques do not sound unfamiliar, from Eusebius' earlier accounts of buildings in Jerusalem. However, and despite hints that one should draw such a conclusion, this was not a church, but rather a large circular mausoleum of the type Galerius had built for himself in Salonica and Maxentius for his family just outside Rome. Indeed, Constantine had built another for himself in Rome.

Constantine as Christ

When news of Constantine's death reached Rome, there were riots. One might expect such a thing during an interregnum, but the citizens rioted not because the force of law was now absent – the seventeen-year-old Caesar Constans was, after all, still in Milan – but rather because of disappointed expectations. They had expected to receive the emperor's body and have it rest in the imperial city. That this did not happen suggested the waning of the city's favoured status. Constantine had never returned to Rome after Fausta's death, although after his victory at the Milvian Bridge he had announced his intention to be buried there and had constructed a mausoleum for himself on an imperial estate some five miles south-east of the city along the Via Labicana (today's Via Casilina). This was formerly the site of the cemetery of the Praetorian Guard, but it also housed a catacomb for Christian burials, including the tombs of some fifty martyrs. A basilica dedicated to the martyrs Marcellinus the deacon and Peter the exorcist (not the apostle) had been built there, and this abutted the circular mausoleum. The interior of the mausoleum was covered in marble and porphyry, and in the mortar of this revetment was discovered, during excavations, a coin of Constantine dated between 324 and 326.

In 326 Constantine had ceded the Sessorian Palace, his Roman base, to his mother Helena as he left Rome for the last time. Two years later, at her death, Helena was interred in Constantine's mausoleum, now known as Tor Pignattara after the clay pots that are visible in its structure. Her body was placed in a porphyry sarcophagus that Constantine had ordered carved, surely to house his own mortal remains (fig. 58). This sarcophagus, moved to the Lateran in the twelfth century, is now in the Vatican Museums. It is decorated on all sides with scenes of battle, not at all fitting for Helena, but the splendour of the piece, in imperial purple stone mined only in one part of Egypt, was paramount. Porphyry had been used frequently in imperial sculpture, not least during the Tetrarchy, but Constantine's reign signalled the beginning of an era when it became *de rigueur* for the sarcophagi of members of the imperial family to be sculpted in the purple marble.

Helena had died aged around eighty, and her passing was marked by the abrupt end in spring 329 of the series of coins her son struck in her honour, as Helena Augusta. Eusebius is peculiarly obscure and obfuscatory when reporting her demise, claiming quite falsely that she had converted to Christianity only at her son's urging (*VC* III.46–7). It was Constantine's policy to obfuscate in this regard since, as we have seen, he wished to prevent criticism of his earlier failure to defend Christians from persecution. Eusebius is similarly conniving in his suggestion that Constantine was present at Helena's death, but he does not indicate where this took place. The scene of filial devotion may have been invented, and there is no suggestion that Constantine accompanied Helena's body as 'she was carried with a great guard of honour to the imperial city, and there laid in the imperial tombs'. The imperial city was then still Rome, although later authors were confused and believed Helena was interred in Constantinople.

That Constantine still intended to be buried in Rome itself until quite late in his life is suggested also by Eusebius' acknowledgement that his mausoleum in Constantinople was conceived not so very long before his death. It was not part of the original plan for the city or the palace complex (see maps 7 and 8). Indeed, 'imperial houses, baths and lamp-stores' were added to the new mausoleum complex, which sat some distance apart from the palace, 'suitably furnished for the guards of that place'. In Constantinople, apart from his imperial forebears, Constantine dwelt in death not with the gods of the Roman pantheon, but rather with Christ's apostles. The design of Constantine's tomb echoed the tomb of Christ at the Holy Sepulchre complex, completed just two years earlier. 'He erected twelve coffins, like sacred statues, in honour and remembrance of the apostolic choir, and placed in the middle of them his own sarcophagus, on either side of which stood six apostles.'

Later authors would suggest that Constantine was *isoapostolos*, 'equal to the apostles'. But this was a conception of the fifth century. It was clear to Eusebius in the fourth that Constantine considered himself not as follower, but leader: he had positioned his sarcophagus in the place of Christ. As Christ ruled in heaven and would return to rule on earth, so Constantine, alone of emperors, continued to rule on earth from heaven. Because 'divine rites and mystic liturgies' were performed over

his tomb, he was 'brought back to life to manage the whole administration, and Victor Maximus Augustus by his very name commands the
government of Rome'. Constantine was thwarted in his desire to be
baptized in the Jordan, but in life he had attained a Christ-like majesty,
as Eusebius opined at some length. In his *Tricennial Oration*, delivered
to the emperor only shortly before his death, Constantine was consistently Christ's 'friend' and emulator, indeed almost his second coming.
Such an idea might be expressed to the emperor while he lived, but it
could not be sustained in death. Constantine's son and longest-lived
successor, Constantius II, rebuilt the Holy Apostles to put his father in
his place, as an adjunct to Christ, his humble door-keeper, in direct
opposition to Constantine's original conception.

The succession

Constantine died on Pentecost, on the fiftieth day after Easter Sunday
counting inclusively as Romans did, and Greeks still do. No day would
have appeared more propitious to Eusebius, for on that day the Holy
Spirit had descended unto the apostles, in whose company Constantine
now moved. According to Aurelius Victor and Eutropius, the usual
comet had foretold his death and heralded his apotheosis. But back on
earth it was a dangerous day, since an interregnum threatened anarchy
and usurpation. His officers, not the bishops, were closest to Constantine
in death as in life, and they arranged affairs appropriately. They did
nothing, suppressing news of the death until Constantius had arrived,
and even then controlling the situation so as to quell the threat of
usurpation until after the funeral and ceremony of apotheosis. The
names of Constantine's generals on his campaign staff are not known,
but it is surely significant that in the following year, 338, both consuls
were generals whose names suggest humble origins, and that they owed
their promotions entirely to Constantine: Flavius Ursus and Flavius
Polemius.

As Constantine's body lay in state, his generals also acted to secure
the succession of his sons alone. Rumours were circulating that
Constantine's brothers had poisoned him. This information is highly
suggestive, revealing that one or both of his younger half-brothers,

Flavius Dalmatius and Julius Constantius, were with Constantine when he left Constantinople to make war on Persia. We cannot know whether the rumours were true or were concocted to justify the murders that ensued. The half-brothers were killed, as was Caesar Hannibalianus, younger son of Flavius Dalmatius, who was married to Constantine's youngest daughter Constantina, and certainly in Constantine's retinue (see stemma 2). A successful campaign would have installed him in the office which he had held in name only for a year or two: 'King of Kings' over the various Caucasian lands east of the Black Sea. Flavius Dalmatius' older son and namesake was murdered probably at Naissus, along with his Praetorian Prefect Valerius Maximus, in August 337. Flavius Dalmatius' appointment as Caesar in 335 had been unpopular with the army, so it would not have been difficult to recruit his killers. Also murdered was an unnamed son of Julius Constantius, the oldest of three. The only members of Constantius Chlorus' second family, with Theodora, to survive the blood-bath were boys considered too young to kill. All would later rise up. Nepotianus, son of Constantine's half-sister Eutropia, made a bid for the throne in 350, ruling the city of Rome for twenty-eight days before he was murdered. Gallus, the older of the two younger sons of Julius Constantius, would be elevated to the rank of Caesar in 351, only to be murdered in 354 for challenging Constantius. Julian, Gallus' younger half-brother, would become both Caesar and Augustus, and is remembered by history as 'the Apostate', Rome's last pagan emperor who died seeking to emulate Alexander and to surpass Constantine, by the conquest of Persia.

Writing in praise of Constantius II some years after the murders but before his own elevation to Augustus, Julian would suggest that his cousin had been 'forced by circumstances and reluctantly failed to prevent others doing wrong'. In its context this is as damning a statement as Julian's later and fuller revelation:

Six of my cousins and his, and my father who was his own uncle, and also another uncle of both of us on the father's side, and my eldest brother he put to death without trial . . . they kept telling us that Constantius acted thus partly because he was deceived and partly because he yielded to the violence and tumult of an undisciplined and mutinous army.

Clearly, matters were beyond the control of the twenty-year-old Caesar Constantius, although he stood to benefit most of all from the carnage. He left Constantinople to meet his brothers at Viminacium (modern Kostolac in Serbia), which was within that region formerly assigned to Flavius Dalmatius. There, in September 337, they each took the title Augustus and agreed upon their portions of the empire. This was confirmed by acclamation of the army and subsequently by the senate on 9 September 337. Constantine II returned to Trier with no more land than before, whereas Constans and Constantius II shared the Balkan territories of their dead cousin, which abutted their assigned lands. Constans received Moesiae, Constantius Thracia. Consequently, the division of empire was thus: Constantius II Augustus ruled all the eastern dioceses, being Thracia, Asiana, Pontica and Oriens, including the imperial capitals Constantinople and Antioch; Constans I Augustus ruled Italy, Africa, Pannoniae and Moesiae, including the cities of Rome, Milan and Carthage, and also Naissus and Sirmium; Constantine II Augustus, from Trier, ruled Gallicae, Viennensis, Hispaniae and Britanniae; and since Constans was still only seventeen, Constantine II served as his brother's guardian. Ominously, he considered Constans' lands also as subject to his guardianship.

Constantine returned to Trier, whence in 338 he launched a campaign against the Germans across the Rhine. Constans took as his new residence his father's birthplace, Naissus, to consolidate his hold on his new territories. Constantius rode east, 'followed by another march under arms', so that 'he stood upon the borders of Persia eager to stain his right hand with blood'. He was less disappointed than Libanius suggests to find the Persians had withdrawn for the winter and that he could return to his new capital on the Bosphorus. As each Augustus consolidated his regime, those who had advised their father in his last years were eliminated. Flavius Optatus, consul of 334 and the first man to hold the elevated rank of patrician after its reintroduction, is revealed by Zosimus to have been murdered. Likewise, the eminent orator Aemilius Magnus Arborius was killed, as Ausonius would later recount. Others simply disappear from the historical and epigraphical record: Evagrius, who was a Praetorian Prefect first in 326 and held that position again in Constantinople when Ablabius was sent to Antioch; Pacatianus,

Constans' Praetorian Prefect; Valerius Felix, Praetorian Prefect of Africa. The eradication of Valerius Maximus, Flavius Dalmatius' Praetorian Prefect, is revealed by an inscription from Tunisia, which dates from between the death of Constantine and the acclamation of his sons as Augusti. The Praetorian Prefects are listed in order of their promotion as follows: L. Pap. Pacatianus, Fl. Ablabius, [space for a scored-out name], C. Annius Tiberianus, Nestorius Timonianus. The name of Valerius Maximus has been chiselled out, an element of the *damnatio memoriae*. The demise of Flavius Ablabius is recounted more fully.

In Constantinople, but briefly, Constantius encouraged Flavius Ablabius to retire to his estates in Bithynia. Within a few months, however, Ablabius received a party of visitors bearing a letter from Constantius. This he must have expected, at least if he saw in the son the father's ruthlessness and hunger for power. The tale is related by Eunapius, in his *Life of the Sophists*, who tells how 'those who delivered the letter into his hands prostrated themselves before him, as Romans are accustomed to prostrate themselves before the emperor':

He received the document with great arrogance, and, freed from all apprehension, he demanded the imperial purple from those who had come, while his expression became more stern, and he inspired terror in the spectators. They replied that their task had only been to bring the letter, but that those who had been entrusted with another mission were at the door. Thereupon he insolently summoned them within, and was inflated with pride. But those who were then admitted were more in number and all carried swords, and instead of the purple robe they brought him 'purple death', and hacked him to pieces like some animal cut up at a public feast. Thus did the shade of Sopater avenge itself on Ablabius 'the fortunate'.

Perhaps Ablabius was arrogant when faced with the young emperor's lackeys, and surely imperious as he faced death at the command of the twenty-year-old. This was the vengeance not of Sopater but of Constantius and his new keepers.

It is at this juncture that Eusebius' testimony ends. He is as silent on the purge of 337 as he was about the deaths of Crispus and Fausta. Instead, he praises only the three sons of Constantine, rewriting the beginning of his *Life of Constantine* to honour the 'new lamps filling the whole earth with radiance ... If previously they still shared the honour of Caesars, now they have been declared *Imperatores Augusti*, singled out with their father's honours.' The only hint of what had so recently taken place is the suggestion that certain of those close to the father had only pretended to be Christians and were no longer at court. Eusebius died in 339, not knowing how far the sons would continue their father's policies, nor whether the division of empire would spark a further round of civil wars.

Tensions soon emerged between Constans and his older brother Constantine II, fomented by officials on both sides seeking to advance their own interests. On 8 January 339, Constantine addressed an edict (*CTh* 12.1.27) to the proconsul of Africa, a subordinate of Constans. In the following year, Constantine set off with his army, ostensibly to lend aid to Constantius in the east. As he entered Constans' territory, it was alleged that he was seeking to establish control of Italy and Africa. We cannot know whether this is true, or a fabrication to justify what happened next. As he approached Aquileia, Constantine's troops were caught in an ambush by a force despatched by Constans. Enjoying none of his father's good fortune, Constantine II was killed and his body cast into the river Alsa. He was shown by this fate to be not a true emperor but a tyrant like Maxentius, cast into the Tiber. His name would be scratched from inscriptions by his brother, his memory damned as surely as his father's unfortunate rivals.

And so, from 340, Constantius and Constans ruled as Augusti in a new Dyarchy, each holding one half of the empire. Constantius did not seek to challenge Constans, nor did he reproach him for their brother's murder. Instead, he devoted himself to the war with Persia, spending the better part of the following decade in a regular routine: winter in Antioch, summer campaigning. He made only a few brief trips to Constantinople. Constans travelled more extensively through his western provinces, in 342 alone visiting his residences in Naissus, Sirmium, Trier, Aquileia and Milan, and in 343 crossing briefly and for the only time into Britain to suppress a potential revolt. Although he made war successfully on the traditional enemies, he acquired a reputation for living decadently and failing properly to reward the army. Indeed, prurient authors would accuse him of debauchery and pederasty, and would suggest that this earned him the disfavour of his men and of God. According to Aurelius Victor, 'he was detestable because of the depravity of his subordinates and passionate in his greed and his contempt for the soldiers'. Consequently, in 350:

In the tenth year after his triumph [over Constantine II in 340] he was overthrown by the criminal actions of Magnentius, although he had certainly suppressed the uprisings of foreign tribes. Because he had treated too attentively the hostages taken from them, rather attractive boys whom he had sought out and paid for, it was justifiably believed that he burned with a passion of this kind. But would that these vices had continued! Everything was devastated by the awful savage character of Magnentius, as is natural with a barbarian . . .

Magnentius was a Gaul, born at Amiens to a Frankish mother by a British father.* He was not a Christian. He had risen through the ranks from common soldier to general, and this suggests that he had served for long years under Constantine himself, certainly in 324 although not as early as 312. On 18 January 350 at Autun, Magnentius was acclaimed by his troops led by Marcellinus, commander of Constans' bodyguard. Constans was murdered shortly afterwards as he fled south, at a fortress called Helena in the foothills of the Pyrenees.

The loyalty of Gaul, Spain and Britain seems to have been Magnentius' immediately, but he had to win over Italy and Africa. One of the few survivors of the 337 purge, Nepotianus, the son of Constantine's half-brother, was able to seize control of Rome for a month in June 350 but could not resist Magnentius' general Marcellinus. The usurper's army proceeded south, securing Africa very swiftly. More problematic was Pannonia, where Vetranio, Constans' Master of the Foot (*magister peditum*), was proclaimed emperor. It would appear that this was done at the behest of Constantina, Constans' sister, then resident in Rome, who took it upon herself to act in the interests of the Flavians. Vetranio swiftly advanced his claim to represent the family of Constantine, and began issuing coins in his own name and that of Constantius, declaring them both to be Augusti. This contradicts contemporary written sources, which suggest he was granted only the rank of Caesar. Some of Vetranio's

---

* His heritage is disputed but there were as yet no Bretons, so Magnentius' father cannot reasonably have been from that region of Gaul.

coins bear the legend HOC SIGNO VICTOR ERIS, 'by this sign you shall become Victor' (fig. 59). Vetranio was from Upper Moesia, not far from Constantine's birthplace, and he was sufficiently old that he might have fought for Constantine in the 310s. Perhaps his coins are intended to suggest that he too witnessed the famous vision in 310, or 312. It is certain that he wished thereby to associate himself with the victorious legacy of Constantine. Magnentius also issued coins, at first in his own name and that of Constantius, whom he claimed as a fellow Augustus, and later also for Vetranio. The numismatic record suggests a more complicated and nuanced picture than is painted by the historians.

Vetranio's elevation was initially supported by the only remaining son of Constantine, Constantius, who was tied down in the east by a Persian assault on Nisibis. It appears he sent a diadem to the general before he was able to head west in person, in winter 350. He did so in haste to engineer the general's abdication, which he achieved at Naissus on Christmas Day 350, offering Vetranio a generous annual stipend and lands to which he might immediately retire. In his place, shortly afterwards, Constantius elevated to the rank of Caesar his cousin Gallus, another of the youths to survive in 337, whom he imagined he might control more easily. Gallus had limited military experience and did not enjoy the support of the army, so it was considered safe to send him east, to maintain an imperial presence in Antioch. Constantius, meanwhile, remained at Sirmium on the Sava–Danube frontier, which served as a base for his campaign against Magnentius the following summer. The two armies met at Mursa, a fortress a short distance north-west of Sirmium, on 28 September 351. Accounts of the Battle of Mursa contradict each other, although all suggest that there was carnage on both sides. According to an account preserved only far later, in the twelfth-century history by Zonaras, Magnentius lost two-thirds of his men and Constantius four of every ten men, and those from a much larger force. Julian, on the other hand, would claim a decisive victory for Constantius and the heavy cavalry of the eastern regiments. Zosimus, following Eunapius, provides a full description:

Magnentius closed in on Mursa and set fire to its gates, thinking that if the iron-bound wood yielded to fire, he would open up the way into the city for his army. But this did not come to pass, as men on the walls extinguished the fire with lots of water. So, when he heard of Constantius' approach, Magnentius devised the following scheme: there was a stadium outside the city, originally designed for gladiatorial contests, which was overgrown with woods. Here he concealed four companies of Gauls and ordered them, when Constantius approached . . . to attack him unawares, so as to surround and annihilate his men.

The ruse failed, and 'it was he who was defeated in the ambush'. So, the armies met in battle on the plain outside Mursa, and 'great numbers fell on both sides' before Constantius' men gained the upper hand. Well after dark, 'Magnentius' army was utterly routed, with immense slaughter of men, horses and other animals'.

Constantius attributed his victory to God and announced that it had been foretold in a dream that he would avenge the murder of his brother. A far more impressive portent would soon become known to him.

Constantius Victor

Fourteen years after his death, Constantine's vision of the cross was once again brought before the public's gaze and imbued with still greater meaning, still within the context of imperial victory. On 7 May 351, according to a letter he sent to Constantius II, Cyril of Jerusalem, having recently taken up his bishopric, witnessed the appearance of a cross of light above Jerusalem. This second apparition has received but a fraction of the attention lavished on Constantine's vision, and all modern commentators appear content to regard it as a solar halo, despite its appearance in the morning. In his letter Cyril describes the appearance 'during the holy days of Pentecost, on the Nones of May, at around the third hour of the day [nine o'clock on the morning], of an immense cross formed from light, in the sky, which stretched above the holy Golgotha as far as the holy Mount of Olives'. It was visible to all in the city for several hours, brighter than the sun, and hordes flocked into the churches, young and old, men and women, locals and foreigners, Christians and others, intoning 'as if from one mouth the name of Jesus Christ, their Lord'. Cyril offers the vision to Constantius as a greater gift than the earthly crowns with which others had honoured him, and as concrete proof of divine favour for his rule, so that he might confront his 'enemies with greater courage'. The cross is a 'trophy of victory', specifically of Christ's victory over death, but also a sign that Constantius has God as his ally, and that he might 'bear the trophy of the cross, the boast of boasts, carrying forward the sign shown to us in the skies, of which heaven has made an even greater boast by displaying its form to human beings'.

Given the similarity in the language he employs to that of Eusebius, writing a little more than a decade earlier in the same part of the world, it is striking that Cyril did not compare the 'immense cross formed from light' to that which Constantine and his troops were now believed to have witnessed four decades earlier. The most obvious reason for his omission was that Constantius had not witnessed the vision in person. Therefore, it allowed Cyril to offer himself as interpreter, and to promote his own interests and those of his see, Jerusalem. J. W. Drijvers has shown that Cyril's letter must be understood as the first of a series of measures to establish the True Cross as a central motif in Jerusalem's emergence as the holiest site in Christendom. Cyril was at that time in conflict with Acacius, the Arian metropolitan of Caesarea, whose inter-ests were well represented at Constantius' court, and he surely saw the apparition as a means to raise Jerusalem's profile. Moreover, since Eusebius had preceded his pupil Acacius in the see of Caesarea, one might understand Cyril's desire to suppress information on Constantine's vision, which Eusebius had so assiduously refined and disseminated from his base in Palestine. As interpreter of the apparition, therefore, Cyril kept Jerusalem to the fore, praising Constantius' piety as surpass-ing that of his most God-beloved father of blessed memory, by whose prayers the soterial wood of the True Cross had been found in Jerusalem and the Holy Places revealed. Whereas Constantine was blessed with revelations from Jerusalem's earth, his yet more pious son received his revelation from the heavens above the city, thus fulfilling the evangelist's prophecy (Matthew 24:30) that 'the sign of the Son of Man will appear in the sky'.

Constantius embraced the vision of the cross as his own, and at the Battle of Mursa the truth of Cyril's claims was demonstrated, when

Constantius defeated Magnentius. Constantius celebrated this victory only belatedly, with a triumphal *adventus* into Rome in 357. The significance of the delay is surely that he wished to emulate his father, who had celebrated his victory over Maxentius in Rome. Naturally, panegyrists drew parallels between the two episodes, including Themistius (*Oration* 3.44b), who delivered an oration in Rome representing the senate of the city of Constantinople. But it is an historian who presents the fullest account of Constantius' Roman *adventus* of 357: Ammianus Marcellinus (XVI.10). In a passage that draws on Xenophon's description of the Persian ruler Cyrus, Ammianus describes Constantius' deportment as he entered Rome on a 'golden carriage in the resplendent blaze of shimmering precious stones' between 'twin lines of infantrymen with shields and crests gleaming with glittering rays, clad in shining mail'.

Accordingly, being saluted as Augustus with favouring shouts, while hills and shores thundered out the roar, [Constantius] never stirred but showed himself as calm and imperturbable as he was commonly seen in his provinces. For he both stooped when passing through lofty gates (although he was very short), and as if his neck were in a vice he kept the gaze of his eyes straight ahead, and turned his face neither to the right nor the left, but (as if he were a lay figure) neither did he nod when the wheel jolted, nor was he ever seen to spit, or to wipe or rub his face or nose, or to move his hands about.

Sabine MacCormack likened the image the emperor sought to project to an icon, set apart from and unmoved by the furore around him. And one can indeed appreciate this comparison when observing Constantius' portrait on a *largitio* bowl, now at the Hermitage (fig. 60). Although Hellenistic models might be cited, Constantius had adopted the style of his father in his later years, placing himself between his subjects and the *summus deus*, the god of the Christians.

Ammianus, a pagan, was silent about the incorporation of any explicitly Christian elements into the celebrations. While he disapproves of Constantius' attempt to secure a triumph for victory in a civil war, he gives no indication that the emperor attributed this victory to the god of the Christians. This silence has led some to suggest that Constantius was seeking to appease the still largely pagan Roman senate; a proposition that may be dispensed with on the grounds that it was on this occasion that he ordered the removal from the senate house of the pagan altar to Victory that had been installed by Augustus.* Moreover, there may be evidence that, far from setting aside his Christianity, Constantius paraded it before the senate, earning the opprobrium of the pagan historian Eunapius, writing c.400, whose work has been preserved only in fragments in later works (largely by Zosimus, as we have seen many times). David Woods has identified in one of the most controversial fragments (fragment 68, preserved as *Excerpta de sententiis* 72) an account of the same victory procession in Rome, where 'a Persian, an *eparch* in Rome . . . reduced the success of the Romans to mockery and laughter'. He did this by 'assembling many small [painted] panels in the middle of the hippodrome' which revealed to those there assembled that the victory was not due to 'the bravery of the emperor or the strength of the soldiers, or anything that was a proper battle':

Instead [on one of the painted panels] a hand extended as if from the clouds, and by the hand was written 'The Hand of God driving off the barbarians'. (It is shameful but necessary to write this down.) And on the other side [was written], 'The barbarians fleeing God', and other things even more odious and stupid than these, the nonsense of drunken painters.

Of course drunken painters were not responsible for the display, but the emperor's image-makers, who would have ordered the 'Persian' and his troops to march through the streets to the hippodrome bearing these images painted on both sides of placards, as was a regular feature of triumphal celebrations. Woods has identified the 'Persian' as the elder Hormisdas, brother of Shapur II of Persia, who defected to Rome in c.324, and who is credited with a clever quip in Ammianus' account of Constantius' Roman visit (XVI.10.16). Woods's argument is ingenious, and thus his conclusions may be questioned. However, I find them most convincing, and the sentiment behind the display, which Eunapius found so repugnant, to be emblematic of Constantius' understanding of his victory over Magnentius. Constantius had seen that coins struck to mark his father's apotheosis in 337 featured the 'Hand of God'

---

* The altar of Victory would be replaced by Julian and removed again by Gratian; then restored by Eugenius and removed for the final time by Theodosius.

(fig. 57). His own right of succession had now been demonstrated conclusively by the reappearance of that helping hand, in the same form as it had appeared to Constantine: a cross of light in the sky guaranteeing his victory. Moreover, his army was responsible for reminding the citizens of Rome that Constantius had inherited his father's divine support, as demonstrated at Jerusalem in May 351 and at Mursa the following September. In victory the emperor himself sat motionless and expressionless above the mêlée, an object of veneration second only to the god he worshipped. He was truly the son and heir of Victor Constantine.

Christian victory

By the end of the 350s Constantius had consolidated his hold on power through the elimination of several rivals. In 354 he commanded the murder of Gallus Caesar, whom he had raised in March 351. Gallus died at Pola, the same Istrian town in which Crispus had been poisoned in 326. In his place, the following November, Constantius raised Gallus' half-brother Julian, known to history as 'the Apostate', the last pagan Roman emperor. Julian obliged Constantius to recognize him as Augustus in 360, but the two men were on course for war when Constantius died, in November 361. The brief pagan interlude of Julian's reign served only to sharpen the Christian triumphalism that attended his death in Persia, falling like Valerian in war against the Persian infidel because he had scorned the one true god. What then was a Christian to make of the devastating defeat of the Roman army at the Battle of Adrianople in August 378, where the devout Christian emperor of the east, Valens, fell with two-thirds of his men, slaughtered by the Goths? That was simple, for, as St Ambrose observed, Valens was an Arian, whereas Gratian, emperor of the west, was assured of victory by virtue of his orthodoxy.

It fell to Theodosius (379–95), chosen to replace Valens, to institute orthodox Christianity as the religion of the Roman state, and to insist that all worship his god as their own. But still victory was his alone when Theodosius took the field against the last pagan pretender, Eugenius. According to Rufinus of Aquileia (XI.33), 'he prepared for war by arming himself not so much with weapons as with prayers and fasts, guarded not so much by the nightwatch but by nightly prayer vigils'. As matters went against the emperor at the Battle of Cold River, he lay prostrate and prayed, shouting that his campaign had been undertaken for Christ in order to exact just retribution 'lest the Gentiles ask, Where is their God?' (Psalms 113:30). Consequently, a wind blew up of such strength and direction that it whipped the arrows unleashed by Eugenius' archers back against them. So inspired were Theodosius' officers that one of outstanding piety, a certain Bacurius, fought through Eugenius' bodyguard to kill him. Orosius (390–418), writing only shortly afterwards, placed emphasis still more singularly on Theodosius, who was now deserted by his men, but prostrated himself on the battlefield and maintained a vigil throughout the night, leaving 'pools of tears which he had paid as the price for heavenly assistance'. The following morning, he rose and threw himself into the thick of battle, certain of victory even if nobody else should follow him, and assisted by the whirlwind, the result was 'determined from heaven between the party which without the help of men placed his faith humbly in God alone, and the party that most arrogantly trusted in its own strength and in idols'.

Rufinus' account of the public liturgical events that Theodosius had staged before he left Constantinople shows how far matters had proceeded since Constantine had allowed his troops a day of rest on Sundays and encouraged them to march under his *labarum*. Such ceremonies would grow ever more central to military preparations as the late Roman world gave way to the Byzantine. In the camps the ritual life of the army was transformed. The mobile tent in the centre of the marching camp, once known as the *aedes*, the temple and treasury where the standards were stored and venerated, became a chapel. It was here that the units prayed together on holy days, but also 'on the actual day of battle before anyone goes out the gate', as is prescribed in Maurice's *Strategikon* of the later sixth century. Maurice further required that the standards be blessed a day or two before battle; that the *Trisagion* – 'Holy God, Holy Mighty One, Holy Immortal One, have mercy on us' – be sung by each unit early in the morning and late at night, before and after all duties; and that, as each unit marched out of camp, it should cry in unison 'God is with us' thrice. Military services would become increasingly complex, as later military manuals reveal.

One can also discern a shift from the traditional theology of victory, centred on the 'manly aggressiveness' (*virtus*) of the commander, to a theology that rewarded personal piety. The new theology, moreover, accommodated the purity of each individual soldier and his correct faith. This is clearly reflected in the adaptation of the *sacramentum*, the military oath which had caused consternation among third-century Christian commentators, but, as preserved by Vegetius (II.5.3), was now sworn: 'By God, Christ, and the Holy Spirit, and by the majesty of the emperor, which second to God is to be loved and worshipped by the human race.' No longer was the *numen* (divine quality) of the emperor worshipped, but rather one swore loyalty to his 'majesty', divinely given and guided.

In the reign of Justinian we see how Christian liturgical celebrations had replaced key holidays recorded in the third-century *feriale* (religious calendar). According to Corippus, in a panegyric celebrating John Troglyta's victories in North Africa, the enemy determined to attack on a holy day, perhaps simply a Sunday, when 'The Roman soldiers, occupied with their customary rites, will fear no battle'. But the general John and his second Ricinarius anticipated the attack, and like Theodosius at Cold River, spent the night before in prayer and the spilling of tears. As the sun rose, so their Christian soldiers trooped out with their standards to a tent in the centre of the camp, a mobile chapel, where a priest draped the altar and conducted the regular service. The congregants wept and together wailed: 'Forgive our sins and the sins of our fathers, we beseech You, Christ.' John, the general, was with them on his knees, more tears 'pouring from his eyes like a river' as he intoned a long prayer for victory. Once the priest had performed the Eucharist, it was shown that 'the gifts were acceptable to the Lord of heaven, and at once sanctified and cleansed' the army. Victory was assured, and those who would die did so purified by their tears and the sanctified elements. This, then, was the legacy of Constantine, the Christian Victor.

Conclusion

Only a shadow of the true Constantine has emerged in these pages, a shifting shade cast by the refulgent images created of and for him through three decades in power. He was a devout son of pious parents, who rushed across the empire to his father's deathbed. He was the one true heir of Constantius Chlorus and of Claudius Gothicus, recognized by the armies of the north and vindicated by victory in the east. He was a Herculian Caesar, kinsman of Maximian and Maxentius, who witnessed Apollo and venerated Sol Invictus. He was the new Alexander, gazing to the heavens, sharing a virile head of hair and other attributes with his divinized forebear. But he was also the new Moses, leader of the elect, who forged a new ark, the *labarum*. He was, in death, a second Christ surrounded by his apostles, but later only equal to the apostles. He was Victor Constantine, the greatest emperor, conqueror of the empire's barbarian foes, a singular sovereign in an age of Tetrarchs and Dyarchs, founder of the second Rome. The later reputation of Constantine the Great attests to the potency of these various images and to the success of his efforts to damn the memories and appropriate the achievements of his rivals.

In contrast to his many public images, of Constantine's private life and views we have only rare hints, and to seek more in the sources is to submit them to a critical scrutiny they cannot bear. His letters and speeches were drafted by a changing staff over his long reign, his coins designed and struck by mint workers not always abreast of current motifs and propaganda imperatives. The major monuments and luxury objects produced in his honour were designed and crafted by a range of patrons and artists whose agendas did not always, if ever, match the emperor's own. Still, we have used them all where we can and with suitable caution to advance key themes. Constantine assigned great value to army and family. He rewarded loyalty handsomely, but would sacrifice anyone to defend his position and reputation. Honour was paramount to him, and he legislated his own preferred morality. He was short-tempered and stubborn, vain and narcissistic, as one might expect from a channel for divine grace. Rumours suggest that he was sensitive to balding and that he brought people close by handing out nicknames at court. He was a lofty sovereign on a high throne, decked out in silk and gold, the heir to Diocletian's style and methods of governance, but like his mentor, he was also a man of the camps and fellow soldier who loved and was loved by his men.

There can be no doubt that Constantine was a charismatic and effective commander, who first demonstrated his ability in war in Galerius' Persian campaigns of the 290s. As a general he was generous, minting and distributing coins in vast numbers to reward and magnify his glorious army. He was also deplorably brave and foolhardy, as he demonstrated by his willingness to march on Rome in 312 and to fight personally before the walls of Turin and in the bloody Battle of Verona. He continued to defy odds, and those who fought in his armies trusted in him and the demonstrated fact that to follow him limited one's chance of death, defeat and dishonour. There seems no better way to explain this than in Constantine's own terms: that his valour and manly aggressiveness, his impulsive *virtus*, was rewarded with spectacular good fortune, *felicitas*. We need not take the further step of suggesting that his successes in war demonstrated divine favour for his undertakings, but it is no surprise that Roman authors, not least Christian Roman authors, saw the imperial theology of victory in action. The god of the Christians was the new greatest god, the divine companion and patron of Constantine.

We have no coherent account of Constantine as commander on which to draw. The only full consideration of Constantine by one who knew him personally is given by Eusebius of Caesarea, who met the emperor on rare occasions and received formal letters from him more frequently. Eusebius wanted the emperor's sons to remember their father as a devout

Christian leader. The heirs would determine the fate of their father's experiment with imperial Christianity even as they fought over his victorious legacy. Eusebius' Constantine was, therefore, far from rounded. He shares only his biographer's concerns and views, appearing to spend all his time and energy promoting Christianity. Certainly Constantine did devote much time and many resources to promoting the faith he came to embrace as his own over long years. Constantine's conversion was a process that took him from a vision in 310, through divine visitations in a number of dreams, to his acceptance in 324 that he fought in the name of the singular god worshipped by his instructors and companions, Ossius of Cordoba and Lactantius. Once the truth of his new faith was clear to him, as emperor he demanded that all Christians understand and worship God in the same manner. While toleration was legislated for those who had not yet followed Constantine's path to enlightenment, Christian schismatics and heretics, those who recognized different authority or defended distinct dogmatic principles, were to be persuaded or, if necessary, forced into unity. And yet through his life, Constantine's own understanding of the faith changed with his advisers and spiritual guides, as Lactantius and Ossius departed and Eusebius of Nicomedia rose to prominence. The universal persecution of Christians was ended, but it was no longer a safe time to be a questioning Christian. Now the diversity of early opinion could no longer stand, and to argue was to challenge imperial authority. Synods were called to end discussion, not to facilitate it.

Constantine required unity of faith to guarantee the continued favour of his god, the god of victory. This god was recognized by a wider range of believers than had hitherto been conceivable. Constantine's conversion promoted the further spread of Christianity in the Roman world, but it did not begin that process. Christianity had been spreading long before his intervention. Indeed, in the decades before Constantine came to power, Christianity was already a dominant faith in many of the eastern provinces, notably in North Africa, Syria and what had now come to be known as the Holy Places; it had also attracted a significant minority of adherents throughout Asia Minor and Anatolia. Imperial patronage for those communities considered orthodox certainly encouraged further conversions, and the formal introductions of Christianity in Armenia and Georgia can be dated to Constantine's reign. But it was also in the eastern lands and North Africa, where Christianity had its deepest roots, that the problem of sectarian strife arose.

The context for the emperor's contribution, the interface between faith and power in the third-century Roman world, allows us properly to delimit his contribution. It was to allow Christianity to spread into areas it might otherwise not easily have reached: into the less urbanized provinces of the north-west and into the army camps. The emperor's conversion was emulated by commanders in his army and those who coveted promotion. The rank and file, whose personal faith had always run parallel to their obligations to the imperial cult and formal *religio*, now also embraced Christianity. They enjoyed for the first time a day of rest each week, a Sabbath, distinct from those days prescribed in the *feriale*. In battle, they recognized the power of the Christian god, the greatest god, to protect and save, and when they were discharged, these soldiers took their new faith home. Christianity spread into areas to the north and west, to fix new roots in the provinces of Gaul, Britannia and Hispania, and beyond into the lands of the Alemans and Sarmatians and Goths, barbarian lands whence the Roman army increasingly drew its recruits. As a consequence of Constantine's successes, and more certainly of the extraordinary efforts made to spread news of their miraculous inspiration, Christianity was considered the religion of victory. Over time, also, chapels were added to camps, portable lead tanks allowed for baptism, chaplains accompanied the legions into battle. None of this would have been possible without Constantine. But Constantine was no holy warrior, still less a crusader. He was a Roman emperor whose fate was determined within the strictures of the imperial theology of victory.

Three centuries after Constantine's death, Islam would rise in the deserts of the Arabian peninsula and sweep into the lands where Christianity had emerged. Muslims conceived of paradise as an oasis, the anti-desert, a fertile garden where they might retire from the heat of the mundane. Christians articulated their heaven as the city of God, free of poverty, disease and time. The contrast between these conceptions is telling, and it would not have been so striking had Christianity emerged not in the densely populated cities of the Roman east, but in the sparsely settled and wooded lands of the north, where Constantine's conversion allowed it to flourish as a religion of victory. Meanwhile, in the east, an ideological reorientation took place within early Byzantium. Emphasis shifted from the emperor as divinely inspired, to individual soldiers, whose spiritual purity became essential to the empire's success or, increasingly, its failure. As late Rome lost confidence in its traditional symbols of power, new motifs emerged, including the tears and chastity of soldiers. The pure, penitent and chaste were prepared to receive spiritual rewards for their sacrifice. This idea was borrowed into Islam, forming the kernel of jihad.

Glossary

adventus A formal imperial entry into a city, far more frequent than a triumphal entry and procession (*triumphus*).

askesis Discipline, more particularly acts that demonstrate one's commitment to a cause, also the root of the term 'ascetic'. Bishops, like 'holy men' and monks, were expected to perform acts of *askesis* to consolidate their spiritual authority.

Augustus The title reserved for the senior emperor or emperors (pl. *Augusti*), distinguished from their junior partners, Caesars.

catechumen A Christian convert under instruction prior to baptism. It was not regular practice to baptize infants, and not all were accepted as catechumens.

centuria The century, the basic unit of the Roman army, comprising eighty men (and not, as one might guess, one hundred men). It was made up of *contubernia* (tent groups, sing. *contubernium*) of eight to ten men.

chi-rho A Christogram, or sign of Christ, formed from the two Greek letters that begin his name, chi (X) and rho (P).

cohort A unit of the Roman army. The traditional strength of the cohort was six centuries (of eighty), with the first century being double strength; actual numbers varied between units.

comes Literally 'companion' (pl. *comites*). When used on coins, it might refer to one who consorted with the gods, and later was used to refer to the emperor's closest companions and advisers, becoming an elevated rank and taking on the meaning of 'count'.

comitatus Originally meaning 'retinue', a group assigned to the person of the emperor. It came to mean a personal bodyguard and later a larger expeditionary force (the *comitatenses*), to be distinguished from those stationed in garrisons at the frontiers (*ripenses*).

consul Once the highest elected office for a senator in the Roman republic, this honorific position was entirely in the gift of the emperor. The ordinary consuls gave their names to the year in the Roman calendar, and hence to be appointed consul was a great and distinctive honour.

cursus publicus The official Roman courier service and postal system, which stretched across the whole empire, delivering official messages and transporting officials from station to station.

damnatio memoriae The destruction of memory and legacy that took place when an enemy was defeated or a rival killed. The deceased's actions and achievements were erased from the historical record, his or her name excised from inscriptions, and his or her existence ignored in future orations and narratives.

divus A minor divinity, usually a deified emperor (feminine, *diva*, although this is less common; pl. *divi*), distinct from the gods of the pantheon, each of which was a *deus*.

felicitas The divine gift of good fortune, most often manifested by victory, given as a reward for imperial *virtus*.

feriale A calendar prescribing rituals and ceremonies to be performed on certain days by state officers and, notably, those in the army. A version of an army calendar, the *Feriale Duranum*, has survived.

genius The guardian spirit of almost anything, whether animate (a military unit) or inanimate (a grain store), the *genius* was commonly portrayed as a nude young man, frequently holding a cornucopia.

henotheism Adherence to a particular god out of several, generally a 'greatest god', who might preside over other, lesser deities. Distinct from monotheism, which professed a single god.

invictus Unconquered, or unconquerable, this epithet was accorded to the Sun god, Sol, but also to emperors.

labarum An imperial standard topped with the chi-rho, manufactured by Constantine to be used as a palladium, or protective device, during battle; also, a channel for divine grace, later used as the imperial sceptre.

magister May be translated as 'master' as in the case of the *magister peditum* (Master of the Foot), *magister equitum* (Master of the Horse) and *magister officiorum* (Master of Offices, head of the palatine administration, the emperor's chief-of-staff).

numen A spirit or divine quality. The *numen* (pl. *numina*) of the emperor or emperors was venerated rather than the mortal man.

obverse The front of a coin ('heads'), on which the portrait of an emperor appeared, allowing a variety of designs on the reverse.

panegyric A speech delivered in praise of someone, most often an emperor.

princeps The first or leading citizen, later translated as 'prince'. It is used in the construction *princeps iuventutis*, 'prince of the youth', a title of Republican origin, once used to identify the leading boy in the Game of Troy. It later passed to the chief of the equestrian order, but under the principate came to be used to designate the scion of the imperial house who was designated to succeed. Often written *princeps iuventatis*, but one should distinguish between *iuventas* (gen. *iuventatis*), which describes the condition of early manhood, and *iuventus* (gen. *iuventutis*), meaning more exactly 'young men collectively', the latter having a military tone.

quadriga A chariot drawn by four horses, employed in processions and associated in iconography with the Sun god, Sol Invictus.

quaestor Among the highest offices within the palatine administration, the *quaestor* was the emperor's principal private secretary and held the rank of *comes*.

quinquennalia Five-year anniversary celebrations, celebrated with great ceremony, including processions, orations and public prayers (*vota*). Coins were issued and distributed as gifts (donatives), principally to the army. Similar, still more splendid celebrations marked each successive five years, especially the ten-year (*decennalia*), twenty-year (*vicennalia*) and thirty-year (*tricennalia*) anniversaries.

religio The collection of cult practices and rituals that supported the Roman state and, particularly, imperial enterprises. 'Religion' is not a particularly accurate translation into English.

rosaliae Rose festivals, dates in the *feriale* which for the army became associated with veneration of the standards (*signa*).

sacramentum An oath, but here particularly the solemn oath sworn by soldiers. None has survived before a Christianized version in the treatise by Vegetius (*c.*AD 400).

signa Roman military standards (sing. *signum*), including the legion's eagle (*aquila*) and the flag standard of a constituent unit (*vexillum*). The standard was carried by the *signifer*.

Sol Invictus The 'Unconquered' or 'Unconquerable Sun', an eastern god equated with the Roman god Apollo.

SPQR *Senatus Populusque Romanus*, 'the senate and people of Rome'.

summus deus Literally the 'highest god' or 'greatest god', the ultimate guarantor of victory.

Tetrarchy The rule of four emperors, two senior Augusti and two junior Caesars, as distinct from Dyarchy, the rule of two, and Pentarchy, the rule of five.

traditores Literally 'handers-over', referring to those Christians who during the Great Persecution surrendered holy vessels and scripture to the authorities. From this term we derive 'traitor'.

triumphus The triumphal entry into and procession through a city by a victorious emperor, and various associated rituals. In Greek this is the *thriambos*.

tropaeum The 'trophy', a cruciform Roman symbol of victory, later used as a battle standard. A precursor of the *labarum*.

vexillation A unit of the army constructed by drawing smaller groups (usually cohorts) from several regiments, initially for expeditionary undertakings or specific campaigns; in later years the groupings took on a greater permanence.

virtus A quality or group of qualities that earns an individual divine favour, the root of the English word 'virtue' but rather broader than that. As understood within the imperial theology of victory, it can be translated as 'manly aggressiveness' or 'valour', the reward for which is *felicitas*.

vota Public prayers offered for the emperor, notably at his anniversary celebrations.

Abbreviations

ANRW *Aufstieg und Niedergang der römischen Welt*, eds H. Temporini and W. Haase (Berlin and New York, 1972–)

CAH *The Cambridge Ancient History*, 2nd edn, vols 12 and 13, eds Averil Cameron et al (Cambridge, 1997, 2005)

CIL Corpus of Latin Inscriptions. *Corpus Inscriptionum Latinarum*, eds T. Mommsen et al, currently 17 multi-part vols (1893–)

CTh Theodosian Code. *The Theodosian Code and Novels and the Sirmondian Constitution*, trans. C. Pharr (Princeton, 1952)

DOP *Dumbarton Oaks Papers* (Cambridge, MA and Washington, DC, 1941–)

HE Eusebius, *Ecclesiastical History. Eusebius, History of the Church*, trans. G. A. Williamson (Harmondsworth, 1965)

ILS Selected Latin Inscriptions. *Inscriptiones latinae selectae*, 5 vols, ed. H. Dessau (Berlin, 1892–1916)

JRS *Journal of Roman Studies*

PLRE *Prosopography of the Later Roman Empire*, vol 1, eds A. H. M. Jones, J. R. Martindale and J. Morris (Cambridge, 1971)

RIB *The Inscriptions of Roman Britain, I. Inscriptions on Stone*, eds R. G. Collingwood and R. P. Wright, 2nd edn with addenda and corrigenda by R. S. O. Tomlin (Stroud, 1995)

RIC *The Roman Imperial Coinage*, eds H. Mattingley et al, 10 vols (London, 1923–94)

VC Eusebius, *Life of Constantine*, trans. Averil Cameron and S. G. Hall (Oxford, 1999)

Primary Sources

Most of the pertinent primary sources are listed within the bibliographical essays that follow, broken down by chapter. The secondary works listed in the essays are merely those that I read in writing this book and should in no way be considered a complete record of scholarship devoted to Constantine. I have indicated how I have used many, and where I have taken a different line. Interested readers seeking English translations of key sources might start with the excellent recent translation of the *Vita Constantini*: Eusebius, *Life of Constantine*, trans. Averil Cameron and S. G. Hall (Oxford, 1999), and the Penguin translation of Eusebius' *Ecclesiastical History*: Eusebius, *History of the Church*, trans. G. A. Williamson (Harmondsworth, 1965). The former contains the fullest account of Constantine's actions, although it is far from comprehensive. The structure of the *Life*, or *VC*, suggests that Eusebius composed it in several stages, and for distinct reasons, modifying earlier content in the process. One hypothesis holds that the work was conceived as a continuation to his *Ecclesiastical History*, which ended in 324. However, events and encounters encouraged the author to modify his work and rewrite the earlier section as a laudatory apologia for Constantine's rise to sole power, which can usefully be contrasted with the tenth book of the *HE*. Eusebius met the emperor for the first time in person at the Council of Nicaea in 325, and subsequently delivered speeches to him in 335, in praise of the construction of the Church of the Holy Sepulchre in Jerusalem, and in 335–6 for Constantine's *tricennalia*, or thirty-year celebrations. He announced his intention of attaching these speeches to the *VC*, and similar subject matter is covered in the body of the text. The final stage of composition and revision was highly political, occurring as Constantine's heirs seemed poised to destroy his legacy. This took place before Eusebius' own death in May 339, but after 9 September 337, for Constantine's three sons are called Augusti in the *VC*'s introduction and conclusion. Before their father's death they were only Caesars.

One cannot rely on Eusebius for historical 'facts', any more than one can rely on the rhetorical material preserved in the invaluable *Panegyrici Latini*: C. E. V. Nixon and Barbara T. Rodgers, *In Praise of Later Roman Emperors. The* Panegyrici

Latini (Berkeley, Los Angeles and Oxford, 1994). Balder, but still heavily interpolated, is the *Origo Constantini*, which can be read as 'The Origin of Constantine', trans J. Stevenson, in Lieu and Montserrat, *From Constantine to Julian: Pagan and Byzantine Views. A Source History* (London and New York, 1996), pp. 39–62; or in an older, less reliable translation appended to the third volume of the Loeb Ammianus Marcellinus, trans. J. Rolfe. Now more difficult to find, but certainly essential, are Lactantius' *On the Deaths of the Persecutors*: Lactantius, *De Mortibus Persecutorum*, trans. J. L. Creed (Oxford, 1984); and Zosimus, *New History*, trans. R. Ridley (Canberra, 1982). A recent translation of Philostorgius, *Church History*, by P. Amidon (Atlanta, 2007) is very helpful. Many additional works are translated in the marvellous series Liverpool Translated Texts for Historians, including Lactantius' *Divine Institutes*, Aurelius Victor, Optatus' *Against the Donatists*, the *Easter Chronicle*, and Constantine's own *Oration to the Saints*. One must turn frequently to the translated excerpts in J. Stevenson, *A New Eusebius. Documents Illustrating the History of the Church to* AD 337, rev. W. H. C. Frend (London, 1987).

Bibliographical Essays

Works devoted entirely to Constantine are legion, but A. H. M. Jones, *Constantine and the Conversion of Europe* (London, 1948), remains of great value. The best introduction to earlier literature is contained in the notes of N. Baynes, 'Raleigh Lecture on History: Constantine the Great and the Christian Church', *Proceedings of the British Academy* (1929): 341–442. Great scepticism about the sincerity of Constantine's conversion was earlier evinced in J. Burckhardt, *Die Zeit Constantins des Grossen* (Basel, 1853), and his views were made more widely known and enduring by more recent translations of the work. In contrast, T. D. Barnes, *Constantine and Eusebius* (Cambridge, MA and London, 1981) presents Constantine as a proselytizing convert from 312, enhancing the sympathetic Christian portrait painted by A. Alföldi, *The Conversion of Constantine and Pagan Rome*, trans. H. Mattingly (Oxford, 1948). Two excellent recent interpretations are: in German, T. Grünewald, *Constantinus Maximus Augustus. Herrschaftspropaganda in der zeitgenössischen Überlieferung*, Historia Einzelschriften 64 (Stuttgart, 1990); and in English, C. M. Odahl, *Constantine and the Christian Empire* (London and New York, 2004). Recent edited collections include S. N. C. Lieu and D. Montserrat, eds, *Constantine. History, Historiography and Legend* (London and New York, 1998); and N. Lenski, ed, *The Cambridge Companion to the Age of Constantine* (Cambridge, 2006). The latter has been invaluable in writing this book, and individual chapters are referred to frequently below. An impressive new analysis of Constantine's empire appeared when most of the research and writing for this project was complete: R. Van Dam, *The Roman Revolution of Constantine* (Cambridge, 2007), but not too late for me to incorporate some fine comments and observations where these supported my own interpretation (on family and hair).

Introduction

On Constantine and Christianity in Britain, one might start now with E. Hartley et al, eds, *Constantine the Great. York's Roman Emperor* (York, 2006). See also J. P. C. Kent and K. S. Painter, *Wealth of the Roman World, AD 300–700* (London, 1977); J. M. C. Toynbee, 'A new Roman pavement found in Dorset', *JRS* 54 (1964): 7–14; Katherine M. D. Dunbabin, *Mosaics of the Greek and Roman World* (Cambridge, 1999); and M. W. Herren and Shirley A. Brown, *Christ in Celtic Christianity: Britain and Ireland from the fifth to the twelfth century* (Woodbridge, 2002). Essential inscriptions are collected in *RIB*. For those in Britain, Constantine has always exerted a fascination, such that in 1951, for the Colchester Cathedral Festival, part of the Festival of Britain, Dorothy L. Sayers penned a play relocating the emperor to Colchester. Colchester's coat of arms features a cross sprouting shoots, an allusion to the legend that Constantine's mother, Helena, discovered the True Cross, Christ's crucifix, a life-giving relic. The story first emerged half a century after Helena's death, and has persisted to the present day, so that when one sees statues and paintings of Helena she is inevitably holding a cross. Colchester's claim goes still further: that Helena was the daughter of a Celtic king, born in Colchester. Her alleged father, 'Old King Cole', is the 'merry old soul' of nursery rhyme, and the story entered the literate imagination through Evelyn Waugh's novel of 1950, simply called *Helena*. So potent was her legacy that more than a hundred churches and chapels were devoted to Helena throughout England and Wales. See J. W. Drijvers, *Helena Augusta: The Mother of Constantine the Great and Her Finding of the True Cross* (Leiden, 1992); A. Harbus, *Helena of Britain in Medieval Legend* (Cambridge, 2002).

In the centuries that followed Helena's death, many other places laid claim to her birth and her body. Trier, in particular, where she had first lived as the mother of a reigning emperor, was advanced through the Middle Ages as the place of her birth, seeking to displace Drepanum. This was no easy task, as Constantine had renamed that town Helenopolis. Depictions of St Helena, together with her son, featured in churches throughout medieval Europe, notably in a town in Bulgaria, now named simply Constantine and Helena. See H. A. Pohlsander, *Helena: Empress and Saint* (Chicago, 1995), which provides chapters on Helena in later religious literature and art.

Chapter 1: Religion in the Later Roman Empire

To find a definition for *religio* and much else one might now start with C. Ando, *The Matter of the Gods: Religion and the Roman Empire* (Berkeley, Los Angeles and London, 2008). I thank Anthony Kaldellis for this reference and others (and apologize that I did not follow his insistence that I call Salonica either Thessalonica or Thessalonike). Roman army religion has generated a fairly large but far from comprehensive bibliography. The standard work before the publication of the *Feriale Duranum* was A. von Domaszewski, *Die Religion des römischen Heeres* (Trier, 1895). The *Feriale Duranum* is considered in great detail by A. D. Nock, 'The Roman army and the Roman religious year', *Harvard Theological Review* 45 (1952): 187–252; J. F. Gilliam, 'The Roman military *Feriale*', *Harvard Theological Review* 47 (1954): 183–96. The full text is published at R. O. Fink, A. S. Hoey and W. F. Snyder, 'The *Feriale Duranum*', *Yale Classical Studies* 7 (1940): 1–222. It is revised at R. O. Fink, *Roman military records on papyrus* (Cleveland, 1971), pp. 422–9, and reproduced by J. Helgeland, 'Roman army religion', in *ANRW* II 16.3, pp. 1470–1555, at 1481–7. The date of the papyrus is considered at H. W. Benario, 'The Date of the *Feriale Duranum*', *Historia* 11 (1962): 192–6. On the calendar as a means to Romanize recruits, see I. P. Haynes, 'The Romanisation of religion in the *auxilia* of the Roman imperial army from Augustus to Septimius Severus', *Britannia* 24 (1993): 141–57. I discovered Georgia L. Irby-Massie, *Military Religion in Roman Britain* (Leiden, 1999), only after I had completed this chapter, but would recommend it highly, not least for its catalogue of pertinent inscriptions.

The most important source collection for Roman Britain is R. G. Collingwood and R. P. Wright, *The Inscriptions of Roman Britain*, I. *Inscriptions on Stone*, 2nd edn with addenda and corrigenda by R. S. O. Tomlin (Stroud, 1995), cited throughout by its standard abbreviation *RIB*. On the Maryport altars, see *RIB*, pp. 274–80, 774, nos. 815–35; R. Davis, '*Cohors I Hispanorum* and the garrisons of Maryport', *Transactions of the Cumberland and Westmoreland Antiquarian and Archaeological Society*, 2nd series 77 (1977): 7–16; S. S. Frere, 'M. Maenius Agrippa, the "*Expeditio Britannica*" and Maryport', *Britannia* 31 (2000): 23–8. Frere counts twenty altars to Jupiter Optimus Maximus, and re-dates the foundation of Maryport to 125. See also D. J. Breeze, 'The regiments stationed at Maryport and their commanders', in R. J. A. Wilson, ed., *Roman Maryport and its Setting* (Kendall, 1997), pp. 67–89. New altars were evidently made annually over a period of around fifteen years, with only one altar ascribed to the unit but not its commander (no. 815 in the *RIB*). Four are inscribed with the name of the tribune Marcus Maenius Agrippa (AD 124–7; nos. 823–6), another four with that of the tribune Gaius Caballius Priscus (128–31; nos. 817–20), and three more with that of the prefect Lucius Cammius Maximus (133–5; nos. 827–9). The sixth and last commander, the prefect Helstrius Novellus, set up one altar in 137 (no. 822). The brief tenure of the prefect Marcus Censorius Cornelianus is not represented by an altar to Jupiter Optimus Maximus (IOM), although he dedicated one to Jupiter Augustus (no. 814) in 132. The fifth commander, Lucius Antistius Lupus Verianus (136), is not represented, although the inscriptions on two altars (nos. 834, 835) are largely illegible.

On the imperial cult, one might start with A. D. Nock, 'The emperor's divine *comes*, *JRS* 37 (1947): 102–16. The literature is now vast, and a comprehensive bibliography is contained in the multiple volumes by D. Fishwick, *The Imperial Cult in the Latin West. Studies in the Ruler Cult of the Western Provinces of the Roman Empire* (Leiden, 1987–). Many of the articles cited are by Fishwick himself, including several on the *numina*, including D. Fishwick, 'Imperial sceptre heads in Roman Britain', *Britannia* 19 (1988): 399–400. For the cult in the east, see S. Price, *Rituals and Power. The Roman Imperial Cult in Asia Minor* (Cambridge, 1984), and G. Bowersock, 'The imperial cult: perceptions and persistence', in his *Selected papers on Late Antiquity* (Bari, 2000), pp. 43–56.

For devotion to military standards, one might start with A. S. Hoey, 'Rosaliae Signorum', *Harvard Theological Review* 30 (1937): 15–35; M. P. Speidel and A. Dimitrova-Mileva, 'The cult of the genii in the Roman army and a new military deity', in *ANRW* II 16.2, pp. 1542–55. The Corbridge relief was examined by I. A. Richmond, 'Roman legionaries at Corbridge', *Archaeologia Aeliana*, 4th series, 21 (1943): 163ff. The Vardulli, an auxiliary force temporarily stationed at Corbridge (probably in AD 161–3), have earned a fair amount of attention. Veterans of the unit 'and their children for posterity' were granted citizenship in AD 98 (*CIL* xiii. 3606). A vexillation of the Vardulli was present at milecastle nineteen on Hadrian's Wall (later second century), where it erected an altar to the *Matres*, before moving to High Rochester. Certainly by *c*.175, the cohort was in garrison at Lanchester (Longovicium) in Co. Durham, where they erected an altar to Jupiter. See P. J. Casey, M. Noel and J. Wright, 'The Roman fort at Lanchester, Co. Durham: a geophysical survey and discussion of garrisons', *Archaeological Journal* 149 (1992): 69–81.

A willingness to use modern sociological insights into war was evinced by R. MacMullen, 'The legion as a society', *Historia* 33 (1984): 440–56, and has since become fashionable. Seminal works are E. Shils and M. Janowitz, 'Cohesion and disintegration in the Wehrmacht in World War II', *The Public Opinion Quarterly* 12 (1948): 280–315; M. Janowitz, *The Professional Soldier. A Social and Political Portrait*, revised edn (New York, 1971); A. Kellett, *Combat Motivation* (Boston, 1982). On more recent developments, I have used T. P. Odom et al, 'Transformation: victory rests with small units', *Military Review* (May–June 2005): 81–5.

Useful overviews of Roman military standards are provided in G. Webster, *The Roman imperial army*, 3rd edn (Norman, OK, 1998); and P. Southern and K. Ramsey Dixon, *The late Roman army* (London, 1996). On the eagle standard, one can turn with great profit to M. P. Speidel, 'Eagle-bearer and trumpeter. The eagle-standard and trumpets of the Roman legions illustrated by three tombstones recently found at Byzantion', *Bonner Jahrbücher* 176 (1976): 123–63. Speidel also lists inscriptions commemorating another thirty-two known *aquiliferi* (four only partial names or anonymous), which show that it was possible to become eagle-bearer with less than one year of service, but which indicate more clearly that the office was attained later in a career, as a reward for bravery and service. Four men held the position of *signifer* before promotion to *aquilifer*. It is very likely that duties were shared, and this appears to be confirmed by the fact that Surillio's tombstone was raised by his colleague Aurelius Zanax, surely also an *aquilifer*. One might compare Surillio's with the tombstone of Pintaius, the *signifer* of the *Cohors V Asturum*, an infantry cohort of the *auxilia*. The carved relief is now to be found in Bonn (*CIL* xiii. 8098; *ILS* 2580; mid-1st cent AD), and is ably described by Webster, *Roman Imperial Army*, p. 149: 'He [Pintaius] appears to be wearing a bear-skin head-dress with a pair of arms ending with extending claws across his chest; the standard terminating in a spear-head bears two wreaths, the lower a plain disc similar to those on the centurial standards of legions, below which is an eagle with extending wings holding a lightning flash in its talons, while below the hand is a thin crescent above a globe. The whole thing would seem to be too elaborate for a centurial standard and may be that of the unit itself.'

Besides the depictions of *vexilla* at Benwell and Corbridge, a third relief from Britannia was found at Ramshawfield, a mile from the fort of Chesterholm (Vindolanda) on Hadrian's Wall. This is no longer extant, and all that remains is a dubious sketch by J. Horsely from 1732, of a standard between a Pegasus (winged horse, left) and a Capricorn (goat-fish, right), the flag of which appears to bear the inscription III CH VEXI. However, the legend given by Collingwood and Wright, *RIB*, p. 537, no. 1707, text is 'leg(ionis) II vex[illum]', attributing the discrepancy to a preference of Collingwood for a variant reading by Huebner. See also M. Speidel, 'The army at Aquileia, the Moesiaci Legion, and the shield emblems in the *Notitia Dignitatum*', *Saalburg-Jahrbuch* 45 (1990): 68–72, at 68–9; reprinted in M. Speidel, *Roman Army Studies* II (Stuttgart, 1992), pp. 414–18, where carved reliefs on the sarcophagus of M. Aurelius Sossinus, a *vexillarius* of the *legio IV Flavia*, shows two *signiferi*, each bearing a *vexillum* marked 'EX AQUIL', which Speidel interprets as 'Exercitus Aquileiensis' (not 'ex Aquileia'). If the reliefs illustrated actual *vexilla*, these will have identified a composite force drawn partly from Sossinus' legion. The bronze roundel from Gaul is discussed at Southern and Dixon, *Late Roman Army*, p. 125, which includes a sketch and a reference to P. J. Casey, *The Legions in the Later Roman Empire*, Fourth Annual Caerleon Lecture (Cardiff, 1991). See also R. Tomlin, 'The legions in the late empire', in R. J. Brewer, ed., *Roman fortresses and their legions* (London and Cardiff, 2000), pp. 159–78.

Besides the new book by Ando, cited above, works by Ramsay MacMullen are excellent places to start when considering the religious devotion of Romans. His *Paganism in the Roman Empire* (New Haven and London, 1981), pp. 5–7, supplies the chart of, and commentary on, dedicatory inscriptions. Dionysus features there as Liber Pater. The cult of Dionysus forms the denouement of R. Turcan, *The Cults of the Roman Empire* (Oxford, 1996), pp. 291–327. There are several well-illustrated studies of the mosaics of Paphos, Cyprus. For the House of Aion, see W. Daszewski,

Dionysos der Erlöser: griechische Mythen im spätantiken Cypern (Mainz, 1985). The argument is summarized in English in W. Daszewski and D. Michaelides, *Mosaic Floors in Cyprus* (Ravenna, 1988). On the House of Dionysus, see C. Kondoleon, *Domestic and Divine: Roman Mosaics in the House of Dionysos* (Ithaca, NY, 1995). She focuses on the second-century mosaics. For an excellent overview one can now turn to K. Dunbabin, *Mosaics of the Greek and Roman World* (Cambridge, 1999), which has a chapter on Hellenistic pebble mosaics. G. Bowersock, *Mosaics as History* (Cambridge, MA, 2006), has recently argued that one must view the popularity of Dionysus and Heracles as a reflection of the popularity of mime and pantomime in the late antique world.

The seven Walters sarcophagi, all from the tomb of the Calpurnii, were studied by K. Lehmann-Hartleben and E. C. Olsen, *Dionysiac Sarcophagi in Baltimore* (Baltimore, 1942). This identifies the trophies on the so-called Victory sarcophagus as *vexilla*, suggesting an equivalence with ships' ensigns, which were apparently loosely associated with Bacchus. For a broader context see R. Turcan, *Les sarcophages romains dionysiaques* (Paris, 1966), where the victorious message is made manifest, especially at pp. 456–72; and the massive F. Matz, *Die dionysischen Sarkophage*, 4 vols (Berlin, 1968–75), in the ongoing German Archaeological Institute corpus of sepulchral sculpture, *Die antiken Sarcophagreliefs*. Two useful overviews of twentieth-century work (early and late) on sarcophagi, are provided by A. D. Nock, 'Sarcophagi and Symbolism', and B. C. Ewald, 'Review article: Death and Myth: new books on Roman sarcophagi', both in the *American Journal of Archeology*: 50 (1946): 140–70; 103 (1999): 344–8. A large bibliography is provided by B. Andreae, in *ANRW* II 12.2 (1981), pp. 3–64.

The brief surveys of Cybele and Isis are provoked by MacMullen's analysis, and by R. Stark, *Cities of God* (for which see the following chapter). A more recent two-volume general interpretation of great use is M. Beard, J. North and S. Price, *Religions of Rome, 1: A History; 2: Sources* (Cambridge, 1998). One can read far more in L. Roller, *In Search of God the Mother: the Cult of Anatolian Cybele* (Berkeley, 1999), who disassociates the arrival of Cybele in Rome and the end of the Punic Wars, but acknowledges the force of the later myth that she was a bringer of victory. For Christian attacks on Cybele, see A. T. Fear, 'Cybele and Christ', in E. Lane, ed., *Cybele, Attis and related cults* (Leiden, 1996), pp. 37–50, and in the same volume K. Summers, 'Lucretius' Roman Cybele', pp. 337–65, assesses that author's account of the ecstatic rites in the first century BC. On Isis see R. Witt, *Isis in the Ancient World* (Baltimore, 1997), a reprint of a 1971 classic (*Isis in the Greco-Roman World*), and John Ferguson, *The Religions of the Roman Empire* (London, 1970), where one may also find the prayer to Asclepius. A survey of the sites devoted to Isis is provided by R. A. Wild, 'The known Isis-Serapis sanctuaries from the Roman period', *ANRW* II 17.4, pp. 1739–1851.

The classic studies of the cult of Jupiter Dolichenus are by P. Merlat: *Répertoire*

des inscriptions et monuments figurés de culte de Jupiter Dolichenus (Paris, 1951), and
Jupiter Dolichenus. Essai d'interprétation et de synthèse (Paris, 1960). Of the more
than two hundred and fifty inscriptions Merlat collated from across the empire,
he found that four-fifths were military. Merlat's interpretation has been superseded
by M. Speidel, *The Religion of Jupiter Dolichenus in the Roman Army* (Leiden, 1978),
who argues instead for greater emphasis on the unity of the civilian and military
aspects of the cult, and suggests that only forty percent of the extant inscriptions
mention soldiers or units. One might also read with profit the German essay by
M. Hörig, 'Iupiter Dolichenus', *ANRW* II 17.4, pp. 2136–79, which provides a survey
of the cult's presence in various provinces. On the temple at Ribchester, see I.
Richmond, in *Archaeologia Aeliana* (1945), where the inscription is considered at
greater length. On the phrase 'ex responsu', at p. 25: 'Indeed, the only [god] whose
cult supplies evidence of a frequent and almost regular habit of thus communicating behests is Iuppiter Dolichenus, whose temples were of elaborate Mesopotamian
type and whose worship was introduced into Britain in the second century and
became popular among the soldiery in the third.'

The widespread fascination with the mysteries of Mithras – it has its own *Journal
of Mithraic Studies* – is in inverse proportion to the amount of solid evidence for
the cult's practices and rites. A very full collection of papers from a seminar held
in Rome, and with special reference to the evidence for the cult and its rites from
Rome and Ostia, *Mysteria Mithrae*, ed. E. Bianchi (Leiden, 1978), attempts a definition of the faith, which contains the following observation: '[Mithra was] a deity
who establishes for mankind an intra-cosmic and extra-cosmic soteriological
perspective, expressed through a symbology not unconnected with fertility, within
a structure of initiation functioning in a particular kind of appointed sanctuaries
[sic], on the basis of the esoteric principle.' Indeed. The follow-up to that learned
symposium convened in 1990, and the papers were published as *Studies in Mithraism*,
ed. J. R. Hinells (Rome, 1994). These include, among several very useful studies, J.
H. W. G. Liebeschuetz, 'The expansion of Mithraism among the religious cults of
the second century', pp. 195–216, which presents a sensible and clear introduction,
and P. Beskow, 'Tertullian on Mithras', pp. 51–60, which sets out all relevant information provided by that Christian apologist. Invaluable, but highly contentious, is
W. M. Brashear, *A Mithraic catechism from Egypt <P. Berol. 21196>*, Supplementband
Tyche (Vienna, 1992). This is not the infamous Mithras Liturgy, published by
Dieterich in 1903 and later debunked by F. Cumont. For that, see now H.-D. Betz,
The 'Mithras Liturgy'. Text, translation and commentary. Studien und Texte zu Antike
und Christentum 18 (Tübingen, 2003).

On Mithraea, one must read E. Sauer, *The end of paganism in the north-western
provinces of the Roman Empire. The example of the Mithras cult*, BAR International
Series 634 (Oxford, 1996). For a fascinating attempt to demonstrate that Roman
Mithraism was not of Persian origin but was developed from the Orion cult, a

'truly Greek religion . . . in Iranian garb', see M. Speidel, *Mithras - Orion. Greek hero and Roman army god* (Leiden, 1980). D. Ulansey, *The Origins of the Mithraic Mysteries* (Oxford, 1989), provides a different outline, and a useful map of the distribution of Mithraea (p. 5), albeit in print almost too tiny to read. Most recently, see R. Beck, *The Religion of the Mithras Cult in the Roman Empire. Mysteries of the Unconquered Sun* (Oxford, 2006), a monographic synthesis of thirty years of articles (collected as *Beck on Mithraism* (Aldershot, 2004)) in which the author places himself in the initiate's boots. Beck's survey of Mithraic scholarship, 'Mithraism since Franz Cumont', *ANRW* II 17.4, pp. 2002–2115, is comprehensive (to 1984), and contains 22 excellent plate illustrations.

Chapter 2: The Rise of Christianity

The chapter's title is descriptive and ostensibly generic, but echoes the titles of two works of great importance: R. Stark, *The Rise of Christianity: A Sociologist Reconsiders History* (Princeton, 1996), and W. Frend, *The Rise of Christianity* (Philadelphia, 1984). Stark's vision is teased out in a series of essays, most delivered as lectures. The book met with a vociferous critical response, not least in a series of rather narrow articles published in the *Journal of Early Christian Studies* 6/ii (1998). Stark has since developed his ideas on the urban character of early Christianity – initially sketched in his chapters 6 and 7, perhaps the weakest in *The Rise of Christianity* – in *Cities of God: The Real Story of How Christianity Became an Urban Movement and Conquered Rome* (San Francisco, 2006). He recounts the familiar explanation of the term pagan. A less attractive explanation suggests that Christians considered themselves to be soldiers of Christ, and hence were drawing a contrast with rustics who did not fight. Other estimates of the numbers of Christians at the end of the third century are far lower, for example only ten percent proposed by H. Drake, *Constantine and the Bishops: The Politics of Intolerance* (Baltimore, 2000). Those who count fewer earlier will attribute far more to Constantine, as does M. Edwards, 'The Beginnings of Christianization', in Lenski, ed., *Age of Constantine*, pp. 137–58. A detailed study in support of one of Stark's assertions can be found in W. V. Harris, 'Child-exposure in the Roman empire', *JRS* 84 (1994): 1–22.

There are many other general accounts of the role of Christianity in the late Roman world, and of the process of Christianization. The following is merely a representative sample of the most recent: G. Clark, *Christianity and Roman Society* (Cambridge, 2005); M. Humphries, *Early Christianity* (New York, 2006); M. Salzman, *The Making of a Christian Aristocracy* (Cambridge, MA, 2002); and some classic studies: P. Brown, *Authority and the Sacred. Aspects of the Christianisation of the Roman World* (Cambridge, 1995); R. Lane Fox, *Pagans and Christians* (Harmondsworth, 1986); R. MacMullen, *Christianizing the Roman Empire (AD 100–400)* (Yale, 1984).

On Christian attitudes to warfare, and Christians in the military, the classic works cited are C. John Cadoux, *The Early Christian Attitude to War. A Contribution to the History of Christian Ethics* (London, 1919; repr. New York, 1982) and Adolf von Harnack, *Militia Christi. Die christliche Religion und der Soldatenstand in den ersten drei Jahrhunderten* (Tübingen, 1905), translated into English as *Militia Christi. The Christian Religion and the Military in the First Three Centuries*, by D. McInnes Gracie (Philadelphia, 1981). More problematic is J.-M. Hornus, *Evangile et labarum* (Geneva, 1960). More recently, see J. Helgeland, 'Christians and the Roman Army, AD 173–337', *Church History* 43 (1974): 149–63; J. Kreider, 'Military service in the Church Orders', *Journal of Religious Ethics* 31 (2003): 415–42. Tertullian's views are well covered in many of these, and also by S. Gero, '"Miles Gloriosus": The Christian and Military Service according to Tertullian', *Church History* 39 (1970): 285–98. On Origen, see in addition *Homilies on Joshua: Origen, Homilies on Joshua*, trans. Barbara J. Bruce, ed. Cynthia White, *The Fathers of the Church* 105 (Washington, DC, 2002). An accessible introduction to Origen is now offered by Anthony Grafton and Megan Williams, *Christianity and the Transformation of the Book: Origen, Eusebius, and the Library of Caesarea* (Cambridge, MA, 2006). The extensive quotations from Origen presented in this chapter are slightly modified from P. Schaff's translations in volumes in the *Ante-Nicene Fathers* series.

Martyrdom has a vast literature, but one might usefully start with the Wiles lectures by G. W. Bowersock, *Martyrdom and Rome* (Cambridge, 1994), a slim volume that complements the classic paper by G. E. M. de Ste Croix, 'Why were the early Christians persecuted', *Past & Present* 26 (1963): 6–38. A useful overview of the Decian persecution is provided by G. Clark, in *CAH* 12, pp. 625–35. J. B. Rives, 'The decree of Decius and the religion of empire', *JRS* 89 (1999): 135–54, argues for the originality of Decius' decree, as a measure to restructure state *religio*. David Woods maintains a marvellous website on the military martyrs, now infrequently updated. For an art-historical overview of major and minor military saints in the eastern canon, one can turn to C. Walter, *The Warrior Saints in Byzantine Art and Tradition* (Aldershot, 2003).

Chapter 3. The Unconquered Emperor and his Divine Patron

The idea that there was a third-century 'Crisis of Empire' has been explored, revised and restored, such that it still retains sufficient force to provide the title of volume 12 of the *CAH* (2nd edn, 2005), retained from A. Alföldi's sixth chapter of its predecessor. General works on the third century are plentiful, and one might recommend: D. Potter, *The Roman Empire at Bay, AD 180–395* (London and New York, 2004); P. Southern, *The Roman Empire from Severus to Constantine*, 2nd edn (London and New York, 2001); M. Christol, *L'empire romain du IIIe siècle. Histoire politique 192–325 après J.-C.*, 2nd edn (Paris, 1997).

On the Roman conflict with Parthia and then the Persians, one might start with

F. Millar, *The Roman Near East, 31 BC–AD 337* (Cambridge, MA, 1994), and the pertinent chapter (ch. 14, pp. 461–80) of the new *CAH* 12, by R. Frye, 'The Sassanians'. The preceding chapter (ch. 13, pp. 440–60), by M. Todd, introduces 'The Germanic peoples and Germanic society'. Recent studies of barbarian 'ethnogenesis' abound. Two of the best are: M. Kulikowski, *Rome's Gothic Wars. From the Third Century to Alaric* (Cambridge, 2006); and John F. Drinkwater, *The Alamanni and Rome 213–496. Caracalla to Clovis* (Oxford, 2007). These are both wonderfully written, and the former is particularly accessible. Occasionally, modern policy wonks venture into ancient – although hardly ever medieval – history and offer useful provocations to specialists. E. Luttwak's *Grand Strategy of the Roman Empire* (Baltimore, 1976), is one such foray, and Luttwak promises to publish a 'Grand Strategy of the Byzantine Empire' soon. One might not consider in quite the same category an essay by B. Bartlett, 'How excessive government killed ancient Rome', *The Cato Journal* 14/ii (1994): 287–303, which argues that the third-century crisis owed much to a failure to pursue Reaganesque policies promoting supply-side economics. For another perspective see K. Hopkins, 'Taxes and trade in the Roman empire (200 BC–AD 400)', *JRS* 70 (1980): 101–25. Recent overviews are presented by M. Corbier in *CAH* 12, pp. 327–439.

My analysis of the emperor and the army follows closely J. B. Campbell, *The Emperor and the Roman Army* (Oxford 1994). This is supplemented by insights from J. Stäcker, *Princeps und miles. Studien zum Bindungs- und Nahverhältnis von Kaiser und Soldat im 1. und 2. Jahrhundert n.Chr.*, Spudasmata 91 (Hildesheim, 2003). S. Wood, *Roman Portrait Sculpture, AD 217–260* (Leiden, 1986), offers descriptive commentary on all the imperial sculptures mentioned, without making mention of triumphal connotations. In contrast to the nude of Gallus, one might enjoy the rather ridiculous placement of Decius' old head on the youthful nude body of Mars (her fig. 46). For the opposite effect, E. Kantorowicz, 'Gods in uniform', *Proceedings of the American Philosophical Society* 105 (1961): 368–93, demonstrates that gods were now increasingly portrayed like emperors, wearing military uniforms and carrying arms.

The titles *invictus* and *victor* are addressed by R. Storch, 'The "absolutist" theology of victory', *Classica et Medievalia* 29 (1968): 197–206; R. Storch, 'The trophy and the cross: pagan and Christian symbolism in the fourth and fifth centuries', *Byzantion* 40 (1970): 105–18; S. Weinstock, 'Victor and invictus', *Harvard Theological Review* 50 (1957): 211–47. Essential in German is P. Kneissl, *Die Siegestitulatur der römischen Kaiser. Untersuchungen zu den Siegerbeinamen des ersten und zweiten Jahrhunderts*, Hypomnemata 23 (Göttingen, 1969). More generally on Roman and Byzantine imperial titles, one might start with M. Peachin, *Roman Imperial Titulature and Chronology, AD 235–284* (Amsterdam, 1990). See also the essential G. Rösch, *Onoma Basileus. Studien zum offizielen Gebrauch der Kaisertitel in spätantiker und frühmittelalterlicher Zeit*, Byzantina Vindobonensia 10 (Vienna, 1978).

The traditional view of Sun worship in the Roman empire, established at the end of the nineteenth century largely by Franz Cumont and his disciples, is that it marked the culmination of a process of 'orientalization' of Roman religion. A century of scholarship was condensed and reconsidered in a monograph by G. Halsberghe, *The Cult of Sol Invictus* (Leiden, 1972). One should read also G. H. Halsberghe, 'Le culte de Deus Sol Invictus à Rome au 3e siècle après J.C.', *ANRW* II.17.4, pp. 2181–201, a summary of the monograph. That traditional view has now been demolished, starting with S. Hijmans, 'The Sun which did not rise in the East: The Cult of Sol Invictus in the Light of Non-Literary Evidence', *Bulletin Antieke Beschaving* 71 (1996): 115–50, which takes issue with Halsberghe, arguing for continuity between a native Roman Sun god, Sol Indiges and Sol Invictus, and against the equivalence of Sol Invictus and Elagabal. Hijmans presents an excellent survey of the iconography of Sol, which is expanded and augmented by P. Martens, *Helios und Sol. Kulte und Ikonographie des griechischen und römischen Sonnengott* (Istanbul, 2002), which concludes with an extensive typological catalogue of images. This is among the wave of recent, and excellent, scholarship on the worship of Sol. A comprehensive overview is offered by S. Berrens, *Sonnenkult und Kaisertum von den Severern bis zu Constantin. I (193–337 n. Chr.)*, Historia Einzelschriften 185 (Stuttgart, 2004). Imperial and divine gestures, for example Sol's raised right hand, may be considered in a broader context by turning to R. Brilliant, *Gesture and Rank in Roman Art* (New Haven, 1963).

A recent 'Routledge imperial biography', A. Watson, *Aurelian and the Third Century* (London and New York, 1999), updates the classic study in French by L. Homo (1904). It also presents an excellent summary of research on the third-century 'crisis'. An accessible study which covers Aurelian's victory over Zenobia, R. Stoneman, *Palmyra and its Empire: Zenobia's Revolt against Rome* (Ann Arbor, MI, 1992), has now been supplemented by the French work of a Polish scholar: T. Kotula, *Aurélien et Zénobie* (Warsaw, 1997).

The information presented in the complex and compelling *Historia Augusta* can never be taken at face value. Keys to understanding the text can be found in several works by the late Sir Ronald Syme, and now in the papers collected in the published proceedings of a regular colloquium, the *Historiae Augustae Colloquia*. Although there is no consensus, a convincing line of argument posits a single author for the whole work, which is presented as the collected writings of six separate writers. The author is perhaps merely the redactor of the first part of the work, and the author of those parts attributed to Trebellius Pollio and Flavius Vopiscus, which include the lives of Claudius II Gothicus and Aurelian. He was writing in the 390s, but presents the work as one composed in the later third century. He draws on a posited lost compilation of imperial biographies, the so-called *Kaisergeschichte*, and much contemporary panegyric, and has a penchant for inventing documents and letters to insert in his narrative. See T. D. Barnes, 'The sources of the *Historia*

Augusta (1967–92)', *Historiae Augustae Colloquium Maceratense* (Bari, 1995), pp. 1–28; and D. den Hengst, 'The discussion of authorship', *Historiae Augustae Colloquium Perusinum* (Bari, 2002), pp. 187–95. Many of our author-redactor's sources are contemporary with events they describe, including a lost panegyrical life of Claudius upon which he clearly draws. On this see A. Lippold, 'Claudius, Constantius, Constantinus. Die V. Claudii der *HA*. Ein Betrag zur Legitimierung der Herrschaft Konstantins aus stadtrömischer Sicht', *ibid.*, pp. 309–43, who argues further that one must view the original life as part of a programme devised by the senate in Rome to flatter Constantine's attempts to link himself to Claudius. The contrasting visions of Aurelian and Constantine are discussed by H. Brandt, 'Die "heidnische Vision" Aurelians (*HA*, A 24, 2–8) und die "christliche Vision" Konstantins des Grossen', *Historiae Augustae Colloquium Maceratense*, pp. 107–17, who determines that the author wrote a conscious rejoinder to Eusebius' account, thus inventing the whole affair. I prefer to follow Berrens, *Sonnenkult*, pp. 89–126, in seeing a more complex relationship between the texts, and noting that Aurelian's actions are entirely consistent with claims that he had a vision, if not quite in the form reported in the *HA*. Constantine was far from the first emperor to have, or to claim to have, such a vision.

Chapter 4. The Tetrarchy

One might now most easily start with R. Rees, *Diocletian and the Tetrarchy* (Edinburgh, 2004), which offers a brief but insightful overview as an introduction to a collection of translated sources and images. The pertinent chapters of D. S. Potter, *The Roman Empire at Bay, AD 190–395* (London, 2004), are typically excellent. S. Corcoran, *The Empire of the Tetrarchs. Imperial Pronouncements and Government, AD 284–324* (Oxford, 1996), offers a careful articulation of the nature of Tetrarchic government through the study of extant documents, notably rescripts (replies to petitions, letters sent to individuals) and edicts (general pronouncements). W. Seston, *Dioclétien et la Tétrarchie, I, Guerres et réformes (284–300)* (Paris, 1946), never proceeded to a second volume, but presents an elegant narrative so far as it goes. One must also read parts of F. Kolb, *Diokletian und die erste Tetrarchie* (Berlin, 1987), which is as forbidding as S. William, *Diocletian and the Roman Recovery* (London, 1985), is approachable.

Tetrarchic art once received short shrift, but now has more sympathetic commentators. Jutta Meischner, 'Die Porträtkunst der ersten und zweiten Tetrarchie bis zur Alleinherrschaft Konstantins: 293 bis 324 n. Chr.', *Archäologischer Anzeiger* (1986/i): 223–50, sketches the stylistic development of portrait busts from the accession of the Caesars (traditionally called 'expressive realism') through the second Tetrarchy ('a harmonization and consolidation of form') to the final defeat of Licinius by Constantine. She offers fresh insights into the portraits of Constantine in Basel, Licinius in Istanbul, and the square-jawed Tetrarch of Malibu. Catherine Walden,

'The Tetrarchic Image', *Oxford Journal of Archaeology* 9 (1990): 221–35, offers a rather tepid overview with no original insights, but it is in English. R. Rees, 'Images and image: a re-examination of Tetrarchic iconography', *Greece and Rome* 40 (1992): 181–200, places necessary emphasis on the homogeneity of images and the *concordia* implied thereby. The classic study by H. P. L'Orange, *Art Forms and Civic Life in the Later Roman Empire* (Princeton, 1965), retains great value, although I have diverged from his judgement on numerous occasions. L'Orange, and many following him, claim that the Venice and Vatican Tetrarchs are all the same height, but this is, at least to my sight, quite wrong: there is a clear difference, clearest at eye level, between Augusti and Caesars. For the heavenward-gazing Alexander, see H. P. L'Orange, *Apotheosis in Ancient Portraiture* (Oslo, 1947).

In addition to the general works listed above, important commentary on the Caesars at war is provided by: T. D. Barnes, 'Imperial campaigns, AD 284–311', *Phoenix* 30 (1976): 174–93; E. Eichholz, 'Constantius Chlorus' invasion of Britain', *JRS* 43 (1953): 41–6; P. J. Casey, *Carausius and Allectus: the British Usurpers* (London, 1994); and R. C. Blockley, 'The Romano-Persian treaties of 299 and 363', *Florilegium* 6 (1984): 28–49. The sculptures on the Arch of Galerius are treated by H.-P. Laubscher, *Der Reliefschmuck des Galeriusbogens in Thessaloniki* (Berlin, 1975), who relied on photographs from the 1930s, as the reliefs today are so badly abraded. (Indeed, between my taking the pictures included in this book in 2003/4 and returning in 2007, the reliefs were encased in perspex for restoration work. They are now once again uncovered.) The scenes described in this chapter are all from the triumphal, rather than the narrative, sequence according to Laubscher's typology: B II 20 ('Triumphales Siegesbild'), B II 21 (Triumphale Repräsentation der Tetrarchen'), B II 22 ('Victorien'), and B II 17 ('Siegesopfer Diocletians und des Galerius'). See also the long and important article by H. Meyer, 'Die Frieszyklen am sogennanten Triumphbogen des Galerius in Thessaloniki. Kriegschronik und Ankündigung der zweiten Tetrarchie', *Jahrbuch des deutschen archäologischen Instituts* 95 (1980): 374–444, for a reconstruction of the narrative of the campaign. He suggests that the triumphal procession, in which one sees a *quadriga* pulled by elephants (Laubscher's B III 23), was an element of the *vicennalia* celebrations of 303, allowing us to date that structure precisely to 304. In English, see M. S. Pond Rothman, 'The Thematic Organization of the Panel Reliefs on the Arch of Galerius', *American Journal of Archaeology* 81/iv (1977): 427–54, which insists on viewing the arch within its broader context, the imperial palace complex. She is more traditional in dating the dedication of the arch to 303. Her broader argument, and its potency, may be seen in two pithy sentences: 'Galerius's victory over Narses was both an event in time and place and a foreordained revelation of the Tetrarch's invincibility. The scenes of the barbarian migration and the victor's clemency and of the imperial *adventus*, *adlocutio*, and sacrifice, for example, recall both particular occurrences and the rich historical and representational traditions of official ceremonies.'

A comparandum for the battle scene, and indeed for a second eroded *virtus augusti* panel, was offered by R. Garucci, 'Brass medallion, representing the Persian Victory of Maximianus Galerius', *Numismatic Chronicle*, 2nd series, 10 (1870): 112–18, on the reverse of which a mounted emperor's horse rears over a representation of various Persians in diverse states of submission and defeat. A Victory flutters over the emperor, placing a wreath on his head, while he wields a spear. Although the emperor in this scene on the arch also has a raised right arm, it is impossible to imagine that he once held a spear. Rather, he was surely empty-handed, like the emperor of the Ludovisi Sarcophagus.

On the Tetrarchic army, see A. H. M. Jones, *The Later Roman Empire, 284–602*, 3 vols (Oxford, 1964), esp. II 607–86; P. Southern and K. Ramsey Dixon, *The Late Roman Army* (London, 1996); M. Nicasie, *Twilight of Empire. The Roman army from the reign of Diocletian until the Battle of Adrianople* (Amsterdam, 1998); D. Hoffmann, *Das spätrömische Bewegungsheer und die Notitia Dignitatum*, 2 vols, Epigraphische Studien 7/i–ii (Düsseldorf, 1969–70). My brief account of organizational changes is a synthesis, far too neat in places, of a number of vexed questions and debates. M. Speidel, 'Raising new units for the late Roman army: *auxilia palatina*', *DOP* 50 (1996): 163–70, is particularly useful on the Regii.

The currency edict of September 301 survives in just a single inscription from Aphrodisias, published with commentary as K. Erim, J. Reynolds and M. Crawford, 'Diocletian's currency reform: a new inscription', *JRS* 61 (1971): 171–7. The edict of maximum prices is translated by Rees, *Diocletian*, pp. 139–46, and a version from Aphrodisias is published by K. Erim et al in *JRS* 60 (1970): 120–41. J. P. Roth, *The Logistics of the Roman Army at War (264 BC–AD 235)* (Leiden, 1998), posits that one army *modius* was the daily ration of a *contubernium*, and consequently that a cohort required 60 *modii*, and a legion 600 *modii*, of pulses and grains each day.

In the suggestion that all four Tetrarchs met in 303, and that here it was determined to promote Maxentius and Constantine, I have followed T. D. Barnes, 'Emperors, panegyrics, prefects, provinces and palaces (284–317)', *Journal of Roman Archaeology* 9 (1996): 532–52, correcting his own account in *The New Empire of Diocletian and Constantine* (Cambridge, MA, 1982). On the celebrations of 303 see M. McCormick, *Eternal Victory*, pp. 19–20. The statues are considered by H. Kähler, *Die Fünfsäulendenkmal für die Tetrarchen auf dem Forum Romanum* (Berlin, 1964), and more recently by P. Bruggisser, 'Constantin aux rostres', *Historiae Augustae Colloquium Perusinum*, eds G. Bonamente and F. Paschoud (Bari, 2002), pp. 73–91.

The intellectual climate of Nicomedia in 302–3 is explored articulately by E. DePalma Digeser, *The Making of a Christian Empire. Lactantius and Rome* (Ithaca, NY, 2000), pp. 1–17. The contribution of Hierocles and a response by Eusebius are considered by T. D. Barnes, 'Sossianus Hierocles and the antecedents of the "Great Persecution"', *Harvard Studies in Classical Philology* 80 (1976): 239–52, which also supplies the date for Diocletian's rescript against the Manichaeans. Further works on the persecution abound. The most perspicacious and original analysis of Lactantius' *On the Deaths of the Persecutors* is A. Søby Christensen, *Lactantius the Historian* (Copenhagen, 1980). This proposes that, contrary to the standard view, Lactantius did not compose his work in the west, having fled Nicomedia, but rather used a Latin historiographical source, the notorious lost *Kaisergeschichte* identified as a common source for Aurelius Victor and the *Historia Augusta*. There are also many useful insights into the employment of quotations from Virgil and 2 Maccabees, although one must turn to Creed's introduction to his English translation for fuller commentary on the latter.

Chapter 5. Constantine Invictus

The events of the second Tetrarchy are recounted in the general works listed above. Of those works devoted to Constantine, Odahl, *Constantine and the Christian Empire*, is strong on these early years, although his commentary tends to attribute more to Constantine's various merits and virtues than to luck and chance. The suggestion that Constantine and Maxentius were to be designated Caesars owes much to Barnes, *Constantine and Eusebius*. The claim that both Severus and Maximinus Daia were related to Galerius must also be credited to T. D. Barnes, 'The wife of Maximinus', *Classical Philology* 94 (1999): 459–60. However, I have not seen it suggested elsewhere that Galerius obliged Diocletian to bring forward the date of his abdication, nor that the original plan was to allow Maximian to celebrate his own *vicennalia*. Scholars have hitherto wavered between trusting Lactantius' claims, that Galerius forced Diocletian to step down, and the implications of several panegyrics, that a plan was in place before 305. My hypothesis allows both to be true. I extend this original line of reasoning to suggest that Galerius had sanctioned Constantine's succession when he allowed him to join the dying Constantius. The only bone of contention between the two men, therefore, was the rank at which Constantine acceded, and his willingness to accept recognition as Caesar, not as Augustus, speaks volumes. The panegyrist of 307 will shortly afterwards praise him for such humility.

The essential panegyrics are translated with full commentary by Nixon and Rodgers, *In Praise of Later Roman Emperors*, relevant parts of which draw upon C. Nixon, 'The panegyric of 307 and Maximian's visits to Rome', *Phoenix* 35 (1981): 70–6. On Maximian more generally, those with Italian can read A. Pasqualini, *Massimiano Herculius* (Rome, 1979). The essential starting point for those interested in Maxentius is M. Cullhed, *Conservator Urbis Suae. Studies in the politics and propaganda of the emperor Maxentius*. Acta Instituti Romani Regni Sueciae, 8 (Stockholm, 1994). The date of the final rebellion of Maximian against Constantine is disputed. Most now favour 310, and dispense with the notion that the father-in-law was pardoned, then later killed. However, there seems to be no good reason to dispose of Lactantius' explicit testimony that this occurred, even if we must dispense with the story he supplies. It would surely have been unnecessary to propagate an elaborate fiction involving a second plot if time had not passed between Maximian's rebellion and his death, and had there been no need to explain away Constantine's apparent willingness to renege on an agreement. Thus I have suggested that the pardon was, in fact, a negotiation, the terms of which Constantine violated by killing his father-in-law. Opting for 309 as the date of the rebellion also fills an awkward gap in coverage of events, for without this plot, Constantine and Maximian appear to have done nothing at all in the year after the meeting at Carnuntum.

Trier staged a magnificent exhibition in 2007, to mark the 1700th anniversary of Constantine's elevation in the city. The catalogue showcases many of the pieces displayed at York in 2006, but also much more besides, notably many pieces from the Balkans. See *Imperator Caesar Flavius Constantinus. Konstantin der Grosse* (Mainz, 2007), with accompanying CD-ROM and colloquium volume. Roman Trier has, as one would expect, a large literature in German, and even a journal devoted to it: *Trierer Zeitschrift*. An elegant, if dated, English overview is offered by Edith M. Wightman, *Roman Trier and the Treveri* (London, 1970). R. Van Dam, *The Roman Revolution of Constantine* (Cambridge, 2007), pp. 62–78, is now important. More broadly, but still with great emphasis on Trier, see R. Krautheimer, 'The Constantinian basilica', *DOP* 21 (1967): 115–40. On the paintings of the imperial residence, one might start with I. Lavin, 'The ceiling frescoes in Trier and illusionism in Constantinian painting', *DOP* 21 (1967): 97–113, which conveys the wonder of the discovery, and the state of play when fewer than half the images had been restored. A fuller account is to be found in E. Simon, *Die konstantinische Deckengemälde in Trier* (Mainz, 1986), with colour photographs, and a convincing demonstration that this was Fausta's chamber, not that of the younger Helena, Crispus' wife, as has also been maintained. The Eagle Cameo, also called the Ada Cameo, has been interpreted variously, as is shown schematically by H. Pohlsander, 'Crispus: brilliant career and tragic end', *Historia* 23 (1984): 79–106, at 93–5. It is interpreted differently to our preferred solution by M. Henig, in Hartley et al, eds, *Constantine*, pp. 71, 73, following Diana E. E. Kleiner, *Roman Sculpture* (New Haven and London, 1992), pp. 430, 441–2. Both suggest that the two sons are Constantine II and Constantius II. But if the gem were produced between 318 and 324 as they argue, the absence of Crispus is glaring and inexplicable. Constantine made no attempt to distinguish between his sons by Fausta and his son by Minervina, despite the encouragement offered by the orator of 307 that he might do so. Indeed, after the deaths of Maximian and Maxentius, Constantine had no reason to honour the 'Herculians' over his first-born heir. This is reflected in his actions, raising Crispus to the rank of Caesar on the same day as Constantine II. Crispus' absence from a family portrait, therefore, would have been unthinkable before 326. His presence to the side of Fausta, the mother, on a cameo celebrating an occasion specific to Constantine II (his birth) makes perfect sense. The same identifications were made long ago by J. M. C. Toynbee in *Trierer Zeitschrift* 20 (1951): 175–7, and again in the *JRS* 50 (1960): 271–3, refuting a suggestion by A. Alföldi that the cameo was re-cut from a first-century original. Odahl, *Constantine and the Christian Empire*, also in agreement, offers further bibliography at p. 327.

Constantine's vision has a vast literature. For scepticism on the need to find a rational or natural explanation for Constantine's vision, see Averil Cameron, 'Constantine and Christianity', in Hartley et al, eds, *Constantine*, pp. 96–103, and O. Nicholson, 'Constantine's vision of the cross', *Vigiliae Christianae* 54 (2000): 309–23. We shall trust these for now, and turn to the larger body of literature when considering the later re-vision, in chapter 7. The road to Rome and the fateful Battle of the Milvian Bridge is equally well covered, and I have restricted my account for the most part to following that presented nearest to the events themselves, by the panegyrist of 313. To this I have added some insights from an account offered by a second panegyrist, Nazarius, reflecting on the outcome in 321. One might use far more, although with care. Among Nazarius' flights of fancy is the suggestion that Constantius, Constantine's father, was seen leading an army of heavenly beings who declaimed 'We seek Constantine, we go to help Constantine.' Eusebius reports, a decade or more afterwards, a quite different vision, and I have made only limited use of his account here. The sixth-century pagan historian Zosimus recounts additional useful details, which clarify some confusion about when and how the Milvian Bridge was cut, and its relationship to the pontoon bridge.

Chapter 6: Constantine and Rome

My analysis of Maxentius' Rome owes much to M. Cullhed, *Conservator Urbis Suae. Studies in the politics and propaganda of the emperor Maxentius*. Acta Instituti Romani Regni Sueciae 8 (Stockholm, 1994), ch. 3, incorporating observations and alternatives suggested by J. Curran, *Pagan City and Christian Capital. Rome in the Fourth Century* (Oxford, 2000), ch. 2. The chapter heading is taken from the revelatory study, R. Ross Holloway, *Constantine and Rome* (New Haven, 2004), which expands upon that author's earlier works. One might also consult H. Lepin and H. Ziemssen, *Maxentius. Der letzte Kaiser in Rom* (Mainz, 2007), which has excellent colour photos. There is now also a useful but rather derivative article in honour of Averil Cameron, by J. W. Drijvers, 'Eusebius' *Vita Constantini* and the construction of the image of Maxentius', in *From Rome to Constantinople*, eds H. Amirav and B. ter Haar Romeny (Leuven, 2007), pp. 11–27. Just as recently, R. Van Dam, *The Roman Revolution of Constantine* (Cambridge, 2007), pp. 79–97, offers interesting commentary, and his line complements that taken here, stressing the importance of establishing a new Flavian imprint on the established cityscape. On the colossal statue, and the theory of extramission whereby beams were believed to project forth from the eyes, see L. Safran, 'What Constantine Saw. Reflections on the Capitoline Colossus, Visuality and Early Christian Studies', *Millennium* 3 (2006): 43–73. Anthony Kaldellis drew this to my attention.

On the triumph in Late Antiquity, one must start with M. McCormick, *Eternal Victory. Triumphal rulership in late antiquity, Byzantium, and the early medieval West* (Cambridge and Paris, 1986), and Sabine MacCormack, *Art and Ceremony in Late Antiquity* (Berkeley, Los Angeles and London, 1981). A critical reflection on ceremonial as portrayed in medieval sources is offered by P. Buc, *The Dangers of Ritual. Between Early medieval Texts and Social Scientific Theory* (Princeton, 2001). A similarly critical stance informs M. Beard, *The Roman Triumph* (Cambridge, MA, 2007), who writes of 'rituals in ink' and the futility of searching for the standard triumph, its route and requirements.

My analysis of the Arch of Constantine draws heavily on Holloway, *Constantine and Rome*, pp. 19–56. More expansive thoughts on the re-use of sculpted materials, *spolia*, are offered by J. Elsner, 'From the culture of spolia to the cult of relics: the Arch of Constantine and the genesis of Late Antique forms', *Papers of the British School at Rome* 68 (2000): 149–84, although Elsner makes much of Constantine's choices that I, following Holloway, have attributed to Maxentius. Elsner's essential point, that this was an age in which the appropriation of the past was advanced, is well taken and one cannot but relish his observation that 'the designers of Constantine's monuments employed this new style of syncretistic bricolage to brilliant and incremental effect'. Elizabeth Marlowe, 'Framing the sun: the Arch of Constantine and the Roman cityscape', *Art Bulletin* 88 (2006): 223–42, presents a compelling new view of the significance of Sol Invictus, identifying the alignment of the colossal statue with the arch. The suggestion that the Capitoline bronze of Constantine formed part of the Colossus is advanced by S. Ensoli, 'I colossi di bronzo a Roma in età tardoantica', in S. Ensoli and E. La Rocca, eds, *Aurea Roma* (Rome, 2000), 66–90. Information on the discovery of the marble plinth of Maxentius' earlier colossus of Romulus, which was discovered incorporated into the arch's roof, was initially provided by P. Peirce, 'The Arch of Constantine. Propaganda and Ideology in Late Roman Art', *Art History* 12 (1989): 387–418. That paper argues generally for Constantine's appropriation of older sculpture in order to present his reign as a new 'Golden Age', which intention can easily be transferred to, or have been absorbed from, Maxentius.

In the very week that the typescript of this book was finished, I received in pre-publication form from the author a compelling new study on the arch, and in particular on its inscription, that I would have wished to incorporate more than I have. N. Lenski, 'Evoking the pagan past: *Instinctu divinitatis* and Constantine's capture of Rome', *Journal of Late Antiquity* 1 (2008): 206–59, assigns the arch to the senate, which seeks to persuade the emperor that his victory has been awarded by a pagan deity. The inscription is the key, and the phrase *instinctu divinitatis*, translated as 'by divine instigation', is shown to recall the Republican war ritual of *evocatio*, whereby a city's (here Rome's) tutelary deity is summoned in anticipation of an assault. Lenski also draws attention to the coincidence between the end of Tarquin and of Maxentius 'by instigation of the god(s)', and evaluates critically the article by L. J. Hall, 'Cicero's *instinctu divino* and Constantine's *instinctu divinitatis*: The Evidence of the Arch of Constantine for the Senatorial View of the "Vision" of Constantine', *Journal of Early Christian Studies* 6 (1998): 647–71.

The development on the Appian Way is addressed by A. Frazer, 'The iconography of the emperor Maxentius' buildings in Via Appia', *The Art Bulletin* 48 (1966): 385–92. The *damnatio memoriae* of Maxentius is summarized well in Grünewald, *Constantinus Maximus Augustus*, pp. 64–71, with very useful commentary on the orations by Nixon and Rodgers, *In Praise of Later Roman Emperors*, pp. 288–385. On Constantine's use of the term 'tyrant' I have not followed suggestions by T. D. Barnes, 'Oppressor, persecutor, usurper: the meaning of "tyrannus" in the fourth century', *Historiae Augustae Colloquium Barcionense* (Bari, 1996), pp. 55–65, that this was imbued with an overtly Christian meaning, preferring the more general analysis of A. Wardman, 'Usurpers and internal conflicts in the 4th century AD', *Historia* 33 (1984): 220–37. Nor have I followed Holloway especially closely in his analysis of Rome's Constantinian churches, at *Constantine and Rome*, pp. 57–119.

Licinius' clash with Maximinus Daia is covered in most general accounts of Constantine's reign; that between Constantine and Licinius is covered in all. The fact that no coins celebrating Constantine's *decennalia* were minted in lands under Licinius' control indicates two things: first, that relations between the two men had soured considerably between 313 and 315; and second, that the battles between them at Cibalae and on the Plain of Arda, which would deliver certain mints in the Balkans to Constantine, did not take place until after his *decennalia* year, which ended in July 316. This is significant, for many written sources date the breach between Constantine and Licinius to 314. P. Bruun was the first to propose that one must re-date the breach to 316. The arguments for and against are well summarized by T. G. Elliot, *The Christianity of Constantine the Great* (Scranton, PA, 1996), pp. 121–7, although one cannot accept his observation (p. 121) that the matter has been concluded in favour of 316 by reference to images of Licinius on the Arch of Constantine (C. Ehrhardt, 'Monumental evidence for the date of Constantine's first war against Licinius', *Ancient World* 23 (1992): 87–96), for these sculptures have since been shown to be of Constantius Chlorus, not Licinius. Coins from the ephemeral reign of Valens, the border general, suggest he held the title Augustus, not merely Caesar (*RIC* VII, ed. Bruun, pp. 644, 706). (The same goes for Martinianus, Licinius' creation in 324, suggesting that Licinius may have intended the promotions to replace Constantine as Augustus.) Odahl, *Constantine and the Christian Empire*, pp. 163–5, 338–9, gets to grips with Balkan geography and the itineraries of the protagonists. The inscription at Arycanda in Lycia is *CIL* III. 12132.

Chapter 7. Constantine's Conversion

The growth of the Moonies, and the observations that altered the manner in which we understand conversion, are contained in J. Lofland, *Doomsday Cult. A Study of Conversion, Proselytization, and Maintenance of Faith* (Englewood Cliffs, NJ, 1966). Karl F. Morrison, *Understanding Conversion* (Charlottesville and London, 1992), presents a compelling critique of the 'peripety paradigm', setting up very useful distinctions between the experience of conversion as a phenomenon, the name by which it is called ('conversion'), and the process of thinking that went into the naming (hermeneutics: the study of understanding). The redemption tale of George W. Bush was famously expounded in a profile by Nicholas Kristof, 'How Bush came to tame his inner scamp', *New York Times*, 29 July 2000. Barack Obama's conversion story appears more sociologically informed, as related by Andrew Sullivan, 'Goodbye to all that', *The Atlantic Monthly*, December 2007, quoting from the stump speech.

It is perhaps unwise to introduce here the *Life of Antony*, for the date of its composition and its authorship are both vexed, and have generated a large secondary literature. A direct comparison with the *Life of Constantine*, positing interesting similarities, is offered by Averil Cameron, 'Form and Meaning: the *Vita Constantini* and the *Vita Antonii*', in *Greek Biography and Panegyric in Late Antiquity*, eds T. Hägg and P. Rousseau (Berkeley and Los Angeles, 2000), pp. 72–88. One might note that the disputed author of the *Life of Antony*, Athanasius, was an enemy of Eusebius and a central figure in the disputes over Arius, and also those following Constantine's death, in which context the *Life of Constantine* was revised and completed.

J. H. W. G. Liebeschuetz, *Continuity and Change in Roman Religion* (Oxford, 1979), pp. 277–91, offers a concise, nuanced and convincing summary interpretation of Constantine's gradual conversion, with references to earlier literature. The most important guide to Constantine's Christian education is now Elizabeth DePalma Digeser, *The Making of a Christian Empire. Lactantius and Rome* (Ithaca and London, 2000). This brilliant study shows quite how much Constantine owed to Lactantius, most clearly to the ideas set out in his *Divine Institutes*. Constantine emerges from her pages no longer either the righteous Christian advocated by T. D. Barnes, or the equivocating politician of J. Burckhardt, but rather as an advocate of concord, insisting that the path to salvation be open to all who venerated a *summus deus*. Her endnotes are replete with remarkable insights and fuller commentaries than can be supplied in the succinct text, notably a wonderful summary of the secondary literature devoted to Constantine's alleged prohibition of sacrifice.

The influence of Lactantius' language and thought is shown clearly in Constantine's letter to the bishops after Arles. Here Constantine wrote that the 'Eternal and incomprehensible goodness of our God will by no means allow the human condition to continue to stray in darkness (*divitius in tenebris oberrare*), nor does it permit the abhorrent wishes of certain men to prevail to such a degree that he fails to open up for them with his most brilliant beams of light (*praeclarissimis luminibus*) a path to salvation.' In the very first page of the *Divine Institutes* (I.1.6), devoted similarly to false religion, Lactantius had expressed similar sentiments in similar, often identical terms: 'God has not allowed man in his search for the light of wisdom to continue to stray (*divitius errare*), wandering in inescapable darkness (*tenebras*) . . . [but] opened man's eyes and made him a gift of the acquisition of truth . . . then to show the errant wanderer the path to salvation.' On all this see C. Odahl, 'Constantine's Epistle to the Bishops at the Council of Arles: A Defense of Imperial Authorship', *Journal of Religious History* 17 (1993): 274–89; and the recent translation of the letter in M. Edwards, trans., *Optatus: Against the Donatists* (Liverpool, 1997). One must see also, of course, the full translation of *Lactantius. Divine Institutes*, trans. A. Bowen and P. Garnsey (Liverpool, 2003). A translation of, and full commentary on, Constantine's *Oration to the Saints* is included in M. Edwards, *Constantine and Christendom* (Liverpool, 2003). Edwards's preferred date and location, 315 in Rome, are quite different to those proposed by others, most notably Barnes, who in his *Constantine and Eusebius*, pp. 73–6, favoured either Sardica or Salonica in a year between 321 and 324, but later determined it was given at Nicomedia in 325, in his 'Constantine's speech to the Assembly of the Saints: place and date of delivery', *Journal of Theological Studies* 52 (2001): 26–36. H. A. Drake, *Constantine and the Bishops: the Politics of Intolerance* (Baltimore, 2000), pp. 292–7, argues that the true value of the speech is its 'timelessness'.

Constantine's legislation is to be found principally in the *Theodosian Code*, trans. C. Pharr (Princeton, 1952), with many subsequent reprints. It is approached in the round by Elliot, *The Christianity of Constantine the Great*, pp. 97–114, and C. Humfress, 'Civil law and social life', in Lenski, ed., *Age of Constantine*, pp. 205–25. Extremely useful articles are collected in J. Harris and I. Wood, eds, *The Theodosian Code* (Ithaca, NY, 1993), especially D. Hunt, 'Christianising the Roman Empire: the evidence of the code', pp. 143–58, and J. Evans Grubbs, 'Constantine and imperial legislation on the family', pp.120–42, which provides a summary of her book, *Law and Family in Late Antiquity: the Emperor Constantine's marriage legislation* (Oxford, 1995). Specific points are addressed by Digeser, *The Making of a Christian Empire*, pp. 121–4. For a brief restatement of the traditional view, see J. Rodalnus, *The Church in the Age of Constantine. The Theological Challenges* (London, 2006), pp. 41–4.

For Sol on coins, one must start with the many and varied works of P. Bruun, most notably his seventh volume of *RIC*, which is essential (*Constantine to Licinius: AD 313–337*), but see also C. H. V. Sutherland and R. A. G. Carson, *RIC* VI. I was greatly helped by Bruun's 'The victorious signs of Constantine: a reappraisal',

Numismatic Chronicle 157 (1997): 41–59, a copy of which he gave me in Helsinki in 1999, but which I subsequently mislaid in Madison, WI. On specific issues one must consult A. Alföldi, 'The helmet of Constantine with the Christian monogram', *JRS* 22 (1932): 9–23; K. Kraft, 'Das Silbermedaillon Constantins des Grosses mit dem Christusmonogramm auf dem Helm', *Jahrbuch für Numismatik und Geldgeschichte* 5–6 (1954–5): 151–78; and the collected articles by Maria R.-Alföldi, *Gloria Romanorum. Schriften zur Spätantike*, Historia Einzelschriften 153 (Stuttgart, 2001). The helmet badge showing the chi-rho discovered in the Meuse Valley in the Netherlands can be seen in the Trier exhibition catalogue (cited in full above) at p. 154, being catalogue no. I.13.124.

Rather than select those issues or features which appear to support a particular interpretation, for example that Constantine rapidly embraced Christianity and its symbols (the chi-rho, or a cross-sceptre), one must be willing to consider multiple messages conveyed by the whole extant coinage of the period, and reflect on how these related to or diverged from earlier coin types. Numerous detailed studies by Patrick Bruun have established beyond doubt that one cannot identify Constantine the Christian on his coins. On the delayed disappearance of Sol from Constantine's coins, Bruun posits that the lag of a year or two even after the defeat of Licinius can be explained by an absence of close supervision of the bronze coinage before *c*.324, and the habit of mints, particularly those distant from the emperor, of using dies until they were worn out. Gold and silver were always more closely monitored, and often produced in the presence of the emperor and his court by mobile mints. Alföldi, *Conversion of Constantine*, pp. 57–9, offers an alternative interpretation for the disappearance of Sol, observing instead a reversal of roles, where the Sun is magnified through Constantine's glory, and a perceived equivalence of Sol and Christ is gradually eliminated. R. Leeb, *Konstantin und Christus: die Verchristlichung der imperialen Repräsentation unter Konstantin dem Grossen als Spiegel seiner Kirchenpolitik und seines Selbstverständnisses als christlicher Kaiser* (Berlin, 1992), expands and revises these arguments.

All major secondary works include an account of the campaign that culminated at Chrysopolis. Odahl, *Constantine*, pp. 162–201, styles it an 'Eastern Crusade'. The *Origo* (V.21) suggests that it was the Goths, not the Sarmatians, who invaded while Constantine was at Salonica. The suggestion that Constantine defeated both the Goths in 322 and the Sarmatians in 323 has been dispensed with by T. D. Barnes, 'The victories of Constantine', *Zeitschrift für Papyrologie und Epigraphik* 20 (1976): 149–55. See also M. Kulikowski, 'Constantine and the northern Barbarians', in Lenski, ed., *Age of Constantine*, pp. 347–76, at p. 359 (in contrast to Lenski's own preference for two campaigns, p. 75); and M. Kulikowski, *Rome's Gothic Wars* (Cambridge, 2007), pp. 81–4. The inscription from Salsovia is *ILS* 8940.

On Eusebius the literature is vast. The best place to start is with the many articles by T.D. Barnes, and his books, cited above. One might then turn for some discussion or disagreement on particular works to: A. Louth, 'The date of Eusebius' *Historia ecclesiastica*', *Journal of Theological Studies* 41 (1990): 111–23; R. W. Burgess, 'The dates and editions of Eusebius' *Chronici canones* and *Historia ecclesiastica*', *Journal of Theological Studies* 48 (1997): 471–504. The recent *Cambridge History of Early Christian Literature*, ed. F. Young et al (Cambridge, 2004), is excellent, but one should also consult relevant chapters in the *CAH* 12 and 13, and now the second part of Anthony Grafton and Megan Williams, *Christianity and the Transformation of the Book: Origen, Eusebius, and the Library of Caesarea* (Cambridge, MA, 2006).

On the *labarum*, one might still usefully start with M. Rostovtzeff, 'Vexillum and victory', *JRS* 32 (1942): 92–106, which discusses earlier developments of military standards (*vexilla*), including the addition of crowns, eagles and victories at the lance tip, where Constantine was to incorporate the chi-rho. H. Grégoire, 'L'étymologie de «Labarum»', *Byzantion* 4 (1927–8): 477–82, first suggested that the odd name *labarum* was derived from *laureum*, a vulgar Latin name used in the camps for the *vexillum*. Barnes, *Constantine and Eusebius*, pp. 44, 306, favoured a Celtic etymology, noting the origins of many of Constantine's troops. Weiss, 'Vision of Constantine', 255 (see immediately below), also suggests a Gallic word, *labaros*, meaning something like 'resounding, eloquent, speaking, talkative, loud'. Leeb, *Konstantin und Christus*, argued convincingly that the *labarum* should be dated no earlier than the final war against Licinius.

If one believes in the veracity of Constantine's vision, then the place to start is now P. Weiss, 'The vision of Constantine', *Journal of Roman Archaeology* 16 (2003): 237–59, a revised translation of a German article published in 1993, which has reinvigorated debate by proposing a single 'vision' of a solar halo in 310. His conclusions differ from those of an earlier proponent of a single vision, H. Grégoire, 'La vision de Constantin «liquidée»', *Byzantion* 14 (1939): 341–51, reprising and defending an earlier paper. Baynes, 'Constantine the Great and the Christian Church', cited above, draws attention to letters sent to *The Times* between April 1929 and April 1930, regarding a cross visible 'athwart the sun . . . when the sun was high in the sky'. An alternative and far less likely explanation is offered by M. DiMaio, J. Zeuge and N. Zotov, '*Ambiguitas Constantiniana*: the *caeleste signum Dei* of Constantine the Great', *Byzantion* 58 (1988): 333–60 at 341–50, developing F. Heiland, 'Die astronomische Deutung der Vision Kaiser Konstantins', in *Sondervertrag im Zeiss-Planetarium-Jena* (Jena, 1948). These papers suggest that the vision took place in September 312 when the planets Jupiter, Saturn and Mars were aligned in the constellations of Capricorn and Sagittarius. Later in October 312, Venus was also virtually in line with Jupiter, Saturn and Mars. A fixed line of visible stars crossed this axis, creating a cross, and one could discern at the end of this line Vega, the brightest star in the configuration, at which point the line would have appeared to curve out and back towards itself. It was this configuration of planets and stars, it is argued, that Constantine saw and turned in his favour as he approached Rome, claiming to have had an explicatory dream. Although such a configuration would have been visible to all at night, it would not have been clear during the day. Eusebius maintained that the vision took place during the afternoon, while the sun was high in the sky, which would have obscured, not illuminated, an alignment of planets. Weiss's interpretation is far better, as it offers a longer time-frame and contradicts none of the key elements of the various accounts. As he notes, no source states that the vision took place immediately before the Battle of the Milvian Bridge, although Constantine's dream, which offered him the means to interpret it, did.

Chapter 8. Constantinople

On Constantinople the two scholars to follow are Cyril Mango and Gilbert Dagron, in numerous contributions over half a century. One might start with the papers in their co-edited volume, *Constantinople and its Hinterland* (Aldershot, 1995), and with G. Dagron, *Naissance d'une capitale: Constantinople et ses institutions de 330 à 451* (Paris, 1974; 2nd edn 1984), which omits archaeology. This is remedied by C. Mango, *Le développement urbain de Constantinople (IVe – VII siècles)* (Paris, 1990), a short book which is nonetheless usefully summarized in his important paper 'The development of Constantinople as an urban centre', most easily accessed in his collection *Studies on Constantinople* (Aldershot, 1993). Most recently, see Mango's provocative essay 'Constantinople: capital of the *oecumene?*', in E. Chrysos, ed., *Byzantium as Oecumene* (Athens, 2005), pp. 319–24. The street plan of Constantinople is studied by A. Berger, 'Streets and public spaces in Constantinople', *DOP* 54 (2000): 161–72, to which I owe the revelation (not spelt out therein) that Licinius was responsible for developing Byzantium. All references to Septimius Severus' building campaigns post-date the fourth century, as was shown by Dagron (*Naissance d'une capitale*, pp. 15–19). Fergus Millar, *The Emperor in the Roman World*, 2nd edn (Ithaca, NY, 1992), pp. 40–57, offers a useful introduction to Tetrarchic capitals and the special status of Constantinople. The telling example of Aphrodisias, to which I refer later in the chapter, is at pp. 342–3.

My preferred plan for the Daphne Palace follows M. J. Featherstone, 'The Great Palace as reflected in the *De Cerimoniis*', in F.-A. Bauer, ed., *Visualisierungen von Herrschaft*, Byzas 5 (2006): 47–61, and J. Kostenec, 'The heart of the empire: the Great Palace of the Byzantine emperors reconsidered', in K. Dark, ed., *Secular Buildings and the Archaeology of Everyday Life in the Byzantine Empire* (Oxford, 2004), pp. 4–36. Kostenec suggests that the best comparison to be drawn is with the so-called palace of Maximian in Cordoba. But as M. Kulikowski (*Late Roman Spain and its Cities*, pp. 116–20) has observed, following Barnes (*New Empire*, pp. 56–60), there is no evidence for Maximian's protracted presence in Spain during his war to recover North Africa in the 290s. Moreover, drawing upon the Spanish

CONSTANTINE

excavation reports and research by Javier Arce, Kulikowski's description of the palace highlights quite how dissimilar it was to the Daphne, except for the superficial resemblance of their enclosed semi-circular courtyards. Nonetheless, the complex at Cordoba, now called the Cercadilla Palace, is clearly a Tetrarchic undertaking. G. Dagron, *Emperor and Priest. The Imperial Office in Byzantium* (Cambridge, 2003), pp. 85–7, supplies excellent illustrations of the imperial palace in its more developed form, proposing a plan for the Daphne quite different from Kostenec's. The juxtaposition of the hippodrome and palace in all imperial residences of the Tetrarchs was noted by M. Vickers, 'The hippodrome at Thessaloniki', *JRS* 62 (1972): 25–32, and the role of the hippodrome as imperial space has been elaborated by C. Heucke, *Circus und Hippodrom als politischer Raum* (Hildesheim and Zürich, 1994), and many others.

On the statues gathered in the city, one must start with C. Mango, 'Antique statuary and the Byzantine beholder', *DOP* 17 (1963): 55–75, and proceed to S. G. Bassett, 'The antiquities in the hippodrome of Constantinople', *DOP* 45 (1991): 87–96, and S. G. Bassett, '*Historiae custos*: sculpture and tradition in the Baths of Zeuxippos', *American Journal of Archeology* 100 (1996): 491–506; both refined in Bassett, *The Urban Image of Late Antique Constantinople* (Cambridge, 2004). The catalogue there provided is invaluable, but one must be wary of the historical commentary. Bassett attributes the pre-Constantinian rebuilding to Septimius Severus with reference to two sixth-century and two twelfth-century sources, without considering whether these might be inaccurate or skewed. One can turn for more sophisticated correctives to Bassett's sometimes literal readings to A. Kaldellis, 'Christodoros on the statues of the Zeuxippos Baths: a new reading of the *ekphrasis*', *Greek, Roman and Byzantine Studies* 47 (2007): 361–83. On the statue of Constantine standing on his column and its alleged association with Sol, see G. Fowden, 'Constantine's porphyry column: the earliest literary allusion', *JRS* 81 (1991): 119–31, which also posits that the later fourth-century life of Elagabalus, contained in the *Historia Augusta*, was composed as a satire on the life of Constantine.

The idea that Constantinople was a new Christian capital was most eloquently expounded by R. Krautheimer, *Three Christian Capitals* (Berkeley and Los Angeles, 1982), before it was demolished by Mango. On the senate, one should start with Dagron, *Naissance*, pp. 119–210, then turn to an insightful article by P. Heather, 'New men for new Constantines? Creating an imperial elite in the eastern Mediterranean', in P. Magdalino, ed., *New Constantines* (Aldershot, 1994), pp. 11–33. These ideas are incorporated into P. Heather, 'Senators and Senates', in *CAH* 13, pp. 184–210.

On the new image forged by Constantine, one might usefully start with a sceptical survey of the limitations of assessing the small and uncertain oeuvre, by J. Elsner, 'Perspectives in art', in Lenski, ed., *Age of Constantine*, pp. 255–77. All the works here mentioned are addressed by Kleiner, *Roman Sculpture*, and the three works in the Met are explored further in C. A. Picon et al, *Art of the Classical World in the Metropolitan Museum of Art* (New York, 2007). For busts of the Tetrarchs, see Jutta Meischner, 'Die Porträtkunst der ersten und zweiten Tetrarchie bis zur Alleinherrschaft Konstantins: 293 bis 324 n. Chr.', *Archäologischer Anzeiger* (1986/i): 223–50. On Alexander, see H. P. L'Orange, *Apotheosis in Ancient Portraiture* (Oslo, 1947), and on Constantine's incipient baldness, Van Dam, *Roman Revolution of Constantine*, pp. 17–18. Constantine the new Moses is considered by E. Becker, 'Konstantin der Grosse, der "neue Moses". Die Schlacht am Pons Milvius und die Katastrophe am Schilfmeer', *Zeitschrift für Kirchengeschichte* 31 (1910): 161–71. See also two articles by Claudia Rapp: 'Imperial Ideology in the Making: Eusebius of Caesarea on Constantine as "Bishop"', *Journal of Theological Studies* 49 (1998): 685–95; and 'Comparison, paradigm and the case of Moses in panegyric and hagiography', in M. Whitby, ed., *The Propaganda of Power: The Role of Panegyric in Late Antiquity* (Leiden, 1998), 277–98. The Red Sea sarcophagi are studied in detail by Clementina Rizzardi, *I sarcophagi paleocristiani con rappresentazione del passaggio del Mar Rosso* (Faenza, 1970), who provides a descriptive catalogue with extensive bibliography for each piece. More generally, see J. Lassus, 'Représentations du «Passage de la Mer Rouge» dans l'art Chrétien d'Orient et d'Occident', *Mélanges d'archéologie et d'histoire* 46 (1929): 159–81. The Arles sarcophagi are best seen in the catalogue of the Musée de l'Arles Antique, ed. C. Sintès (Arles, 1996). Most recently, Jas Elsner has considered the scenes on these sarcophagi in an as yet unpublished paper entitled '"Pharaoh's army got drowned": some reflections on Jewish and Roman genealogies in early Christian art', presented at the 3rd Lavy Colloquium, 'Jewish and Christian Art', at Johns Hopkins University, Baltimore on 11 October 2007. I disagree with his conclusions.

T. F. Mathews, *The Clash of Gods. A reinterpretation of early Christian art*, 2nd edn (Princeton, 1999), pp. 75–7, too easily dismisses Eusebius and neglects the other sources compiled by Becker. Mathews, arguing against the notion that Christian art drew upon imperial models, prefers to see Moses as prefiguring Christ in defeating the evil Pharaoh. Focusing on a most striking sarcophagus, one of four from the Church of St Trophîme in Arles, Mathews suggests that it belongs stylistically to the reign of Theodosius I (379–95), thus far later than Constantine's reign and Becker's proposed model, the battle scene on the Arch of Constantine. 'Becker made an ideological muddle of the subject,' Mathews suggests, and since the scene departs from scripture in portraying Pharaoh's death, therein lies the clue to its interpretation: Pharaoh is dressed as the Roman emperor, whereas Moses is dressed like Christ as citizen philosopher, thus striking blows against imperial oppression. But here Mathews fails to acknowledge that Maxentius was also a Roman emperor, so he may indeed be Pharaoh, whose troops were driven into the Tiber by Constantine. One would expect him to be dressed in a 'military tunic and cuirass . . . covered by a chlamys'. Becker may very well have been correct.

Chapter 9. Victor Constantine

On Constantine as Victor, see H. A. Drake, *In Praise of Constantine: A Historical Study and New Translation of Eusebius'* Tricennial Orations (Berkeley, 1976). There is little else. On imperial power and Christianity, one must now start with G. Dagron, *Emperor and Priest. The Imperial Office in Byzantium* (Cambridge, 2003), which devotes a chapter to Constantine. Seminal work on triumphal rulership in Rome was undertaken by G. C. Picard, *Les trophées romains. Contribution à l'histoire de la religion et de l'art triomphal de Rome* (Paris, 1957), whose thesis built on extensive foundations laid in numerous articles by J. Gagé, notably his 'Stavros Nikopoios. La victoire impériale dans l'empire chrétien', *Revue d'histoire et de philosophie religieuses* 13 (1933): 370–400. Here and elsewhere, one cannot ignore M. McCormick, *Eternal Victory. Triumphal rulership in late antiquity, Byzantium, and the early medieval West* (Cambridge and Paris, 1986). On triumphal art and architecture, one must start with Sabine MacCormack, *Art and Ceremony in Late Antiquity* (Berkeley, Los Angeles and London, 1981).

The Great Cameo is addressed by A. N. Zadoks Josephus Jitta, 'Imperial messages in agate, II', *Bulletin Antieke Beschaving* 41 (1966): 91–104; and by F. Baster, 'Die grosse Kamee in den Haag', *Bulletin Antieke Beschaving* 43 (1968): 2–22. More generally, see F. Althaus and M. Sutcliffe, eds, *The Road to Byzantium. Luxury Arts of Antiquity* (London, 2006), and the art historical papers in Hartley et al, *Constantine* (cited above), which place the cameos discussed here in a broader context. The quotation from Peter Brown, on the Calendar of 354, is from *Authority and the Sacred*, pp. 12–13.

The lives and deaths of Crispus and Fausta are considered in all general accounts of Constantine's reign, but especial attention is accorded by H. Pohlsander, 'Crispus: brilliant career and tragic end', *Historia* 33 (1984): 79–106; and by D. Woods, 'On the death of the empress Fausta', *Greece and Rome* 45 (1998): 70–86, who displays his familiar careful attention to the sources. I have adopted his translations and followed his suggestion on Fausta's possible abortion.

The Goths receive far fuller coverage than the Sarmatians, thanks to their later 'successes'. See M. Kulikowski, 'Constantine and the northern Barbarians', in Lenski, ed., *Age of Constantine*, pp. 347–76; and also his *Rome's Gothic Wars*, pp. 83–102. P. Heather, 'Goths and Huns, c.320–425', in *CAH* 13, pp. 487–515, summarizes earlier work. On Libanius' testimony on the Goths (*Oration* 59.39) and Sarmatians (59.29), see M. Wiemer, 'Libanius on Constantine', *Classical Quarterly* 44 (1994): 511–24, who further suggests that in *Oration* 59 Libanius was drawing on Eusebius' *Life of Constantine*. See also P.-L. Malosse, 'Libanius on Constantine again', *Classical Quarterly* 47 (1997): 519–24, whose reading presents Libanius as far more slippery and pointed in his allusions in *Oration* 59. A full translation of the oration is provided in S. Lieu and D. Montserrat,

From Constantine to Julian: Pagan and Byzantine Views (London and New York, 1996), pp. 147–209.

On excavations at Sirmium, see I. Popović, 'Marble sculptures from the imperial palace in Sirmium', *Starinar* 56 (2006): 153–66. There is far less commentary on the Belgrade Rider than one might expect. Good pictures can be seen in *Imperator Caesar Flavius Constantinus*, the catalogue of the Trier exhibition, where it was recently displayed. G. Bruns, *Staatskameen des 4. Jahrhunderts nach Christus Geburt* (Berlin, 1948), observed wisely that we cannot date the cameo any more precisely than the fourth century, although she preferred the second half of that century.

On the army in the fourth century there are many important and provocative essays, some already cited, including: A. D. Nock, 'The Roman army and the Roman religious year', *Harvard Theological Review* 45 (1952): 187–252; R. MacMullen, 'The legion as a society', *Historia* 33 (1984): 440–56; R. Tomlin, 'Christianity and the late Roman army', in Lieu and Montserrat, eds, *Constantine* (cited above), pp. 21–51; and the collected papers of M. Speidel. Archaeological surveys used here include: H. von Petrikovits, 'Fortifications in the north-western Roman Empire from the third to the fifth centuries AD', *JRS* 61 (1971): 178–218; P. Petrović, 'Les fortresses du Bas-Empire sur les limes danubiènnes en Serbie', in W. S. Hanson and L. J. F. Keppie, eds, *Roman frontier studies 1979* (Oxford, 1980): 757–74; and now J. J. Wilkes, 'The Roman Danube: an archaeological survey', *JRS* 95 (2005): 124–225. Most recently, see M. Kulikowski, 'Constantine and the northern Barbarians', in Lenski, ed., *Age of Constantine*, pp. 347–76; H. Elton, 'Warfare and the military', ibid., pp. 325–46. The quotation from Peter Brown can be found in his *Authority and the Sacred*, p. 45.

Chapter 10. Constantine Maximus Augustus

The administrative reforms initiated by Diocletian and developed under Constantine are addressed very succinctly by E. Lo Cascio, 'The Emperor and his Administration', in *CAH* 12, pp. 170–83; and C. Kelly, 'Emperors, Government and Bureaucrats', *CAH* 13, pp. 138–83. More fully on Constantine, see C. Kelly, 'Bureaucracy and Government', in Lenski, ed., *Age of Constantine*, pp. 183–204, which I have followed closely, although I have not adopted his position that the Praetorian Prefects did not yet administer regional prefectures. Barnes, *New Empire*, pp. 201–8, supplies an edition of and commentary on the *Verona List*; at pp. 199–200, he supplies a list of dioceses and their emperors; at pp. 91–109, an annotated list of ordinary consuls, from which my own abbreviated list is drawn. The careers of many are traced in the *PRLE*, where Ablabius is Ablabius 4, pp. 3–4. Eunapius, in his *Lives of the Sophists* (VI.3.1–7), suggests that at his (humble) birth in Crete there was a prophecy that his mother had almost given birth to an emperor. He was appointed vicar of Asiana (324–6), and promoted to Praetorian Prefect in 329, which office he held until his exile by Constantius II. His daughter Olympias was betrothed (as an infant) to Constans, and later married to Arasces, king of Armenia (see Ammianus Marcellinus XX.11.3), certainly before 358, probably in 354. His son Seleucus (= *PLRE*: Seleucus 1, pp. 818–19) was, therefore, father of a second Olympias, b. 361. Evagrius (= *PLRE*: Evagrius 2, pp. 284–5), who probably replaced Ablabius as Constantine's Praetorian Prefect in 336, when Ablabius was seconded to Constantius, had earlier been Praetorian Prefect in 326 and 329, and then was seconded to Constantine II in Gaul in 330–1. On the administration of the east, and the Antioch statue base, see F. Millar, *The Roman Near East, 31 BC–AD 337* (Cambridge, MA, 1994), p. 210; D. Feissel, 'Une dédicace en l'honneur de Constantin II César et les préfets du prétoire de 336', *Travaux et Mémoires* 9 (1985): 421–34. On the *comites*, see Millar, *Emperor in the Roman World*, pp. 117–20, from which I have taken the examples of Acacius and Strategius.

On Indian gems and jewels, see A. Ghosh, *An Encyclopaedia of Indian Archaeology* (Leiden, 1990), pp. 216–24. On diamonds, and their uses in engraving, see L. Gorelick and A. J. Gwinnett, 'Diamonds from India to Rome and beyond', *American Journal of Archeology* 92 (1988): 547–52. On elephants and tigers, see G. Jennison, *Animals for Show and Pleasure in Ancient Rome* (Manchester, 1937), and D. F. Lach, *Asia in the Making of Europe, II: A Century of Wonder* (Chicago, 1977), pp. 172–4. Both consider the Barberini Diptych to be of Constantine, which is no longer believed to be the case, although the emperor clearly resembles other portraits of Constantine. Elephants appear on another famous diptych of the late fourth century depicting the apotheosis of an emperor (possibly Julian), now in the British Museum, for which see J. Elsner, *Imperial Rome and Christian Triumph* (Oxford, 1998), pp. 30–2.

The war with the Persians is covered in all general accounts, and the broader context sketched elegantly by E. Key Fowden, 'Constantine and the Peoples of the Eastern Frontier', in Lenski, ed., *Age of Constantine*, pp. 377–98. For the various versions of events, see G. Fowden, 'The last days of Constantine: oppositional version and their influence', *JRS* 84 (1994): 146–70, at 146–53, which offers more detail than in his equally compelling account of Constantine's path to 'crusade' in G. Fowden, *Empire to Commonwealth. Consequences of Monotheism in Late Antiquity* (Princeton, 1993), pp. 80–99. On Aphrahat, see T. D. Barnes, 'Constantine and the Christians of Persia', *JRS* 75 (1985): 126–36. For the later legendary victories, see S. Lieu, 'Constantine in legendary literature', in Lenski, ed., *Age of Constantine*, pp. 298–321.

The *Tricennial Oration* is translated by H. A. Drake, *In praise of Constantine: a historical study and new translation of Eusebius'* Tricennial Orations (Berkeley, 1976). Helena's life, death and legacy are treated exhaustively by H. Pohlsander, *Helena: Empress and Saint* (Chicago, 1995). On her pilgrimage, see E. D. Hunt, *Holy Land Pilgrimage in the Later Roman Empire, AD 312–460* (Oxford, 1982), pp. 28–49; and especially J. W. Drijvers, *Helena Augusta: The Mother of Constantine the Great and the Legend of her Finding of the True Cross* (Leiden, 1992). Drijvers believes Eusebius' claim that Constantine converted his mother, and posits that she died in Trier. There seems no good reason to accept either suggestion. Drijvers explores in great detail the sources for the legend of Helena and the invention of the True Cross, although the excerpts I quote from Rufinus are taken from P. Amidon, trans., *The Church History of Rufinus, Books 10 and 11* (Oxford, 1997). It is rather far-fetched to suggest, as Drijvers does, that Constantine relied on his aged mother to enforce an unpopular policy of Christianization in Palestine. However, elsewhere Drijvers has made a very strong case for correlating the rise of the significance of the True Cross and that of the status of Jerusalem in the later fourth century: J. W. Drijvers, *Cyril of Jerusalem. Bishop and City* (Leiden, 2004).

Egeria's pilgrimage has long been available in translation, and many appear online. The fullest recent guide to Constantine's building activity in the Holy Land and to pilgrimage is G. Stemberger, *Jews and Christians in the Holy Land. Palestine in the Fourth Century* (Edinburgh, 2000), pp. 48–85, 86–120. E. D. Hunt, *Holy Land Pilgrimage*, pp. 3–27, presents a neat summary, although one might beware the observation that the mosaic at Santa Pudenziana in Rome presents an accurate representation of the churches in Jerusalem and Bethlehem. If the scene does strive for accuracy, the mosaic, traditionally dated to the 390s, may be a little later, as it shows a bejewelled golden cross upon Golgotha, which was placed there only in the reign of Theodosius II, for which see K. Holum, 'Pulcheria's Crusade AD 421–2 and the ideology of imperial victory', *Greek, Roman and Byzantine Studies* 18 (1977): 153–72. For a debate on the mosaic, compare T. F. Mathews, *The Clash of Gods. A reinterpretation of early Christian art*, 2nd edn (Princeton, 1999), pp. 92–114, and J.-M. Spieser, 'The representation of Christ in the apses of early Christian churches', *Gesta* 37 (1998): 63–73. The classic account of Christ's tomb is C. Coüasnon, *The Church of the Holy Sepulchre in Jerusalem* (London, 1941), which must now be read alongside M. Biddle, *The Tomb of Christ* (Stroud, 1999).

Chapter 11. Constantine and the Bishops

This chapter takes its title, and much of its inspiration, from the marvellous book by H. A. Drake, *Constantine and the Bishops: the Politics of Intolerance* (Baltimore, 2000). Drake considers the 'real significance' of Constantine's reign to be the relationship he established with the bishops, which was still subject to negotiation in 335, where he chooses to start. A key argument he advances, which I have chosen not to develop explicitly, is that access was key: all power structures operate through access, and Constantine now granted that to bishops. Bishops, rather like senators, had greater prestige, but they also had constituencies whose views were now represented in a bottom-up fashion; but as importantly, from the top down, Constantine now had influence with powerful lobbying groups and one of the most fervent, vocal groups in contemporary society. Drake emphasizes that his manipulation of bishops was crucial to Constantine's agenda, since they had a right to impose his will on their flocks, and hence could affect how the parishioners acted, including how they carried out official duties if and when they entered public life. Drake rehearses some arguments more succinctly in his 'The Impact of Constantine on Christianity', in Lenski, ed., *Age of Constantine*, pp. 111–36.

Equally important, and in some regards a corrective to Drake, is Claudia Rapp, *Holy Bishops in Late Antiquity. The Nature of Christian Leadership in an Age of Transition* (Berkeley, 2005), despite being 'a study that deemphasizes the reign of Constantine and that, instead of treating it as a watershed . . . follows the continuous flow of developments, both in Christian culture and in the Roman empire'. At pp. 125–31 Rapp also suggests: 'Moses was considered the biblical model par excellence for bishops, especially among Greek authors.' Here she summarizes her 'Imperial Ideology in the Making: Eusebius of Caesarea on Constantine as "Bishop"', *Journal of Theological Studies* 49 (1998): 685–95; and 'Comparison, paradigm and the case of Moses in panegyric and hagiography', in M. Whitby, ed., *The Propaganda of Power: The Role of Panegyric in Late Antiquity* (Leiden, 1998), 277–98. But we cannot go so far as she in supposing that in taking Moses as the model of leadership one can explain away Eusebius' comment that Constantine was a 'bishop'. The references are 'no longer puzzling' thanks to G. Dagron, *Emperor and Priest. The Imperial Office in Byzantium* (Cambridge, 2003), pp. 133–4, who from a close reading of Eusebius' Greek observes: first, that Constantine's claim was no more than a claim, demonstrated by the use of the conditional tense and the telling 'perhaps'; and second, that in a very real sense, Constantine, as yet unbaptized, was outside the Church. Dagron also observed that Eusebius' clever use of the verb 'to watch over' (*episkopein*) with the noun 'bishop' (*episkopos*) serves not to assert Constantine's priestly status, but rather to undermine it, 'making the [ostensibly Christian] words commonplace and diffusing their charge'. Older studies, which establish the broad context for Constantine's quips, include J. Straub, 'Constantine as *koinos episkopos*. Tradition and innovation in the representation of the first Christian emperor's majesty', *DOP* 21 (1967): 37–55; and his older (1957) paper 'Kaiser Konstantin als *episkopos ton ektos*', republished in J. Straub, *Regeneratio Imperii* (Darmstadt, 1972), pp. 119–33.

The classic study of the Donatists is W. H. C. Frend, *The Donatist Church. A Movement of Protest in Roman North Africa* (Oxford, 1952; repr. 1970). More recently, and in contrast, M. Tilley, *The Bible in Christian North Africa* (Minneapolis, 1997), 'privileges the specifically religious character of the Donatist controversy'. Tilley also translated *Donatist Martyr Stories* (Liverpool, 1997), including the *Sermon on the Passions of Saints Donatus and Advocatus*. The 'Catholic' side before Augustine is set out in M. Edwards, trans., *Optatus: Against the Donatists* (Liverpool, 1997), from which quotations from the translated letters of Constantine to the bishops Aelafius and Celsus are taken. Shorter translations of these and much else can be found in Stevenson, *A New Eusebius*, pp. 297–312. J. Rodalnus, *The Church in the Age of Constantine. The Theological Challenges* (London, 2006), pp. 37–41, offers a useful summary, and Drake, *Constantine and the Bishops*, pp. 212–21, is excellent.

The literature on Arianism is substantial, that on Arius somewhat less so. An excellent place to start is C. Haas, 'The Arians of Alexandria', *Vigiliae Christianae* 47 (1993): 234–45, which explores social, topographical and urban contexts with extensive but not exhaustive bibliography. Constantine's treatment of heretics and schismatics is traced by Drake, *Constantine and the Bishops*, building upon observations from his 'Lions into Lambs', *Past and Present* 153 (1996): 3–36, at 29–31. I do not see, as Drake does, that Constantine became less tolerant even as he professed toleration for all, but rather that his intolerance was directed in different directions. Perspicacious commentary on Eusebius is provided, as ever, by Cameron and Hall, *Life of Constantine*, pp. 306–8. For the role of Ossius of Cordoba, see H. Chadwick, 'Ossius of Cordova and the presidency of the Council of Antioch', *Journal of Theological Studies* 9 (1958): 292–304; and more fully, V. C. de Clercq, *Ossius of Cordova. A Contribution to the History of the Constantinian Period* (Washington, DC, 1954). The ecclesiastical politics of Constantine's last decade, to which I have devoted too little space, are covered in a sophisticated manner by Drake, *Constantine and the Bishops*, pp. 3–9, 258–352, who avers that in his dealings with the bishops in this period 'Constantine lost control of the agenda, and, ultimately, he lost control of the message'. The details can best be gleaned from Barnes, *Constantine and Eusebius*, pp. 224–44. Barnes's position is set out well and briefly in his '*Constantine, Athanasius and the Christian Church*', in S. Lieu and D. Montserrat, eds, *Constantine. History, Historiography, Legend* (London, 1998), pp. 7–20.

If one might be permitted to conclude with another's words, no judgement on Constantine's dealings with the Church is more astute than that of F. Millar, *The Emperor in the Roman World*, 2nd edn (Ithaca, NY, 1992), pp. 551–607, at 551: 'If we look back from the end of Constantine's reign over the relations of church and emperor, we can see mirrored in them almost every one of the distinct features of the imperial monarchy which we have observed in operation in other contexts: the emperor's personal pronouncement of decisions and verdicts; the addressing of accusations and petitions to him; his conferment of privileges, and his decisions on the exclusion or inclusion or marginal cases; confiscation and restoration of property; the issuing of *edicta* and general *epistulae*, and before that for a long period only of *rescripta* in answer to *consultationes* by governors, or to letters from *koina* or cities.'

Chapter 12. Death and Succession

On Constantine's death, the commentary by Cameron and Hall on Eusebius, *Life of Constantine*, pp. 339–50, is a superb guide to the issues. See also R. Burgess,

"'Achyron" or "proasteion". The location and circumstances of Constantine's death', *Journal of Theological Studies* 50 (1999): 153–62. For the various later sources that treat of Constantine's baptism and death, see G. Fowden, 'The last days of Constantine: oppositional version and their influence', *JRS* 84 (1994): 146–70, at 153–70.

On travel by road in the Roman empire, see L. Casson, *Travel in the Ancient World* (Baltimore, 1974), pp. 176–96. On the *cursus publicus*, see A. M. Ramsay, 'The speed of the Roman Imperial Post', *JRS* 15 (1925): 60–74; and especially C. W. J. Eliot, 'New evidence for the speed of the Roman Imperial Post', *Phoenix* 9 (1955): 76–80, which examines the rate of dissemination of news of the death of Pertinax. I used online moon phase and sunrise/sunset calculators to determine conditions in Turkey in May 337. On the *Antonine Itinerary*, see N. Reed, 'Pattern and purpose in the *Antonine Itinerary*', *American Journal of Philology* 99 (1978): 228–54, who suggests it shows routes by which military provisions should be transported. J. Wilkes, 'Frontiers and Provinces', *CAH* 12, pp. 212–68, makes full use of the *Antonine Itinerary*, with the section pertinent here at p. 240.

I have in my description of Constantine's apotheosis diverged from the clearest analysis, by S. Price, 'From noble funerals to divine cult: the consecration of Roman emperors', in D. Cannadine and S. Price, eds, *Rituals of Royalty. Power and Ceremonial in Traditional Societies* (Cambridge, 1987), pp. 56–105. I have followed Price in drawing from Cassius Dio and Herodian, but sought out standard translations. Price suggests that Constantine had no pyre, whereas I believe Eusebius has suppressed that aspect of the ceremonial. For more on the afterlife and the symbolism of *consecratio*, see MacCormack, *Art and Ceremony*, pp. 93–127; Dagron, *Emperor and Priest*, pp. 135–8.

Helena's mausoleum is reported in F. Deichmann and A. Tschira, 'Das Mausoleum der Kaiserin Helena und die Basilika der Heilige Marcellinus und Petrus an der Via Labicana vor Rom', *Jahrbuch des deutschen Archäologischen Instituts* 72 (1957): 44–110; with insights and images in Holloway, *Constantine and Rome*, pp. 86–109; J. Elsner, *Imperial Rome and Christian Triumph* (Oxford, 1998), pp. 20–2, 160–1.

The origins of the Church of the Holy Apostles in Constantinople is discussed most convincingly by C. Mango, 'Constantine's mausoleum and the translation of relics', *Byzantinische Zeitschrift* 83 (1990): 51–61. For once I have not used the translation by Cameron and Hall, but rather have followed Mango. He argues for the attribution of the mausoleum to Constantine, and of the adjacent basilica to Constantius. Confusion may have arisen, he notes, because Constantius repaired his father's mausoleum following an earthquake. This develops the detailed study by G. Downey, 'The builder of the original Church of the Apostles at Constantinople. A contribution to the criticism of the *Vita Constantini* attributed to Eusebius', *DOP* 6 (1951): 51–80, esp. 69–71, and the long note 58, which maintains that the mausoleum and basilica were contemporaneous constructions by Constantius. Most recently, traces of the Church of the Holy Apostles, which was hitherto imagined to have been eradicated by Mehmet the Conqueror after 1453, were discovered at the foundation of Mehmet's mosque: K. Dark and F. Özgümü , 'New evidence for the Byzantine Church of the Holy Apostles from Fatih Camii, Istanbul', *Oxford Journal of Archaeology* 21 (2002): 393–413.

That Eusebius was clearly willing to compare Constantine to Christ is noted by Drake, *Constantine and the Bishops*, pp. 304–8. Dagron, *Emperor and Priest*, pp. 132, 135–43, also notes this and expands on the notion that the emperor was 'equal to the apostles'. The comparison with Christ is most fully developed by R. Leeb, *Konstantin und Christus: die Verchristlichung der imperialen Repräsentation unter Konstantin dem Grossen als Spiegel seiner Kirchenpolitik und seines Selbstverständnisses als christlichen Kaiser* (Berlin, 1992). A more succinct overview is afforded by K. M. Setton, *Christian Attitudes towards the Emperor in the Fourth Century* (New York, 1941), pp. 40–56.

On the wars of succession, see now the succinct overview by D. Hunt, 'The Successors of Constantine', in *CAH* 13, pp. 1–43; and R. Frakes, 'The Dynasty of Constantine down to 363', in Lenski, ed., *Age of Constantine*, pp. 91–107. M. Di Maio and W. H. Arnold, '"*Per vim, per caedem, per bellum*": a study of murder and ecclesiastical politics in the year 337', *Byzantion* 62 (1992): 158–211, offers a thorough review of all pertinent literature, although I find much of the conjecture unconvincing (viz., a forged will discovered by Eusebius of Nicomedia). On the events of 340, see generally A. Wardman, 'Usurpers and internal conflicts in the 4th century AD', *Historia* 33 (1984): 220–37, which offers an excellent analysis. T. D. Barnes, *Constantius and Athanasius* (Cambridge, MA, 1993), pp. 218–28, provides a remarkably useful summary of known imperial itineraries, 337–61. I have not incorporated the interesting analysis of W. Portmann, 'Die politische Krise zwischen den Kaisern Constantius II. und Constans', *Historia* 48 (1999): 301–29, for reasons of space.

Constantius' wars with Magnentius and his triumph are addressed well and concisely by Potter, *Roman Empire at Bay*, pp. 471–6, and at greater length by J. Drinkwater, 'The revolt and ethnic origin of the usurper Magnentius (350–353), and the rebellion of Vetranio', *Chiron* 30 (2000): 131–59; B. Bleckmann, 'Constantina, Vetranio und Gallus Caesar', *Chiron* 24 (1994): 29–68. On the coins see K. Shelton, 'Usurpers' coins: the case of Magnentius', *Byzantinische Forschungen* 8 (1982): 211–35; P. Bastien, *Le monnayage de Magnence (350–353)* (Wetteren, 1953 and 1983); and A. Dearn, 'The coinage of Vetranio: imperial representation and the memory of Constantine the Great', *Numismatic Chronicle* 163 (2003): 169–91.

In J. W. Drijvers, *Cyril of Jerusalem. Bishop and City* (Leiden, 2004), one can read more on Cyril's letter of 351, which is edited and translated in E. Bihain, 'L'épître de Cyrille de Jérusalem à Constance sur le vision de la croix (BHG³ 413)', *Byzantion* 43 (1973): 264–96; and E. Yarnold, *Cyril of Jerusalem. The Early Church Fathers* (London, 2000), pp. 68–70. On Ammianus Marcellinus, see J. Matthews, *The Roman Empire of Ammianus* (London, 1989); J. W. Drijvers and D. Hunt, eds,

The Late Roman World and its Historian. Interpreting Ammianus Marcellinus (London and New York, 1999), which contains the important paper by D. Woods, 'A Persian at Rome. Ammianus and Eunapius, *Frg. 68*', pp. 156–65. The *largitio* bowl is illustrated in context in J. P. C. Kent and K. S. Painter, eds, *Wealth of the Roman World* (London, 1977), pp. 15–62.

For the non-Arian opinion on the Battle of Adrianople, see Ambrose, *De Fide* II, 136–43; trans. P. Schaff, *Ambrose, Selected Works and Letters* (Grand Rapids, MI, 2004), pp. 431–3; cited by F. Heim, *La Théologie de la victoire de Constantin à Théodose* (Paris, 1992), p. 127. There were also 'pagan' reactions: Libanius (*Oration* 34.1) saw the defeat as divine retribution for the demise of Julian, whereas Ammianus Marcellinus (XXXI.4.9) blamed the officers 'with stained reputations', who 'as if at the command of some adverse deity, were . . . given command of armies'. See J. Straub, 'Die Wirkung der Niederlage bei Adrianopel auf die Diskussion über das Germanenproblem in der spätrömischen Literatur', in his *Regeneratio Imperii* (Darmstadt, 1972), pp. 195–219. Other key sources: Orosius, *The Seven Books of History against the Pagans*, trans. R. Deferrari (Washington, DC, 1964), pp. 345–6; *The Church History of Rufinus of Aquileia, Books 10 and 11*, trans. P. Amidon (Oxford, 1997). The Christian military oath is preserved at *Vegetius: Epitome of military science*, trans. N. P. Milner (Liverpool, 1993), p. 35. On Corripus, see *Flavii Cresconii Corippi Iohannidos seu de bellis Lybicis libri VIII*, eds J. Diggle and F. Goodyear (Cambridge, 1970), pp. 173–8; G. Shea, trans., *The Iohannis or De Bellis Lybicis of Flavius Cresconius Corippus* (Lampeter, 1998), pp. 196–8; *Maurice's Strategikon*, trans. G. Dennis (Philadelphia, 1984). Excellent commentary is contained in M. McCormick, *Eternal Victory*, pp. 245–6. More recently, see the first chapter of D. Bachrach, *Religion and the Conduct of War, c.300–1215* (Woodbridge, 2003).

Index

tax 64–5, 100–1
  Aphrodisias 204
  Rome 118
Temple of Artemis Azzanathkona 15
Temple of Bel 24
Temple of Roma and Venus 144
Temple of Romulus 150
Terentius 24
Terme, Museo Nazionale delle, Rome 75
Tertullian 41, 49, 52, 54, 55–8, 61
Tervingi 225–6
Tetrarchy 87–109
  Second 114–16, 117
Tetricus, C. Pius Esuvius 80
Thaiphali 225
Thecla, St 59
Theodora 4, 116, 130
Theodosian Code 140, 174, 230, 231, 271
Theodosius 72, 195, 256, 300, 301
Theology of Victory 7, 9, 71–5, 79, 83, 87, 91, 95,
  132, 138–40, 156, 189, 302, 304, 306
Theophanes Confessor 249
theosis 266
Tiberianus, Annius 245, 246, 292
Tiberius 17, 30, 69, 74
Ticinum medallion 173
Timonianus, Nestorius 245, 246, 292
titulus 254
traditores 259–60
Trajan 22, 23, 46–7, 140
  Dacian campaigns 74
  Dacian wars 66
  Great Trajanic Freize 155
  Trophy 74
Trier 3, 71, 94, 104, 119, 124–7, 131, 136, 163, 166,
  169–70, 179, 219, 221, 223, 225, 227, 246, 275
triumphus 29, 146–7
Troglyta, John 302
trophy, *tropaeum, tropaion* 70, 74–5, 151, 161,
  183–7, 216, 217, 229, 248, 297
Troy 192
True Cross 253–5, 297
Turin 133
Twelfth Legion Fulminata 54–5
Tyre 255, 274–5

Ulfilas 226
Ulpius Chresimus, Marcus 32

Ulpius Silanus 81–2
Ursus, Flavius 289

Valens 165, 166, 195, 300
Valeria 107, 162
Valerian 62, 78, 88, 248
Valerianus, Titus Flavius 22
Valesianus, Anonymus *see Origo Constantini*
Vandals 99
Vardulli 35–6
Varus 23
Vatican 34, 84, 85, 86, 92, 208, 287
Vegetius 302
Velia 143–4, 150
Verona 132, 133–4
Verona List 236–7
Vetranio 294–5
vexillations 99
vexillum 22, 23–4, 185, 186
vicarius 237
Victor, Aurelius 93, 150, 220, 246, 289,
  294
Victoria 74, 129, 153
Victorinus 124
Victor title 8, 215–17
Virgil 192
virtus 72–3, 81, 95
vows 25–6

Walesby 233
Walters Art Museum, Baltimore 27
warfare, Christian attitudes 49–54
warrior saints 59–61
water, Constantinople 194–5
Weiss, Peter 188
Willingham Fen 18
women
  Christianity 39–42
  martyrs 59–60
Woods, David 222, 299

Yerebatan Sarayı 195

Zenobia 80, 82, 83, 260
Zonaras 3–4, 222, 223, 295
Zosimus 116, 164, 165, 179, 180, 181, 205,
  221–2, 223–4, 225, 231, 233, 272, 291, 295–6,
  299